THE UNIVERSAL WAY OF SALVATION IN THE THOUGHT OF AUGUSTINE

T&T Clark Studies in Ressourcement Catholic Theology and Culture

Edited by
Matthew Levering
Tracey Rowland

THE UNIVERSAL WAY OF SALVATION IN THE THOUGHT OF AUGUSTINE

Thomas P. Harmon

LONDON • NEW YORK • OXFORD • NEW DELHI • SYDNEY

T&T CLARK
Bloomsbury Publishing Plc, 50 Bedford Square, London, WC1B 3DP, UK
Bloomsbury Publishing Inc, 1359 Broadway, New York, NY 10018, USA
Bloomsbury Publishing Ireland, 29 Earlsfort Terrace, Dublin 2, D02 AY28, Ireland

BLOOMSBURY, T&T CLARK and the T&T Clark logo are trademarks of Bloomsbury Publishing Plc

First published in Great Britain 2024
Paperback edition published 2026

Copyright © Thomas P. Harmon, 2024

Thomas P. Harmon has asserted his right under the Copyright, Designs and Patents Act, 1988, to be identified as Author of this work.

For legal purposes the Acknowledgments on p. vii constitute an extension of this copyright page.

Series design by Annabel Hewitson
Cover image: Saint Augustine Writing Miniature taken from De civitate Dei by Saint Augustine of Hippo (354–430). 1459 (miniature). Artist: Polani, Nicolo (15th century) / Italian. (Photo © Photo Josse / Bridgeman Images)

All rights reserved. No part of this publication may be: i) reproduced or transmitted in any form or by any means, electronic or mechanical, including photocopying, recording or by means of any information storage or retrieval system without prior permission in writing from the publishers; or ii) used or reproduced in any way for the training, development or operation of artificial intelligence (AI) technologies, including generative AI technologies. The rights holders expressly reserve this publication from the text and data mining exception as per Article 4(3) of the Digital Single Market Directive (EU) 2019/790.

Bloomsbury Publishing Plc does not have any control over, or responsibility for, any third-party websites referred to or in this book. All internet addresses given in this book were correct at the time of going to press. The author and publisher regret any inconvenience caused if addresses have changed or sites have ceased to exist, but can accept no responsibility for any such changes.

A catalogue record for this book is available from the British Library.

Library of Congress Cataloging-in-Publication Data
Names: Harmon, Thomas P., author.
Title: The universal way of salvation in the thought of Augustine / Thomas P. Harmon.
Description: 1. | London : T&T Clark, 2024. | Series: T&T Clark studies in ressourcement Catholic theology and culture | Includes bibliographical references and index.
Identifiers: LCCN 2023055196 (print) | LCCN 2023055197 (ebook) | ISBN 9780567712127 (hardback) | ISBN 9780567712172 (paperback) | ISBN 9780567712134 (pdf) | ISBN 9780567712165 (ebook)
Subjects: LCSH: Augustine, of Hippo, Saint, 354-430. | Universalism.
Classification: LCC B655.Z7 H37 2024 (print) | LCC B655.Z7 (ebook) | DDC 234–dc23/eng/20240424
LC record available at https://lccn.loc.gov/2023055196
LC ebook record available at https://lccn.loc.gov/2023055197

ISBN: HB: 978-0-5677-1212-7
PB: 978-0-5677-1217-2
ePDF: 978-0-5677-1213-4
ePub: 978-0-5677-1216-5

Series: T&T Clark Studies in Ressourcement Catholic Theology and Culture

Typeset by Newgen KnowledgeWorks Pvt. Ltd., Chennai, India

For product safety related questions contact productsafety@bloomsbury.com.

To find out more about our authors and books visit www.bloomsbury.com and sign up for our newsletters.

CONTENTS

Acknowledgments   vii

INTRODUCTION   1

Part I
SETTING UP THE ARGUMENT ABOUT THE UNIVERSAL WAY OF SALVATION

Chapter 1
POLITICS, PERCEPTION, AND RELIGION FROM REPUBLIC TO EMPIRE   15

Chapter 2
RELIGIOUS UNIVERSALISM IN THE LATE ROMAN EMPIRE AND THE ARGUMENTS OF PORPHYRY OF TYRE   31

Chapter 3
THE FEW, THE MANY, AND THE UNIVERSAL WAY OF SALVATION IN AUGUSTINE'S EARLY WORKS   47

Part II
CHRIST'S MEDIATION OF THE UNIVERSAL WAY OF SALVATION

Chapter 4
HUMAN WHOLENESS AND THE UNIVERSAL WAY OF SALVATION IN THE *CITY OF GOD*   67

Chapter 5
PLATO ON THE DIVISIONS AMONG HUMAN BEINGS   75

Chapter 6
AUGUSTINE'S ENGAGEMENT WITH PLATONIC POLITICAL PHILOSOPHY ON IGNORANCE AND DIFFICULTY   85

Chapter 7
AUGUSTINE'S ARGUMENT WITH PORPHYRY ON THE UNIVERSAL WAY OF SALVATION   98

Chapter 8
CHRIST THE MEDIATOR OF THE UNIVERSAL WAY OF SALVATION 120

Chapter 9
CHARITY, JUSTICE, AND RECONCILIATION IN THE TRANSPOLITICAL
CITY OF GOD 133

Part III
THE UNIVERSAL WAY OF SALVATION AND AUGUSTINE HIMSELF

Chapter 10
HUMAN WHOLENESS IN THE *CONFESSIONS* 149

Chapter 11
AUGUSTINE'S PHILOSOPHIC ASCENT 161

Chapter 12
SALVATION FOR THE PHILOSOPHER AND THE
NONPHILOSOPHER: THE CASES OF VICTORINUS AND ANTHONY 185

Chapter 13
AUGUSTINE'S MORAL AND RELIGIOUS CONVERSION: SOUL AND
BODY, FEW AND MANY 199

CONCLUSION 213

Bibliography 215
Index of Names 231
Index of Subjects 235

ACKNOWLEDGMENTS

I would first of all like to thank my wife, Catherine Harmon, for her untiring support, limitless patience, and loving encouragement; for the myriad helps from my grandparents, Neil and Gini Harmon; and grateful thanks to my parents, Rodney and Suzanne Harmon, who were my first models of faith seeking understanding.

I want to thank the Scanlan Foundation for funding the research chair I occupy at the University of St. Thomas, which allowed me the time to complete this book. I received several helpful grants from the University of St. Thomas faculty development committee, for which I am grateful. I would never have crossed the finish line without the encouragement and persistence of Tracey Rowland and Matthew Levering, my series editors. I am also very grateful for the patience and good cheer of my Bloomsbury editors, Anna Turton and Jack Curtin.

Over the years, I have had many conversations that shaped the development of this book. My unending gratitude goes to everyone who has helped me think through both the parts and the whole, especially: Stephen F. Brown, Marc D. Guerra, Fr. Matthew L. Lamb, and Peter Augustine Lawler. Special thanks also to my supportive colleagues from across several institutions: Andrew J. Hayes, Christopher P. Evans, Michael Boler, Michael P. Barber, John Kincaid, and Fr. Andrew Younan.

INTRODUCTION

Platonic philosophy divides human beings into two types: the philosophers and the nonphilosophers, or the wise and the foolish, or the few and the many.[1] Those who are able to pursue wisdom are able to live lives of genuine virtue and to become at least somewhat happy. Those who are unable to pursue wisdom pursue ultimately unsatisfying ends such as glory or sensual pleasure. The division between the few and the many is what accounts for the necessity of the many to believe noble lies[2] and for the difficulties attending the possibility of the rule of philosophers,[3] to choose two of Plato's most famous teachings as illustrations. Because of the quite different ends of the ways of life lived by the two types of human being, it is difficult, verging on impossible, for the two groups to share any kind of truly common life. As a result, the Platonic philosopher takes an ironic stance toward the multitude, manifested most eminently in Socrates' own famous irony.[4] The purpose of Socratic irony is to simulate commonality where little or

---

1. See, inter alia, Plato, *Republic*, 493e–494a; *Apology of Socrates*, 25b.
2. See Plato, *Republic*, 414b–c, and *Laws*, 663d–e.
3. See Plato, *Republic*, 473d.
4. See Augustine, *ciu. Dei*, 8.4. Unless otherwise indicated, all references to the English translation of *De ciuitate Dei* will be from the Bettenson translation. As Leo Strauss puts it, "[The philosopher] is ultimately compelled to transcend not merely the dimension of common opinion, or political opinion, but the dimension of political life as such; for he is led to realize that the ultimate aim of political life cannot be reached by political life, but only in a life devoted to contemplation, to philosophy." Leo Strauss, *The Rebirth of Classical Political Rationalism*, ed. Thomas L. Pangle (Chicago: University of Chicago Press, 1989), 60. See Douglas Kries' insightful article, "Augustine as Defender and Critic of Leo Strauss' Esotericism Thesis," *Proceedings of the American Catholic Philosophical Association*, vol. 83 (2009), 241–52 at 243–6 and Michael P. Foley, "Commentary," in Augustine, *Against the Academics*, trans. Michael P. Foley (New Haven: Yale University Press, 2019), 115–215 at 201–13, for helpful discussions of Augustine's grasp of Platonic esotericism. Also see Pierre Manent, *Metamorphoses of the City: On the Western Dynamic*, trans. Marc LePain (Cambridge, MA: Harvard University Press, 2013), 269–73.

none in fact exists.⁵ Since there are these serious divisions between the two basic types of human beings, it is impossible, on the basis of Platonic thought, for all human beings to share a single, universal way of salvation whereby the entirety of a human being is made whole and is made whole together with other types of human beings in a universal community.

In the *City of God*, St. Augustine tells his reader that his philosophic interlocutor, Porphyry of Tyre, had not been able to find a "universal way for the liberation of the soul" (*liberandae animae uniuersalis uia*).⁶ Porphyry, Augustine argues, spurned Jesus Christ, who was the true mediator of the way of salvation open in principle to all human beings and all types of human beings. The argument between Augustine and Porphyry about the universal way of salvation is central to the work as a whole. It is key to the theoretical argument of the *City of God*, but it also picks up on a vitally important thread in pagan-Christian controversy in the late Roman Empire. The enormous expansion of Rome and its transition from republic to empire had far-reaching political, psychological, and religious effects. The psychological and political transformations in Rome were also accompanied by religious transformations as Roman religion moved more and more in the direction of the worship of world-spanning and cosmic gods. These various expansions gave rise to new problems, both theoretical and practical, about how to incorporate all manner of human beings into some kind of unity. Questions about unity among human beings quite naturally brought to the fore questions about what constitutes the wholeness of each, single human being, both in the here-and-now and after death. Augustine takes great pains to clarify the intimate link between those two problems, the wholeness of the single human person and the wholeness of the race of human beings, as well as the unique ability of Christ the mediator to solve both problems in his one act of redemption.

The most authoritative opinions about the prospects for a universal way of salvation coming from religion or philosophy were not very encouraging. Polytheistic religion, no matter its movement toward a more unitary understanding of the pantheon as time went on, was dogged by divisions of various types. Philosophers, as was becoming increasingly well known, tended to hold out one type of salvation for themselves and another for nonphilosophers based on the difference in capacity of various people to rise to the contemplation of eternal things. This latter situation proved to be both a rhetorical and theoretical problem for advocates of pagan religion and fertile territory for Christian apologetics.⁷ Augustine addresses himself to the various religious problems of pagan polytheism throughout the *City of God*, but it is this scandalous position especially

---

5. For a more fulsome, dedicated treatment of Plato's presentation of Socratic irony, see Ronna Burger, "Socratic Eironeia," *Interpretation: A Journal of Political Philosophy*, vol. 13, no. 2 (May 1985), 143–9.

6. *Ciu. Dei*, 10.32.

7. See Michael Bland Simmons, *Universal Salvation in Late Antiquity* (Oxford: Oxford University Press, 2016), x.

of his Platonic philosophic interlocutors that he is addressing in the *City of God* regarding the universal way of salvation.

Augustine knows of the classical political problem of the division between the few and the many with respect to their ability to attain the truth. In classical philosophy—especially Platonic philosophy—the division persists due to the limiting factors of human nature, in spite of any philosophic ministrations. "The many are vulgar," Veronica Roberts Ogle explains, "and in the classical world, there did not yet exist a widespread belief that they could be rescued from this. The Christian teaching that all are capable of being liberated was new. It was not, Augustine thinks, something that could come from the world."[8] But Augustine is able to resolve the division on a higher, theological plane through access to faith in the Incarnate Word of God. What is at stake is whether the many or only a few, select souls, can in principle live according to highest wisdom. For Augustine, the Incarnate Word grants the possibility of participation in a universal way of salvation open in principle to all human beings because Christ brings together in himself God and man, soul and body, intellect and will, and—through his loving, sacrificial passion and death—inaugurates the Catholic Church, in which all are capable of becoming members of his one body. Augustine also recognizes that the divisions afflicting human nature have their origins in sin, and therefore a solution on the basis of natural human resources will not get to the root of the problem.

For Augustine, the Incarnation of the Word of God overcomes the bifurcation between the few and the many that, on human terms, is unbridgeable. With the coming of Jesus Christ, wisdom is now available even to the many since the Divine Wisdom in person, the Word of God, has become flesh. Augustine nevertheless affirms the reality of the division between the wise and the foolish.[9] He only

---

8. Veronica Roberts Ogle, *Politics and the Earthly City in Augustine's City of God* (Cambridge, UK: Cambridge University Press, 2021), 87.

9. This judgment about the two classes of human beings influences the way Augustine himself writes. He says,

> For through [Moses] God has adapted the sacred writings to many men's interpretations, wherein will be seen things true and also diverse. Surely I myself—and I speak this fearlessly from my heart—if I were to write anything for the summit of authority, I would prefer to write in such a manner that my words would sound forth the portion of truth each one man could take from these writings, rather than to put down one true opinion so obviously that it would exclude all others, wherein there was no falsity to offend me. *Conf.*, 12.31.42.

As Frederick Crosson notes,

> These levels of meaning in a text will be accessible to "certain souls dedicated to intelligible things" but not to "other souls given over to things of sense," (13.18.22) for the latter, "still little ones and carnal (*animalibus*)," their beliefs will be strengthened in a childlike way, but "other men ... see the fruits that lie therein ... and look carefully at them and feed on them (12.28.37)."

refuses to grant it absolute status.[10] Augustine and his Platonic interlocutors make different judgments about the causes of the division among men and the effect of the division on the philosopher. The Platonic philosopher seems to think that the division is a result of nature. If the division is natural, there is not much the philosopher can do to bridge the chasm between the two types of men other than attempt to attract those few young men who have the necessary natural abilities for a life in philosophy. For the rest of the multitude, the philosopher must content himself with the attempt to moderate some of the more harmful consequences of its foolishness through the exertion of indirect influence on the city, for example, in the private conversations of Socrates, the lionization of philosophy in Plato's dialogues, or the revisionist theology of Varro or Porphyry.

In contrast, Augustine argues that the observable division between men and the limited distribution of natural abilities that allow men to pursue wisdom are only natural in a mitigated sense, since human nature is wounded by historical sin.[11] Further, this would affect all people—philosophers and nonphilosophers—alike.

Frederick Crosson, "Structure and Meaning in St. Augustine's Confessions," *Proceedings of the American Catholic Philosophic Association*, vol. 63 (1989), 84–97 at 90. See also the very beginning of Augustine's *De Trinitate*, where he is at pains to show how he writes in such a way that two classes of people, one given over to things of sense and the other pursuing intelligible things, are able to find the "portion of truth" appropriate to his own condition therein:

> The reader of this treatise on the Trinity should know beforehand that our pen is on the watch for the sophistries of those who consider it beneath their dignity to begin with faith, and who are thus led into error by their immature and perverted love of reason. Some of them attempt to transfer the ideas of corporeal things, which they have experienced through their bodily senses, or have grasped by their native human ingenuity and assiduous application, or by the help of art, to incorporeal and spiritual substances so as to measure and explain the latter by the former.

Augustine, *Trinity*, trans. Stephen McKenna, CSSR (Washington, DC: Catholic University of America Press, 2002), 1.1.1. The *Confessions* passages cited by Crosson lay the accent on the apparently docile simple believer, whereas the *Trinity* passage lays the accent on the obstinacy of some whose minds are carnal. For a taxonomy of the various types of simple believers, see Michael Cameron, *Christ Meets Me Everywhere* (Oxford: Oxford University Press, 2012), 62–3. I have tried to take Augustine's own advice as to how to read him into consideration in my own interpretation of his texts as found in this present work. The English text translation of the *Confessions* used herein is Augustine, *Confessions*, trans. F. J. Sheed (Indianapolis, IN: Hackett, 2006).

10. As Douglas Kries notes, "Augustine does not assert that the Platonic distinction between knowledge and opinion, the intelligible and the sensible, the wise and the unwise, has simply disappeared. But now, with the advent of Christian faith, there is a promising and realistic way for the many to move from the lower category to the higher." Kries, "Esotericism Thesis," 247.

11. See Augustine, *lib. arb.*, 3.18.173–9.

Human nature before sin did not suffer from the harmful divisions to which it is subject afterwards. Before the Fall, men enjoyed the harmony of right order, in which the body is subject to the soul, the sensitive soul is subject to reason and will, and reason and will are subject to God.[12] In this harmonious state, man's mind and his will are fixed upon God and, insofar as he considers created things, he refers them to God with praise and thanksgiving. Through sin, man violently disorders his mind and will; he wrenches them away from their proper object, the eternal things of God, and toward temporal things to the exclusion of God. Through the free choice of his will, man voluntarily subjected himself to the twin punishments of *ignorantia* and *difficultas*.[13] The divisions the philosopher observes after the Fall were therefore not always present. Because of the social and corporate nature of human beings,[14] the condition of disorder inaugurated by Adam and Eve is inherited by their descendants.[15]

Ignorance and difficulty manifest differently in the philosopher and the nonphilosopher, but Augustine insists that both suffer from them.[16] All men share in the consequences of the Fall; but since there are many temporal goods, some of which are nobler than others, divisions among men arise as to the grade of temporal goods they now pursue. Those who pursue baser goods are baser men, while those who pursue nobler goods are nobler men. Nevertheless, all men without grace pursue temporal goods to the exclusion of God—even the philosopher—who pursues the good of his own mind without praising and thanking God for it.[17] Because he pursues knowledge as the distinguishing mark of his way of life, the philosopher dismisses faith as the right guide to living an excellent life and regards revelation as suspect unless he is able to verify it according to the standard of his own reason. But it is not at all clear that all of the wisdom man desires or needs is available to his unaided reason. By insisting on this standard, the philosopher may very well unreasonably and precipitously rule out of court the avenues toward wisdom he most needs.

The desire for certain knowledge of the right order of things is what accounts for Augustine's immature, youthful turn to Manicheanism. But Manichean fables and superstitions do not keep Augustine's interest for long. Philosophy succeeds where Manicheanism does not, since philosophy actually provides a way to arrive at the truth of things. Augustine's burning passion throughout his life is for wisdom. He reports that he is definitively transformed in his nineteenth year when he reads Cicero's exhortation to philosophy, the *Hortensius*. Augustine says the book "changed my affections" toward "wisdom itself."[18] The way of life of

---

12. See, among many, many other texts, Augustine, *uera rel.*, 15.32.
13. See Augustine, *lib. arb.*, 3.18.178.
14. See Manent, *Metamorphoses*, 283, for an incisive treatment of this topic.
15. See Augustine, *lib. arb.*, 3.20.186–92.
16. See also Manent, *Metamorphoses*, 271.
17. See, inter alia, *conf.*, 5.3.5. See also Rom. 1:21, which is Augustine's source text in Scripture for these discussions.
18. *Conf.*, 3.4.7.

philosophy[19] and the way of life of Christianity as it is lived out concretely in the Church are, for St. Augustine, the two great candidates for the highest way of life because they are the only options that hold out hope for reaching true wisdom. Augustine chooses Christianity because he finds that Christianity, not philosophy, holds out the best hope to satisfy his desire for wisdom. This is because Christianity addresses itself to the reunification of the elements that philosophy separates, namely, in Manent's phrasing, "between the philosopher or wise man and the 'vulgar,' the latter deriving from the separation and even the rupture between the soul and the body that is the condition and achievement of philosophy."[20]

For Augustine, whereas philosophy perpetuates divisions within man between body and soul, mind and imagination, and among men, specifically between the philosophic few and the nonphilosophic many, Christianity holds out hope that man can be made whole through faith, or the loving knowledge of God as Father, Son, and Holy Spirit on the basis of the merciful and loving condescension of the divine Wisdom who has become incarnate. Human wholeness, broken by sin, is available to man through the mysteries of Christ's incarnation and redemptive work under two aspects. First, Christ makes man whole in himself; second, Christ reconfigures the whole body of men in his own body, the Church.

The question of wisdom and human wholeness comes to the fore dramatically as Augustine narrates his intellectual conversion in the *Confessions*. Any reader of the *Confessions* must ask the question upon finishing Book 7: Why was philosophy not enough for Augustine? What more did he need? The peak of Augustine's contemplations before his conversions happens in *conf.* 7.17.23 when he briefly grasps *that which is*, the unchanging being that has been the object of his search since he was awakened to the possibility of contemplative wisdom by Cicero.[21] Why doesn't that brief grasp lead inexorably to the banishing of his ignorance and difficulty in a stable adherence to the moral order? Why did it instead compound the pain of his ignorance and difficulty, deepening the divisions within himself and between him and others? To answer these questions, it is necessary to examine Augustine's full teaching on the obstacles to human flourishing and their effects on different types of men and on men when they gather to live together.

Both philosophy and Christianity attempt to address man's woeful condition by presenting a mode of discerning the right order of things and then a way in which to live in accord with it. That is why Augustine identifies the obstacles to human flourishing as ignorance and difficulty, which prevent the mind from knowing the right order of things and the will from choosing to live in accord with that order.

---

19. Philosophy, that is, as Augustine is most apt to consider it. In this book, I will follow Augustine's usage when he refers to "philosophy" or "philosophers." For a key text in Augustine's taxonomy of philosophers, see Augustine, *ciu. Dei*, 8.1.

20. Manent, *Metamorphoses*, 294. Manent observes that there is a parallel, for Augustine, between the Jewish separation of the chosen people from the nations and the separation between the philosopher and the nonphilosopher.

21. See *conf.*, 7.17.23.

Throughout most of what is commonly called the autobiographical part of the *Confessions*, Books 1–9, Augustine struggles mightily against his ignorance. He especially attempts to overcome his crude confusion of sensible and intelligible reality. Without the ability to distinguish these two orders of reality, Augustine has no hope of distinguishing the soul from the body or the human from the divine. He can, therefore, hardly expect to discern and live in accord with the order of creation if he cannot distinguish, on the one hand, between the different orders of creation, and on the other hand, between creatures and the Creator himself. This inability, therefore, stands at the heart of Augustine's troubles. When he makes his contemplative breakthrough to grasp unchanging being in *conf.* 7, he is able finally to touch that which he has most ardently desired and that which he has thought up to that point would finally put him on the way to happiness. It does not.

Because human beings are composed of body and soul, human wholeness must include both body and soul. Further, since the ravages of sin are the result of human choice, any solution to human troubles must address the miserable state of the postlapsarian will. Ignorance and difficulty must therefore be dealt with by focusing on their common root: sin. Human happiness concerns *both* the theoretical and moral life. Augustine's ascent to *that which is* remains, therefore, abortive and unstable not only because there is something wrong with his mind, but also because his will is divided. Contemplation on its own can do nothing to heal his will; instead, it increases his pain by making the object of his burning desire appear to him closer than ever, while yet remaining beyond his reach because of the "half-maimed" condition of his incontinent will.[22]

Since Augustine affirms the reality of the division of the human race into two classes of men, one of whom is given over to the pursuit of the sensible while the other seeks wisdom, he must affirm not only that the source of the salvation of each class of men is the same, but also that the salvation of each type of man is received differently according to his different constitution. In other words, while the humble acceptance of the humble mediator is the only way of salvation for all men, the humility of the advanced believer will express itself differently from the humility of the simple believer. As Augustine puts it elsewhere, there is only one truth, "which all men hear in the same measure when it is publicly spoken, but which each one appropriates in his own measure."[23] Augustine is simultaneously an everyman character in the *Confessions* and also an unrepeatable individual. He is an everyman in that his problems have the same root as anyone's problems, that is, in sin. But he is also no bland cipher: his personality and genius leap off of every page of the *Confessions*.

Augustine was a student of Platonic philosophy, although he read more of what have come to be known as "Neoplatonic"[24] texts than the Platonic dialogues

---

22. *Conf.*, 8.8.19.
23. *Jo. ev. tr.*, 98.2.
24. Joshua Parens clarifies by saying,

> I use the term "Neoplatonism" (a modern invention) to distinguish Plato proper from the authors that the Church Fathers such as Augustine referred to loosely as

themselves.[25] He carried into his theology the difference between the simple and the advanced believer, based on Paul's distinction between those who are capable of being fed meat versus those who are capable of being fed only milk.[26] Generally speaking, few Augustine scholars remark very much on the distinction or credit it

> "Platonism." The mainstay of the Neoplatonists was the assertion in Plato's *Republic*, book 6, that the good is beyond being (509b), which led to an intensification of Socratic dualism—and eventually to an antipolitical animus among thinkers such as Plotinus and Proclus.

Joshua Parens, *Leo Strauss and the Recovery of Medieval Political Philosophy* (Rochester, NY: University of Rochester Press, 2016), 156, n. 16. Parens is right to notice the antipolitical character of "Neoplatonism." See also Manent, *Metamorphoses*, 307.

25. See Lewis Ayres's treatment of the question of which Platonic books Augustine had read in *Augustine and the Trinity* (Cambridge, UK: Cambridge University Press, 2010), 13–18. According to Frederick Van Fleteren,

> Augustine had only a modest knowledge of Greek. For example, even in his maturity he could criticize Latin biblical translations by reference to Greek, but no more. Therefore, we conclude that Augustine knew Plato exclusively through secondary sources. Almost certainly he read Plato's *Timaeus* in Cicero's Latin translation (*cons. Ev.* 1.22.35), *Phaedrus*, and *Republic* through encyclopedias, doxographies, or other authors.

Frederick Van Fleteren, "Plato, Platonism," in *Augustine through the Ages: An Encyclopedia*, ed. Allan D. Fitzgerald, OSA (Grand Rapids, MI: Eerdmans, 1999), 651–4 at 651. Van Fleteren mentions several of the main authors from whom Augustine got his secondary knowledge of Plato: Virgil, Cicero, Varro, Plotinus, Apuleius, and Porphyry. As Robert Crouse helpfully observes, "for well over a century now, no aspect of Augustinian studies has been more marked by controversy than the question of his 'Platonism.'" R. Crouse, "*Paucis Mutatis Verbis*: St. Augustine's Platonism," in *Augustine and His Critics*, ed. R. Dodaro and G. Lawless (London: Routledge, 2000), 37–50 at 37. See also the chapter "Interlude: Plotinus, Porphyry and Augustine's Platonic Sources" in *Augustine's Early Theology of Image: A Study in the Development of Pro-Nicene Theology*, ed. Gerald Boersma (Oxford: Oxford University Press, 2016). John Peter Kenney assigns the reason for the controversy: "In the history of scholarship the relation of Augustine's thought to Platonism has at times been neuralgic, a proxy for larger struggles over the nature and shape of Christian theology." Kenney, writing sixteen years after Crouse, judges that the "specific question of Augustine's relation to Platonism has assumed a relative tranquility of late, as scholarship has come to a more capacious understanding of Hellenistic Judaism, Early Christianity, and Platonism itself." John Peter Kenney, "'None Come Closer to Us Than These:' Augustine and the Platonists," *Religions*, vol. 7, no. 9 (2016), 1–16 at 1.

26. See 1 Cor. 3:2 and Heb. 5:12.

Introduction 9

with having a significant influence on Augustine's thought as a whole.[27] An exception to the rule of scholarly neglect of Augustine's thought concerning the few and the many is French political philosopher Pierre Manent.[28] In his *Metamorphoses of the City*, Manent aptly highlights the bishop of Hippo's enormous debt to, as well as his criticisms of, his philosophic teachers.

---

27. In addition to Pierre Manent, the most outstanding in this latter group are Ernest L. Fortin and James V. Schall. In the other direction, one can note the otherwise very interesting volume, *Augustine and Politics*, edited by Doody, Hughes, and Paffenroth. None of the authors included in the volume takes up the distinction between the few and many in a thematic way. See *Augustine and Politics*, ed. John Doody, Kevin L. Hughes, and Kim Paffenroth (Lanham, MD: Lexington Books, 2005). There seems to be a similar *aporia* in a later book in the same series. See *Augustine and Philosophy*, ed. Phillip Cary, John Doody, and Kim Paffenroth (Lanham, MD: Lexington Books, 2010). Johannes Brachtendorf writes of the division between the learned and unlearned in his chapter in the latter volume. He says,

> The great humans—and Augustine obviously counts the evangelist John among them—can see; they dispose of the noetic vision of the divine, and simultaneously they trust in the cross in order to traverse the sea and arrive at the envisioned reality. Through philosophy they possess the highest form of knowledge, and through religion their will is entirely oriented towards God. To philosophize and to believe, to see the good itself and to love it above everything else, this is the best way to live according to Augustine.

He continues, referring to the little ones: "For those who cannot see also reach the longed-for homeland if they simply board the ship of faith and trust that it will bring them to the desired place." Johannes Brachtendorf, "Augustine on the Glory and the Limits of Philosophy," in *Augustine and Philosophy*, ed. Phillip Cary, John Doody, and Kim Paffenroth (Lanham, MD: Lexington Books, 2010), 3–22 at 7. This is basically correct, but may leave the reader wanting more. Brachtendorf does not, for instance, connect Augustine's division of Christians into great ones and little ones to the Platonic division between philosophers and nonphilosophers. These books seem representative of the field of Augustinian studies as a whole. It is not that there is no way to study Augustine's political thought or his engagement with Platonic philosophy profitably without adverting directly to the distinction between the few and the many in Augustine's thought; quite the contrary. My point is only to emphasize that this is a neglected approach that can shed light. In another vein, John M. Rist calls Augustine's identification of Carneades in *c. acad.*, 3.17.37–39 as a practitioner of esotericism a "strange claim, of uncertain origin." See Rist, "On the Nature and Worth of Christian Philosophy: Evidence from the *City of God*," in *Augustine's City of God: A Critical Guide*, ed. James Wetzel (Cambridge, UK: Cambridge University Press, 2012), 205–24 at 207. For an insightful response to the alleged strangeness of Augustine's claim, see Foley, "Commentary," 202 and following.

28. See, especially, the section of Manent's *Metamorphoses of the City* entitled "The Critique of the Pagan Sages." Manent, *Metamorphoses*, 269–73. See also ibid., 292–318.

In Manent's view, elucidated in a section dedicated to the thought of Augustine within his *Metamorphoses of the City*, "Christianity's point of impact is the separation between the few and the many. What Christianity attacks is not social or political inequality but the pertinence of the distinction between the few and the many, the philosopher and the nonphilosopher, with regard to the capacity to attain or receive the truth."[29] For the best of the pagan philosophers—in Augustine's view, the Platonists—human beings are ineluctably and irresolvably divided into the few and the many on the basis of their capacity to attain the truth and then live by it. To attain the truth requires an arduous ascent to transcend the shadowy realm of history to reach the light of eternal truth, undertaken through the ascetical intellectual endeavors of a rare and distinctive human type: the philosopher.[30] The multitude of human beings are consigned to the realm of history and opinion. This situation is summed up admirably in Plato's famous description of the divided line and the allegory of the cave in the *Republic*. The philosopher lives according to what is highest in him—his intellect—which is capable of transcending the realm of history and opinion. The multitude lives either according to spiritedness or appetite, neither of which is able to ascend to grasp eternal truth. Because the intellectual and moral gifts necessary for philosophic transcendence are distributed so sparsely by nature, the division between few and many is unbridgeable with the resources of nature. The best that can be hoped for in human affairs for the multitude is that, through chance, the multitude may come to be ruled—indirectly and imperfectly—by the wise. That chance occurrence, however, is understood by the Platonists to be unlikely in the extreme. The multitude does not know where to look for wisdom and likely would not like it if it were found. Christianity, however, breaks things wide open: the Incarnation of the Word resolves what is irresolvable by nature through a humble descent of the transcendent, eternal truth into history. It is possible, in Augustine's account, for even those human beings who are ruled by their appetites or spiritedness to grasp the savior who has walked among them. Through Christ's act of redemption, they can be transformed and, through faith in Christ, they can attain the truth and live according to it, even to some degree in this life. St. Augustine's argument with Porphyry of Tyre about the universal way

---

29. Manent, *Metamorphoses*, 272. This is the basis of Augustine's argument, for example, with Porphyry in the *ciu. Dei* over the universal way of salvation. See *ciu. Dei*, 10.32.5–7. He also dedicates the first part of *uera rel.* to an evaluation of Platonic esotericism. He says there, "However philosophers may boast, anyone can understand that religion is not to be sought from them. For they take part in the religious rites of their fellow-citizens, but in their schools teach divergent and contrary opinions about the nature of their gods and of the chief good, as the multitude can testify." Augustine, *Of True Religion*, trans. J. H. S. Burleigh (Chicago: Regnery, 1959), 5.8. All translations from *uera rel.* are from the Burleigh translation.

30. Roberts Ogle puts it well: "Philosophy, almost by definition, is reserved for the few. Few have the opportunity to transcend the horizon communicated to them by the city, and even fewer have the desire." Roberts Ogle, *Earthly City*, 77.

of salvation essentially concerns the cause for hope of all types of human being for salvation by the mediation of the Incarnate Word through his Church and sacraments.[31]

The Plan of This Book

The present volume is divided into three parts with distinct goals. Part I strives to give the proper context to Augustine's argument in the *City of God* about the universal way of salvation, both by presenting the topic as it was discussed among Augustine's Roman predecessors—especially Porphyry—and in exploring his treatment of the universal way of salvation earlier in his writing career. In Part I, the context and contours of the controversy over the universal way of salvation as it arose historically will be established. It will become clear that Augustine was thinking about the universal way of salvation throughout his literary career, not just late in the game when he wrote the *City of God*. Accordingly, the reader will see how Augustine discusses the topic of the universal way of salvation quite early on, with his *Epistula 1*, *Contra Academicos*, and *De uera religione*. Part I should give the reader an orientation to the argument between Augustine and Porphyry in the *City of God* both among historical events and other thinkers, as well as in some of Augustine's earliest writings.

Part II directly addresses Augustine's critique of Porphyry of Tyre's soteriological proposals in the *City of God*. This section also provides a look at the particularly theological way in which Augustine addresses the division between the few and the many and the anthropological features of that division, which concerns the

---

31. Before the argument proceeds too far, it is important to clarify what sense of "universalism" is involved. The contemporary discussion of universalism tends to involve Hans Urs von Balthasar's "Dare We Hope" thesis, or David Bentley Hart's even stronger version, found in his most recent book, which argues about whether or not all human beings might or might not be saved. See Hans Urs von Balthasar, *Dare We Hope "That All Men Be Saved"?* (San Francisco: Ignatius Press, 2014) and David Bentley Hart, *That All Shall Be Saved* (New Haven: Yale University Press, 2021). There is also a more ancient debate about universalism, which oftentimes centers around the writings of Origen of Alexandria. See Origen, *On First Principles*, 1.6 and 3.6, inter alia. The other sense of universalism is the offer of salvation to all types of human beings (leaving none out of the offer). It is the latter sense, in conversation with the Platonic tradition and especially the Platonic exposition of the tripartite soul, which would leave genuine salvation only to a single type of human being, which is discussed in the present volume. It is not the intention behind this present volume to offer a global defense of Augustine's views, only to give an account of the warp and woof of his argument on these matters with his Platonic interlocutors; to show why Augustine thought he had the better argument; and then to give a theoretical account of the foundations, scope, and implications of Augustine's position, especially by reference to several of his most important works.

distinction between practical and theoretical excellence and the distinction between the mind and the soul's lower powers. In short, Augustine develops an argument that the division between the few and the many is the result of historical sin and its consequences: ignorance, affecting the mind; and difficulty, affecting the will; and not a result of nature. Part II particularly treats Christ's mediation of the universal way of salvation as it affects the relations among human beings, although it will begin to become clear that the problems of the few and the many, and the problems attending the mind and will, are intimately and inextricably connected. The solution to the problem of human division will itself therefore need to be singular and unitary, capable in itself of effecting a universal reconciliation in a single act, in contrast with Porphyry's tripartite soteriological proposal in which, in the final account, it must be said that three separate ways of salvation are provided for three groups of human beings that remain, finally, divided.

The question that ought to arise at this point is, granted Christ's mediation of the universal way of salvation's effects on relationships among human beings, how does Christ's mediation affect the individual human being? And how does that effect on the individual human being's soul relate to the way of salvation that incorporates, in principle, all human beings? Part III will provide answers to those questions by examining Augustine's narration of his own life, in which the drama of salvation plays itself out and in which the attentive reader can see all of the forces playing out in Augustine's soul that play out in the *City of God*'s discussions of the relations among human beings. The parts of the soul and the ways of life based on them are intimately related in Augustine's thought just as much as in the thought of the various philosophers Augustine learns from and argues with. Taken together, Augustine's treatment of the universal way of salvation as it flows among men in society and as it flows through the individual both involve the reconciliation of elements divided by the effects of sin. The healing of divisions among human beings and within human beings, in the thought of Augustine, is effected by the same agency: the redemptive action of the Incarnate Word.

Part I

SETTING UP THE ARGUMENT ABOUT THE UNIVERSAL WAY OF SALVATION

Chapter 1

POLITICS, PERCEPTION, AND RELIGION FROM REPUBLIC TO EMPIRE

William Shakespeare and Pierre Manent's insights about the psychological and political transformations in the Romans wrought by the metamorphosis of Rome from city to empire illuminate the context of religious controversy in the late Roman Empire, which centered on (1) universal salvation and (2) who can offer it most plausibly and effectively. As Michael Bland Simmons has demonstrated thoroughly, the argument over universal salvation stretches over centuries and involves many of the leading lights in both pagan and Christian intellectual circles. The controversy over the possibility of a universal way of salvation is the linchpin of the argument of St. Augustine's *De ciuitate Dei*, especially in his argument with the Neoplatonist philosopher, Porphyry of Tyre.

Augustine's argument ultimately rests on the Incarnation of the Word of God in Jesus Christ. The hypostatic union provides the basis for Christ's mediation of the universal way of salvation to all human beings. The warp and woof of Augustine's Christological argument for Christ's mediation of a universal way of salvation constitutes the main focus of the present volume. In this Chapter 1, the decidedly *Roman* context of that argument will be made clear—which nevertheless does not detract from its relevance outside the Roman context. This chapter turns first to Manent's observations on the metamorphosis of Rome from city to empire, and then to the transformations in Roman religion wrought by the new imperial context, especially in the hands of the philosopher Porphyry of Tyre, who offers an alternative to the Christian universal way of salvation based on Christ's mediation that Porphyry and, most probably, the emperor Diocletian, hoped would be enticing enough to Romans to weaken the attractions of Christianity. Next, this chapter explores the psychological transformations Shakespeare narrates in his Roman trilogy that open the way for the political transformations brilliantly described by Pierre Manent and the religious transformations so thoroughly documented by Michael Bland Simmons.[1] Finally, the chapter will conclude with a brief reflection

---

1. Shakespeare's Roman plays are deeply indebted to Plutarch. Paul A. Cantor argues convincingly that "Shakespeare's debt to Plutarch was deeper and more extensive than has often been supposed, and that he penetrated to the core of the Greek author in a profound way, despite having read him in a translation that was twice removed from the

on the ways in which Porphyry's arguments in favor of a pagan universal way of salvation unintentionally laid the groundwork for the Constantinian revolution in Roman religion, which itself gave rise to problems in how both pagans and Christians were to understand the relationship between Christianity and politics, and which Augustine took great pains to address.

There is a long history of thinking about the rise of Christianity in terms of the changes in the late Roman Empire. One widespread opinion is that Christianity is to blame for the corruption of the Roman Empire. Nietzsche[2] and Gibbon are the most famous advocates of that position, along with many of Augustine's pagan opponents in the *City of God*. But Shakespeare shows the various transformations that open the way for Christianity already in motion before Christ is born, as will be discussed later in the present chapter. The political and geographic extension of the empire breaks open Roman perceptions, expanding—and diluting—them, making Romans much more interested in the universal, the cosmopolitan, and the boundless as their political experience decompresses. That dynamic already indicates a certain weakening of Roman politics and public spiritedness. It is no surprise that Roman religion would follow upon Roman politics and perceptions as the subject matter of religion moves from the gods of the city of Rome to world-spanning and cosmic gods. Even the famous—and questionable—otherworldliness of Christianity, Shakespeare seems to show, has its parallels in the Roman religion that results from the transformation from city to empire. Liebeschuetz even goes so far as to write,

> The "imperial theology" of the tetrarchy is without parallel in the history of imperial Rome. Jupiter and Hercules had of course always been part of Roman religion, and the emphasis given to these two divinities marks a revival of Roman religion and a retreat from the Greek and Near Eastern worship of Sol that had been favored by Aurelian. Nevertheless the mythological construction of the theology as a whole is un-Roman. It is obviously derived from Hellenistic theories of kingship, and related to the theological framework in which Eusebius was to place the Christian monarchy of Constantine. One can go further. The imperial theology of the greatest of the persecutors had important features in

---

original." Paul A. Cantor, *Shakespeare's Roman Trilogy: The Twilight of the Ancient World* (Chicago: University of Chicago Press), 183.

2. Although, as Cantor points out, Nietzsche's thought about the interplay of Christianity and Rome is more complex than it at first appears in works such as *The Antichrist*. See Cantor, *Shakespeare's Roman Trilogy*, 104–8, 119–24, and 130–4. Shakespeare and Nietzsche recognize that the critical transformations that paved the way for Christianity occurred before the advent of Christianity. For Nietzsche, Rome's corruption made the rise of Christianity possible—and perhaps only a corrupt Rome would have given rise to Christianity. But the critical weakening of Rome happened before Christianity came onto the scene and therefore Christianity could not have been the sole or main cause of Rome's corruption.

common with the religion which they persecuted. Jupiter is the supreme god. His son, Hercules, acts as his executive representative, and as a benefactor of man. The resemblance to Christian theology is obvious. Of course, imperial theology makes use of this pattern a second time: Jupiter and Hercules are each represented on earth by a "Son." The pagan state religion and Christianity were never closer in theology than at the time of the Great Persecution.[3]

Liebeschuetz is right about the resemblance, which was both exploited and misunderstood to great effect in the Arian controversy, as Erik Peterson has convincingly shown in his classic essay, "Monotheism as a Political Problem: A Contribution to the History of Political Theology in the Roman Empire."[4] It ought to surprise no one, therefore, that religious universalism and a universal way of salvation would become a flashpoint for religious and political controversy as the new faith vied with the old paganism—revised and revived by Christianity's political, religious, and philosophic opponents—for who could provide the most plausibly universal way of salvation, which would comport best with Rome's newly universalized perceptions and longings.

Pierre Manent convincingly argues that the phenomenon of Rome's metamorphosis from city to empire, which he calls "Caesarism," is not provided for in classical political thought. Manent's unique and groundbreaking contribution to political science is his observation that, in addition to political regimes, there also exist political forms. The factual basis of Manent's observation is simply that both the ancient city and the modern nation have the same variety of regimes, but the ancient city is not the same as the modern nation. In addition to city and nation, Manent identifies two, other political forms: empire and Church. Rome is a monarchy—an imperial monarchy, or empire—that follows a republic that has ceased to be able to govern itself. This order is a novel one, not appearing in the Greek experience.[5] For Manent, Rome therefore represents a unique case.[6]

Through the dynamic of competition for honor among the patricians, the Roman body eventually outgrows its republican soul. Rome's base is extended through conquest by the turning of its citizens' competition with each other outwards. The dynamic comes to an end when there can no longer be any competition because one among the patricians has so clearly and obviously

---

3. J. H. W. G. Liebeschuetz, *Continuity and Change in Roman Religion* (Oxford: Clarendon Press, 1979), 243.

4. Erik Peterson, "Monotheism as a Political Problem: A Contribution to the History of Political Theology in the Roman Empire," trans. Michael J. Hollerich, in Peterson, *Theological Tractates*, ed. Hollerich (Palo Alto, CA: Stanford University Press, 2011).

5. See Manent, *Metamorphoses*, 114.

6. "For the first time, a city, the most compact and dense political form, was expanding in an effort to encompass the whole world." Pierre Manent, "Birth of the Nation," *City Journal* (Winter 2013), https://www.city-journal.org/html/birth-nation-13529.html, accessed September 2, 2021.

achieved supremacy.[7] At one point, Caesar had rivals like Brutus and Cicero. But at some later point, Caesar's accomplishments mount up so high as to make any comparison of equality ridiculous. At that point, the republican principle of equality fails.[8] Manent explains the phenomenon of Caesar, writing,

> This extraordinary elevation of a citizen above those who were his equals presupposes a considerable modification of the form of the city. For such an elevation to be possible, its base—which is the city itself—must first have been considerably extended to be able to sustain this elevation. The surface area of the base, dare I say, must be proportional to the height of the new prince. The narrow city, "where all that is odious becomes even more odious," had to undergo such an extension and deformation, such a distention, that the laws of hate and love, the chemistry of the passions, were profoundly modified.[9]

Finding itself extended—or distended—in territory, Caesar's soul then gives the vertical dimension to the imperial body, replacing the republican soul.[10] But the consequences are far reaching: "The political and moral order becomes blurred or, better, indeterminate."[11] The compression of the republican civic political form allows not only for a "readily surveyable" territory on a human scale proportioned to human eyesight, but also clarity of deliberation in bringing thought and action together: the readily surveyable city is at least in principle comprehensible to its citizens' eyesight: not so the empire. To comprehend the empire by sight would

---

7. Allan Bloom argues, "Caesar is the peak and the end of that old order. Republican Rome had existed and flourished on two conditions—external warfare and domestic faction. Caesar, in principle, ended both of these conditions, which are undesirable in themselves; in so doing, he rendered it no longer necessary to have Romans." Allan Bloom, "The Morality of the Pagan Hero: *Julius Caesar*," in *Shakespeare's Politics*, ed. Allan Bloom with Harry V. Jaffa (Chicago: University of Chicago Press, 1981), 79.

8. Timothy W. Burns notes an important paradox in Shakespeare's depiction of Caesar:

> Unlike the rest [of the patricians], [Caesar] cannot be moved. But then he alone deserves to rule. So devotion to the republican principle of equality under the law must acknowledge the superior worth of him who is unsurpassingly devoted to such equality. Republicanism, by its own principle, points to the rule of one, to monarchy, as surely as it points away from despotism.

Timothy Burns, *Shakespeare's Political Wisdom* (New York: Palgrave Macmillan, 2013), 37.

9. Manent, *Metamorphoses*, 132.

10. David Lowenthal points out that Shakespeare's Julius Caesar even seems to plan for his own assassination to, in a way, release his spirit from the confines of his limited body so as to found a new, imperial regime. See David Lowenthal, *Shakespeare's Thought: Unobserved Details and Unsuspected Depths in Thirteen Plays* (Lanham, MD: Lexington Books), 102–4.

11. Manent, *Metamorphoses*, 132.

take godlike vision and to bring thought and action together in the empire would require something like divine providence.

The blurring of political and moral orders leads also to the weakening of human associations. The universality of the empire, Manent indicates, is a vague thing and induces vagueness. That vagueness is responsible for a new notion, found in Cicero, of the fellowship of the human race.[12] The new situation brings massive problems with it. Despite the empire's pretensions, Manent argues,

> It is impossible to consider humanity as such as a political form. In both cases, human action as *ratio et oratio* tends to detach itself from any political form as well as any political regime. It is no longer located in a concretely determined political order but in an order that will later be called *civilization* or what Cicero himself begins then to call the "universal society of the human race." *Ratio et oratio* are independent of any concrete political operation; they are at the service of a general morality, detached from political forms, in all political conditions, for the citizen of the smallest city as well as the emperor of Rome.[13]

At the same time as human action becomes detached from political regime and political form, it also privatizes.[14]

The attempts to update the pagan religions of Rome for the new imperial situation are all efforts at a new mediation between the human and the divine. There is an important transformation Manent notices between the Platonic treatment of religion in the context of the city and the Platonic treatment of religion in the context of the empire with regard to mediation. Manent explains,

> Such a transformation profoundly modifies human life; it modifies the life of the gods no less. This is indeed the context in which Augustine's critique has its target and meaning: the pagan religion with reference to which the Christian religion discloses its proper character most clearly is not the pagan religion of the cities in its original spontaneity; I might say, it is the religion of the cities that have undergone two important and related transformations, the intellectual transformation produced by Platonism and the political transformation produced by the passage from city to empire.[15]

As life in the empire depoliticizes, so also does Roman religion. But it is also important to note that Manent affirms that Plato's reform was a genuine reform, which introduced two, new ameliorations: first, that any god must be good; and second, that no god is subject to corruption. This more satisfactory and fitting understanding of the divine makes the problem of mediation more urgent, since

---

12. See Manent, *Metamorphoses*, 134. See also Cicero, *De officiis*, 1.16.52–4.
13. Manent, *Metamorphoses*, 135.
14. Manent also confirms Shakespeare's insight about privatization. See ibid., 143.
15. Ibid., 307.

it emphasizes the otherness of the divine.[16] The suitable mediation, Augustine argues, is the one provided by the Incarnation. It is important to emphasize that the difference between the pagan attempt at mediation and the Christian attempt at mediation is not the tired old saw about the relationship between the world and the otherworldly. In different senses, the Roman civic attempt at mediating the human and the divine, the imperial Roman attempt at mediating the human and the divine, and the Christian attempt to mediate the human and the divine all have components of the worldly and the otherworldly. Manent's understanding of political form is especially important for the topic at hand because it shows the ways in which all three attempts were attempts at dealing with the same problem, but in different circumstances (political, religious, perceptual) and with different resources (primarily, the Incarnation itself).

These transformations in pagan religion give rise to the problem of mediation, which can be briefly explained: "How can humans enter into relation with gods that are surely good but who have nothing to do with humans? … Through what mediator or mediators can humans enter into relation with gods that are so conceived?"[17] The perverse situation of a depoliticized, Platonized pagan religion gives rise to a search for mediators, the conclusion of which Plato probably never envisaged. What is between gods and men? The demons are those amalgams of the divine and the human. The problem with the demons is that they share the passions with humans. As Manent comments, the religion of Platonists like Apuleius compels its worshippers to honor as gods those whom one would never want to resemble.[18] The problem, as Augustine sees it, is that the "Platonists" have not found the correct mediator.

Remarkably, Shakespeare's Roman trilogy of *Coriolanus*, *Julius Caesar*, and *Antony and Cleopatra* confirm Manent's observations about the distention of Rome and the effects of Rome's metamorphosis from city to empire. The play dealing directly with the metamorphosis is *Julius Caesar*. Cassius' description of Julius Caesar, quoted at the beginning of this chapter, puts the matter starkly: Caesar's enlargement is a mortal threat to Rome, or at least, to Roman republicanism— which is the same thing to an austere citizen of the old republic like Cassius.[19] Cassius' lines encapsulate nicely the extraordinary metamorphosis Caesar catalyzes: from civic republic to empire. That shift, as Pierre Manent brilliantly demonstrates, is unprecedented, ushering something new into the world, a new

---

16. See ibid., 314.
17. Ibid., 308.
18. Ibid., 309.
19. Shakespeare sums up the contrast between the old-school republican Cassius and the new style of man suited for the new empire when he has Julius Caesar say, "Let me have men about me that are fat, Sleek-headed men, and such as sleep o' nights. Yond Cassius has a lean and hungry look. He thinks too much. Such men are dangerous." *Julius Caesar*, I.ii.192–5. The implicit contrast is with Antony, whose attraction to the luxuries of private life are unfolded in *Antony and Cleopatra*.

political form not anticipated by the *politike* of Plato or Aristotle. As Manent demonstrates, the extension—or distention—of Rome geographically across the world of the Mediterranean and Europe dissolves her civic form and, with the magnification of Julius Caesar, becomes something new. That new political form transforms Roman perceptions so that the city of Rome shrinks, with the world—or as close to it as humanly possible—taking its place.[20] New perceptions produce a new mentality that extends not only to politics but also to Roman religion, both suppressing the old civic paganism and opening up the possibility—first psychologically and then in actuality—of a new sort of religion. The new religion will be concerned not only with present benefits but also the afterlife, and not only with the benefit of fellow citizens of the city of Rome but with the salvation of any who might come under Rome's imperial aegis—in principle, all human beings without exception. The new psychological conditions not only explain the new space for the cult of the emperor, the new place for Jupiter, and the wholly new dedication to Sol Invictus,[21] it also opens room for a vastly different type of religion, which firmly sets paganism aside: Christianity.

This chapter uses the same justification for turning to Shakespeare in order to understand Rome that Pierre Manent uses:

> I propose to interrogate Shakespeare. Since this approach is not obvious, I owe the reader a brief explanation. Shakespeare's Roman plays follow faithfully Plutarch's *Lives*. A historian and philosopher, Plutarch was admired by Montaigne and Rousseau for his acute judgment of human actions and for his skill in revealing the bases of these actions. The drama of the theater adds to these qualities, for it is all about action, and there all speech serves action or is bound up with it, thus bringing to the surface, by its very form, the springs of human endeavor. Shakespeare's Roman plays thus make available to us not, of course, a historical document, but an interrogation or inquiry into the motives of the actors of the Roman Republic, the regime that left the deepest mark on the history of Europe and of the West.[22]

Shakespeare's Roman trilogy of plays drawn from source material in Plutarch, which includes the tragedies of *Coriolanus*, *Julius Caesar*, and *Antony and Cleopatra*, provides—among other things—a literary narrative of Rome's transformation from city and republic into empire. The fulcrum of the trilogy is *Julius Caesar*,

---

20. Andrew Fichter argues that Antony and Cleopatra "pursue the logic of transcendence to the point where it verges on a new perception of the universe." Andrew Fichter, "*Antony and Cleopatra* and Christian Quest," in *Shakespeare's Christian Dimension: An Anthology of Commentary*, ed. Roy W. Battenhouse (Bloomington, IN: Indiana University Press, 1994), 500.

21. See Liebeschuetz, *Continuity and Change in Roman Religion*, 243.

22. Pierre Manent, "The Tragedy of the Republic," *First Things* (May, 2017), https://www.firstthings.com/article/2017/05/the-tragedy-of-the-republic, accessed December 29, 2021.

where Shakespeare allows the reader to see the transition in motion. Paul A. Cantor argues, "In Shakespeare, the movement from *Coriolanus* to *Antony and Cleopatra*—and hence from the Republic to the Empire—transforms the Romans from citizens to subjects. What the conspirators hold against Julius Caesar is precisely that he is turning noble Romans into bondsmen."[23] In the republic, men are driven by honor, especially honor given by equals who are seen to be equals. The desire for honor is motivated by the spirited part of the soul, which demands that virtue be rewarded and vice punished. The tragedy of Coriolanus concerns what happens when human spiritedness is purified and separated from all other forces that play on the soul and thereby made supreme. Jan H. Blits argues, "Coriolanus's spirited opposition to everything in his nature except spiritedness gives rise to his spirited opposition to his enemies in battle. Seeking to be altogether spirited, he is always at war against others."[24] Blits also points out that the purification of Coriolanus' character leads to a deep tension. Coriolanus both desires honor and repudiates it. Blits explains,

> Loving excellence and victory, he loves honor. There is, consequently, a theatrical element in much that he does. To be looked up to, he must be looked at … . But Coriolanus also repudiates honor, for its pursuit implicitly denies the self-sufficiency of virtue. Not only does honor depend on others and is only as good as those who bestow it, but the desire for it implies that virtue is not an end in itself, but rather a means to a further end— "[a] bribe to pay [one's] sword" (1.9.38).)[25]

The reason behind the office of the consul seems to be to keep the patrician love of honor in check by subjecting it to the need for the ratification of the plebeians, who are "chiefly characterized in terms of their appetite."[26] By contrast, Coriolanus seems to desire to excise the aspects of the city not predominantly driven by the spirited praise of virtue, which aspects he regards as contemptible.

As befits a story about honor given among peers who must be known as peers, *Coriolanus*' action is concrete, making frequent reference to various built features of the city of Rome so that the city itself becomes a kind of character in the play. This can only happen because the city of Rome is, in the time of Coriolanus, of a human scale that allows citizens to observe each other's actions. The city of Rome in *Coriolanus* seems to match the description Aristotle gives of a city's physical character: that its population and its territory are "readily surveyable."[27] By

23. Cantor, *Shakespeare's Roman Trilogy*, 106.
24. Jan H. Blits, *Spirit, Soul, and City: Shakespeare's* Coriolanus (Lanham, MD: Lexington Books, 2006), 2.
25. Ibid., 4.
26. Paul Cantor, *Shakespeare's Rome: Republic and Empire* (Chicago: University of Chicago Press, 2017), 71.
27. Aristotle, *Politics*, trans. Carnes Lord, University of Chicago Press (Chicago: 1984), 7.5.2. Leo Strauss expands: "A city is a community commensurate with man's natural powers

contrast, the nation as a political form can only be surveyed through the faculty of imagination. Hugh Liebert argues, "The nation is essentially an 'imaginary community,' for it is too large to be known in any other way."[28] Liebert continues, "The nation does not abjure every appeal to the immediacy of vision, however. The nation can be seen as a whole via figurative representation, as when we view the shape of the nation on a map, and in national symbols—that is, visible but reproducible objects—such as flags, coins, and portraits."[29] But the nation also "is not merely imagined but imagined in a particular way," according to Liebert, "and this is important, because it is possible to imagine one's political body not as a community set apart but as a community that incorporates the whole. This imaginary universal community is what I have called the empire."[30] The shift from the immediacy of vision, which is capable of taking in only the enclosed space of the compressed political form of the city gives way to the ever-expanding empire and the vagaries of imagination, not subject to the limitations of the human sense of sight, but also less capable of orienting and sustaining concrete human action on a human scale.

The gods of the city of Rome in *Coriolanus* are straightforward and concerned with the well-being of the city. If you are victorious or successful, the gods favor you; if not, not. Shakespeare even goes out of his way to minimize the role of priests and prophets in *Coriolanus*. Cantor observes, "In *Coriolanus*, he contradicts his source in Plutarch by all but excluding priests from his portrait of republican Rome."[31] Shakespeare depicts the increasing role and authority of priests and soothsayers as the Roman trilogy progresses, which seems to go hand in hand with an increasing obscurity and distance of the gods and an increasing loss of confidence in human agency.

In *Julius Caesar*, Shakespeare shows the implosion of the republican way of life to be the effect of the man Julius Caesar. If the republican way of life depends on the desire for honor given among peers and equals,[32] the obviously peerless Julius Caesar destroys the ground of equality necessary for honor-seeking.[33] The

---

of firsthand or direct knowledge. It is a community which can be taken in in one view, or in which a mature man can find his bearings through his own observation, without having to rely habitually on indirect information in matters of vital importance." Leo Strauss, *Natural Right and History* (Chicago: University of Chicago Press, 1965), 131.

28. Hugh Liebert, *Plutarch's Politics: Between City and Empire* (Cambridge, UK: Cambridge University Press, 2016), 70.

29. Ibid., 70, n. 91.

30. Ibid., 71.

31. Cantor, *Shakespeare's Roman Trilogy*, 110.

32. See Michael Platt, *Rome and Romans According to Shakespeare* (Lanham, MD: University Press of America, 1983), 100–1.

33. Allan Bloom puts it well:

> *Julius Caesar* is the story of a man who became a god. Beyond his merely human achievements—the destruction of the Republic and the establishment of a universal

realization of what Caesar portends is what motivates the bitter but also deadly serious speech by Cassius at the beginning of this chapter:

CASSIUS
Why, man, he doth bestride the narrow world
Like a Colossus, and we petty men
Walk under his huge legs and peep about
To find ourselves dishonorable graves.[34]

The various contentions for honor among the Roman nobility has finally produced a figure that towers so far above the rest that there can no longer be any more contention.[35] In the meantime, those very contentions have extended Rome far beyond what it had been in its primitive beginnings in *Coriolanus* by motivating noble Romans to win glory in conquest.[36] In order to take the measure of such an extended or distended Rome, one might say, a colossus is needed. No petty man will do.

In *Julius Caesar*, the religion of the Romans has a very different character from that in *Coriolanus*. There are portents in the heavens, and even the earth seems to be unstable.[37] The difference is stark. Cantor notes, "In [*Julius Caesar*] the Romans do make reference to the heavens … . In *Coriolanus*, most of the references are to parts of the city. Menenius asks in Act 5, 'See you yond coign o' the capital?'"[38]

> monarchy—he was worshiped [sic] as a divinity, as were many of those who inherited his name. His appearance ended forever the age of human heroes. Caesar brought to fulfillment the end implied in all heroic ambition; he proved himself the best of all men. He had no competitor; he was benefactor without being beneficiary. Finally, his spirit ruled Rome, conveyed the sole title to legitimacy, and punished all offenders against it. He was, in short, self-sufficient.
>
> Bloom, "Pagan Hero," 75.

34. William Shakespeare, *Julius Caesar*, I.ii.135–8. All references to Shakespeare's plays are from *The Complete Works of Shakespeare*, ed. David Bevington (New York: Longman, 1997).

35. The potential for a Caesar was always there from the beginning, Shakespeare shows. Cantor remarks, "The city is potentially too dependent on its great leaders, as we see when Coriolanus almost brings it to its knees single-handedly. If one of the patricians could master his rivals in the political competition in the city, he could take it over completely." Cantor, *Shakespeare's Roman Trilogy*, 30. Platt points out the effects Caesar has on both of Rome's classes, the plebs and the patricians: "To the plebs [Caesar] offers comfortable self-preservation without political rights or duties. Upon the patricians, he imposes much the same; he deprives them of the pursuit of honor, the leading aim of their lives and the foundation of their political rights and duties." Platt, *Rome and the Romans*, 192.

36. "The passions which are unsatisfied within the city spill out in the direction of conquest; the turbulence in the city leads to war with other cities." Platt, *Rome and Romans*, 122.

37. See *Julius Caesar*, I.iii.3–13.

38. Shakespeare, *Coriolanus*, V.iv.1.

When he looks up, he still sees a Roman building, but in *Julius Caesar* when the Romans look up they see the heavens being torn apart."[39] The disorientation the characters in *Julius Caesar* experience renders the city less distinct than it was in *Coriolanus*. In *Coriolanus*, as Michael Platt observes, "The Roman city is dedicated to nothing higher than itself; its gods are native, civic, and local, not transcendent and universal."[40] The distention of Rome through conquest seems to have torn it open somehow—no longer able to shelter its residents, provide for the mutual observation of citizen peers, and fix its citizens' horizons. The scale of the action and the characters' perceptions have altered to something more than human. The superhuman character of the action and setting of the play is reinforced by the role that soothsayers, dreams, and ghosts play. Rome is no longer something that is "readily surveyable," at least not by human sight. The breaking open of Rome also seems to open it to a religion whose gods are no longer native, civic, and local but rather transcendent and universal.

If the city of Rome becomes indistinct and fragmented in *Julius Caesar*, it virtually exits the scene in *Antony and Cleopatra*. Imperial modes and perceptions are at the forefront of *Antony and Cleopatra*, moving toward the limitless extent of the empire, an unleashing of new types of desires, and toward the satisfactions of private life and away from the satisfactions of public life. The effect, Cantor argues, is that, "In the sprawling, cosmopolitan world of *Antony and Cleopatra*, the Romans lose their ethical and political bearings and as a result even their faith in human agency."[41] What begins in *Julius Caesar* with the cracking open of Rome is brought to its full realization in *Antony and Cleopatra*. Even the battles that are fought in *Antony and Cleopatra* are fought for the most part on the indeterminate and expansive sea. There are no sea battles in *Coriolanus* or *Julius Caesar*.

Roman republican ethics and politics take their bearings from honor and the drive especially among the patricians to seek honor. Cantor argues, however,

> In the Empire, the rewards of public life begin to look hollow, whereas private life seems to offer new sources of satisfaction. The change from the era of the Republic might be conveniently summed up in the formula: the Imperial regime works to discourage spiritedness and encourage eros, or, more accurately

---

39. Paul A. Cantor, "Shakespeare and Politics: *Julius Caesar*," lecture 1 of 3; https://thegreatthinkers.org/shakespeare-and-politics/lecture-course/?video=4, accessed September 1, 2021. See also Platt, *Rome and Romans*, 52–3.

40. Platt, *Rome and Romans*, 147. Platt suggests that the key to Rome's restless lust for conquest is its lack of a true foundation. Rome's subsequent deeds seek in some way to make up for the absence of an origin. Accompanying Rome's martial deeds is a long, cooperative work of rhetoric and mythology attempting to cover over the lack of a true foundation. See ibid., 148–9.

41. Cantor, *Shakespeare's Roman Trilogy*, 106.

expressed, by removing the premium the Republic places on spiritedness, the Empire sets eros free with a new power.[42]

The satisfactions of love between Antony and Cleopatra occupy the same position as the satisfactions of honor in *Coriolanus*.[43] After all, as Cleopatra exclaims, "'Tis paltry to be Caesar."[44] The reason it is paltry to be Caesar is because Caesar puts an end to the honor-seeking that characterizes the noble patrician class of the republic. Caesar makes all Romans into bondsmen, thereby diminishing them. What good is honor received from bondsmen? As Cantor puts it, "Above all what the Republic offers and the Empire denies is a sense of being honored by one's equals. The Emperor has no equals and, instead of accepting recognition of his worth freely given by fellow citizens, he can only experience what amounts to the submission of slaves to his will."[45] With the way of life based on the public pursuit of honor foreclosed, even Rome's most outstanding men are bound to seek private satisfactions.

Antony and Cleopatra ends up being a love story between the titular characters. Antony turns his back on his wife, Octavia, the very image of the Roman patrician matron, in favor of the exotic Cleopatra. Cantor explains, "Cleopatra is a potent symbol of the seemingly infinite proliferation of new human possibilities unleashed by the imperial regime and the revaluation of traditional values; as Enobarbus says of her, "Age cannot wither her, nor custom stale / Her infinite variety. Other women cloy / The Appetites they feed, but she makes them hungry / Where most she satisfies; for vilest things / Become themselves in her, that the holy priests / Bless her when she is riggish."[46] Cleopatra is herself an index of the transformation

---

42. Cantor, *Shakespeare's Rome*, 128. Platt points out what Caesar means for politics in Rome: "The rule of a god is unpolitical and destroys the life of honor." Platt, *Rome and Romans*, 189–90.

43. Platt notes, "In Pompey and throughout the play we see the fading of Roman virtue. It survives, but fitfully, in the intermittent courage of Antony; in his magnanimity it glows but ember-like; and in his sensuality it bows before a new god, both un-Roman and uncivil, Eros." Platt, *Rome and Romans*, 259. Although, as Platt points out later, this eros is a remarkably infertile eros. Ibid., 271.

44. Shakespeare, *Antony and Cleopatra*, V.ii.2.

45. Cantor, *Shakespeare's Rome*, 129–30. Platt likewise argues,

But the impact of Caesar seems to reach beyond politics. In ordering that no images be hung with Caesar's trophies, the Tribunes seek to prevent a feared event; Caesar may "soar above the view of men / And keep us all in servile fearfulness" (I.i.74-75). To be above the view of men is to be outside politics which is intimately connected with "other men," but to be so elevated, nevertheless, has this effect on politics and other men: it makes them servile.

Ibid., 189.

46. Cantor, *Shakespeare's Roman Trilogy*, 117–18. For the passage from the play, see *Antony and Cleopatra*, 2.2.234–9.

of Roman desires from the concrete and particular desire to serve the concrete and particular city to the limitlessly fecund Cleopatra, whose limitless possibilities open up like the expansive horizons of the empire itself.

As perceptions and politics change, so also does religion. The priests who are most prominent in *Antony and Cleopatra* are the Egyptian priests of Cleopatra's court. No longer will the gods and the religion of the empire have a straightforward relationship to the city of Rome. In fact, as Cantor points out,

> The most striking supernatural incident in *Antony and Cleopatra* is not the entrance but the exit of a god, suggesting that, whatever will replace it, the traditional Roman religion is coming to its end. The eery scene when "the god Hercules, whom Antony lov'd, / Now leaves him" (IV.iii.16-17) seems to have more than personal significance, faintly suggesting as it does the motif of the flight of the pagan gods, familiar to us from Milton's "Nativity hymn." In another scene with symbolic resonance, Shakespeare shows the world of classical antiquity drunk and reeling, involving in song the god of an Eastern mystery religion (II.vii.113-118). Perhaps Shakespeare realized that when Rome turned to foreign gods like Bacchus, it was a sign of the city's decline, and the beginning of a process that eventually dissolved the ancient world.[47]

What sort of god, what sort of religion is portended? Shakespeare ends his Roman trilogy with a hint, or more than a hint, of what is to come. The distention of the city of Rome through conquest and the appearance of the figure of Julius Caesar have forced it to metamorphose into something else. Allan Bloom observes, "Julius Caesar has prepared the way for monarchy and peace; within that peace can be sown the seeds of a new faith which exalts peace. The old gods leave with the last warrior. The old order and its characteristic man must pass before the new one can grow."[48] Having been cracked open and then had its extent brought to heel by the height of the Colossus, Caesar, Roman perceptions, and politics move in the direction of the limitless and universal. Cantor comments,

> Perhaps one universal deity is needed to correspond to the universal Emperor in the world of *Antony and Cleopatra*. Cleopatra's dream of Antony can be interpreted as an attempt to create the myth of such a universal god: His face was as the heav'ns, and therein stuck / A sun and moon, which kept their course, and lighted / The little o' th' earth. His legs bestrid the ocean, his rear'd arm / Crested the world [V.ii.79–83].[49]

---

47. Cantor, *Shakespeare's Rome*, 145.
48. Bloom, "Pagan Hero," 79.
49. Cantor, *Shakespeare's Rome*, 145.

Shakespeare (perhaps uncharacteristically) avoiding implausible anachronism, does not directly mention Christianity, but the Eastern-ness of the new god seems deliberate. The corruption of the republic leads to the empire.

The emphasis on the sterility of the ascendant Roman *eros*, which tends to issue only in the exhaustion of the Romans and of the Roman way of life, seems to point to the source both of a new vitality and the fulfillment of Roman immortal longings in the birth of the Christ child, which will inaugurate a confrontation on the Roman imperial scene.[50] Shakespeare shows the inchoate transformation through Cleopatra.[51] The change from city to empire inaugurates a change in longings. Shakespeare therefore confirms the observations of both Simmons and Manent regarding the metamorphoses in perception, politics, and religion.

As the tragedy of Rome unfolds, Shakespeare shows the gradual depoliticization of Rome. As Manent puts it,

> *Coriolanus* is the most completely political play. It is exclusively and one might say obsessively political: The city is the beginning and the end of all the actions of all the characters. In contrast with the civic closure of *Coriolanus*, *Antony and Cleopatra* deals only with the division or unity of the "world." There is even, beginning in the first lines, the question of finding out a "new heaven, a new

---

50. See Platt, *Rome and Romans*, 272–3. Platt pointedly observes that "of the eight references to Herod which appear in Shakespeare's works, five occur in *Antony and Cleopatra*: I.ii.27; III.iii.3; III.iii.4; III.vi.73; IV.vi.14." Ibid., 275–6, n. 12. Roy Battenhouse argues that Shakespeare may be using Antony as a kind of "perverted likeness to Christ," so that the world of Christianity can be seen to be present by its absence. See Battenhouse, "Shakespeare's Augustinian Artistry," in Battenhouse, *Shakespeare's Christian Dimension: An Anthology of Commentary* (Bloomington: Indiana University Press, 1994), 45. Maurice Hunt explains, "A Christian tradition reaching back into the Middle Ages construed the defeat of Julius Caesar's assassins and the ascendancy of an absolute ruler, Augustus Caesar, as necessary for the establishment of the so-called *pax Romana*, the universal peace cited in Isaiah 39.8 as a condition for the Messiah's birth." Maurice Hunt, "A New Taxonomy of Shakespeare's Pagan Plays," *Religion and Literature*, vol. 43, no.1 (Spring 2011), 29–53 at 30. Octavius himself in IV.vi.5–7 of *Antony and Cleopatra* says

> OCTAVIUS
> The time of universal peace is near.
> Prove this a prosp'rous day, the three-nooked world
> Shall bear the olive freely.

51. Joseph Alulis observes, "'Tis paltry to be Caesar; Not being Fortune, he's but Fortune's knave' (V.ii.1-3). She takes her bearings by something beyond the realm of fortune. But everything in the sphere of time, as subject to change, is governed by fortune. What makes life better is to look to what is beyond time, that is, eternal." Joseph Alulis, "'The Very Heart of Loss': Love and Politics in *Antony and Cleopatra*," in *Shakespeare and the Body Politic*, ed. Bernard J. Dobski and Dustin Gish (Lanham, MD: Lexington Books, 2013), 31–48 at 46.

earth." The aging imperator and the sorceress of the Nile seek to fill, by their passion alone, a world that is henceforth without a city and deserted by the gods of the city.[52]

The external expansion of perceptions experienced by the title characters leads to a privatization of desires. By transcending the closed city, human beings living in the context of the imperial form are pushed away from politics and toward the private sphere. It is in private that they will now pursue their various satisfactions. But their new perceptual framework of the entire world is with them even in private. They begin to want a private transcendence of the political order, which the old civic paganism of the civic temples and public sacrifices limps to satisfy. They are searching in this new context for a new mediation between the divine and the human. Into this gap many new expressions of religiosity will step.

The new imperial form has certain advantages over the old civic form. Manent clarifies that while the city enjoyed liberty, that liberty was purchased at the cost of restlessness, whereas the empire provides peace, albeit at the cost of domination under a master.[53] After the bloody history of the republic, the new *pax Romana* has much to recommend it. Still, as Manent observes, "Whatever its historical success, which stems perhaps above all from the civic energies it still harbors, an inner weakness affects the Roman imperial form. It is far from satisfying the aspirations awakened by the original experience of the city."[54] What Manent notices here is the much-publicized weakening or corruption of the Roman regime. If the new political form is incapable of satisfying human longings, those longings will not simply go away. They will seek satisfaction elsewhere. For Augustine, the city of God—among other things—features both a type of universality analogous to imperial universalism and also the intimacy of the city. Hugh Liebert observes,

> It is possible, however, to conceive of a situation in which vision is set free from its natural limits as we know them, and thus to transpose the form of the city into a universal key. Tocqueville discerns this sort of form when he describes God's vision … . This form, then, would be both visible (insofar as God can count the hairs of one's head) and universal (insofar as no one's head is excluded). If we refer to the universal imaginary form as empire, we might refer to this universal form as the City of God.[55]

The way of life of the city of God, it almost goes without saying, brings unique perils and problems. The bifocalism of the Middle Ages with its two swords and the struggle to make practical sense out of the mixture of the earthly city with the

---

52. Manent, "Tragedy of the Republic."
53. Manent, *Metamorphoses*, 105.
54. Ibid., 143.
55. Liebert, *Plutarch's Politics*, 72.

city of God in the practical realm loom on the horizon. At the same time, the way of life of the city of God is not only suited to the context of an imperial earthly city. The city of God is, however, admirably suited to address the longing for the satisfactions of the private sphere, but a private sphere capable of transcending the ends of political life, to be found in the context of the late Roman Empire.

Chapter 2

RELIGIOUS UNIVERSALISM IN THE LATE ROMAN EMPIRE AND THE ARGUMENTS OF PORPHYRY OF TYRE

The salvation sought by Romans begins to have an increasingly otherworldly orientation at the same time as it detaches itself from the political common good of Rome. This new situation cannot but give rise to a transformation in religious longing. The new mystery religions and the theurgical rites encouraged by, for instance, Porphyry of Tyre address the change in mentality of the Romans. They are oriented toward the longing for personal salvation and detached from political community. They are, therefore, private and also able to make less of the differences in customs and personal station inherent in an expansive empire than the older civic religion of Rome.

Michael Bland Simmons documents the struggle of paganism to adapt to the new situation while entering into conflict with Christianity. Simmons boldly argues, "The first Christian emperor did not cause an unprecedented cultural and political revolution: He simply embraced a movement already experiencing exponential growth, whose universalism was the most suitable for a successful politico-cultural unification program, which his predecessors failed to achieve due to the pluralistic, inclusive, and quite fluid nature of pagan views on salvation."[1] The metamorphosis of Rome from city and republic into empire has fundamentally altered Roman perceptions, extending or distending them to match the extended or distended territory of the burgeoning empire. In decompressing Rome, Romans moved increasingly to achieve their various types of human satisfactions in private and detached from politics. The political institutions and religious longings of the people followed suit. Christianity comes to sight as finely suited to the times, bearing a universal way of salvation for (in principle) all types of human beings based on the mediation of the Word made flesh, without destroying or washing out distinctive differences among particular peoples and ways of life.

In the context of the late Roman Empire, pagan religion went through a reorientation to match the metamorphosis of Rome itself. The well-documented

---

1. Simmons, *Universal Salvation*, 209.

proliferation of mystery religions was proof that the old-time Roman paganism already was deficient in addressing the longings of the people it used to serve. In that context, Simmons explains, "This perception that Christ alone offered universal salvation regardless of one's social, economic, gender, class, racial, age, and even moral status was an increasingly attractive component that gave it the edge in its competition with all the other salvation cults" in Rome.[2] There were many attempts, sometimes deliberate and sometimes not, on the part of pagan religions to adapt to the times and the new political and cultural situation Rome's metamorphosis brought about: the various mystery religions, the spread of Gnosticism, and even the emphasis on the world-spanning or cosmic aspects of the old mainstays of the Greek and Roman pantheon to make them more suitable to the new situation.

The adoption of the cult of Sol Invictus by the emperor Aurelian and subsequent emperors—up to and including Constantine until his conversion to Christianity—seems to have been an attempt to adapt a figure familiar from old-time Roman paganism to fit the new needs of expansive, imperial Rome. The emperors had other needs, too: the extent of the empire meant that it was always in danger of fracturing. A more universal religion would serve as a valuable support to the increasingly difficult task of keeping the empire unified. The various crises the Empire suffered in the third century[3] made the effort to bind the empire together more and more pressing. As Simmons notes, "The centerpiece of imperial policies whose primary goal was to bring about unity during the third century was a developing religious universalism."[4] The center of the centerpiece, therefore, was the work of the Neoplatonic philosopher Porphyry of Tyre, author of the greatest and most extensive attempt to refashion the religion of Rome to suit the times. In making the monumental effort to provide what must be considered the most impressive alternative to the Christians' universal way of salvation in Christ, Porphyry positioned himself as the late Roman Empire's greatest intellectual opponent of Christianity.

Simmons exhaustively documents the preoccupation of Christian intellectuals with Porphyry's arguments in his *Contra Christianos*.[5] The sheer frequency of engagement with his arguments shows that the Christians, at least, took Porphyry's arguments to be formidable enough to need a response. The persistence of engagements across time—Simmons notes Christian responses from Arnobius *c*. 302–5 all the way to Damascene Studites in 1500–77—shows

---

2. Ibid., x.

3. See Averil Cameron, *The Later Roman Empire* (Cambridge, MA: Harvard University Press, 1993), 1–12; Liebeschuetz, *Continuity and Change in Roman Religion*, 223–5; Stephen Williams, *Diocletian and the Roman Recovery* (New York: Routledge, 1985), 15–23, inter alia.

4. Simmons, *Universal Salvation*, 187.

5. See ibid., 52–91. See also Wilken, who remarks, "Porphyry's writings claimed the attention of several generations of Christian intellectuals." Robert L. Wilken, *The Christians as the Romans Saw Them* (New Haven: Yale University Press, 1984), 126.

that the anti-Christian party in many other time periods also judged Porphyry's arguments to be formidable.⁶

As Augustine himself reports, Porphyry had not come across a "universal way for the liberation of the soul" (*liberandae animae uniuersalis uia*).⁷ For Porphyry, on the one hand, there is no single way to salvation open to all types of human beings. In this, Porphyry is at one with his Platonic forebears. On the other hand, motivated by the Christian challenge, Porphyry took his task to be to offer salvation to all types of human beings within a renewed form of paganism. Given that, for Porphyry, there is a division between the few capable of philosophy and the many, who are not, so far as their ability to attain and live according to wisdom, there cannot be a single way of salvation. That means both that salvation for the different groups of human beings happens by different methods and also that the salvation they receive is different.

Porphyry's schema involved, in Simmons's words, "A comprehensive soteriological paradigm whose individual stages served the purpose of cleansing that part of the soul that was appropriate for the recipient's spiritual or metaphysical level."⁸ Porphyry delineated the types of human beings on the basis of which part of the soul dominates within them: appetites, spiritedness, or reason. On the basis of which part of the soul dominates, there is a distinct way of salvation and a distinct type of salvation; nevertheless, Porphyry was able to offer something he could plausibly say was universal salvation by holding out hope of some type of salvation to all types of human beings.⁹ For Christianity, the universal way of salvation is Christ and the salvation all receive through Christ is essentially the same, even though it may be experienced differently according to the different gifts of grace received by the saved. There is what may be called a "dual soteriology"¹⁰ in the scholarly literature on Porphyry's writings.¹¹

---

6. See Simmons, *Universal Salvation*, 187, where he summarizes the context and effects of Porphyry's soteriological proposal.

7. Augustine, *ciu. Dei*, 10.32.

8. Simmons, *Universal Salvation*, 20.

9. Ibid., 24.

10. Ibid., xi.

11. See ibid., xi, for Simmons's complete treatment. Simmons also identifies a third way of salvation for the neophyte Neoplatonic philosopher. See ibid., 137. Porphyry offers this median way most clearly in his *Letter to Marcella*. Simmons explains the three ways concisely:

> This provided his readers, starting with the masses, moving to the novice philosophers, and ending with the mature Neoplatonic philosophers, three distinct ways of salvation for the soul designed for the cleansing of that part existing at the ontological and spiritual level of the recipient. The first way was for the lower or spiritual part of the soul and emphasized the importance of the traditional cults, including the practice of animal sacrifice, and theurgical rituals. The other two ways were designed for the novice and mature Neoplatonic philosopher, respectively. (Ibid., 39.)

To sum up, there are three paths to salvation in Porphyry's writings. The first path of salvation is for the multitude—those who are ruled by appetite—and involves theurgical and other rituals.[12] This way cleanses the lower soul alone and not the intellectual soul. That is to say, the first way cleanses the parts of the soul that are below the divided line in Plato's image,[13] the ones that are conditioned by matter. The second or median way belongs to the neophyte Neoplatonic philosopher and involves the practice of the virtue of continence, which cleanses the median, spiritual, soul by way of moral virtue. It is a transitory stage as the practitioner attempts to transcend the body and the material conditions that limit his or her soul. Strictly speaking, this median way does not yet achieve the salvation of the third way and has not yet succeeded in transcending the body or moving beyond the theurgical rites of the first way, nor has it arrived yet at the transition to the higher sections of the divided line image. While the second way is distinct from the first way in offering a different method—the practice of continence as opposed to reliance on theurgy—the salvation offered is the same: a resting point in the ethereal realm.[14] The third and final way involves "philosophical salvation for the mature Neoplatonic philosopher through discursive thought including the practice of the contemplative virtues and

---

12.

The salvific function of theurgy enabled Porphyry to offer a way of salvation for the masses that, incorporated within the context of ancestral Greco-Roman religious tradition, will have provided the following benefits: (a) cleansing the spiritual soul (but not the intellectual soul); (b) breaking the bonds of fate; (c) eschatologically enabling the soul to exist in the Ethereal Realm before its next reincarnation; and (d) offering the possibility for those with the requisite aptitude to move beyond this first path of salvation and learn the basic philosophical principles conducive to weaning the soul from an attachment to corporeal reality and orienting itself toward the initial phases of contemplation upon intelligible reality. (Ibid., 49.)

13. See Plato, *Republic*, 509d–511e.

14.

In conjunction with a lengthy process of training whereby the novice philosopher underwent intensive studies of the Platonic dialogues and mathematics possibly lasting from ten to fifteen years, there was initiated an ontological and epistemological *conversion* of the mind from being dependent upon *doxa* and *pistis* to an intermediate stage by means of dianoia, which enabled the mind to contemplate intelligible reality. The class of virtues stressed was the Purificatory, and Porphyry greatly accentuated *continentia/sophrosyne* as the main virtue at this level that was salvifically efficacious, the benefits being that, not only can the spirited soul be cleansed by the virtue of continence, but it is ontologically at a better position now to move on to the final stage. (Simmons, *Universal Salvation*, 220.)

focusing upon the *nous*; the paradigmatic virtues that focused upon the One; and not being involved in the traditional rites and practices of the religious cults."[15] This third way cleanses the intellectual soul and, at its term, brings the soul of the philosopher into union with the One. The philosopher has no need of theurgy or the rites that belong to it and, while continence is the necessary condition for the practice of the contemplative virtues, continence itself is not directly involved in the contemplation of intelligible realities.[16]

What Porphyry really offers is a coordinated system of three different ways of salvation with different types of salvation as their terms. But, as Augustine noticed, there is a real question about whether the cleansing of the spiritual soul and the ascent to the ethereal realm after death ought to be called salvation at all, according to Porphyry's highest (philosophic) principles. Porphyry himself says in *On Abstinence*,

> First then, you should know that my discourse will not offer advice to every human way of life: not to those who engage in banausic crafts, nor to athletes of the body, nor to soldiers, nor sailors, nor orators, nor to those who have chosen the life of public affairs, but to the person who has thought about who he is and whence he has come and where he should try to go, and who has principles about food, and about other proper behavior, which are different from those in other ways of life.[17]

---

15. Simmons, *Universal Salvation*, 219.
16. Porphyry remarks,

> So we too shall sacrifice. But we shall make, as is fitting, different sacrifices to different powers. To the god who rules over all, as a wise man said, we shall offer nothing perceived by the senses, either by burning or in words. For there is nothing material which is not at once impure to the immaterial. So not even *logos* expressed in speech is appropriate for him, nor yet internal *logos* when it has been contaminated by the passions of the soul. But we shall worship him in pure silence and with pure thoughts about him. We must, then, be joined with and made like him, and must offer our own uplifting as a holy sacrifice to the god, for it is both our hymn and our security. This sacrifice is fulfilled in dispassion of the soul and contemplation of the god.

Porphyry, *On Abstinence from Killing Animals*, trans. Gillian Clark (London: Bloomsbury, 2014), 2.34.2–3, 163–4. Elsewhere in the same work, Porphyry calls the philosopher "the priest of the god who rules all," ibid., 2.49.1.176; and teaches, "We say with good reason that the philosopher whom we describe, who is detached from external things, will not importune the *daimones* or be in need of diviners or the entrails of animals, for he has practiced detachment from the things with which divination is concerned." Ibid., 2.52.2.178.

17. Ibid., 1.27.1.104.

Gillian Clark offers a candid assessment:

> How many souls are blessed? In *On Abstinence*, escape from the body is essential for those who aspire to liberate the soul from the body and achieve the blessed life. They are an acknowledged minority, a spiritual elite of priests and ascetics in various ethnic traditions and of "true philosophers" among philosophers, who understand the true purpose of life and practice detachment from the needs of the body so that their soul may return to God. What about the working classes, the *banausoi* with their vulgar ideas, their material satisfactions and their failure to understand, who need the concessions made by civic laws? Have we any reason to think that Porphyry at any time sought a universal way of salvation accessible even to them? Bluntly, no.[18]

At most, the universality of salvation can only occur through successive metempsychotic life cycles in which the transmigrated soul is able to pass each stage gradually. To say the least, Porphyry's coordinated, gradated, successive schema asks quite a bit of his audience and the potential practitioners of his revived and modified paganism. Augustine's relative silence on the matter of Porphyrian metempsychosis may be an index of how credible Augustine's audience took it to be—that is, not credible enough to warrant the systematic dismantling to which Augustine subjects Porphyry's recommendation of theurgy.

The Neoplatonists are sometimes accused of being indifferent to politics. For instance, R. F. Hathaway explains what distinguishes Neoplatonism from Plato by pointing out that Neoplatonism omits Socratic political philosophy "by demoting the moral or political virtues to minimal conditions of the 'purification' or theological virtues."[19] Ernest L. Fortin observes a "shift from the political to the apolitical" in Plotinus' reinterpretation of the cave and, more broadly, in Neoplatonist doctrine as a whole.[20] Fortin argues,

> At the risk of considerable oversimplification, one could say that Neoplatonism first comes to sight as an attempt to solve the problem raised by the famous discussion of the Good in the *Republic*. The remarkable feature of Plato's method of procedure is that, while it describes the ascent to the Good or superessential principle which, like the sun in the invisible world, is the cause of the being of all things and their knowability, it does not furnish any indication as to how one

---

18. Gillian Clark, "Augustine's Porphyry and the Universal Way of Salvation," in *Studies on Porphyry*, ed. George Karamanolis and Anne Sheppard (London: Institute of Classical Studies, University of London, 2007), 127–40 at 139.

19. R. F. Hathaway, "The Neoplatonist Interpretation of Plato: Remarks on Its Decisive Characteristics," *Journal of the History of Philosophy*, vol. 7, no. 1 (January 1969), 19–26 at 20.

20. Ernest L. Fortin, *Collected Essays, vol. 1, The Birth of Philosophic Christianity: Studies in Early Christian and Medieval Thought*, ed. J. Brian Benestad (Lanham, MD: Rowman & Littlefield, 1996), 196, n. 110.

descends from that highest principle to the lower levels of everyday existence. The hiatus was pointed out by Aristotle, who objected to the Platonic approach on the ground that it was incapable of providing practical guidance in human affairs. Neoplatonism countered the objection in a novel way, not by attempting to fill the lacuna, but by replacing the imperfect constructions in which human initiative and freedom play a preponderant role with an eternal and unchangeable model articulating the structure of the intelligible world. In the process, however, the properly political dimension of Plato's thought was to all intents and purposes discarded. The net result was a natural, metaphysical, and mystical Platonism, inspired in largest measure by the *Timaeus*, the *Parmenides*, or the *Phaedo*, and all but totally divorced from the political context in which Platonic philosophy in its native form was imbedded.[21]

In one sense, the observations of Hathaway and Fortin are correct and Pierre Manent's observations support them, as the next chapter will show. But if the Neoplatonists are to be true followers of Plato, their political philosophy would need to be properly attuned to the political circumstances they find themselves in rather than the "context in which Platonic philosophy in its native form was imbedded," which was vastly different from the ones they found themselves in. As Pierre Manent points out, the operative political form in the time of the Neoplatonists is not the *polis* but rather the empire, with its distended borders and cosmic scale, washed-out differences among particular cities, and movement toward an indistinct universality.[22] It should therefore be no surprise that Socratic political philosophy embedded in the Greek *polis* gives way before a very different expression of philosophy that has its home in the imperial political form.

If the resultant Neoplatonic philosophy can be called apolitical, it is apolitical because of the difference between the civic and imperial form, which Manent already compares as the political to the apolitical—even while still insisting on calling the empire a *political* form. In another way, there should be no problem calling Neoplatonic philosophy, especially the philosophy of Porphyry, political, since he is addressing his thought to the political circumstances of the Roman Empire. Leo Strauss explains, "Political philosophy is that branch of philosophy which is closest to political life, to non-philosophic life, to human life."[23] The

---

21. Fortin, *The Birth of Philosophic Christianity*, 186.

22. Hathaway and Fortin's criticism of Neoplatonism in terms of its "rigid dogmatism" (Fortin, *Birth of Philosophic Christianity*, 186) as contrasted with "Socratic dialectic as revealing the aporetic nature of the moral questions" (Hathaway, "Neoplatonist Interpretation of Plato," 20) seem right. But even these ways the Neoplatonists—especially Porphyry—chose to present philosophy may have been more influenced by the rhetorical circumstances conditioned by the empire as opposed to the *polis*. See also Manent, *Metamorphoses*, 136.

23. Leo Strauss, *What Is Political Philosophy?* (Chicago: University of Chicago Press, 1988), 10.

political philosophy of Porphyry would have to seem apolitical because the political life of the late Roman Empire has become comparatively apolitical, especially when compared to the Athens of Socrates and Plato. After all, Porphyry deals with a world in which "the difference between cities pales, where their sufficiency and impenetrability pales," in the words of Manent.[24]

Porphyry's anti-Christian writings ought to be considered works of political philosophy in a way analogous to the way in which Augustine considered Varro's *Antiquitates* to be works of political philosophy. Varro's intention was to massage and therefore moderate Roman religious institutions in a subtle way that improved them without disrupting their beneficial effects or drawing the ire of their nonphilosophic devotees.[25] Porphyry's intention seems to have been to defend (pagan) Roman religion and the empire that depended on it for its unity, even its political unity, against the (perceived) threat posed by Christianity.[26]

Not only is it possible to consider the Neoplatonic philosophy of someone like Porphyry to be political philosophy, but recent scholarship has been moving in the direction of placing Porphyry and his anti-Christian writings at the center of the Great Persecution initiated by Diocletian.[27] In other words, Porphyry the philosopher put his philosophic mind and pen at the service of the emperor's political deliberations and actions. Most of the evidence for Porphyry's personal

---

24. Manent, *Metamorphoses*, 136.

25. "Augustine thus understands Varro to have bowed to his political community's customary beliefs," Mary M. Keys clarifies, "and indeed to have sought to purify and strengthen their myths about the gods." Mary M. Keys, "Books 6 & 7: Nature, Convention, Civil Religion, and Politics," in *The Cambridge Companion to Augustine's City of God*, ed. Fr. David Vincent Meconi, SJ (Cambridge, UK: Cambridge University Press, 2021), 102–21 at 105.

26. Stephen Williams argues, "Porphyry was concerned not only with the truth and falsity of Christianity, but primarily its revolutionary threat to traditional culture." Williams, *Diocletian and the Roman Recovery*, 163. David Neal Greenwood concurs, arguing,

> Porphyry did not view traditional religion as the highest reality or expression of divinity, but rather, a legitimate reflection of it. He held that civic religion was still necessary for the sake of society, a view similar to that of his predecessor Celsus, if more sophisticated. He tied the identity and health of the state to correct worship of the divine.

David Neal Greenwood, "Porphyry, Rome, and Support for Persecution," *Ancient Philosophy*, vol. 36 (2016), 197–207 at 200.

27. There is still a lively debate about Porphyry's involvement in the Great Persecution. Greenwood gives a helpful overview of the debate in his article "Porphyry, Rome, and Support for Persecution," 198–9. Greenwood ends up concluding that it is more likely that Porphyry was involved. See ibid., 204. From what I can tell, Greenwood's opinion, that it is more likely that Porphyry was involved in the Great Persecution, seems to be the opinion the current scholarly consensus favors. See the footnote immediately following this one.

2. Arguments of Porphyry of Tyre   39

participation in Diocletian's court and the planning of the Great Persecution at Nicomedia in 303 is indirect, from sources like Arnobius, Eusebius, and Lactantius, who speak of a philosopher involved in the proceedings and whose descriptions seem to match Porphyry.[28] It is impossible to say for certain that this figure was Porphyry, but it seems likely. Simmons argues,

> It is difficult to argue convincingly against the view that Porphyry not only attended the imperial conference in the period preceding the Great Persecution in February A.D. 303, but also that he and other anti-Christian writers like Sossianus Hierocles offered a proactive, positive soteriological message for all the classes and ethnic groups of the Roman Empire in order to revitalize religious and philosophical paganism in conjunction with Diocletian's New Imperial Theology. As a result of these imperial policies, Porphyry's *De pholosophia ex oraculis* was written to foster religious unity, offer new hope, check the spread of Christianity, revive the pagan cults, and provide unprecedentedly the *via salutis* on a comprehensive scale to all his readers.[29]

If, as seems likely, Porphyry was the philosopher at Diocletian's court in Nicomedia, he was already involved in politics. Digeser argues, "The third-century Platonists cultivated a relationship with the Roman equivalent of Plato's tyrant, the emperor at the imperial court: so Plotinus and Gallienus, but also Porphyry and Diocletian's Nicomedian court."[30] Porphyry's arguments against the Christians and in favor of an alternative schema for universal salvation therefore also need to be seen as political, especially in the terms Strauss speaks about political philosophy being that branch of philosophy that is closest to political life—the political life to which Porphyry's philosophical presentation of religion is closest, of course,

---

28. Jeremy M. Schott marshals much of the evidence in the appendix to his book, *Christianity, Empire, and the Making of Religion in Late Antiquity*. See Jeremy M. Schott, *Christianity, Empire, and the Making of Religion in Late Antiquity* (Philadelphia: University of Pennsylvania Press, 2008), 179–85. For other significant scholars who share Schott's judgment, see the following: Henry Chadwick, *The Sentences of Sextus* (Cambridge, UK: Cambridge University Press, 1959), 66; Liebescheutz, *Continuity and Change in Roman Religion*, 248; Wilken, *Christians as the Romans Saw Them*, 134–5; 159; Elizabeth DePalma Digeser, "Lactantius, Porphyry, and the Debate Over Religious Toleration," *The Journal of Roman Studies*, vol. 88 (1998), 129–46 and, *A Threat to Public Piety: Christians, Platonists, and the Great Persecution* (Ithaca, NY: Cornell University Press, 2012), 131; Michael Bland Simmons, "Graeco-Roman Philosophical Opposition," in *The Early Christian World*, vol. 2, ed. Philip Esler (London: Routledge, 2000), 133; Timothy Barnes, *Constantine: Dynasty, Religion, and Power in the Later Roman Empire* (Oxford: Wiley-Blackwell, 2011), 110; 89; 186; Simmons, *Universal Salvation*, 23–4; 90; 137; 187.

29. Simmons, *Universal Salvation*, 90. See also Simmons's even stronger claims in *Universal Salvation*, 137.

30. Digeser, *Threat*, 89.

imperial political life, giving rise to a very different treatment of politics and religion from what would be found in the Greek *polis*.

The effort to understand Porphyry's philosophic treatments of religion also requires an effort to understand the choices involved in Porphyry's decision to weigh in. If the decision to publish the *Contra Christianos* and the *Philosophia ex Oraculis* were political choices, then he could have made another choice given another prudential judgment. His sole concern in his decision to publish, in other words, was not merely to publicize what he understood to be the truth of things. He could have remained silent; he could have judged (as Constantine did later) that the religion that best matched the needs of the empire was Christianity rather than a revived and modified paganism. It is possible, as Elizabeth DePalma Digeser does, to interpret Porphyry's choice to support a revived paganism against the new Christian faith as simply a case of Porphyry reviewing the evidence for Christianity and finding it wanting. For instance, Digeser points out,

> Although Porphyry had voiced the latter concern as an argument against the Iamblichaean enthusiasm for eating sacrificial meat, his qualms also pertained to the sacrament of the Eucharist. In other words, Porphyry's arguments against the Origenists' reading scripture as a coherent whole led to the conclusion that Jesus was not divine. Porphyry's conclusion that Jesus, however pious and inspired a teacher, was a mere man—a position that harks back to Ammonius's view—allowed his readers to infer that the sacramental transformation of the wine and bread into a dead man's blood and body was a polluting, evil daemon-attracting ceremony carried out by ignorant priests.[31]

But no one who has gone carefully through Augustine's sifting of Porphyry's recommendation of theurgy can think at the end of it that Porphyry was firmly convinced of the existence of the *daemones*, either. So in between two, fabulous religions (to Porphyry's mind)—ancient Roman paganism and novel Christianity—what motivated Porphyry's choice to support one and oppose the other?[32] For Porphyry, as for Marcus Varro before him, the Roman religion is the bulwark of the Roman way of life. As Jeremy Schott puts it,

> Porphyry, of course, had his own rationale for supporting tradition. While the simpleminded might cultivate piety to avoid the wrath of neglected gods, Porphyry thought that traditional religion was beneficial to the worshiper. By adhering to tradition, the human soul progresses in virtue and becomes more like God; this is the sort of cultivation that makes cities and peoples endure.[33]

---

31. Digeser, *Threat*, 164.

32. Of course, there are also the reports that Porphyry suffered abuse at the hands of Christians in his youth. It would be impossible to say what kind of role—if any—those youthful experiences had in motivating Porphyry's actions against Christianity beyond the valuation of the reasons he actually gives. See Simmons, *Universal Salvation*, 10.

33. Schott, *Christianity, Empire, and the Making of Religion in Late Antiquity*, 77.

Christianity, on the other hand, was a novelty and had nothing to do—apparently—with the shoring up of Roman tradition. Dedication to the new creed could not but weaken Romans' attachment to the empire, which was already suffering from divisions. If the bulwark of Roman life were to dissipate under the influence of Christianity, there would be nothing else of sufficiently solid substance available to uphold Roman virtue—certainly not what appeared to him to be the tenuous Christian proposition that faith in Christ could suffice to undergird a way of life or support peoples in widely different circumstances with very different manners and customs. He had, after all, already offered sophisticated arguments purporting to show that Christianity was a ridiculous fable, especially attacking the veracity and coherence of the Christian (and Jewish) Scriptures.

If, as it seems reasonable, one can assume that Porphyry and the tetrarchy were of one mind about what made the Great Persecution necessary, one gets confirmation in their emphasis on the importance of the passing on and living out of Roman traditions in the edict of Galerius proclaiming an end to the persecution. Schott reports, "As he lay dying in 311, Galerius, now the senior member of the tetrarchy after Diocletian's retirement, ordered an end to the persecution. His edict confirms that concern for tradition was one of the principal reasons for beginning the persecution eight years earlier: Christians had 'abandoned the way of life of their own fathers.' The notion that the safety and success of the empire depended on the traditional worship of the traditional gods was shared by emperors and intellectuals."[34] Far from the indifference to empires Fortin attributes to the Neoplatonists,[35] Porphyry shows himself both concerned about and active in imperial politics, putting his vast talents at the service of preserving the imperial form.

It is remarkable how quickly the Roman Empire moved from active persecution to benign toleration of Christianity with the ascension of Constantine. The Christian claim to offer a universal way of salvation struck a chord in the new situation inaugurated by Rome's metamorphosis from city to empire. "Christianity," Simmons argues, "was the *only* religion in the Roman Empire that offered universal salvation: Constantine acknowledged this fact and knew that the time had come for the emperor officially to embrace it; Porphyry came to the same conclusion, but opted for the creation of his tripartite soteriology to compete with

---

34. Schott, *Christianity, Empire, and the Making of Religion in Late Antiquity*, 76. The Edict Serdica of Galerius, preserved by Lactantius, says among other things, "We had earlier sought to set everything right in accordance with the ancient laws and public discipline of the Romans and to ensure that the Christians too, who had abandoned the way of life of their ancestors, should return to a sound frame of mind." He is later concerned to note that "very many, however, persisted in their determination and we saw that these same people were neither offering worship and due religious observance to the gods nor practicing the worship of the god of the Christians." See Lactantius, *De Mortibus Persecutorum*, ed. and trans. J. L. Creed (Oxford: Clarendon, 1984), 34.

35. Fortin, *Birth of Philosophic Christianity*, 187.

Christian universalism."[36] But next to Christianity's elegant and straightforward soteriology, in which one salvation is made available in principle to all through the one mediation of Christ who unites eternity and time, divine and human, in himself, Porphyry's alternative was clunky and ill-suited to the new perceptual and political situation, despite its utilization—with modifications appropriate to the empire—of traditional Roman religion.

Christianity was no passing fad and was, to some degree, capable of undergirding an imperial way of life that incorporates many different peoples with their varying manners and customs no less than the polytheistic Roman religion Porphyry sought to revive. Constantine's judgment was opposite to Porphyry's. For Constantine, Christianity was precisely what could serve to support imperiled imperial unity. Constantine himself declares in his *Oration to the Saints*:

> There is one overseer for all existent things, and that everything is subjected to his sole rulership, both things in heaven and those on earth, both natural objects and organic bodies. For if there were not one but many authorities over these innumerable things, there would be share-outs and divisions of elements and [things told in] ancient myths; envy and avarice, dominating according to their power, would mar the harmonious concord of the whole, as many disposed in different ways of the shares allotted to each, and took no thought to maintain the whole world in the same state and according to the same principles.[37]

It is impossible not to hear in Constantine's description of God's monarchy the reflection and justification of his own monarchy. But from another perspective, it was precisely the thought that earthly rulership and divine rulership track so closely with one another that led Christianity's Roman critics to regard it as politically dangerous. Just as one, universal God rules over all the other particular gods of the local cults in the Roman Empire, so also the emperor rules over the various peoples. Erik Peterson observes, "It was Porphyry, as we have seen, who preserved Philostratus' critique of monotheism, and it is certainly not too bold to suspect that the thought of the Pythagorean Onatus, according to which rulership could exist only over beings of like nature and that therefore God must rule over other gods, was also taken over by Porphyry from Pythagorean speculation."[38] "Because the Christians understand themselves as a faction," Peterson explains, "as the faction of the One God, their monotheism is itself tainted with faction and

---

36. Simmons, *Universal Salvation*, 198. Emphasis in original.

37. Constantine, *Oration to the Saints*, trans. Mark Edwards, in Edwards, *Constantine and Christendom* (Liverpool: Liverpool University Press, 2003), 1–62 at 3.

38. Peterson, "Monotheism," 85. See also Willem Den Boer, "A Pagan Historian and His Enemies: Porphyry against the Christians," *Classical Philology*, vol. 69, no. 3 (1974), 198–208 at 206.

excludes the worship of other gods. The monotheism of the Christians is 'revolt' in the metaphysical world, but as such it is at the same time revolt in the political order."[39] Christianity, which denies that God rules over other gods—because there is no other god—would then appear to be straightforwardly political and inherently revolutionary. It would dissolve the particular cults with their particular gods, with necessary—and drastic—political ramifications.[40]

The *pax Romana*, to the Romans, seemed to depend on the empire's ability to subsume particular nations with their gods under the imperial political superstructure and the imperial cult. Christian rhetoricians took things even further, identifying polytheism itself with the warring state of particular nations and peoples. Christians like Eusebius and Constantine cleverly utilized the empire's own self-understanding, as called to "pacify, to impose the rule of law, to spare the conquered, battle down the proud," in the famous verses of Virgil.[41] That means that, as Peterson argues, "in principle, Augustus inaugurates monotheism, as Eusebius's assertions make clear, and Constantine only fulfills what Augustus had begun," and further, "the political idea that the Roman Empire does not lose its metaphysical character when it shifts from polytheism to monotheism, because monotheism already existed potentially with Augustus, is now linked with the rhetorical-political idea that Augustus is a foreshadowing of Constantine."[42] Constantine comes to sight, then, as bringing about the full implications of Rome's shift to empire and the universalism of the Christian God, and Christian soteriology comes to sight as what allows the empire to reach its full potential.

Constantine and Porphyry alike saw the implications of Christianity for the empire. But whereas Porphyry attempted to demolish the upstart religion because he judged the newcomer to be incapable of supporting a Roman Empire, Constantine saw the promise of Christianity for imperial unity precisely in its ability to offer a universal way of salvation. As Liebeschuetz argues,

> It appears that Constantine, supported by his "court theologian" Eusebius, concluded that cultural and political unification without doctrinal uniformity was impossible, and every one of his predecessors in the purple failed to unify the empire because paganism was incapable of providing the very thing that Christianity could offer, namely, universal salvation based upon the ideal of uniform beliefs and practices, a uniformity which was not achieved until many years later beginning with the Theodosian settlement.[43]

---

39. Peterson, "Monotheism," 88.
40. See Peterson: "Whoever destroys the national cults is therefore in the final analysis also destroying ethnic particularities, and at the same time attacking the Roman Empire, in which there is room for the national cults as well as for ethnic particularities." Ibid., 88.
41. Virgil, *Aeneid*, 6.1153-4. Translations of Virgil's *Aeneid*, unless otherwise noted, are from Virgil, *Aeneid*, trans. Robert Fitzgerald (New York: Alfred A. Knopf, 1992).
42. Peterson, "Monotheism," 97.
43. Liebeschuetz, *Continuity and Change in Roman Religion*, 197.

Constantine and Eusebius' insight seems to have been that polytheism itself was ill-suited to undergird the way of life of an empire because of its inherent, metaphysical factionalism—despite Porphyry's attempts to jury-rig Roman religion to provide a semblance of a universal way of salvation.

But Eusebius and Constantine's solution to one problem ended up giving rise to another, more serious problem. The Eusebian-Constantinian rhetorical strategy successfully carves out a space for Christianity in the empire, but also threatens to turn Christianity into something crudely political, effectively transforming the Christian faith into a civic substitute for Roman imperial theology. As Peterson points out, that is what makes Arianism look so politically enticing and goes a long way in explaining its popularity at the time. As Reinhard Hütter writes about Peterson's essay,

> Based on his rigorous study of Roman political theology and of the theology of the Church Fathers, Peterson demonstrates that monotheism as a political problem originated in the Hellenistic transformation of the covenantal authority of God over Israel into the political authority of the secular ruler. This collapse of a singular divine authority into a singular political authority was one reason Arianism (a view that subordinated Christ to the Father's supreme and singular divinity) was attractive for many emperors after Constantine, and why Arianism took on a second life among the Germanic tribes dominated by their ruler kings.[44]

Orthodox Trinitarianism could not provide the politically useful models that Arianism could. What could the *homoousios* possibly mean in the light of a mentality that sees the divine court and the earthly court as tracking so closely together? It is much easier to map the ontological hierarchy involved in Arian conceptions of the Christian God onto the Roman imperial hierarchy. Hütter explains,

> Christianity's trinitarian dogma, however, undermined the Hellenistic doctrine of divine monarchy, and with it the theological warrants for a political "monotheism" that merged secular and sacred authority into the singular person of the supreme or autocratic ruler. Any analogy between the triune God and the autocratic state—and for that matter any analogy between the triune God and whatever form of human governance—had to fail and will have to fail in the future.[45]

It is no exaggeration to say, along with Joseph Ratzinger, that "the ecclesiastical belief in the Trinity shattered the politically usable moulds, destroyed the potentialities

---

44. Reinhard Hütter, "Dogma's Defender," *First Things* (May 2012), https://www.firstthings.com/article/2012/05/dogmas-defender, accessed June 9, 2022.

45. Ibid.

of theology as a political myth, and disowned the misuse of the Gospel to justify a political situation."[46] It is not, therefore, possible to use Christianity as a superior imperial theology and, further, Christianity cannot serve the same role to shore up Roman imperial unity.

Between Constantine and Augustine, Porphyry's arguments did not go away, despite the attempts by Christians to suppress Porphyry. Julian the apostate very likely revived and recirculated the writings of Porphyry in his campaign to suppress Christianity and replace it once again with a more traditional form of Roman religion.[47] The resultant situation calls Christianity's place in the Roman

---

46. Joseph Ratzinger, *Introduction to Christianity*, trans. J. R. Foster (New York: Herder and Herder, 1969), 121. Peterson summarizes his own argument as follows:

> Monotheism as a political problem had originated in the Hellenistic transformation of the Jewish faith in God. Insofar as the God of the Jews was amalgamated with the monarchical principle of the Greek philosophers, the concept of the divine Monarchy at first acquired the function of a political-theological propaganda formula for Jews. This political-theological propaganda formula was taken over by the Church in its expansion into the Roman Empire. It then met up with a concept of pagan political theology, according to which the divine Monarch indeed reigned, but the national gods had to rule. In order to counteract this pagan theology, tailored to fit the Roman Empire, it was asserted from the Christian side that the national gods could not rule at all, because national pluralism had been suspended by the Roman Empire. In this sense the Pax Augusta was then interpreted as the fulfillment of the Old Testament eschatological prophecies. Nevertheless, the doctrine of the divine Monarchy was bound to founder on the trinitarian dogma, and the interpretation of the Pax Augusta on Christian eschatology. In this way, not only was monotheism as a political problem resolved and the Christian faith liberated from bondage to the Roman Empire, but a fundamental break was made with every "political theology" that misuses the Christian proclamation for the justification of a political situation. (Peterson, "Monotheism," 104.)

47. See Simmons, *Universal Salvation*, 68 and Schott, *Christianity, Empire, and the Making of Religion in Late Antiquity*, 53. Alexandre Kojève argues,

> As Emperor, Julian is especially concerned with those who are quite young, physically or mentally. He wants them to be told edifying myths in believable forms in order that their way of life may be ameliorated. Practically, Julian is concerned with educating the people whom he has, as Roman Emperor, consented to govern. And the philosopher seems to have been firmly convinced that the Emperor could save his empire only by having his subjects told pagan myths, and this in such a way that the great majority would begin again to believe them.

Alexandre Kojève, "The Emperor Julian and His Art of Writing," in *Ancients and Moderns: Essays on the Tradition of Political Philosophy in Honor of Leo Strauss*, ed. Joseph Cropsey (New York: Basic Books, 1964), 95–113 at 108.

Empire into question once again. That new situation is the subject of Augustine's *City of God*, in which Augustine has to perform a careful two-step to articulate and maintain Christianity's transpolitical status. For Augustine, Christianity is not crudely political, but neither is it totally apolitical, and it is certainly not revolutionary or antipolitical. First, Augustine must convince the patriotic Roman that his excessive attachment to Rome is bad; but second, in doing so, he must not detach the patriotic Roman altogether from Rome.[48]

The metamorphosis of Rome from city to empire involved the transformation of Roman perceptions and politics, which inevitably gave rise to a new religious situation in which the cosmic and world-spanning becomes the horizon of the Roman imperial subject. Rome's movement toward expansion, political and moral indistinctness, depoliticization, and privatization called for a religious reformation of sorts. The older, particularistic pantheon no longer had the power either to move Romans or to bind together the increasingly far-flung empire. The move from city to empire especially changed the requirement for the mediation between the Roman people and the divine. Rather than being a novel, foreign agent responsible for the corruption of Rome, Christianity possessed a key feature that allowed it to take advantage of the historical moment: its ability to provide a genuinely universal way of salvation. Its way of salvation based on the Incarnation and inaugurating a transpolitical way of life in the Church did not solve the political problem presented by the metamorphosis of Rome from city to empire, but it did provide a new way of grounding Roman life, a way that does not require the dissolution of particularities related to political or cultural factors. In order to add both theoretical depth as well as more historical context, it is time to turn directly to the metamorphosis of Rome from city to empire.

---

48. These arguments will be gone through in greater detail in later chapters of the present volume.

Chapter 3

THE FEW, THE MANY, AND THE UNIVERSAL WAY OF SALVATION IN AUGUSTINE'S EARLY WORKS

Now that the historical context of the controversy about a universal way of salvation has been established, it is possible to turn to Augustine himself. The place Augustine takes up the universal way of salvation most directly and most extensively is the *City of God*. As befits such an important topic, however, Augustine is concerned to address it throughout his writing career. Already from the beginning of his writing career, the contours of his treatment of the topic are visible. The framing of the topic by Platonic philosophers is especially important, since Augustine is at pains to address the Platonic division between the few and the many, the philosophers and the nonphilosophers even as early as his first epistle and his first published dialogue, *Contra Academicos*. One implication of that Platonic division is the esoteric manner of philosophic writing, which seeks to prevent the nonphilosophers from penetrating into the inner sanctum of philosophy, for which they would be unprepared and which could have disastrous consequences both for them and for philosophers.[1]

---

1. There are plenty of indications that Augustine was aware of the esotericism of Platonic writing. There are three texts in particular other than the *City of God* where Augustine addresses philosophic esotericism: His First Letter, the first seven chapters of *De uera religione*, and *Contra academicos* 2.10.24. The dissembling of philosophers and statesmen, or lies about their true thoughts about the divine, is one of the main themes of the *City of God* and can be found in many, many places. For an excellent discussion of Augustine's relationship to esoteric writing, see Kries, "Reason in Context," 214–52 at 243–6. See also one chapter in particular from Fortin, *Birth of Philosophic Christianity*, 79–93, entitled "Augustine and the Problem of Christian Rhetoric." Although Augustine did not engage in what could be called esoteric writing himself, as Fortin points out, "There is evidence that Augustine shared with his predecessors, both pagan and Christian, the view that the whole truth in matters of supreme moment can be safeguarded only if its investigation is accompanied by a prudent reserve in the expression of that truth." Ernest L. Fortin, "Augustine," in *History of Political Philosophy*, ed. Leo Strauss and Joseph Cropsey (Chicago: University of Chicago Press, 1987), 176–205 at 178. For evidence, Fortin points to the following texts: *ciu. Dei* 8.4; *c. acad* 2.4.10, 2.10.24, 3.7.14, 3.17.38, 3.20.43; *epp.* 118.1 and 1. I would also add *Trin.*, 1.1.1 and *c. mend.*, 10.23. Fortin also

In the present chapter, some of Augustine's very early works will be examined to see how they treat the topic of the universal way of salvation in conversation with Platonic interlocutors to show that Augustine is concerned with the topic not only in his late period of writing, but also from his earliest days as a Christian writer. Accordingly, Augustine's concern with this topic will be traced in a few of his earlier works, especially his *First Letter*, *Against the Academics*, and *Of True Religion*, which are among the writings commonly understood by Augustinian scholars to belong to his early period, appearing very soon after his conversion and before he was ordained a priest. *Against the Academics* is his earliest extant work[2] and likely the first work he wrote after his conversion. *Of True Religion* is likely the last work he wrote before his ordination.[3] Van Fleteren argues, "An analysis of the content and structure of the *De uera religione* shows that it is, for all intents and purposes, a summary of Augustine's early thought."[4] The *First Letter* is likely the earliest letter from Augustine and is written specifically about the topic of esotericism in *Contra Academicos*. These works have been chosen, therefore, to demonstrate the concern with our topic in the bookend works of Augustine's early period. The argument here will provide the beginnings of an appraisal for how Augustine's treatment of the topic of the division between the few and the many and the universal way of salvation changed throughout his writing career, especially before and after the traumatic sack of Rome by Alaric in 410 AD, after which the question gained more political urgency.

Augustine writes his first letter in 386, the year of the famous garden conversion scene narrated in *Confessions* Book 8 and the year before his baptism into the Catholic Church. As G. R. Evans describes it,

---

helpfully clarifies, saying, "It should be added that, whereas some of the earlier Church Fathers like Clement of Alexandria and Origen defended the use of noble lies in the common interest, Augustine denounces all lies, salutary or otherwise, as intrinsically evil and, following a precedent he alleges to have been set by Christ, admits only of indirect forms of concealment, such as omissions and brevity of speech." Fortin, *Birth of Philosophic Christianity*, 179–80. Ryan Balot argues convincingly that Augustine regarded the pedagogical esotericism as a trap by which the best Romans were ensnared by demons "to further the corruption of the city by deceiving even the best individuals and keeping them out of sight, thereby diverting them from their proper roles as leaders and ethical examples." Ryan Balot, "Truth, Lies, Deception, Esotericism: The Case of St. Augustine," in *Augustine's Political Thought*, ed. Richard J. Dougherty (Rochester, NY: University of Rochester Press, 2019), 173–99 at 179.

2. See Josef Lössl, "The One (*unum*)—A Guiding Concept in *De uera religione*: An Outline of the Text and the History of Its Interpretation," *Revue des Études Augustiniennes*, vol. 40 (1994), 79–103 at 79.

3. Ibid.

4. Frederick Van Fleteren, "Augustine's *De vera religione*: A New Approach," *Augustinianum*, vol. 16, no. 3 (1976), 475–97 at 497.

In Milan Augustine came into contact with a circle of philosophers, Zenobius, Hermogenianus, Manlius Theodorus, who met from time to time as a society. These were "renaissance" men, adherents of a Platonism reborn, who thought of themselves not as "Neo"-Platonists, but as *Platonici*. Platonism had been brought alive again in Italy by the works of two Greek Academicians of the third century: Plotinus and his pupil Porphyry.[5]

The letter itself is a response to Hermogenianus, who had written to Augustine after receiving his copy of *Contra Academicos*. Augustine specifically wanted to have Hermogenianus' comments on his own treatment of Academic esotericism in the dialogue. Esotericism pertains to the topic of the universal way of salvation because it indicates a cleft between groups about their ability to attain and understand the truth. In his *Retractationes*, Augustine explains his purpose in writing *Contra Academicos*: "I wrote, first of all, so that, with the most forceful reasons possible I might remove from my mind—because they were disturbing me—[the Academics'] arguments which in many men instill a despair of finding the truth and prevent a wise man from giving assent to anything or approving anything at all as clear and certain, since to them everything seems obscure and uncertain."[6]

It is natural for Augustine to be taking up the topic of esotericism at this juncture. The great struggle in his own life at that point had been between the claims of philosophy done under the tutelage of the *Platonici* (see, especially, *Confessions*, Book 7) and the claims of Christianity. As he tells it in the *Confessions*, the struggle concerns the Christian insistence on the need for a mediator between God and Man, namely Jesus Christ as the Incarnate Word of God, over and against the merely intellectual ascent of the *Platonici*. The first book he writes after his conversion in the garden at Milan is the *Contra Academicos*, taking up in large part the problem of the esotericism of the philosophers. The concern boils down to this: is there a single, unified way of salvation for all men that provides for the integration of the whole of the human being and the whole of the human race? If not, is it possible to call the multiple ways of salvation true ways of salvation? Do they not, each of them, leave something integral to the human being cut off from salvation: the higher soul with the intellect or the lower soul with the senses and passions? After all, just because one is not a philosopher, that does not mean one has no intellect; just because one is a philosopher, that does not mean one has no passions.[7]

---

5. G. R. Evans, *Augustine on Evil* (Cambridge, UK: Cambridge University Press, 1993), 17.

6. Augustine, *Retractations*, trans. Sister Mary Inez Bogan (Washington, DC: Catholic University of America Press, 1968), 1.1.

7. For contrast, see the opinion articulated by Leo Strauss that, "If striving for knowledge of the eternal truth is the ultimate end of man, justice and moral virtue in general can be fully legitimated only by the fact that they are required for the sake of that ultimate end or that they are conditions of the philosophic life. From this point of view the man who

It is precisely on the basis of the capacity of the nonphilosopher to attain or receive the truth that St. Augustine provides a critique of Porphyry in Book 10 of the *City of God*, probably finishing Book X of the *City of God* around 415, which is, as it were, at the beginning of the latter stages of Augustine's writing. Augustine says that the eminent Platonist has not come across a universal way for the liberation of the soul (*liberandae animae uniuersalis uia*).[8] Instead, what Porphyry does provide are two separate ways of "purification" (*purgatio*) that liberate the soul: one affecting the higher or intellectual soul (*intellectualem animam*), one affecting only the lower or "spiritual" soul (*ipsam spiritalem*) through theurgy.[9] The first way is for those few who are capable of philosophy; the second is for the multitude who for whatever reason are not capable of the philosophic life.

The concern about philosophic esotericism runs from the very first book Augustine writes after his conversion, all the way through his later writings, and it seems that the concern is tied consistently to engagement with Porphyry. Porphyry's positions about the different ways to salvation, Michael Bland Simmons argues, "was the closest that Greco-Roman polytheism ever came to a semblance of universalism, which was, in turn, constructed as a counter-assault upon Christian claims that in Christ alone was found the *via salutis universalis animae liberandae*,"[10] the universal way of the soul's liberation. As mentioned in the previous chapter, Simmons and others report intriguing evidence that Porphyry was involved in the imperial effort to craft a message against Christianity on the basis of a pagan universal under Diocletian's Great Persecution, giving the topic great practical and political urgency as well.[11] Porphyry's fame as a great Roman philosopher as well as his influence on Augustine's philosophic development would have put Porphyry's concerns at the forefront of Augustine's own consideration of the theoretical and practical matters involved in esotericism and universal salvation. Augustine's arguments with the Platonists, therefore, would have been not only exercises in theorizing but had very serious practical and political implications as well.

As Augustine puts it in *Contra Academicos*, "One should think that in Plotinus Plato lives again."[12] It is to Plotinus and Porphyry that Augustine refers, as well as others like Cicero and (the much earlier) Carneades the Cyrene, when he refers to "academicians [*academici*]." He says of the "academicians" in the *First Letter*, that their "influence has always weighed strongly with me."[13] Indeed, the subject of

---

is merely just or moral without being a philosopher appears as a mutilated human being." Strauss, *Natural Right and History*, 151.

8. *Ciu. Dei*, 10.32.

9. Ibid., 10.27.

10. Michael Bland Simmons, *Universal Salvation*, 24.

11. See ibid., 18; 30; 32. See Chapter 2 of the present volume for an extended discussion.

12. *C. acad.*, 3.18.41.

13. Augustine, Augustine, *Letters*, vol. 1, trans. Sister Wilfrid Parsons, SND (New York: Fathers of the Church, 1951), *ep. 1*. English translations from *epp* will be from Parsons's translation.

the letter is to ask Hermogenianus to comment on a draft of Augustine's dialogue *Contra Academicos*, especially regarding Augustine's discussion of the esotericism of the *academici*, which he treats in the conclusion of Book 3 of *Contra Academicos*.

Augustine frames the esotericism of the Academy in terms of its exoteric skepticism. The philosophers of the Academy utilize a skeptical public front to provide the necessary cover to allow the philosophers to conceal their true knowledge and teachings from the multitude. That being said, Augustine is worried not only about the capacity of the nonphilosopher to arrive at the truth, but also the capacity of anyone at all to do so. Augustine in the *Confessions* describes the Academy's exoteric stance, where he says, "The notion began to grow in me that the philosophers whom they call Academics were wiser than the rest, because they held that everything should be treated as a matter of doubt and affirmed that no truth can be understood by men."[14] In the *First Letter*, Augustine explains the necessity for this concealment: "If any untainted stream flows from the Platonic spring, it seems to me that in these times it is better for it to be guided through shady and thorny thickets, for the possession of the few, rather than to wander through open spaces where cattle break through, and where it is impossible for it to be kept clear and pure."[15] The philosophers' concealment of their true opinions is requisite to maintain the purity of the truth against the misconstrual of those whose minds are not capable of understanding. What is particularly the danger in this instance? The opinion that the soul and body are identical. Augustine attributes to Zeno the opinion that God is fire, the soul is mortal, and "in this world nothing is done except by matter [*corpus*]," and there is nothing beyond the sensible world.[16] It was on the basis of Zeno's materialism, Augustine speculates, that Zeno's fellow Academic, Arcesilaus, began to hide the truth about the distinction between the sensible and intelligible world even from fellow members of the Academy, a practice that persisted down through Carneades' day and even to Cicero's.[17]

Augustine identifies the confusion of soul and body as his own major theoretical difficulty in the *Confessions*, which itself leads to the even more harmful opinion that there is no significant difference between the substance of the soul and the substance of God—or in other words, that while God may be greater than the soul, the two substances belong to the same order of being. The inability to conceive of spiritual substance is unraveled by Augustine in *Confessions* Book 7 under the tutelage of the *libri Platonicorum*, the books of the Platonists. Augustine reiterates in *Contra Academicos*, saying, "Plato sensed that there are two worlds: one intelligible (in which the truth itself dwells) and the

---

14. *Conf.*, 5.10.19.

15. Augustine, *ep.*, 1.1.

16. See *c. acad.*, 3.17.38. All translations of *c. acad.* are from Augustine, *Against the Academics*, trans. Michael P. Foley (New Haven, CT: Yale University Press, 2019).

17. Ibid. Foley notes, "Cicero calls Zeno an ignoble wordsmith (*ignobilis verborum opifex*) in the *Tusculan Disputations* 5.12.34." Foley, in Augustine, *Against the Academics*, 267, n. 161.

other sensible (which we obviously sense through sight and touch)."[18] Through the course of Book 7, Augustine is able to grasp immaterial substance—the intelligible world—and therefore to understand the relationship between the sensible and the intelligible. Augustine's accomplishment is extraordinary and one that he knows is rare: very few are able to do the same.[19] His knowledge of immaterial substance therefore also makes him aware of the reasons underlying the Platonists' philosophic esotericism.

In his letter, Augustine both explains the Academy's reasons for employing philosophic esotericism and approves of their esoteric practice. He ventures, "I think the method of concealing the truth is a useful invention."[20] Augustine's narration of the theoretical difficulty he himself had in conceiving of spiritual substance provides the groundwork for the distinction between the few and the many for Augustine. The few, having undergone the ascetic rigors of philosophy, are capable of conceiving spiritual substance. Consequently, those few who are successful in conceiving of spiritual substance are capable of distinguishing body and soul, creator and creature, as well as understanding that evil is not a substance of its own. Augustine's basis for distinguishing the few and the many is therefore quite similar to the one given by Socrates in Plato's *Republic* in the image of the divided line[21] and the allegory of the cave.[22]

Augustine nevertheless does not think that philosophic esotericism is useful in his own day. What has changed since latter days? He observes,

> In this age, since we find no true philosophers—and I consider that those who go around dressed in philosophers' cloaks are quite unworthy of that honorable title—men need to be led back to the hope of discovering the truth, especially those who have been deterred from understanding things by the subtlety of Academic phrases. Otherwise, what was devised in its time for the uprooting of deep-seated error might now begin to be a hindrance to the cultivation of knowledge.[23]

---

18. Augustine, *c. acad.*, 3.17.37. "Platonem sensisse duos esse mundos, unum intellegebilem, in quo ipsa ueritas habitaret, istum autem sensibilem, quem manifestum est nos uisu tactuque sentire."

19. See Porphyry's account of Plotinus and his own experiences on this score in Porphyry, "On the Life of Plotinus and the Arrangement of his Work," in Plotinus, *Enneads*, trans. Stephen MacKenna (London: Faber and Faber, 1966), at #23.

20. Augustine, *ep.*, 1.1. Foley also notes that "although Augustine praises the Academics for their initial prudence, he is not entirely complimentary about the long arc of their work, describing the literary tradition that they developed over time as 'inflated,' or bloated (3.18.41)." Foley, "Commentary," 204.

21. See Plato, *Republic*, Book 6, 509d–511c.

22. See ibid., 514a–520a.

23. Augustine, *ep.*, 1.1.

Augustine seems to think that in his own day, the exoteric skepticism of the Academy discourages not only the unworthy, but absolutely everybody, from seeking the truth. Academic skepticism dashes hopes that human beings might be able to come to know any truth at all. He seems worried that the *academici* are starting to believe their own exoteric teachings. Augustine speaks here not just in the abstract, but also out of his own experience. He admits that when he was younger, "the arguments of the Academicians seriously deterred me from this undertaking," namely, the search for the truth in hope of really coming to know the truth. His argument in the *First Letter* tracks his narration of his movement toward skepticism in *Confessions* Books 5–6. He declares in his *Retractations* that he was only able to avoid succumbing to the Academy's exoteric skepticism "by the help and mercy of the Lord."[24]

It is not as clear in these earlier works what need those few who are capable of distinguishing the intelligible and sensible world have of Christ's mediation, which is the linchpin of his discussion of the universal way of salvation in *City of God* X and in *Confessions* Books 7–9. Instead, his emphasis is on the impotence of philosophy to provide a way of salvation for the many. As he says in Book 3 of *Contra Academicos*,

> For this philosophy is not the philosophy of this world that our Sacred [Scriptures] most rightly detest but of the other, intelligible world to which that most subtle Reason would never call back souls blinded by the multiform darkness of error and smeared by the deepest filth from the body had not the Supreme God, out of a certain clemency for the multitude, humbled and lowered the authority of Divine Understanding all the way into the human body itself, so that having been roused up not only by His precepts but His deeds, souls could return to their very selves and even gaze upon their homeland without the bickering of disputations.[25]

Augustine points out that the solution to the problem of salvation has to address both mind and body. The solution available in the Incarnation works by uniting the divine mind to the human body (there is more to it than that, of course—he is no Apollinarian). There is therefore a fit between the ailment and the remedy. Likewise, Augustine insists that the remedy is applied by Christ not only through

---

24. *Retr.*, 1.1.1.
25. Augustine, *c. acad.*, 3.19.42.

> Non enim est ista huius mundi philosophia, quam sacra nostra meritissime detestantur, sed alterius intellegibilis, cui animas multiformibus erroris tenebris caecatas et altissimis a corpore sordibus oblitas numquam ista ratio subtilissima reuocaret, nisi summus deus populari quadam clementia diuini intellectus auctoritatem usque ad ipsum corpus humanum declinaret atque summitteret, cuius non solum praeceptis sed etiam factis excitatae animae redire in semet ipsas et respicere patriam etiam sine disputationum concertatione potuissent.

his teaching or precepts (*praecepti*) but also by his deeds (*facti*). The remedy available in Christ, therefore, is unified, offering in the one remedy the unification of body and soul, teaching and deeds.[26] The hint of what is to come is already present: the unified remedy in Christ is also the universal way for all human beings; the unity of the remedy is what grounds and provides for its universality.

Augustine begins the *De uera religione* with high praise for Platonic philosophers, especially for Socrates and Plato. Socrates and Plato did not believe in the gods worshipped popularly in the temples, Augustine remarks. Socrates, whom Augustine says some call "bolder than others [*audacior ceteris*],"[27] tried to point out the absurdity of popular religion, Augustine contends, by swearing oaths "by a dog or a stone or any other object that happened to be near him or came to hand."[28] There was a sense or a suspicion among the wider people, Augustine says, that the philosophers did not believe in the gods worshipped popularly, that "what the philosophers observed along with the people in the way of religious rites was something quite different from what they defended in private, or even in the hearing of the people."[29] But as long as the philosophers attended the public rites in the temples and gave an outward show of support, there was no problem.

In the much later *City of God*, Augustine develops this argument further when he critiques Rome's civil religion and criticizes the philosophers for dissimulating. He chides the philosophers for seeking freedom of mind while they are forced to endure slavery in body to the false religion of the temples. The gulf between their mental lives and their public lives is yet another division Augustine notices as showing that the way of life they follow is deficient.[30] In *De uera religione*,

---

26. Augustine also emphasizes that Christ offers personal assistance. See *c. acad.* 2.1.1. Ryan N. S. Topping correctly notices that "the necessity of prayer figures prominently within the moral argument of the dialogue." Ryan N. S. Topping, "The Perils of Skepticism: The Moral and Educational Argument of *Contra Academicos*," *International Philosophical Quarterly*, vol. 49, no. 3 (Sept. 2009), 333–50 at 336.

27. *Uera rel.*, 2.2.

28. Ibid. "Per canem quemlibet et lapidem quemlibet et quidquid iuraturo esset in prompt et quasi ad amnum occurrisset."

29. Ibid. 1.1. "Apparet aliud eos in religione suscepisse cum populo et aliud eodem ipso populo audiente defendisse priuatim."

30. Van Fleteren writes,

> According to [Augustine], ancient philosophy was characterized by disagreements between schools of philosophy. Further, a lack of harmony existed in the lives of most philosophers between their convictions and their worship. While they knew of the existence of the one true God, they worshipped the pantheon of pagan gods. Christ and his Church overcame both the plurality of doctrines and the disharmony between doctrine and worship. In regard to the former, Christ saw the same end for man (union with the one true God) as the Platonists had, but, in addition, unlike Socrates and Plato, he was able to persuade the mass of mankind to pursue it. (Van Fleteren, "Augustine's *De vera religione*," 480)

Augustine's focus is to show that the philosophers acknowledged a division between what was possible to expect of the few with respect to living a life in accordance with wisdom, and what is possible to expect of the many with respect to living a life according to wisdom. He observes,

> Nothing hinders the perception of truth more than a life devoted to lusts and the false images of sensible things, derived from the sensible world and impressed on us by the agency of the body, which beget various opinions and errors. Therefore the mind has to be healed so that it may behold the immutable form of things which remains ever the same, preserving its beauty unchanged and unchangeable, knowing no spatial distance or temporal variation, abiding absolutely one and the same.[31]

Absent the knowledge of the eternal, human beings are destined to misdirect their thoughts and actions, being unable either to rank the importance of created things compared with each other or to see how created things ought to turn us toward God in both thought and action. The result is a disordered and unhappy life in the here-and-now, which is also cut off from obtaining eternal life. The soul whose thoughts and actions are so disordered, he writes,

> Is weakened by love of things that come to be and pass away, or by pain at losing them,[32] so long as it is devoted to the custom of this life and to the bodily senses, and becomes vain among vain images, it laughs at those who say that there is something which cannot be seen by the eyes, or conjured up by any phantasm, but can be beheld by the mind alone, by the intelligence.[33]

To make his point, Augustine imagines a hypothetical conversation between Plato and a student of his. The student tells Plato that he has become convinced of the reality of the intellectual soul, its distinction from the body, and its superiority; and that contemplation of eternity is superior to the enjoyments of the body and

---

31. *Uera rel.*, 3.3. "Nihil magis impedire quam uitam libidinis deditam et falsas imagines rerum sensibilium, quae nobis ab hoc sensibili mundo per corpus impressae uarias opiniones erroresque generarent; quamobrem sanandum esse animum ad intuendam incommutabilem rerum formam et eodem modo semper se habentem atque undique sui simile pulchritudinem nec distentam locis nec tempore uariatam, sed unum atque idem omni ex parte seruantem."

32. See Augustine's description of this same phenomenon in his own life in *conf.* 4.4-8, where he describes the death of an unnamed friend. He says that his fault was in "loving a mortal man as if he were never to die." *Conf.*, 4.8.

33. *Uera rel.*, 3.3. "Sed dum nascientur atque transeuntium rerum amore ac dolore sauciatur et dedita consuetudini huius uitae atque sensibus corporis inanibus uanescit imaginibus, irridet eos, qui dicunt esse aliquid, quod neque isitis uideatur oculis nec ullo phantasmate cogitetur, sed mente sola et intellegentia cerni queat."

its senses. But, the imaginary student of Plato implies, it is one thing for he himself to believe these things, who is after all a direct pupil of Plato and, presumably, someone singularly capable of undertaking the hard asceticism demanded by the philosophic way of life. For the few among the mass of human beings capable of such feats, there is already philosophy. But what about those who either cannot or, because of a variety of factors, simply will not undertake the rigors of philosophy in order to pursue the truth, and therefore to reap the rewards of a rightly ordered way of life? The imaginary pupil supposes,

> Now, if some great and divine man should arise to persuade the peoples that such things were to be at least believed if they could not grasp them with the mind, or that those who could grasp them should not allow themselves to be implicated in the depraved opinions of the multitude or to be overborne by vulgar errors, would you not judge that such a man is worthy of divine honors?[34]

The philosopher might be able to grasp the concept of eternity, or the intellectual soul, with the mind, but the nonphilosopher would not. Nevertheless, where knowledge is unavailable, belief might still be possible. What Augustine refers to in the latter part of this imaginary pupil's statement is the Platonic noble lie. To "allow themselves to be implicated in the depraved opinion of the multitude" is the dissimulation of the Platonic noble lie, which Augustine criticizes—especially in the *City of God*, where Augustine blames philosophers and leading men of Rome for misleading the multitude about the truth, giving them over to false gods and demons.[35]

Augustine imagines an answer that Plato would give to his imagined student. Plato, Augustine proposes, would reply,

> That could not be done by man, unless the very virtue and wisdom of God delivered him from natural environment, illumined him from his cradle not by human teaching but by personal illumination, honoured him with such firmness and exalted him with such majesty, that he should be able to despise all that wicked men desire, to suffer all that they dread, to do all that they marvel at, and so with greatest love and authority to convert the human race to so sound a faith. But it is needless to ask me about the honours which are due to the wisdom of God. Being the bearer and instrument of the wisdom of God on behalf of the

---

34. Ibid.

35. See also later in *uera rel.*, where Augustine argues that religion is not to be sought from philosophers, "For they take part in the religious rites of their fellow-citizens, but in their schools teach divergent and contrary opinions about the nature of their gods and of the chief good." *Uera rel.*, 5.8. "Qui eadam sacra suscipiebant cum populis et de suorum deorum natura ac summo bono diuersas contrariasque sententias in scholis suis eadem teste multitudine personabant."

true salvation of the human race, such a man would have earned a place all his own, a place above all humanity.[36]

The import of Plato's imagined reply is that Augustine here acknowledges that nature does not provide for the universal way of salvation. If it could be shown as a matter of historical fact that even the many nonphilosophers could be persuaded that the eternal is superior to the temporal and the soul superior to the body, and that the many could be incorporated into a way of life that prioritizes eternal over temporal and soul over body, then it could only be a feat accomplished by God.

Augustine does not neglect to finish his syllogism. He declares, "Now this very thing has come to pass."[37] Augustine proceeds to show, with scriptural references, how the teaching of Christ does for the many what Plato would only acknowledge could be done for the few with the resources of nature. Augustine regards it to be a proof of the truth of Christianity and Christianity's God that "all nations now are persuaded that these things ought to be believed."[38] The true religion grants access to the universal way of salvation. Continuing even more boldly, Augustine argues that, if "Plato and the rest of them"[39] were to see what Christianity has wrought, they would become Christian, "as many Platonists of recent times have done."[40] Porphyry is a notable exception to the trend Augustine references.[41] Porphyry turns to recommending theurgy to provide for something like a way of salvation for the nonphilosopher as a contrasting alternative to Christianity.

The contemporary popularity of Porphyry's arguments when Augustine is writing is indicated by Augustine's preoccupation with Porphyry's approach.

---

36. Ibid., 3.3.

Ille non posse hoc ab homine fieri, nisi quem forte ipsa dei uirtus atque sapientia ab ipsa rerum natura exceptum nec hominum magisterio, sed intima illuminatione ab incunabulis illustratum tanta honestaret gratia, tanta firmitate roboraret, tanta denique maiestate subueheret, ut omnia contemnendo, quae praui homines cupiunt, et omnia perpetiendo, quae horrescunt, et omnia faciendo, quae mirantur, genus humanum ad tam salubrem fidem summo amore atque auctoritate conuerteret. De honoribus uero eius frustra se consuli, cum facile possit existimari, quanti honores debeantur sapientiae dei, qua gestante ille et gubernante pro uera salute generis humani magnum aliquid proprium et quod supra homines esset mereretur.

37. Ibid., 3.4. "Quae si facta sunt."
38. Ibid., 4.6. "Populis iam omnibus haec credenda persuasa sunt."
39. Ibid.
40. Ibid., 4.7.
41. Augustine may very well have had Victorinus chiefly in mind regarding Platonists who had become Christian, thereby heightening the contrast with Porphyry, for it was Victorinus who had translated Porphyry's works into Latin. Victorinus' own conversion had had a major effect on Augustine's conversion, as the latter narrates it in *Conf.*, 8.4.

Augustine ventures, "I do not know whether such great men would have been prevented [from becoming Christian] by the other vice which prevents present-day pagans, who now concern us, for indeed it is utterly puerile. I mean, of course, their curiosity in inquiring at demons."[42] Porphyry recommends theurgy to the nonphilosopher for the sake of purging the "spiritual," or nonintellectual soul—philosophy is the only sufficient means Porphyry recognizes to purge the intellectual soul. By contrast, Augustine acknowledges that Christian religion is sufficient to purge the mind. The reason is the relationship between history and eternity in the Christian revelation that is to be believed—and in the Incarnation, which is the basis of that revelation. Augustine writes,

> In following this religion our chief concern is with the prophetic history of the dispensation of divine providence in time—what God has done for the salvation of the human race, renewing and restoring it unto eternal life. When once this is believed, a way of life agreeable to the divine commandments will purge the mind and make it fit to perceive spiritual things which are neither past nor future but abide ever the same, liable to no change.[43]

To believe the prophetic history is to believe that the eternal God acts in history for the sake of our eternal good, and is already a step on the way to the purgation of the mind Augustine says that Christianity can effect in the many.

In the *uera rel.*, Augustine is treating true religion, religion that is true by allowing all human beings to know and follow the truth. Paganism, by contrast, in both religion and philosophy, is inherently disunifying.[44] The bulk of *uera rel.*,

---

42. *Uera rel.*, 4.7. "Nescio utrum possent ad ea ipsa, quae appetanda et desideranda esse dixerant, cum istis sordibus uiscoque reuolare. Nam tertio uitio curiositatis in percontandis daemonibus, quo isti maxime, cum quibus nunc agitur, pagani a Christiana salute reuouantur, quia nimis puerile est, nescio utrum tales illi praepedirentur uiri." See Willy Theiler, *Porhyrios und Augustin* (Berlin: Halle, 1933), 160–251 for Theiler's work to identify the Porphyrian component of *uera rel.*

43. Ibid. 7.13. "Huius religionis sectandae caput est historia et prophetia dispensationis temporalis divinae prouidentiae pro salute generis humani in aeternam uitam reformandi atque reparandi. Quae cum credita fuerit, mentem purgabit uitae modus diuinis praeceptis conciliates et idoneam faciet spiritalibus percipiendis, quae nec praeterita sunt nec futura, sed eodem modo semper manentia nulli mutabilitati obnoxia."

44. Lössl observes, "The content of true religion relying on the transcendent One is seen in contrast to the plurality of religions." Lössl, "The One," 79–103 at 99, n. 101. The title, "Of True Religion," itself would have sounded innovative to his Platonist interlocutors. While Van Fleteren points out that the phrase is found in both Tertullian and Lactantius, the concepts of "truth" and "religion" would not have been put together by Plato or his followers. Philosophy seeks truth, the apprehension and judgment of being by the mind; philosophers are the ones who are capable of attaining truth. Religion is a kind of next best substitute for the many nonphilosophers, which does not have truth as its object, but rather exists at the level of custom and myth.

therefore, takes up the topic of unity and disunity, which latter always has sin at its root. It is in this context that Augustine calls the Church "Catholic," meaning "whole" or "universal."[45] In the prologue, Augustine is mostly concerned with pagan philosophers, especially the Platonists, or what would be called nowadays the "Neoplatonists." Gerald P. Boersma has admirably traced the ways in which the ascent to God in *uera rel.* mirrors the ascent to the One found in Plotinus. There are very important differences, however, in how Augustine conceives of human unity.[46] Boersma helpfully explains the important differences between the Neoplatonic ascent to the One and the Christian ascent—namely, the need for grace, the termination of the ascent in the Trinity, and its openness to all human beings in principle.

The differences between the Plotinian ascent to the One, which Plotinus describes as being "the flight of the alone to the alone"[47] in the final phrase of the *Enneads*, and the ascent to the Trinity, the one God who is nevertheless a community of Persons, are quite pointed.[48] For one thing, the ascent is made in an irreducibly Trinitarian and therefore communal context. Although both Augustine and the Neoplatonists are united in identifying a fall from the One to the Many

---

45. See especially *uera rel.*, 7.12–8.14. Lössl, "The One," 99, n. 101.

46. See Boersma, *Image*, 228–54.

47. "Phyge monou pros monon." This is Andrew Louth's translation of the line from *Enneads* VI.9.11, which appeared in Louth, *The Origins of the Christian Mystical Tradition from Plato to Denys* (Oxford: Clarendon, 1981), 51. Kevin Corrigan invites the reader to compare Louth's translation with Stephen Mackenna's "the passing of solitary to solitary" in *Plotinus: The Enneads*, trans. Stephen Mackenna (New York: Burdett, 1992), 709. See Kevin Corrigan, "'Solitary' Mysticism in Plotinus, Proclus, Gregory of Nyssa, and Pseudo-Dionysius," *The Journal of Religion*, vol. 76, no. 1 (Jan. 1996), 28–42 at 28, n. 1.

48. These differences are dramatized in Augustine's *Confessions* in the contrast between Augustine's solitary ascent in *Confessions* 7 under the tutelage of the *libri Platonicorum* and the ascent to the Triune God in Book 9 together with Augustine's mother, Monica. Lössl notes that A. Harnack and G. Boissier published essays in 1888 observing that "Augustine's account of the events of 386 in *conf.* disagreed with what he had written in his early writings. Those had been much more Platonic than Augustine himself would later admit." Lössl, "The One," 80. There is no doubt that Augustine was influenced by the Platonists and that he was writing in a Platonic key; but to notice the superficial similarities between Augustine and his Neoplatonic interlocutors while missing the gigantic gulf, even in his early writings, risks distorting our understanding of Augustine. Augustine certainly does claim of the Platonists that "with the change of a few words and sentiments, they would become Christians, as many Platonists of recent times have done." "Et paucis mutatis uerbis atque sententiis Christiani fierunt, sicut plerique recentiorum nostrorumque temporum Platonici fecerunt." *Uera rel.*, 4.7. But those few words and sentiments (like "humility" and "Trinity") effect a radical alteration in thought and orientation. No one would be more aware of the difference changes in a few words and sentiments could make than Augustine the *rhetor*.

as the primordial human problem, the character of the Fall is quite different. For Plotinus, the fall is primarily metaphysical, a matter of necessity. For Augustine, the fall is a matter of the will, and specifically pride, which seeks to overturn the order of creation, and the order of creature and creator.[49] Augustine explains that the soul, through grace, "will return from the mutable many to the immutable One. It will be re-formed by the Wisdom which is not formed but has formed all things, and will enjoy God through the spirit, which is the gift of God."[50] Augustine thereby invokes all three Persons of the Blessed Trinity and gives brief expression to the individual Missions of the Son and Spirit.

The way of ascent in *uera rel.* is marked by the Missions of the Son and Spirit. The humility of Christ provides the moral exemplar to reverse the harmful pride of human beings. Even more than moral exemplarity, the Incarnation makes it possible for the Church to administer the sacraments. Augustine refrains from discussing the sacraments openly in *uera rel.*, but does not hesitate to allude to them:

> To heal souls God adopts all kinds of means suitable to the times which are ordered by his marvelous wisdom. I must not speak of these, or at least they must be spoken of only among the pious and perfect. But in no way did he show greater loving-kindness in his dealings with the human race for its good, than when the Wisdom of God, his only Son, coeternal and consubstantial with the Father, deigned to assume human nature.[51]

---

49. Although Boersma is right to note that, in *uera rel.*, Augustine's description of the Fall "is given Platonic dress." Boersma, *Image*, 248. Lössl notes, "Not creation as such (being) is responsible for the fall but creation insofar as it wills (not to be creation from God)." Lössl, "The One," 97, n. 78.

50. *Uera rel.*, 12.24. "A multis mutabilibus ad unum incommutabile reuertetur reformata per sapientiam non formatam, sed per quam formantur uniuersa, frueterque deo per spiritum sanctum, quod est donum dei."

51. *Uera rel.*, 16.30. "Sed cum omnibus modis medeatur animis deus pro temporum opportunitatibus, quae mira sapientia eius ordinantur, de quibus aut non est tractandum aut inter pios perfectosque tractandum est, nullo modo beneficentius consuluit generi humano quam cum ipsa dei sapientia, id est unicus filius consubstantialis patri et coaeternus totum hominem suscipere dignatus est." Michael P. Foley explains the discipline of the secret, which Augustine is utilizing here. Foley explains,

> During the age of persecution and for over a century thereafter, the early Church withheld certain aspects of its teaching and practices from nonbelievers and its own catechumens. This judicious reserve chiefly concerned Trinitarian and Eucharistic doctrine, though it also included prayers such as the Apostles' Creed and the Lord's Prayer. Catechumens, for instance, were only allowed to attend the Liturgy of the Word, from the beginning of the Mass until the homily; when the Liturgy of the Eucharist began, they were dismissed. Similarly, catechumens would not be given the Lord's Prayer or the Apostles' Creed until shortly before their baptism, and

Christ therefore provides both the moral exemplar and the healing power through sacraments to enable the ascent to God.

Boersma astutely notices that it is the Spirit's specific role in the ascent to God to enable man to enjoy God. He argues, convincingly, that the *uti-frui* distinction so well developed in *De Doctrina Christiana* is already present in *uera rel.* and that "The Holy Trinity is 'enjoyed' *through* the Holy Spirit, the gift of God."[52] What does this mean for Boersma? He says, "Return to unity, which is the aim of the ascent to God," takes place through a process of "the same seven stages of restoration that [Augustine] also discusses in *De quantitate animae*. The steps describe the ascent from changing, temporal, and material loves to unchanging, eternal, and immaterial loves; it is a gradual acclimatization to the things of the Spirit, through what Augustine describes as 'setting up a ladder to things that are immortal.'"[53] Created things are to be used (*uti*) for the sake of our return to God; but only God is to be enjoyed (*frui*). At the root of the disorder of human beings, in which they fall away from the One willfully through pride and are distracted among the many, therefore, is the improper enjoyment of things that ought to be used, while what ought to be enjoyed—God—is neglected.[54] It is therefore entirely appropriate that the Holy Spirit's assistance in the ascent to God concerns what Boersma calls a "gradual acclimatization to the things of the Spirit."[55] He thereby makes clear how the Missions of the Second and Third Persons of the Trinity, as sent by the First Person of the Trinity (whom Augustine calls *principium*[56]), enable the ascent to God. The Christian ascent to God in the communion of the Blessed Trinity, and with the help of the Trinitarian Persons, is already quite different from the Plotinian flight of the alone to the alone. In order to emphasize the difference, Augustine also uses the term "One" (*unus*) to refer to the divine substance and the Blessed Trinity,[57] making clear that even the ascent to the One, in Christianity, is an ascent to a God who is Triune; that is, who, while one in substance, is three divine Persons.[58] That is why at the conclusion of *uera rel*, in 55.112–13, Augustine

> they were not told the Church's teaching on the Eucharist as the body and blood of Christ until after they were baptized and had received it.

Foley argues further that the discipline of the secret "account[s] for Augustine's circumspect manner of referring to the sacraments in the *Confessions*, a book intended for a general audience." Michael P. Foley, "Glossary of Select Terms," in Augustine, *Confessions*, trans. F. J. Sheed (Indianapolis, IN: Hackett, 2006), 327–34 at 329–30.

52. Boersma, *Image*, 251.
53. Ibid., 248.
54. As Van Fleteren elegantly puts it, "The proud man wishes all things to be subject to himself." Van Fleteren, "Augustine's *De vera religione*," 491.
55. Boersma, *Image*, 248.
56. *Uera rel.*, 55.112.
57. See ibid., 55.113.
58. Lössl's otherwise helpful article on "The One" as a guiding principle in *uera rel.* does bear this serious lacuna: an insufficient emphasis on Trinitarian character of Augustine's

accompanies his use of the term *unus* with immediate reference to the Trinitarian Persons.[59]

Just as he does at the conclusion of *uera rel.*, Augustine also makes reference to the Trinity at the conclusion of *c. acad.* As Foley puts it, at the end of *c. acad.*,

> Augustine's mention of the intelligible world to which both classical philosophy and Christianity point provides a bridge to a brief yet astonishingly rich discussion of the Trinity. In 3.19.42, Augustine tells the group that the Holy Spirit (that most subtle Reason)[60] calls back souls from error and sin by virtue of the fact that God the Father mercifully sent His Son to be conceived of the Virgin Mary and become incarnate. Therefore, the mission of the Holy Spirit, at least in the current era, springs from the mission of the Son, which was initiated by the Father's love for and mercy on humankind.[61]

Even at the outset of his literary career, Augustine is already at pains to show, if subtly, the difference that the Trinitarian Missions make for the way of salvation.

The loving condescension of the Trinitarian Persons is what accounts for the universality of Christianity's way of salvation. On their own, human beings are not capable of overcoming the moral and intellectual consequences of sin, which are what divide human beings into different types. Grace allows for the ascent to God, and not only for the few who are already intellectually gifted. Christ's moral exemplarity and the healing effects of the sacraments on the whole man as they insert each man into a universal body, the mystical body of Christ, who himself unites God and Man in the hypostatic union, provide for the universal way of salvation. That is why Augustine relies so heavily on Nicene orthodoxy in *uera rel.* Augustine there treats of heretics, who remove themselves from Catholic unity. He mentions in particular the Arians and the Photinians, who, he points out, may not

---

"*unum*," and the implications of that Trinitarian view of divine unity for human beings and the universal way of salvation. Boersma's treatment is a significant improvement in this regard.

59. See, for instance, Augustine's declaration, "One God alone I worship, the sole principle of all things, and his Wisdom who makes every wise soul wise, and his Gift whereby all the blessed are blessed." *Uera rel.*, 55.112. "Ecce unum deum colo unum omnium principium et sapientiam, qua sapiens est, quaecumque anima sapiens est, et ipsum munus, quo beata sunt, quaecumque beata sunt." Also see his argument, "Wherefore it befits us to keep and to worship the Gift of God, equally unchangeable with the Father and the Son, in a Trinity of one substance." Ibid., 55.113. "Quare ipsum donum dei cum patre et filio aeque incommutabile colere et tenere nos conuenit: unius substantiae trinitatem unum deum."

60. See also Foley's note, where he argues that "When Augustine speaks of 'That Most Subtle Reason' calling us to the Supreme God thanks to the Incarnation of Divine Understanding, it is likely that he is alluding to God the Holy Spirit, God the Father, and God the Son, respectively." Foley, in Augustine, *Against the Academics*, 270, n. 186.

61. Foley, "Commentary," 209–10.

share religious rites with Catholics.[62] Both Photinus and Arius maintained heresies denying the divinity of Christ and the equality of Word with the Father, which both would have had catastrophic effects on the capacity to account for Christ's ability to mediate a truly universal way of salvation.

Man is made whole because the whole man is tended to—higher soul and lower soul, intellect, passions, and body; the whole man being tended to allows for those men to enter into a universal society, which is constituted and sustained on the basis of the love of God and the love of the image of God in man, taking no account of the temporally bound features connected to mortal particularities. Augustine teaches, "Man is not to be loved by man even as brothers after the flesh are loved, or sons, or wives, or kinsfolk, or relatives, or fellow citizens. For such love is temporal. We should have no such connections as are contingent upon birth and death, if our nature had remained in obedience to the commandments of God and in the likeness of his image."[63] The object and term of the love of Christians is eternal: God and the image of God that participates in God. As such the love that enlivens the Christian way of salvation is capable first of healing divisions within the man, and then of transcending divisions that arise among men on account of sinful distraction among temporal things. Christian love is inculcated through and directed by the worship of the Triune God.[64]

After the sack of Rome in 410 by Alaric, there was a resurgent paganism utilizing anti-Christian arguments about Christianity's responsibility for the weakness of Rome that left her vulnerable to barbarian attack. It makes sense that Porphyry's attempt to find an alternative to Christianity's universal way of salvation on pagan terms would see a revival. Augustine's engagement with those Porphyrian arguments, among others, finds its place especially in the *City of God*. But as has been seen, Augustine concerned himself with those arguments even in his early period, well before the sack of Rome. The form of Augustine's engagement with those Porphyrian arguments is less practically and politically urgent, but it can be seen that Augustine regards Christianity's ability to provide a genuinely universal

---

62. Boersma observes that Augustine uses specifically anti-Arian, Nicene language to describe the Second Person of the Trinity in *uera rel.* See Boersma, *Image*, 249.

63. *Uera rel.*, 46.88. "Sed nec sic quidem ab homine homo diligendus est, ut diliguntur carnales fratres uel filii uel coniuges uel quique cognati aut affines aut ciues. Nam et ista dilectio temporalis est. Non enim ullas tales necessitudines haberemus, quae nascendo et moriendo contingunt, si natura nostra in praeceptis et in imagine dei manens in istam corruptionem non relegaretur."

64. In his *Retractations*, Augustine emphasizes the purpose of *uera rel.* is to show the need to worship God the Trinity. He writes, "At that time I also wrote a book on the true religion. In that book I argued in many ways and to great length that the true religion must adore the one true God, that is, the Trinity, the Father, the Son, and the Holy Spirit." "Tunc etiam De vera religione librum scripsi, in quo multipliciter et copiosissime disputatur unum verum Deum, id est Trinitatem, Patrem et Filium et Spiritum Sanctum, religione vera colendum." *Retr.*, 1.13.1.

way of salvation, with robust intellectual underpinnings, to be a huge asset for Christianity not only for Christians' own *intellectus fidei*, but also in apologetics and for entering into the various contests about the best way of life with which classical Roman intellectuals were so preoccupied. With that said, it is time to turn to Augustine's argument with Porphyry about the universal way of salvation in the *City of God*.

Part II

CHRIST'S MEDIATION OF THE UNIVERSAL
WAY OF SALVATION

Chapter 4

HUMAN WHOLENESS AND THE UNIVERSAL WAY OF SALVATION IN THE *CITY OF GOD*

In the *City of God*, Augustine presents the possibilities for all classes of men, especially the few and the many, to live together in the city of God. This is accomplished through the availability of the universal way of salvation provided by the mediator between God and men, the incarnate Word. Since Porphyry's variegated soteriology is grounded on his particular anthropology, in which the ways of salvation are based on the part of the soul that dominates within each given human being, Augustine joins the argument with him on anthropological grounds. Augustine's anthropology is illuminated by biblical faith and so is informed by the Christian doctrine of original sin and its consequences. Augustine argues that the observable division between men and the limited distribution of natural abilities that allow men to pursue wisdom are only natural in a mitigated sense, since human nature is wounded by historical sin.[1] Further, this would affect all people—philosopher and *hoi polloi*—alike.

Human nature before sin did not suffer from the harmful divisions to which it is subject afterwards. Before the Fall, men enjoyed the harmony of right order, in which the body is subject to the soul, the sensitive soul is subject to reason and will, and reason and will are subject to God.[2] In this harmonious state, man's mind and his will are fixed upon God and, insofar as he considers created things, he refers them to God with praise and thanksgiving. Through sin, man violently disorders his mind and will; he wrenches them away from their proper object, the eternal things of God, and toward temporal things to the exclusion of God. Through the free choice of his will, man voluntarily subjected himself to the twin punishments of *ignorantia* and *difficultas*, consequences of original sin afflicting, respectively, the mind and the will.[3] It is in Christ the mediator's healing

---

1. See *lib. arb.,* 3.18.173–9.

2. See, among many, many other texts, *uera rel.* 15.32. Margaret Miles provides a succinct description of this phenomenon: "The human soul is inferior to God, and the body is inferior to the soul; if the soul is in a state of insubordination to God, it loses its control over its own body." Margaret Miles, *Desire and Delight* (New York: Crossroads, 1992), 62.

3. See *lib. arb.,* 3.18.178. While *ignorantia* and *difficultas* are not found in the *ciu. Dei* with the kind of precision of use as in the *De Libero*, Augustine opens *ciu. Dei* Book 2 criticizing *caecitas* and *parvicacia*, or blindness and weakness, which, as Robert Dodaro notes,

of ignorance and difficulty through overcoming sin that each individual human being is made whole and the obstacles to a universal way of salvation are removed.

Ignorance and difficulty manifest differently in the philosopher and the nonphilosopher, but Augustine insists that both suffer from them.[4] All men share in the consequences of the Fall; but since there are many temporal goods, some of which are nobler than others, divisions among men arise as to the grade of temporal good they now pursue. Those who pursue baser goods are baser men, while those who pursue nobler goods are nobler men. Nevertheless, all men without grace pursue temporal goods to the exclusion of God—even the philosopher—who pursues the good of his own mind without praising and thanking God for it.[5] As Pierre Manent argues,

> The pagan ordering that places the many in the realm of nontruth is subverted by Christianity, which affirms at the same time that all people, absolutely all people, including philosophers, share the same condition of misery and error—they are all "slaves to sin"—and that they are all, absolutely all, including the many, capable of truth, and of the highest truth—"capable of the true God." In this way Christianity humbles the proud and elevates the humble.[6]

Augustine narrates in the *Confessions* how his will was divided between two loves: the love of wisdom and the love of his disordered way of life. Each love is also present as the motivating principle in the two cities Augustine describes in the *De ciuitate Dei*, the city of God and the city of Man. The love that predominates in each city is an indication about who it is who rules in each city. In the city of God, God is loved above all else, and all other things are loved in God. In the city of Man, man pridefully loves himself to the point of contempt for God. Love of God includes the love of the wise order that God has created, while the love of self characteristic of the City of Man entails the preference of the human will and judgment over divine wisdom. Because human beings are afflicted with ignorance and difficulty, they organize their common life around temporal goods rather than eternal goods, in public as they do in private. As a result, life in the City of Man is inherently disunified and disordered, lacking a truly transcendent good

---

"impede the soul from accepting sound doctrine (*doctrina salubris*) and divine assistance (*adiutorium diuinum*), which, when received in faith, enable the mind to perceive errors and arrive at religious and moral truth." Robert Dodaro, *Christ and the Just Society in the Thought of Augustine* (Cambridge, UK: Cambridge University Press, 2008), 43. The parallel with *ignorantia* and *difficultas* should be clear. In *ench.*, 22.81, Augustine also calls ignorance (*ignorantia*) and weakness (*infirmitas*) the "two causes of sin." Augustine, *The Enchiridion on Faith, Hope, and Love*, trans. Albert C. Outler (Washington, DC: Regnery, 1996).

4. See also Manent, *Metamorphoses*, 271.

5. See, inter alia, *conf.*, 5.3.5. See also Rom. 1:21, which is Augustine's source text in Scripture for these discussions.

6. Manent, *Metamorphoses*, 271.

that provides for the unity of the whole man in himself and, therefore, with his fellow human beings. The city of God, however, organizes its life around God, who absolutely transcends the created order, but also mercifully condescends to appear within it through the Incarnation. As the creator of men, God is capable of undergirding human wholeness both within the man and between the man and his fellow men. Because God transcends creation, the city of God participates in God's transcendence by living a transpolitical way of life. It exists alongside the city of Man on earth, even sharing certain limited goods such as temporal peace and security, while reserving to itself determinations about religion, which it receives from God. The love that characterizes the city of God therefore directs its citizens to a transcendent goal and simultaneously orders the love of temporal goods. Love of God and love of neighbor, therefore, are one love, and the love of God and knowledge of God are likewise one act. As Augustine explains in *De Trinitate*,

> When we love our brother from love, we love our brother from God; nor can it happen that we do not love above all else that same love by which we love our brother. From this we conclude that these two commandments cannot be without one another. For since "God is love," he who loves love, surely loves God; but he must needs love love who loves his brother. And, therefore, he says a little later: "He cannot love God whom he does not see, who does not love his brother whom he sees." That he does not love his brother is indeed the reason why he does not see God. For he who does not love his brother is not in love; and he who is not in love is not in God, because God is love. Furthermore, he who is not in God is not in the light, because "God is light and in him is no darkness." If anyone, therefore, is not in the light, what wonder is it if he does not see the light, that is, if he does not see God, because he is in darkness? But he sees his brother with the human sight by which God cannot be seen. If, however, he loved him whom he sees by human sight with a spiritual love, he would see God, who is love itself, with that inner sight by which he can be seen.[7]

---

7. *Trin.*, 8.8.12. The refusal of Augustine, and Victorinus before him, to consort with the Christian multitude before his final conversion shows that he does not love his brother and therefore does not truly know God. The vision of God at Ostia (see *conf.* 9.10.23–6) accomplished in friendly conversation with his unlettered mother, happens after his baptism, whereas the abortive Platonic ascent in *conf.* 7.17.23 is a private ascent. See also Thomas Aquinas, *Summa Theologiae*, I. q. 1, a. 4 and Pope Benedict XVI, *Deus Caritas Est*, #10. Scott MacDonald argues that the problem Augustine discusses, which he calls "Meno's Paradox," contains too strong an insistence on knowledge in the strict sense. MacDonald suggests that, to the question, "Which comes first, knowing God or invoking God?" the answer is, "Believing in God comes first." Scott MacDonald, "The Paradox of Inquiry," *Metaphilosophy*, vol. 39, no. 1 (2008), 20–38 at 24–5. MacDonald later observes insightfully that the search for God who is not known fully has a possibility for success because "God has given us natures that are sensitive to joy and truth, and that, having once

What is required for man to live the way of life Augustine describes are the unity of man's loves and the unity of man's knowledge and love. The whole man must be rightly ordered and harmonious, knowing and loving God and his neighbor in God.

In order for the charity of the city of God to transform men, ignorance and difficulty must be overcome. What is required is a mediator between the transcendent God and sinful human beings. Fallen human nature is subject to the huge divisions noticed by the Platonic political philosophers. The foolish multitude is distracted among temporal things and is incapable of governance by the wise. It pursues fleeting goods like glory or sensual pleasure. The wise few are incapable on their own of transforming fallen human nature from within. There are intractable limits, naturally speaking, based on the division of wisdom and political power. When combined with the uncertainty of eternal life, those limits prevent the wise few from ministering effectively to the multitude. Besides, as Augustine's dramatic narration in the *Confessions* shows, even those who pursue wisdom as a way of life are by no means free from the *consuetudo carnalis*. The wise therefore resort to utilizing noble lies and partially true myths in order to pacify rather than transform the multitude and to keep the multitude from harming the wise.[8] One reason for God's similar treatment of good and bad men with respect to temporal goods and evils is to ensure that the good are free to correct the bad. Nevertheless, Augustine is harder on the philosophers like Porphyry who lived after the Incarnation, since beforehand the universal way of salvation had not yet appeared among men.

Christ the mediator, on the other hand, is the eternal wisdom of God become man. In Christ, God mercifully deigns to present himself among the temporal things by which fallen man is distracted. He can, therefore, lead sinful human beings from a disordered love of the temporal to love of the eternal by focusing their attention on him. Since he is the meeting place of time and eternity, the love of Christ is able to unify human loves and, therefore, to unify human beings. It is Christ who provides for human wholeness, both in the sense of the wholeness of the man himself, and the wholeness of the entire body of men. Human beings no longer have to choose between intellectual excellence and moral excellence, between wisdom and their neighbor. Christ therefore constitutes the universal way of salvation Augustine says that Porphyry could not find.[9] Christ the

---

tasted them, restlessly hunger for true joy and truth itself." Ibid., 37. Robert Dodaro argues, "Augustine equates knowledge of God with love of God. He insists that both knowledge and love of God are received by the soul as one and the same divine grace. God cannot be known in a true sense in any other way." Dodaro, *Christ and the Just Society in the Thought of Augustine*, 162.

8. In this regard, Ernest L. Fortin remarks, "Philosophers may parade as lovers and teachers of moral virtue, but none of them seems to have been eager to place the service of his fellow men above the good of the mind." Fortin, *Birth of Philosophic Christianity*, 87.

9. See *ciu. Dei*, 10.32.5–7.

mediator is able to bring together the two classes of men because Christ is able to unify man in himself, in his body, the Church, which Augustine terms the *totus Christus*.[10]

Now a select group of Augustine's discussions of both ignorance and difficulty in his magisterial *De ciuitate Dei* will be examined. Specifically, this discussion will focus on Augustine's engagement with classical political philosophers and with those philosophers who recommend theurgy on the character of ignorance and difficulty and how these obstacles are best addressed. This will entail a brief, admittedly provisional and incomplete, examination of the positions of some of Augustine's philosophic interlocutors on the nature of ignorance and difficulty drawn from Socrates' proposals in Plato's *Apology of Socrates* and *Republic*. This examination is only intended to limn some of the key features of classical political philosophy's characteristic teachings on the nature of ignorance and difficulty. Augustine's criticisms of these proposals of the *Platonici* as they are found in Book 8 of the *De ciuitate Dei* will then be briefly considered. Particular attention will be paid to Augustine's argument that Christianity is the one, truly universal way of salvation open to all men.[11] Finally, the theological response to Platonic political philosophy's division of men into the wise few and the foolish multitude that Augustine advances in his account of the way of life that is lived by those inhabitants of the city of God will be examined.

In the *De ciuitate Dei*, Augustine shows what advances are possible on the basis of the Incarnation and the Church over the presentation of the relationship between the few and the many in classical political philosophy. As always, it is important to keep in mind Augustine's rhetorical strategies. To modern readers especially, his extreme statements seem to rail against the whole notion and practice of politics. But John von Heyking gives a valuable caution:

> Augustine's antipolitical rhetoric is meant to form the passions of identifiable types of people among his readers. His political speech is intended to form the inordinate passions into ordinate love. His rhetoric appears immoderately antipolitical because he considered most of his audience's passion for political glory inordinate and deformed, and his rhetoric is meant to illuminate goods that transcend politics and to demonstrate how political glory insufficiently secures eternal happiness. Augustine shows how the inordinate desires of his audience degenerate into the lust for domination (*libido dominandi*) if the goals of these desires are taken as the greatest human good.[12]

---

10. See *ep. Jo.*, 1.2 and *s.*, 133.8. For a fine summary of Augustine's doctrine of the *totus Christus*, see David Vincent Meconi, SJ, *The One Christ* (Washington, DC: Catholic University of America Press, 2013), 195–216.

11. See *ciu. Dei*, 10.32.

12. Von Heyking, *Augustine and Politics as Longing in the World* (Columbia, MO: University of Missouri Press, 2001), 20. Roberts Ogle, relying on Pierre Hadot, puts Augustine into a class of authors who write "psychagogy," which she explains:

Augustine writes elsewhere,

> If Plato and the rest of them, in whose names men glory, were to come to life again and find the churches full and the temples empty, and that the human race was being called away from desire for temporal and transient goods to spiritual and intelligible goods and to the hope of eternal life, and was actually giving its attention to these things, they would perhaps say (if they really were the men they are said to have been): That is what we did not dare to preach to the people. We preferred to yield to popular custom rather than to bring the people over to our way of thinking and living.[13]

Leo Strauss expresses the Platonic position by saying:

> When attempting to guide the city, [the philosopher] knows then in advance that, in order to be useful or good for the city, the requirements of wisdom must be qualified or diluted. If these requirements are identical with natural right or with natural law, natural right or natural law must be diluted in order to become compatible with the requirements of the city. The city requires that wisdom be reconciled with consent. But to admit the necessity of consent, i.e., of the consent of the unwise, amounts to admitting a right of unwisdom, i.e., an irrational, if inevitable, right. Civil life requires a fundamental compromise between wisdom and folly, and this means a compromise between the natural right that is determined by reason or understanding and the right that is based on opinion alone. Civil life required the dilution of natural right by merely conventional right. Natural right would act as dynamite for civil society. In other words, the simply good, which is what is good by nature and which is radically distinct from the ancestral, must be transformed into the politically good, which is, as it were, the quotient of the simply good and the ancestral: the politically good is what "removes a vast mass of evil without shocking a vast mass of prejudice."[14]

> Describing the genre of writing known as psychagogy—the art of leading souls to a state of health—Hadot explains that the ancient philosophers believed the human condition was marked by a sickness of soul which prized material things above their true worth; seeking to achieve "the south-after therapeutic and psychagogic effect" for their readers, they meticulously crafted the "formulations necessary" to cure them of such mistaken beliefs. The same can be said of Augustine. Christianizing the genre, to be sure, Augustine attributes our distorted vision to sin and argues with a view to religious conversion. Yet, like all other authors writing works of psychagogy, he seeks to correct the vision of his readers by carefully crafted rhetorical arguments. (Roberts Ogle, *Earthly City*, 3)

13. *Uera rel.*, 4.6.
14. Strauss, *Natural Right and History*, 152–3.

Augustine by no means denies the main Platonic insight articulated here by Strauss: political life requires the dilution of wisdom with the consent of the unwise. Ernest L. Fortin notes,

> Augustine knew very well that for the most part his exalted moral principles were not directly applicable to the conditions of daily life and had to be diluted in order to become effective. Innumerable obstacles, stemming from our bodily and fallen nature, stand in the way of our becoming perfect lovers of justice. Book III of *On Free Choice of the Will* traces them back to two general roots: the "ignorance" that so often clouds our judgment and the "difficulties" that so often hinder the exercise of our free will. Clearly, there are limits to what can reasonably be expected of human beings. To make matters worse, the complexity of the situations in the midst of which one is compelled to act is often such as to make it virtually impossible to satisfy some of the demands of the moral law without violating others.[15]

Augustine only dissents on the necessity of lying, especially of lying about God and religion. According to Augustine, the city's lies and half-truths not only harm the many, who are induced to worship false gods, but also harm the philosophers, who sin against charity in sacrificing their fellow men to demons.

There are very good reasons to suppose that Augustine realizes that the noble lie may have been the best that could be hoped for in the absence of God's intervention through his prophets or in the person of Christ. This is why the post-Christian Porphyry and Apuleius come in for a much more severe criticism in the *City of God* than the pre-Christian Plato or Cicero.[16] As Douglas Kries argues, "perhaps esotericism had once understood the problem as well as was then possible, but that the problem had changed," with the coming of Christ.[17] Because philosophy liberates in mind only, it is open only to the few who are mentally keen and strong enough to undertake its rigors in pursuing the transpolitical goal of wisdom; the multitude is left with the next best option: civil religion and theurgy. The city and its laws are incapable of providing the harmony and peace needed for the city's way of life to be a happy one. Through the grace of Christ, on the other hand, men are

---

15. Ernest L. Fortin, *Birth of Philosophic Christianity*, 34.
16. See also Augustine's first letter, where he says,

> What is more acceptable to the common herd than the idea that body and soul are identical? Contrary to men of this type, I think that that method or art of concealing the truth is a useful invention. But, in this age, since we find no true philosophers—and I consider that those who go around dressed in philosophers' cloaks are quite unworthy of that honorable title—men need to be led back to the hope of discovering truth, especially those who have been deterred from understanding things by the subtlety of Academic phrases. (*Ep.* 1.1)

17. Kries, "Augustine as Defender and Critic of Leo Strauss' Esotericism Thesis," 247.

able to be healed and converted in their whole persons, body and soul—sensitive and intellectual—by the grace of Christ.[18] As a result, they can live according to wisdom in faith with the assistance of grace. Charity, in which knowledge and love are united, directs the whole city of God to its transpolitical[19] goal of communion with the Triune God in eternal life, while upholding the duties of its members to work for the achievement of temporal peace and some approximation of justice that is the earthly city's goal.[20]

---

18. Robert Dodaro argues that the city of God, "in Augustine's view, is largely penitential while it is confined to the earthly city." Dodaro, *Christ and the Just Society*, 4. The city of God therefore endures ignorance and difficulty as punishments, combating them with faith and humility guided by the love of God and neighbor. See Dodaro, *Christ and the Just Society*, 97. The city of God has recognized its sins, confessed them, and asked for aid from God; the earthly city perversely holds its punishments to be sources of pride.

19. Roberts Ogle rightly says that the introduction of "a transpolitical religion" is "nothing less than revolutionary." Roberts Ogle, *Earthly City*, 87.

20. For Plato, the best regime exists in speech only, but not in deed. For Augustine, the best regime is the city of God, which is not a city in speech but in deed. R. A. Markus observes, "Some will be bad, some will be better; only one, the heavenly city, will be good without qualification." R. A. Markus, *Saeculum: History and Society in the Thought of Augustine* (Cambridge, UK: Cambridge University Press, 1970), 66. "By comparison to it," James V. Schall writes, all earthly regimes "are pragmatic and imperfect." James V. Schall, *Reason, Revelation, and Human Affairs: Selected Writings of James V. Schall*, ed. Marc D. Guerra (Lanham, MD: Lexington Books, 2001) 112. As Fortin puts it, for Augustine, "The perfectly just regime has never existed in practice and never will." Fortin, *Birth of Philosophic Christianity*, 26. This is because of ignorance and difficulty. On the other hand, the city of God not identical with Plato's Socrates' city in speech, since the city of God is an actual—although not earthly—city. Robert Dodaro observes, for Augustine, "the classical sense of justice as 'giving to each person his due' is translated into giving to God and to one's neighbor the love which is their due by virtue of the double commandment of love." Robert Dodaro, *Christ and the Just Society*, 4. Charity therefore perfects justice, it does not undermine it. To put it even more simply, Dodaro states, "Human beings, [Augustine] believes, are just insofar as they know and love God." Ibid., 27. The love of God cannot exclude the love of those whom God loves, that is, all men. See *Trin.*, 8.8.

Chapter 5

PLATO ON THE DIVISIONS AMONG HUMAN BEINGS

At this point, it will be useful to pause in order to examine the basic background of the conversation between Augustine and his Platonic interlocutors by looking briefly at the ways in which Plato himself portrays human disunity. Since what is being examined is the split between the few and the many, the philosopher and the nonphilosopher, for our purposes the most useful dialogue to turn to is the *Apology of Socrates*, which portrays the dialogue between the philosopher: Socrates, and the multitude: the "men of Athens."[1]

Plato's analyses of what Augustine will call ignorance and difficulty typically appear in his dialectical accounts of the fundamental differences that separate the philosophic way of life and the moral or political way of life. In these accounts, the Socratic philosopher is seen to be guided by his erotic quest for wisdom; the nonphilosopher or the moral/political man, on the other hand, is guided by the opinions embodied in the city's conventions, customs, and laws.[2] Custom and law, or *nomos*, gain their force in large part through their being linked to the weight of tradition and to the reverence routinely accorded to the ancestral. Socratic philosophy, on the other hand, originates in the discovery of nature and turns on the articulation of the distinction between nature and convention. Nature provides philosophy with principles for the right way of life different from those provided

---

1. Plato, *Apology of Socrates*, 17a, trans. Thomas G. West, in *Four Texts on Socrates*, translated with notes by Thomas G. West and Grace Starry West (Ithaca, NY: Cornell University Press, 1998). All translations from the *Apology of Socrates* are from this version.

2. Leo Strauss writes, "Prephilosophic life is characterized by the primeval identification of the good with the ancestral." Strauss, *Natural Right and History*, 83. He continues by saying, "For one cannot reasonably identify the good with the ancestral if one does not assume that the ancestors were absolutely superior to 'us,' and this means that they were superior to all ordinary mortals; one is driven to believe that the ancestors, or those who established the ancestral way, were gods or sons of gods or at least 'dwelling near the gods.' The identification of the good with the ancestral leads to the view that the right way was established by gods or sons of gods or pupils of gods: the right way must be divine law." Ibid., 83–4. This identification is at the heart of the so-called theological-political problem.

by ancestral law and custom. Because no man is born a philosopher, men are raised and first educated by laws and customs.³

The ambiguous, perhaps hostile, stance that Socratic philosophy seems to take regarding the adequacy and reasonableness of the city's ancestral claims about morality and the laws fuels the drama of Plato's *Apology of Socrates*. Plato reports there that Socrates is charged with corrupting the youth, making the lesser argument the stronger, and not believing in the gods of the city. Socrates identifies two groups of accusers: his old accusers—the comic poet Aristophanes is here named—and his new accusers led by the ambitious young man, Meletus. The old accusers, Socrates says, are more dangerous than the recent accusers because they are "many" and they accused Socrates "long ago, talking now for many years" and "got hold of the many of you from childhood."⁴ These accusers make two particular accusations: that Socrates investigated "the things aloft" and "all the things under the earth, and who makes the weaker argument the stronger."⁵ Further, these old accusers' listeners "hold that investigators of these things also do not believe in gods."⁶ This is exactly how Socrates is portrayed in Aristophanes' *Clouds*, to

---

3. See the indignant argument of the legal apparition in Plato, *Crito*, 50c–e.
4. Plato, *Apology of Socrates*, 18b.
5. Ibid., 18b–c.
6. Ibid., 18c. George Anastaplo gives a plausible explanation as to why these investigations lead to the suspicion of atheism: "The words 'earth' and 'heaven' recall (in the Greek) Gaea and Ouranos—the parents and grandparents of the gods of the city—and this suggests, in turn, Socrates' concern with the origins and hence the nature of the gods. A refined parallel to this couple can be seen in Zeus and Hera, the only Greek gods Socrates invokes by name in this dialogue. Zeus and Hera represent complete divinity, from which all other aspects can be generated. A blending of these two gods into one can be anticipated as the next stage of the development. But the many, it seems, require many gods—and poetry ministers to this need and may have thereby even prepared the way for philosophy. Were not the poets 'the wise men of old?'" George Anastaplo, "Human Being and Citizen: A Beginning to the Study of Plato's *Apology of Socrates*," in *Ancients and Moderns: Essays on the Tradition of Political Philosophy in Honor of Leo Strauss*, ed. Joseph Cropsey (New York: Basic Books, 1964), 16–49 at 31. The raising of questions about the things aloft and the things under the earth therefore calls into question the city's belief in the gods and the city's deployment of the gods as explanations both for cosmic events and historical events concerning itself. Poetry, in teaching about many gods, also teaches about many goods, and therefore cannot help but teach about the gods at war with each other. But philosophy seeks wisdom about the whole, which, as a whole, would be characterized by unity. On the theoretical level, the Christian and Jewish teaching of one God would therefore be more amenable to the philosophic way of life than poetic polytheism. Christian teaching on God as triune and as the Church being Christ's one body with many members is therefore the Christian response to the conflict between the one and the many that partially characterizes the ancient quarrel between philosophy and poetry.

which Socrates alludes without naming later on.[7] Aristophanes' Socrates differs from Plato's Socrates. He seems to have more in common with the pre-Socratics and their "physiology" than with Plato's presentation of Socrates. Socrates even complains in the *Apology of Socrates* that Meletus seems to be confusing him with Anaxagoras, who boldly taught that the sun was a rock and not a god.[8] The bad reputation of Anaxagoras and his fellow physiological philosophers may have poisoned the minds of the Athenians against Socrates, whose way of life would not look much different to them. For example, Socrates evinces from Anytus, one of his three accusers in the *Apology of Socrates*, a harsh denunciation of the Sophists in *Meno* 91c, just before it becomes clear that Anytus is, in fact, "altogether without experience of these men."[9]

The new accusers, represented by Meletus, Anytus, and Lycon, add a further charge to those of the old accusers: "teaching others these same things."[10] It is only these new accusers who actually bring Socrates to court to be tried, so it is warranted to surmise that the addition of the new charge provides the reason for the change. Athens could perhaps tolerate one or a few philosophers with eccentric, ambiguously civic-minded ideas, but Socrates seems to attract followers—and not just any followers, but the sons of respectable citizens in the well-to-do classes. It is a matter of controversy between Socrates and his accusers whether he actually teaches these young men; Socrates declares that such a noble ability is not within his powers.[11] Nevertheless, he does not deny them the opportunity to be present when he examines others. The young men he attracts enjoy watching Socrates examine men believed to be wise, presumably because of the comic pleasure in seeing Socrates demonstrate to the purportedly wise men their foolishness.[12] They

---

7. Plato, *Apology of Socrates*, 18d. The poets, of course, are the prime redactors and keepers of the city's customs. As Ernest L. Fortin notes, "They function both as the unacknowledged legislators of the nation and as instruments used by actual legislators in establishing or perpetuating its religious traditions." Ernest L. Fortin, *Collected Essays*, vol. 2, *Classical Christianity and the Political Order*, ed. J. Brian Benestad (Lanham, MD: Rowman and Littlefield, 1996), 92. For a sustained treatment of what Plato called the ancient quarrel between philosophy and poetry and Augustine's intervention in that ancient argument, see Thomas P. Harmon, "Augustine and the Ancient Quarrel between Poetry and Philosophy," *Antonianum*, vol. XC (2015), 249–74.

8. Plato, *Apology of Socrates*, 26d. Socrates ventures no opinion, either *pro* or *contra* Anaxagoras about the sun's divinity. The reader is left to wonder whether Socrates differs from Anaxagoras in his reserve rather than in his astronomy.

9. Plato, *Meno*, 92b.

10. Plato, *Apology of Socrates*, 19c. Socrates adds, "It is something like this."

11. Ibid., 19e.

12. Socrates' examinations provoke anger, especially when he examines the politicians. When he examines anybody, the one under examination grows angry. When he examines politicians, not only the politician but also those nearby witnessing the examination get angry. Ibid., 21c–d.

then turn around and imitate Socrates' examinations, thus overturning the order in the city in which young defer to old and sons to fathers. This result is exactly what happens in Aristophanes' *Clouds*, which therefore serves as a prescient warning to Socrates. One also notes that the turning of son against father is an image of the turning of the present generation against the ancestral, and therefore old, or divine, which may be the root of the charge of atheism Socrates later provokes Meletus into making. Almost certainly in the background of the accusation is the memory of the infamous Alcibiades, a sometime associate of Socrates, whom Socrates denied teaching but whose evil deeds the city blamed, at least in part, on Socrates' unwholesome influence.[13] The two accusations of impiety are therefore combined with what Leo Strauss calls Socrates' "alleged missionary zeal,"[14] which made Socrates a menace, so his accusers thought, to the city as a whole. Whether Socrates set out to teach his imitators is therefore mostly beside the point. The import of Socrates' alleged impiety is that, in investigating nature, Socrates calls into question the gods, and, at the very least, calls into question the wisdom and desirability of looking to the gods of the city for instruction on how to act. In calling into question the gods of the city, Socrates calls into question the divinity and therefore authority of the city's laws and customs.[15] In influencing the young men of Athens, Socrates could prove to be a destabilizing force on the whole city.

Socrates' apology therefore, as Strauss puts it, "gives an account of Socrates' whole life, of his whole way of life, to the largest multitude, to the authoritative multitude, to the city of Athens before which he was accused of a capital crime; it is *the* dialogue of Socrates with the city of Athens."[16] Against the charge of impiety, Socrates invokes his adherence to his *daimonion* and also tells the story about the Oracle of Apollo, in which the oracle declares that "no one was wiser" than Socrates.[17] He casts his way of life as a divine mission undertaken in response to the message of the oracle. This mission changes in his telling of it from an examination of his fellow men to see whether he could refute the oracle—hardly a particularly pious undertaking—to a service to the god in support of the oracle, and then in a mission to exhort his fellows to care for virtue. He says,

---

13. On this point, Socrates could turn the accusation back on his accusers. As Anastaplo notes, "Does [Socrates] not virtually accuse the city, or at least his old accusers, with having corrupted the youth? All seem agreed that the young have been corrupted." Anastaplo, "Human Being and Citizen," 36, n. 11.

14. Strauss, *Rebirth of Classical Political Rationalism*, 190.

15. For a classic treatment of the relation between the city and its gods, see Numa Denis Fustel de Coulanges, *The Ancient City* (Baltimore: Johns Hopkins University Press, 1980).

16. Leo Strauss, *Studies in Platonic Political Philosophy* (Chicago: University of Chicago Press, 1986), 38. One could also add that the *Apology of Socrates* is the *popular* account and defense of Socrates' way of life, given as it is under compulsion and to the widest possible audience. That being said, Socrates is certainly constrained to offer his defense speech in the *Apology of Socrates*; but his jury is also duty bound to listen to him.

17. Plato, *Apology of Socrates*, 21a.

I, men of Athens, salute you and love you, but I will obey the god rather than you; and as long as I breathe and am able to, I will certainly not stop philosophizing, and I will exhort you and explain this to whomever of you I happen to meet, and I will speak just the sorts of things I am accustomed to: "Best of men, you are an Athenian, from the city that is greatest and best reputed for wisdom and strength: are you not ashamed that you care for having as much money as possible, and reputation, and honor, but that you neither care for nor give thought to prudence, and truth, and how your soul will be the best possible?"[18]

First, Socrates tells his jury that he pursues a transpolitical good, so his way of life does not fall under the city's jurisdiction. He lends emphasis to this claim later on when he tells his acquitters that, if he were to end up in Hades, he would not alter his way of life.[19] Second, against the charge of corruption, he argues that his transpolitical way of life allows him to be of great service to the city by persuading the citizens to care for the higher things rather than the lower. He even makes the bold claim, "And I suppose that until now no greater good has arisen for you in the city than my service to the god. For I go around and do nothing but persuade you, both younger and older, not to care for your bodies and money before, nor as vehemently as, how your soul will be the best possible."[20] Earlier, Socrates had claimed that what distinguishes him from the various kinds of men he examines is that, while none of them knows "anything noble and good, but he supposes he knows something when he does not know, while I, just as I do not know, do not even suppose that I do. I am likely to be a little bit wiser than he in this very thing: that whatever I do not know, I do not even suppose I know."[21] But if Socrates is to rest his case on his benefaction to the city, he would have to claim to have some knowledge of virtue. Strauss makes a suggestion, saying "Socrates denies that he or anyone else possesses knowledge of the greatest things (22d5-8); perhaps badness and goodness as pertinent to the discussion with Meletos do not belong to the greatest things."[22] Socrates' protestations of ignorance therefore perhaps do not apply to the field relevant to the matters dealt with in the *Apology of Socrates*. Socrates claims to pursue wisdom, not to possess it; political matters, therefore, perhaps do not belong to wisdom but to a lower kind of knowledge, a "human wisdom" which Socrates admits to possessing.[23]

---

18. Ibid., 29d–e.
19. See ibid., 40e–41c.
20. Ibid., 30a–b.
21. Ibid., 21d.
22. Strauss, *Studies in Platonic Political Philosophy*, 43.
23. See Plato, *Apology of Socrates*, 20d–e. See also Fortin, *Classical Christianity and the Political Order*, 76: "For all his professed ignorance of the highest matters, Socrates is convinced of the injustice of the laws of Athens and does not hesitate to oppose them when the circumstances demand it." To be *convinced* of the injustice of a law, Socrates must first *know* something about political justice.

As Cicero put it, Socrates "was the first to call philosophy down from the heavens and set her in the cities of men and bring her also into their homes and compel her to ask questions about life and morality and things good and evil."[24] This move, which is part of what Socrates calls his "second sailing,"[25] is the beginning of the examination of opinion necessary to move from opinion to knowledge. Opinion is the unavoidable starting point for the philosopher, from which he desires to ascend in order to attain knowledge. The city and its laws and customs are the most forceful and urgent opinions in human experience, by which every human being is shaped even before he is able to use reason. The ascent from opinion to knowledge therefore has to begin by examining opinion. The initial sense in which Socrates differs from those he examines, therefore, is that Socrates recognizes opinions for what they are. His knowledge of ignorance is simply the knowledge that what is held is opinion and not knowledge. In this respect, it is important to note that the opposite of knowledge for Plato is not lack of knowledge but opinion.[26] Even though his ultimate purpose is to transcend the opinions he dialectically examines, Socrates ends up knowing a great deal about the setting of those opinions in the city, and therefore a great deal about what it is to live well, at least in a qualified sense, in the city. His political philosophy is therefore a consideration of the city that transcends the capability of those whose judgments are encompassed by the city's opinions precisely because his goal is one that transcends the city. Socrates is able to understand virtue, therefore, much better than the nonphilosopher, both in itself as the true virtue that the philosopher seeks in his transpolitical pursuit and the simulacrum of virtue he finds in the city, dedicated as it is to unstable and ultimately unsatisfying political ends.

The bald fact about Socrates' defense speech is that it failed to persuade Athens not to kill him.[27] The lesson of the *Apology of Socrates*, at least on one level, is not to imitate the young men who imitated Socrates, and, therefore, not to imitate Socrates. The philosopher needs some kind of protection and needs to provide some kind of service in order to persuade the city not to deal harshly with him. As James V. Schall puts it,

> The philosopher attempts to deal with the shrewd politician who has the power to kill him. When the politician chooses not to participate in the philosopher's sole protection for his life, namely, in the continuation of honest discourse about

---

24. Cicero, *Tusculan Disputations*, 5.4.10, trans. J. E. King (Cambridge, MA: Loeb Classical Library, 1966). Augustine cites this passage in *ciu. Dei* 8.3.

25. Plato, *Phaedo*, 99d.

26. Meno, who is a kind of collector of opinions in his vast memory, is less able to acquire real knowledge than the unlettered slave boy Socrates corrals.

27. That being said, Plato's *Apology of Socrates* may have succeeded as a defense of philosophy, if only by rehabilitating the reputations of philosophers from the disrepute into which the pre-Socratics had fallen.

what "true politics" really are, we know the philosopher is dead. His only safety is found if the politician will examine the issues with him.[28]

If a great majority of citizens succumb to the *misologia* or hatred of arguments of the *Phaedo* then tolerance for the philosopher, the one who engages in arguments, will end. The philosopher therefore has an urgent need to cultivate those in the city who have not yet been completely given over to *misologia*, who are able to tolerate and perhaps, in exceedingly rare cases, even to live the theoretical way of life.

Politics, and therefore the city, is imperfect because the practical is inferior to the theoretical. That which the life of the city aims at is fulfilled only in the philosophic life.[29] But the philosophic life, as Strauss puts it, for Plato "is accessible only to what he calls good natures, to human beings who possess a certain natural equipment."[30] The service that Socratic political philosophy provides to the city, therefore, is limited by the limits of the city itself. It cannot transform the city into something it is not; nor can it transform human nature so that the many become wise. Nor would the philosopher find this outcome desirable, for he still depends on the city at least to meet his bodily needs. As Strauss says,

> If it is then impossible that the wise can rule the unwise by persuasion and since it is equally impossible, considering the numerical relation of the wise and the unwise, that the wise should rule the unwise by force, one has to be satisfied with a very indirect rule of the wise. This indirect rule of the wise consists in the

---

28. James V. Schall, *Reason, Revelation, and Human Affairs*, 56. Fortin remarks that Socrates' "own public speeches were meant to be more 'persuasive' than genuinely truthful. They were aimed as much at keeping the multitude away from the truth as they were at attracting the few who had proved themselves worthy of it by their ability to penetrate the disguise in which it is habitually cloaked." Fortin, *Birth of Philosophic Christianity*, 8.

29. Strauss argues, "[The philosopher] is ultimately compelled to transcend not merely the dimension of common opinion, or political opinion, but the dimension of political life as such; for he is led to realize that the ultimate aim of political life cannot be reached by political life, but only in a life devoted to contemplation, to philosophy. This finding is of crucial importance for political philosophy, since it determines the limits set to political life, to all political action and all political planning. Moreover, it implies that the highest subject of political philosophy is the philosophic life: philosophy—not as a teaching or as a body of knowledge, but as a way of life—offers, as it were, the solution to the problem that keeps political life in motion." Strauss, *Rebirth of Classical Political Rationalism*, 60.

30. Ibid., 162. James V. Schall comments, "Augustine was aware of philosophic problems that were not met by philosophy but that served as a link to revelation." Schall, *Reason, Revelation, and Human Affairs*, 113. Schall argues that, for Augustine, the incompleteness of both politics and philosophy points beyond itself by allowing one to wonder whether there is something that does offer the completion that politics and philosophy lack, the former more severely than the latter. Schall continues, "The completion of political philosophy does not come about by political philosophy itself." Ibid., 114.

rule of laws, on the making of which the wise have had some influence. In other words, the unlimited rule of undiluted wisdom must be replaced by the rule of wisdom diluted by consent.[31]

Platonic political philosophy, therefore, is a moderate, nonutopian attempt to improve an imperfect situation, which cannot be perfected on its own terms, through influencing the city's customs and laws. The city's religion, of course, falls into the category of the city's custom and laws for the Platonic political philosopher. Because the philosopher's wisdom must be diluted by the consent of the foolish many, the philosopher will have to resort to myths or lies in order to accomplish his goals. Most notable is the "noble lie" of the *Republic*,[32] in which nature, convention, and divinity are all brought together to ensure the highest possible degree of harmony in the city in speech.[33] James Leake remarks,

---

31. Strauss, *The Rebirth of Classical Political Rationalism*, 146.
32. Plato, *Republic*, 414c.
33. For a helpful explanation of the noble lie and its purposes in the *Republic*, see Allan Bloom's interpretive essay in Plato, *The Republic of Plato*, ed. Allan Bloom (New York: Basic Books, 1991), 365–9. For the purposes of the present volume, the relevant point is that, even the most just city, the city founded in speech, depends upon a lie. On the other hand, as Fortin explains,

> unlike his pagan counterparts, Augustine's orator must avoid lies at all costs, even the most harmless ones, lest by indulging in them he should be suspected of lying about the Christian message itself and undermine his own credibility. He may know vastly more than his less learned hearers and is thus often compelled to adapt himself to their limited intellectual capacities, but what he knows is not something other than what every Christian knows or should know. (Fortin, *Birth of Philosophic Christianity*, 7)

But Fortin also explains elsewhere,

> There is evidence that Augustine shared with his predecessors, both pagan and Christian, the view that the whole truth in matters of supreme moment can be safeguarded only if its investigation is accompanied by a prudent reserve in the expression of that truth. The difficulty inherent in the highest truths precludes their being made easily available to all indiscriminately. Not only error but truth itself can be harmful, inasmuch as all men are not equally well-disposed toward it or sufficiently prepared to receive it. (Fortin, *Classical Christianity*, 3)

For Christianity, the only way to attain the highest truth in this life is through hearing; for philosophy, the way to the highest truth available to us is through the direct sight of understanding. Augustine's aversion to lying and Platonic philosophers' instrumental view of lying are explicable on the basis of the place they assign to hearing and seeing and their reasons for doing so in each case.

The unstated assumption on which Socrates bases his argument for the utility and necessity of lies is the hardness of the truth and the irrefragable proneness of most men to live under the protective limitations of illusion or belief. The very best city, ruled by philosophers, nevertheless needs a "noble lie" to deceive and improve the majority of its citizens (*Republic* 413a–415d, 459c, and 377a). The fundamental problem to which Socrates points is that most men love themselves better than they love justice. Therefore certain lies are necessary to strengthen the claim of justice upon them. He does not think that such men can be changed.[34]

The necessity for myth and lies in the foundation and governance of the city both is the result of and points to the fact that the large multitude of men are not wise and therefore cannot be ruled by reason alone. This is one of the interesting parallels brought to light by the *Republic*'s city–soul analogy. Just as the multitude is unable or unwilling to be governed by the wise through reason alone, so also the man is unable to govern his subrational nature by his reason alone. This parallel provides a basis for reflecting on the reasons for both; in other words, Augustine's experience of his rebellious flesh in the *Confessions*, along with his narration of the way in which he dealt with this problem, provides some basis for reflecting on the rebelliousness of the multitude when confronted with real human wisdom. That the flesh could be converted gives warrant to James V. Schall's contention that the Augustine of the *Confessions* is a radical political philosopher.[35] If the flesh can be transformed, even somewhat and as a foretaste of a full transformation available only in the life to come, then the limits of politics are different from what the Platonic political philosopher can discern through the study of fallen human nature.

An analysis of the causes and extent of the foolishness of the multitude in contrast to the wisdom of the wise in the thought of Plato would require much more than can be attempted here, but a few observations are possible. First, Plato speaks of both "phantom" virtue and true virtue:[36] the kind of virtue upheld and championed by the city as city is in fact "phantom" virtue. True virtue, by contrast, is the kind of virtue the philosopher qua philosopher seeks. This kind of virtue is identical with knowledge. "Phantom" or vulgar virtue is imperfect, while true virtue is perfect. As a result, vulgar virtue does not perfect man, while true virtue does.[37]

---

34. James Leake, "On the *Lesser Hippias*," in *The Roots of Political Philosophy*, ed. Thomas L. Pangle (Ithaca, NY: Cornell University Press, 1987), 300–6 at 305.

35. See Schall, *Reason, Revelation, and Human Affairs*, 102. See Adam Thomas's excellent essay, "The Investigation of Justice in Augustine's *Confessions*" on this score, as well, in *Augustine's Political Thought*, ed. Richard J. Dougherty (Rochester, NY: University of Rochester Press, 2019), 105–26.

36. See, for example, the speech of Pausanias in *Symposium* 180c–185c. See also ibid. 212a, in which Diotima distinguishes between true virtue and its phantom images, and *Phaedo* 82a–b.

37. Something similar holds true for Augustine. See *c. acad.* 3.17.37. As Ernest L. Fortin explains, "Simply put, there is for Augustine no such thing as moral virtue properly so

Second, the reason why many are foolish and very few are wise is rooted in nature. Nature usually fails to achieve its goals, and the unhappy numeric distribution of wisdom is the result. For Plato, only the exceedingly rare individual will approach the achievement of his natural end. This perhaps accounts for Socrates' seeming resignation in the face of death.[38] It also explains the claim that the foolishness and viciousness of the multitude may be moderated by a wise constitution and by wisely given customs and laws, but, absent the chance coincidence of wisdom and political power, these things will never cease to exist in the city's multitude. As Socrates famously states, unless "the philosophers rule as kings or those now kings and chiefs genuinely and adequately philosophize, and political power and philosophy coincide in the same place … there is no rest from ills for the cities … , nor I think for human kind, nor will the regime we have now described in speech ever come forth from nature, insofar as is possible, and see the light of the sun."[39] The prospects for such a strange eventuality are extremely dim.

---

called, by which I mean moral virtue unaccompanied by the dianoetic or intellectual virtues." Fortin, *Birth of Philosophic Christianity*, 25.

38. Augustine would, no doubt, call Socrates' resignation "despair." Socrates' "swan song" in *Phaedo* 84e–85b and Scipio's dream in Cicero's *Commonwealth* are also meant to impart some of this philosophic resignation to the audience. Their goal is to moderate the panicked self-assertion of mortal men who rebel frantically against their mortality.

39. Plato, *Republic*, 473d–e.

Chapter 6

AUGUSTINE'S ENGAGEMENT WITH PLATONIC POLITICAL PHILOSOPHY ON IGNORANCE AND DIFFICULTY

Augustine had little direct access to the works of Plato. The most that was available to him seems to have been Cicero's translation of the *Timaeus*.[1] Nevertheless, through his engagement with a variety of thinkers working broadly in the Platonic tradition, Augustine was able to identify the touchstones of Platonic thought and to develop a sophisticated and incisive engagement with that thought, the most extensive and perspicacious of its kind in the early Church. Augustine's engagement with Plato therefore must be found in his engagement with the students of Plato. On the subject of the obstacles to human wholeness, Augustine engages four main philosophers as interlocutors in the *City of God*: Varro, Apuleius, Porphyry, and Cicero. Augustine's engagement with Varro and Porphyry, whom Augustine addresses most directly regarding the universal way of salvation, is the present focus. Both propose to dilute wisdom with consent in different but related ways: Varro by the philosophic improvement of Roman religion[2] and Porphyry by the recommendation of theurgy. Both ways require the deception of the nonphilosopher by the philosopher, which function to accustom the nonphilosophic multitude better for a peaceful life in the city and to keep them away from the inner sanctum of philosophy. Both ways bring to light the limitations of philosophy to improve the lot of the multitude. Augustine seizes on those limitations to compare pagan philosophy to Christianity in terms of the universal way of salvation Christianity makes possible. The necessity of philosophic deceptions, Augustine argues, has been abrogated by the coming of Christ, who heals human nature, tormented by ignorance and difficulty, through

---

1. See Van Fleteren, "Plato, Platonism," 651–4 at 651; John M. Rist, *Augustine: Ancient Thought Baptized* (Cambridge, UK: Cambridge University Press, 2000), 8–9; Douglas Kries, "Augustine's Response to the Political Critics of Christianity in the *ciu. Dei*," *American Catholic Philosophical Quarterly*, vol. 74, no. 1 (2000), 79–93 at 88; Ernest L. Fortin, *Birth of Philosophic Christianity*, 2; 55–6.

2. For an excellent treatment of Augustine's engagement with Roman civil religion, and especially with Varro, see Fortin, *Classical Christianity*, 85–105.

his grace. Christ breaks down the barriers that separate men from God and from each other who have their roots in sin.[3]

Marcus Varro dilutes wisdom with consent by mixing the teachings of natural theology with those of Roman civil religion in his book, *Antiquities*. Rather than overthrowing Roman polytheism, he attempts to make it less harmful. Augustine has plenty of sympathy with Varro's task. "What Varro can and does know with solid certainty, according to Augustine," Mary M. Keys explains, "is that in Varro's own time, Rome's public religion required considerable reformulation and revision in order to move beyond mere convention and toward nature via philosophy."[4] Augustine's criticism of Varro focuses on Varro's reserve in denouncing the false gods of Rome and announcing the truths about God he has discovered through natural theology. Augustine's criticisms of Varro are meant to have a contemporary influence. Varro is long dead, of course, so Augustine's criticisms of Varro are meant to address those of Augustine's own time and later who have followed or will be tempted to follow the same path. Augustine's criticisms of Varro must be understood, therefore, as coming from a time after the birth of Christ. Varro and other pagan philosophers who still deploy myths and lies are understood not to be acting as true benefactors to their fellow citizens in light of the coming of Christ.

Augustine criticizes Varro's reserve in two ways. First, Augustine questions the ability of Varro to accomplish his stated goal to improve the moral lives of Romans.[5] In speaking of the supposedly harmful elements in natural theology—which should be concealed from the multitude—Augustine says,

> But what are the elements which are harmful, if divulged to the general public? "The assertion," says Scaevola, "that Hercules, Aesculapius, Castor, and Pollux are not gods. The learned inform us that they were men, and that they died,

---

3. This is what the reader sees happening between Augustine and Evodius in *lib. arb* and between Augustine and Monica in the vision at Ostia in *conf.*, 9.

4. Keys, "Nature, Convention, Civil Religion, and Politics," 111. Keys continues: "Augustine does not dispute Varro's descriptions of the common people's propensity to keep company with the poets more than with the philosophers (cf. *ciu. Dei* 6.6), and so to follow convention more closely than nature. Neither does Augustine dispute Varro's prescription, to those able and willing, of the philosophic study of nature and endeavor to follow its guidance over that offered by myth (*ciu. Dei* 6.6). That nature—human nature and the nature of divinity or Deity—often is not, yet ought to be, followed in public life and in private, is not in question for Augustine or for Varro." Ibid., 114.

5. Roberts Ogle sums up Augustine's position by saying, "Just as Varro hopes that reading his books will convert others to natural philosophy, but has little way to speak to the culture at large, these philosophers' reinterpretation of the myths bear little fruit; they might interpret the myth of Saturn's cannibalism as an allegory for the changing seasons, but this reinterpretation will not alter the reason why most people enjoy plays about Saturn or worship at his temple (*ciu.* 6.8). In the end, philosophy can only reassure the *literati* themselves; it cannot change the broader culture." Roberts Ogle, *Earthly City*, 82.

in accordance with the human condition." And further, "The allegation that communities do not have true images (*uera simulacra*) of those who really are gods, because the true God (*uerus Deus*) has neither sex nor age, nor has he a defined bodily form." The pontiff did not wish the people to be aware of this; he did not think the statements were untrue (*falsa*). Thus he held that it was expedient for communities to be deceived in matters of religion (*falli in religione*), and Varro himself has no hesitation in saying as much, even in his books on "Divine Affairs." What a splendid religion for the weak (*infirmus*) to flee to for liberation (*liberandus*)! He asks for the truth (*ueritatem*) which will set him free; and it is believed that it is expedient for him to be deceived (*fallitur*)![6]

Varro exacerbates the predicament his nonphilosophic fellow citizen is in by strengthening the bonds of false religion on his soul. The unwise multitude is not capable of the strenuous efforts and the elevating contemplations needed to devote itself to natural theology, and there is nothing that Varro can do to change that. Varro's next best option is to attempt to purify Roman religion through the addition of some of the findings of natural theology, and to fight against the depredations of poetic immorality. But by lying to the multitude, Varro uses his own reputation for erudition and wisdom to persuade the multitude to be content with vice. Although Varro would not have recognized the category, Augustine criticizes him on the grounds of a lack of charity for his fellow man, which lack of charity clearly harms not only his fellow man, but also harms Varro.[7] Augustine summarizes his accusation:

> But the man who despises flattering judgment, also despises baseless suspicions; and yet, if he is a truly good man, he does not regard the salvation (*salutem*) of his fellow-men as of no importance. For so great is the righteousness of one who has his virtues from the Spirit of God, that he loves even his enemies and such is his love even for those who hate and disparage him, that he wishes them to be reformed so that he many have them as fellow-citizens, not of the earthly city, but of the heavenly. As for those who praise him, though he takes little account of their applause, he does not undervalue their love; he does not want to deceive those who praise him, because he would not want to play tricks on those who love him. And for that reason his ardent concern is that praise should rather be

---

6. *Ciu. Dei* 4.27. Dodaro points out, "Political leaders (*principes ciuitatis*) perpetuate such large-scale deception in order to strengthen the bonds of civil society and reinforce their power over their subjects. In doing so, they victimize the weak (*infirmus*) and uneducated (*indoctus*)." Dodaro, *Christ and the Just Society*, 53.

7. Von Heyking puts it well: "Varro failed to speak the truth openly because he lacked the spirit of God and thus the resolve to speak the truth to his fellow Romans." Von Heyking, *Augustine and Politics*, 49.

given to him from whom man receives whatever in him is rightly deserving of praise.[8]

There is pathos in Augustine's treatment of Varro on these points, since it is not at all clear what else Varro could have done. Von Heyking observes, "On the one hand, Augustine admires Varro's prudence in deferring to custom. On the other hand, he appears to have wished that Varro had been able to speak out against the false custom."[9] Augustine's clear strategy is to open the way for the reader to understand Christianity, and of course himself as an expositor of Christianity, as being able to imitate Varro's prudence but to add needed boldness in proclaiming the truth.

Augustine has to perform a careful two-step. He desires to moderate the hold of the city on the souls of unbelievers enough so that they will desire to join the transpolitical city of God, while also strengthening his fellow Christians' commitment to the city so as to uphold temporal peace and the other blessings of civil society. These are goals that pull in different directions. Augustine's solution is to remove from the city the absolute authority to determine laws of religion, but also to make dedication to the city and all of its other laws an obligation based on love of neighbor in other areas.[10] But Augustine's two-step is not without difficulty. Pierre Manent observes,

> The amelioration brought by Christianity could only be indirect, for its intent is not to introduce a new religion into the world in order to improve the world, but to introduce people into a new city in order to sanctify them. The amelioration of human life that we speak of can concern only this zone of uncertain status situated at the interface or intersection of the two cities. And if Christians can legitimately expect to observe indirect positive benefits, they will notice indirect negative effects: by troubling the vicious functioning of the earthly city through the good it brings, Christianity is susceptible of hindering the good effects that the vicious city can produce.[11]

---

8. *Ciu. Dei* 5.19. Oliver O'Donovan observes, "A unified account of justice, which related law to religion, was for [Augustine] a philosophic *sine qua non*." Oliver O'Donovan, "Augustine's *City of God* XIX and Western Political Thought," *Dionysius*, vol. XI (1987), 89–110 at 99. O'Donovan is surely correct that a unified account of justice is indispensable for Augustine, but Augustine recognizes along with his philosophic interlocutors the limitations of philosophy, given the predations of ignorance and difficulty. A unified account of justice that relates law and religion is only possible, in Augustine's view, with the advent of Christianity.

9. Von Heyking, *Augustine and Politics*, 49.

10. "By presenting Christianity as a better religion for the *ciuitas* than Roman civil religion," Roberts Ogle argues, "Augustine suggests that the patriot need not abandon his concern for Rome in order to join the city of God. Instead, it provides a foundation for all the virtues that benefit the political community." Roberts Ogle, *Earthly City*, 115.

11. Manent, *Metamorphoses*, 235.

Christianity can potentially make a bad situation worse when Christians do not attend to the real goods that even bad cities secure. Even bad cities have an admixture of goodness, after all, the disruption of which even in the name of higher things could lead to disaster. Besides, viewed from the standpoint of the city of God, all actual cities are imperfect, and so to that degree qualify as "bad." In addition to his rhetorical move to make sure that Christians do not take the earthly city and its laws as their total horizon, Augustine also brings his considerable rhetorical gifts to bear against any possible antinomian tendencies that Christianity's transpolitical orientation might encourage.[12]

Augustine also criticizes Varro's reserve on the basis of his own religious practice. He says, "What support do you derive, in this quandary, from your learning—which is also merely human, however manifold and immense? You desire to worship 'natural' gods; you are compelled to worship the 'gods of the city.' "[13] Augustine points out that, through the fear of the opinion of the multitude, Varro was compelled to join in the temple worship of the Roman civil religion despite his disbelief in the gods of the city. Varro would not have acknowledged any binding obligation to put himself at risk in order to avoid taking part in external religious observances. But it is precisely this disjunct between thought and deed that Augustine opposes. Augustine, unlike his Platonic interlocutors, stresses the importance of liberation from vice for the body as well as the mind, and the worship of God with the body as well as the mind. The whole man must worship God, and if the whole man does not worship God, then God is not worshipped properly. Both the mind and body are teleologically ordered toward God. It is in light of this particular criticism that Augustine makes his most searing indictment of philosophic reserve. In speaking of Seneca, who went even further than Varro in actually criticizing civil theology in his writing,[14] Augustine says, "But he [Seneca], whom the philosophers, as it were, made free, nevertheless, because he was an illustrious senator of the Roman people, he worshipped what he censured, did what he denounced, and adored what he blamed."[15] Seneca's public position and his private judgments were at odds. That situation, Augustine says, can only be a fake liberation. Augustine continues,

---

12. "Augustine is aware," Roberts Ogle writes, "of the earthly city's constant designs on political life, but he does not concede politics to the earthly city, nor does he make the Church the new realm of politics." Roberts Ogle, *Earthly City*, 143.

13. "Quid tibi humana licet multiplex ingensque doctrina in his angustiis suffragatur? Naturales deos colere cupis, ciuiles cogeris." *Ciu. Dei*, 6.6.

14. Although in *ciu. Dei*, 6.9, Augustine shows that Varro's critique of poetic theology is meant to redound onto civil theology, which, Augustine says, Varro identifies as poetic theology's source.

15. "Sed iste, quem philosophi quasi liberum fecerunt, tamen, quia inlustris populi Romani senator erat, colebat quod reprehendebat, agebat quod arguebat, quod culpabat adorabat." Ibid., 6.10. My translation.

> Doubtless philosophy (*philosophia*) had taught him an important lesson, that he should not be superstitious in his conception of the physical universe; but, because of the laws of the country (*leges ciuium*) and the accepted customs (*moresque hominum*) he also learnt that without playing an actor's part in theatrical fictions, he should imitate such a performance in the temple. This was to take a line the more reprehensible in that he acted this insincere part in such a way as to lead people to believe him sincere (*ueraciter*). The stage-player on the other hand, only aims at giving pleasure by his performance; he has no desire to mislead or deceive (*fallendo deciperet*) his audience.[16]

At least the actors did not expect their audiences to believe the stories performed for them on stage; but Varro and Seneca, in simulating religious devotion, deliberately deceive their fellow men.[17] Ignorance and difficulty therefore entrap not only the multitude, but also the philosopher. Freedom in mind is good, but it is not enough to satisfy.

When he comes to discuss natural theology directly, Augustine shifts to a group of philosophers he simply calls "the Platonic philosophers [*philosophos Platonicos*]."[18] Augustine desires to discuss natural theology with the keenest of philosophers, with those whom Augustine identifies as coming closest to the truth. "The Platonic philosophers" surpass Varro in one crucially important respect. Varro, Augustine says, identifies the soul with the divine, and therefore misses the mark. The group Augustine identifies as Platonists, he says, acknowledges a God who created the world and the soul and therefore stands above it, absolutely speaking. These Platonists, according to Augustine, therefore share the foundational belief of Christian teaching that God is the creator of the world and the soul. This is what makes them the best available philosophic interlocutors with Augustine the theologian on natural theology.

Book 8 of the *City of God* begins by discussing pre-Socratic philosophy and then moves on to Socrates. When Augustine gets to Socrates, he identifies two problems with Socratic philosophy, which then are transferred to Plato and his students. First, Socrates and then Plato concealed their thoughts on the highest good.[19] Augustine says, "The nature of this *Summum Bonum* did not emerge clearly from the discussions of Socrates, his method being to sift every question

---

16. *Ciu. Dei*, 6.10. As Kries observes, there is therefore one important way that "the mythical theology of the poets celebrated in the theaters is better than the civil theology celebrated in the temples." Kries, "Augustine's Response to the Political Critics of Christianity," 89.

17. See Manent, *Metamorphoses*, 272.

18. *Ciu. Dei*, 8.1. My translation.

19. Foley argues, "In fact, the discovery of esotericism was the first intellectual breakthrough that [Augustine] recounts as a Christian author and one that he continued to discuss years later as a bishop." Michael P. Foley, unpublished manuscript, quoted in Kries, "Augustine as Defender and Critic of Leo Strauss's Esotericism Thesis," 249.

by advancing hypotheses and then overthrowing them. And so everyone took from him what he fancied, and set up whatever agreed with his own ideas as the Final Good."[20] Socrates' practice of concealing his thoughts on the highest things, Augustine says, was also shared by his student Plato: "It is well known that Socrates was in the habit of concealing his knowledge, or his beliefs; and Plato approved of that habit. The result is that it is not easy to discover his own opinion, even on important matters."[21] Augustine's observation about the divisions among philosophers is a red thread throughout the rest of the *City of God*. The kind of knowledge the philosophers seek reliably leads to division, given the effect of pride on the sinful soul. The object of philosophy is perfected reason, that is, the perfection of the highest power of the human being. It is much less about handing down opinions or the formation of schools. In fact, the handing down of opinions and the formation of schools militates against the peculiar perfection desired by the philosopher, which can only be achieved through strenuous personal effort and rare natural intelligence. The distinctions in different men's inclinations and abilities therefore give rise to distinctions in their learning. Socrates and Plato concealed their thoughts on the supreme good not only, as it were, to protect philosophy against the contempt of the foolish and base, but also as a pedagogical practice to urge potential philosophers to take up philosophy.[22] The division in the learning of those who take the name of "philosophers" is therefore part and parcel of the philosophic way of life itself. The accompanying sad fact of human desire for glory and to possess first place, which Augustine identifies as the pride of life,[23] also means that some, perhaps most, students of philosophers will desire to start their own schools dedicated to their own opinions, thus enshrining division by setting up different philosophic sects based on each founder's view of the supreme good.

In addition to their internal divisions, philosophers foment divisions among the multitude by their teaching that many gods are to be worshipped.[24] Augustine asks his Platonic interlocutors whether only good gods or both good and evil gods ought to be worshipped.[25] He notes that Plato says that "all gods are good,"[26] which is the reason Augustine gives for why Plato exiled the poets from the city

---

20. *Ciu. Dei*, 8.3.
21. Ibid., 8.4.
22. See *ep.*, 1.
23. See also 1 Jn 2:16.
24. Cavadini argues that, for Augustine, the philosophy of Porphyry "underwrites the splintering of human community fostered by the permission it gives for polytheistic worship such as that endorsed by the Empire." Cavadini, "Ideology and Solidarity in Augustine's *City of God*," in *Augustine's* City of God: *A Critical Guide*, ed. James Wetzel (Cambridge, UK: Cambridge University Press, 2012), 93–110 at 105–6.
25. *Ciu. Dei*, 8.13.
26. Ibid. See Plato, *Republic* 379a–c. This is one area in which Augustine surely would have benefited from greater direct access to Plato's texts. On that score, see also Manent, *Metamorphoses*, 307.

founded in the *Republic*: the poets told false tales about the gods that portrayed the gods as perpetrating crimes and evils.[27] Augustine notices a disjunct between Plato's apparent affirmation of the goodness of all gods and Apuleius' recommendation and practice of theurgy, which is the practice of gaining favors from demons. Apuleius, Augustine notes, does not distinguish between good gods or demons to whom one ought to sacrifice and bad gods or demons to whom one ought not to sacrifice. Apuleius' theurgic practices rest, Augustine observes, on the fact that the demons possess bodies superior to human bodies and can therefore accomplish wonders in the corporeal realm. But the status of their bodies says nothing about their souls, for "an inferior material body may well be the habitation of a superior soul, and an inferior soul may dwell in a superior body."[28] Apuleius' theurgy is therefore the religious equivalent of the poetic theology of the theaters, but shorn of the quasi-innocence of the stage actors, who do not aim for their stories to be believed as true by their audiences.[29] Theurgy occupies a place in Porphyry's writing analogous to the Roman temple worship and the practice of rhetoric in Varro and Cicero: a way to, as it were, purge the passions of the masses who are not capable of the higher purification open to those rare souls who can take up philosophy. Augustine approvingly cites the Roman laws against magic arts as a salutary check on ungodly practices and pits Apuleius against Plato.

There is still a problem even if Augustine's case against Apuleius has been successful, for the question still arises as to whether it is acceptable to worship the "good" demons or gods. For Augustine, worship and sacrifice ascribe ultimacy to the object of worship or sacrifice, hence his frequent warnings that only God the creator, who is a God of all goods,[30] ought to be worshipped. Worship of many gods, even if they are understood as good, implies a metaphysical claim. Any kind of polytheism, in other words, even a polytheism with a Jupiter at the pinnacle of its pantheon, still posits at the very least a tension, if not conflicts, between goods, which is at odds with the Christian doctrine of the creation of the world from

---

27. "Then who are these gods who are at odds with Plato himself on this subject of stage performances? Plato would not suffer the gods to be slandered by false accusations (*falsis criminibus*), while the gods demanded that those slanders should be performed in their honour." *Ciu. Dei*, 8.13.

28. Ibid., 8.15. The consequence is that Augustine exclaims, "It is nothing but folly, nothing but pitiable aberration, to humble yourself before a being you would hate to resemble in the conduct of your life and worship one whom you would refuse to imitate. For surely the supremely important thing in religion is to model oneself on the object of one's worship." Ibid., 8.17.

29. See also Dodaro, *Christ and the Just Society*, 53, n. 113. "In Augustine's view, Porphyry could be associated with Cicero and Varro, insofar as the Neoplatonist philosopher deceives the masses into practicing theurgical arts, even while recognizing that contemplation is purer when it is unaccompanied by superstitious rites."

30. See *ciu. Dei*, 10.3.

nothing by God.[31] Hence, Augustine argues extensively in Book X that, not only should the good gods—or angels, as Christians call them—not be worshipped, but that they themselves desire human beings to worship only God the creator, in communion with them. Any "god" or demon who seems to desire worship must be bad since the desire for worship could only stem from pride and the *libido dominandi*.

The discussion of theurgy in Book 8 sets up Augustine's engagement with Porphyry about the universal way of salvation and the true mediator. Having posited agreement between himself and "the Platonic philosophers" that man's happiness consists in loving and enjoying God,[32] the problem of a mediator comes to the fore, since men are separated from God. The demons appear as candidates to mediate between God and men because they seem to occupy an intermediate position between the divine and the human, being placed in the air. But Augustine points out the incongruity of the supposedly pure gods accepting communications from the foul demons on behalf of men who may be less foul than the demons. Further, the problem at hand is how to grow nearer to God, and Augustine points out that physical proximity is not the kind of proximity that is urgent and desirable. Augustine instead argues, "If man comes near to God in proportion as he grows more like him, then unlikeness to God is the only separation from him, and the soul of man is estranged from that immaterial, eternal and unchangeable being in proportion as it craves for things that are temporal and changeable."[33] God is described as "immaterial, eternal and unchangeable," and man is described as

---

31. Fortin argues, "According to Augustine, the real reason for which the classical scheme is unable to make men virtuous and for which it is convicted by its own standards is not that it is irreligious but that it is intrinsically linked to a false conception of the divinity." Fortin, *Classical Christianity*, 15.

32.

Now we selected the Platonists as being deservedly the best known of all philosophers, because they have been able to realize that the soul of man, though immortal and rational (or intellectual), cannot attain happiness except by participation in the light of God, the creator of the soul and of the whole world. They also assert that no one can attain the life of blessedness, the object of all mankind's desire, unless he has adhered, with the purity of chaste love, to that unique and supreme Good, which is the changeless God.

Elegimus enim Platonicos omnium philosophorum merito nobilissimos, propterea quia sapere potuerunt licet inmortalem ac rationalem uel intellectualem hominis animam nisi participato lumine illius Dei, a quo et ipsa et mundus factus est, beatam esse non posse; ita illud, quod omnes homines appetunt, id est uitam beatam, quemquam isti assecuturum negant, qui non illi uni optimo, quod est incommutabilis Deus, puritate casti amoris adhaeserit. (*Ciu. Dei*, 10.1)

33. "Si ergo deo quanto similior, tanto fit quisque propinquior: nulla est ab illo alia longinquitas quam eius dissimilitudo. Incorporali uero illi aeterno et incommutabili tanto

being unlike God insofar as he longs for temporal and mutable things, which are opposed to two of the three attributes of God listed just prior. The third attribute is corporeality. By omitting the opposite of incorporeal from the list of the things the desire of which makes man unlike God, Augustine implies that desire for the corporeal is not necessarily at odds with a desire for the immutable and eternal. After all, Christians also hope for the resurrection of their bodies. Nevertheless, "It is not by physical elevation, but by spiritual—that is incorporeal—likeness to God that we must ascend to God."[34] Augustine uses his criticisms of theurgy as an occasion to point out the folly of thinking about godliness in spatial terms. Spiritual likeness is the necessary condition of bodily communion in the Resurrection.

Augustine presents Porphyry as holding forth two ways of purification for the soul corresponding to the division of the soul into sensitive and intellectual: theurgy and philosophy.[35] Theurgy, according to Augustine's presentation of Porphyry, is able to perform a kind of purgation of the sensitive soul,[36] but does not affect the intellectual soul.[37] Porphyry therefore recommends sacrifices to demons for those who are incapable of taking up philosophy. This will accomplish a kind

est anima hominis dissimilior, quanto rerum temporalium mutabiliumque cupidior." Ibid., 9.17.

34. "Quoniam non per corporalem altitudinem, sed per spiritalem, hoc est incorporalem, similitudinem ad Deum debemus ascendere." Ibid., 9.18.

35. Although Simmons points out that Porphyry includes a third, median way of salvation suited for the novice philosopher. See Simmons, *Universal Salvation*, 137.

36. Similar, perhaps, to the catharsis of pity and fear Aristotle says tragedy attempts to accomplish. See Aristotle, *Poetics*, 1449b28.

37.

> So one can observe [Porphyry] maintaining two contradictory positions, and wavering between superstition which amounts to the sin of blasphemy, and a philosophical standpoint. For at one moment he is warning us to beware of such practices as fraudulent, fraught with danger in their performance, and prohibited by law, and the next minute he seems to be surrendering to the supporters of magic, saying that the art is useful for the purification of one part of the soul. This is not the "intellectual" element by which is perceived the truth of intelligible realities which have no resemblance to material substances; it is the "spiritual" part of the soul, by which it apprehends the images of material things.
>
> Ut uideas eum inter uitium sacrilegae curiositatis et philosophiae professionem sententiis alternantibus fluctuare. Nunc enim hanc artem tamquam fallacem et in ipsa actione periculosam et legibus prohibitam cauendam monet; nunc autem uelut eius laudatoribus cedens utilem dicit esse mundandae parti animae, non quidem intellectuali, qua rerum intellegibilium percipitur ueritas, nullas habentium similitudines corporum; sed spiritali, qua corporalium rerum capiuntur imagines. (*Ciu. Dei*, 10.9)

In what is otherwise a very fine piece, Cavadini seems to miss the exoteric character of Porphyry's recommendation of theurgy. Cavadini says,

6. Ignorance and Difficulty 95

of purification for them, but only of the sensitive soul. The consequence is, Augustine says, "He admits at the same time that those 'theurgic rites' do not effect any purification of the intellectual soul which would fit it to see God and to apprehend the true realities."[38] But seeing God and apprehending the true realities are what Augustine says makes men happy—not just philosophers, but all men. Porphyry's judgment about who is capable of taking up philosophy and who can only rise as far as the purification of the sensitive soul offered by theurgy is based on his apprehension of nature and its purposes and limits. Because of the limits of nature—as apprehended by Porphyry—the majority of men must give up on wholistic purification, since their intellectual souls are excluded from theurgic ministrations. One might say that the multitude must sacrifice their intellects to purify their imaginations and emotions. In this way, their troubles are papered over, leaving them in a desperate situation: the immediate signs of their distress are hidden through the false purgation of theurgy. They have not achieved any happy purification of their whole persons, nor have they in any way overcome their ignorance or difficulty. There is no way for the foolish multitude, cut off from both faith and reason, to discern between good spirits and bad.[39] It is, however, possible

> Platonism has a vested interest in continuing to tolerate or even to endorse polytheism. Insofar as it is a philosophy of self-purgation available only to the few, based on the purgation of the soul from any connection to the body, the Platonists can glory in their wisdom and appeal to the pride of those less talented by providing access to sacrificial rites that will in effect make them, too, the principles of their own purgation, simply by enacting the rites and so forcing the hand of the gods. Here is reproduced the community that is no community, the community continually degenerating into self-serving domination and subordination, splintered and splintering. (Cavadini, "Ideology and Solidarity in Augustine's *City of God*," 107)

This missing detail ought to be mentioned not to gainsay Cavadini's point, but to make the case that advertence to Porphyry's esotericism would actually strengthen his case. The "community that is no community" and the "splintered and splintering" character that Cavadini notices are actually worse if the few philosophers separate themselves even further by reserving philosophy and the purgation of the intellect to themselves while chaining the many nonphilosophers to the theurgic rites.

38. "Ex quibus tamen theurgicis teletis fatetur intellectuali animae nihil purgationis accedere, quod eam faciat idoneam ad uidendum Deum suum et perspicienda ea, quae uere sunt." *Ciu. Dei*, 10.9.

39. Augustine points out,

> Porphyry relates that those who engage in those polluted rites of purification, with their blasphemous ceremonies, have some marvelously beautiful visions, whether of angels or gods, after the supposed purification. But even if they do in fact see anything of this sort, it is just as the Apostle says: "Satan transforms himself to look like an angel of light" (*angelum lucis*). For it is from the Devil that these phantoms come. The Devil longs to ensnare men's wretched souls in the fraudulent ceremonies

that men whose emotions have been soothed may become more peaceable, in the sense of more adapted to the earthly peace of the earthly city, and less inclined to raise disturbances at least in the short term.

There is a corresponding problem with the philosopher as well. He identifies his good with the good of his intellectual soul. Porphyry's concern with his body is to pacify it to the extent that it does not hinder his contemplations. As Augustine remarks, "Porphyry so often lays it down that one must escape from any kind of body (*omne corpus esse fugiendum*) in order that the soul may dwell with God in blessedness."[40] Just as the multitude of men, that is, men who live according to the desires of their bodies, are incapable of receiving purification so also even the very body of the philosopher himself is incapable of receiving purification. In the absence of the purification of the body, the body must be pacified sufficiently so that the soul is unburdened by its weight. Even for Porphyry the philosopher, there is no way to purify the whole man. He might, therefore, be said to sacrifice his body to the good of his soul. Because of the cleft between body and soul, which corresponds to the cleft between the philosopher and the nonphilosopher, Porphyry, Augustine reports, says, "As yet there has been nothing received by any sect that contains a universal way for the salvation of the soul."[41] Ignorance and difficulty apparently make any kind of universal way of salvation that is open to all men impossible. The best that can be hoped for is that, on the one hand, the men who have better natures can be purified and fulfilled in their better parts, that is, in their intellectual souls, and can, to some extent, behold God and perceive the

> (*fallacibus sacris*) of all those false gods (*falsorum deorum*), and to seduce them from the true worship of the true God (*uero ueri Dei cultu*) by whom alone they are purified and healed. And so, as is said of Proteus, "he turns himself into all shapes," sometimes appearing as a ruthless persecutor, sometimes as a fraudulent (*fallaciter*) helper; in either case, he seeks man's hurt. (*Ciu. Dei*, 10.10)

Dodaro notes,

> As permanent defects of the soul caused by original sin, ignorance and weakness make human beings vulnerable to deception about true religion by demons or other human beings. This deception, which is communicated through different forms of discourse, such as oratory, religious ritual, games and theatrical spectacles, philosophy and literature, is, moreover, the primary means of ensuring continued ignorance and weakness. (Dodaro, *Christ and the Just Society*, 66)

To overcome ignorance and difficulty or weakness, Christianity attacks the adherence of non-Christians to false religion, which is a kind of institutionalization of ignorance and difficulty.

40. *Ciu. Dei*, 10.29. This is also the teaching of the *Phaedo*, although whether either Plato or Porphyry literally meant that the soul must exit the body in order to be happy, leaving it completely behind and separate, is a matter that cannot be resolved here.

41. "Nondum receptum in unam quandam sectam, quod uniuersalem contineat uiam animae liberandae." Ibid., 10.32. My translation.

things that are; on the other hand, the men with worse natures might be soothed into a certain kind of calmness that comports with the requirements for earthly peace and a cessation of some degree of bodily violence.[42] Any possible remedy to the bifurcations involved in Porphyry's thought will have to address both clefts simultaneously.

---

42. Simmons argues, "The final and greatest deficiency of paganism was that it possessed multiple paths to the gods, and hence to 'salvation,' which by the third century must have been perceived by many in the empire as an overwhelmingly confusing jungle of cults." Simmons, *Universal Salvation*, 208.

Chapter 7

AUGUSTINE'S ARGUMENT WITH PORPHYRY ON THE UNIVERSAL WAY OF SALVATION

Political philosopher Pierre Manent argues, "Christianity's point of impact is the separation between the few and the many. What Christianity attacks is not social or political inequality but the pertinence of the distinction between the few and the many, the philosopher and the nonphilosopher, with regard to the capacity to attain or receive the truth."[1] It is precisely on the basis of the capacity of the nonphilosopher to attain or receive the truth that St. Augustine provides a critique of Porphyry in Book 10 of the *City of God*, saying that the eminent Platonist has not come across a universal way for the liberation of the soul (*liberandae animae uniuersalis uia*).[2] Instead, what Porphyry does provide are two separate ways of "purification" (*purgatio*) that liberate the soul: one affecting the higher or intellectual soul (*intellectualem animam*), one affecting only the lower or "spiritual" soul (*ipsam spiritalem*) through theurgy.[3] The first way is for those few who are capable of philosophy; the second is for the multitude of men who for whatever reason are not capable of the philosophic life.

Through his critique of Porphyry on the basis of the concrete way of life lived by Christians, St. Augustine enters into a classic conversation,[4] the boundaries and stakes of which had already been charted out. The classical political problem of the division between the few and the many is that, for the city to be properly ordered in justice, it must be ruled by the wise and according to wisdom; but the wise are few and outnumbered by the many, who are far too attached to their own opinions and customs to allow the wise to rule, even if they could (1) identify the wise

---

1. Manent, *Metamorphoses*, 272. Manent grants that Augustine owes an enormous debt to his philosophic teachers. But his argument also entails a dialectical relationship between them, in which Augustine appears not only as a debtor to his Platonic interlocutors, but also as a critic.

2. *Ciu. Dei*, 10.32.

3. Ibid., 10.27.

4. There are many other places in the Augustinian corpus that Augustine addresses this division. Book X of the *City of God* provides Augustine's most direct and concentrated dialectical engagement with a specific philosopher who is operating in the tradition of Platonic political philosophy on the topic of the division between the few and the many.

and (2) persuade or coerce them to rule—a doubtful proposition in either case. This lamentable situation requires the wise to cultivate ironic distance from the multitude—most famously in the figure of Plato's Socrates. If the wise are to exert any influence on the city, it will have to be indirect and through the utilization of lies—the most famous instance of which is the noble lie in Plato's *Republic*.[5]

In the first part of this chapter, the argument between Augustine and Porphyry on the universal way of salvation will be explored, especially focusing on Augustine's theological argument that the resolution of the division of the few and the many rests on the mediation of the incarnate Word of God in Christ. But the Christian way of life based on the mediation of Christ the Incarnate Word of God does not make it so that "political power and philosophy coincide in the same place," as Socrates puts it in Plato's *Republic*.[6] What this means for Augustine, as will be shown in the second part of this chapter, is that Christianity is transpolitical: it issues forth in no laws or constitutions and demands the foundation—or abolition—of no particular regime or form of government. The good that Christians pursue transcends the good of the political order; nevertheless, Augustine is at pains to make clear that, on the one hand Christianity does not dissolve politics, and on the other hand, faithful Christians can contribute positively to the legitimate political goals of the city, although he does not deny that Christianity makes impossible the perfervid attachment to one's own city that political men may regard as indispensable for the welfare of the city. Augustine seems to think that, on balance and given the other positive contributions Christians make to civic welfare, the potential risks Christianity might pose in directing citizens toward transpolitical goods are risks statesmen ought to be willing to embrace.

The first part of Augustine's *City of God*, which comprises Books I–X, is itself divided in two. Augustine dedicates Books I–V to refuting those who worship false gods for the sake of temporal benefits; he dedicates Books VI–X to refuting those who worship false gods for the sake of "the future life after death."[7] The second part of *The City of God* is dedicated to an examination of the origin, progress, and end of the city of God. Fittingly, Christ the mediator provides the hinge between the two parts: Book X ends with Augustine speaking of Christ the mediator and Book XI begins with Augustine speaking of Christ the mediator. Porphyry occupies the pivotal place in the first part of the *City of God* by way of contrast, for Augustine, in his explication of Christ's mediation. The contrast is between the universal way of salvation provided through Christ's mediation and the bifurcated ways provided by Porphyry's recommendation of theurgy for the purgation of the "spiritual" soul to the nonphilosopher on the one hand, and his recommendation of the purgation of the intellect to those capable of philosophy on the other.

---

5. See Plato, *Republic*, 414b–e. Later on, Socrates says, "It's likely that our rulers will have to use a throng of lies and deceptions for the benefit of the ruled." Ibid., 459c–d.
6. Ibid., 473d.
7. *Ciu. Dei*, 10.32.

Augustine's critique is deeper than what appears at first. It is true that he laments Porphyry's exclusion of the multitude from a fulsome salvation, but his critique does not admit that the only defect in Porphyry's bifurcatory remedies is that the multitude is left out. If that were so, then Augustine would be admitting that the philosopher is capable of salvation without the mediation of Christ. Only the multitude would stand in need of Christ's ministrations. That would leave things almost as they stand with Porphyry: the philosophers would take one way of salvation based on their intellectual capabilities while the multitude would take another way that is opened up for them by Christ. The difference would be that, for Augustine and Christianity, both the few and the many could be saved—but there would remain *two* ways of salvation, one of which depends on Christ and the other of which does not—rather than one, universal way. Augustine's critique is not only that Porphyry excludes the multitude from salvation, but that the bifurcation of ways of salvation also excludes the philosopher from salvation.

Augustine's critique of Porphyry appears in an extended section where Augustine is refuting those who think that angels and demons ought to be worshipped. His basic argument is, "If [an angel] does not worship God, it is wretched, because deprived of God; if it worships God, it will not wish itself to be worshipped in the place of God."[8] Both angels and men ought to worship the one God who is the Creator of all else. If an angel truly worships this true God, then he will not want to be worshipped in God's place. Any angel who seems to want to be worshipped in God's place is evil. If an angel desires worship for himself in order to be a mediator between the human being offering worship and God, that angel is a deceiver. Mediation happens on the basis of commonality between both sides of the mediation. All the demon can claim is that it has a superior nature to man and, by virtue of that superior nature, stands between man and God and so can act as a proper mediator. But the angel or demon is not placed between men and God; on the contrary, demonic wickedness makes the demon inferior to the human being in a crucial respect. Besides, the assumption of a continuum from human to angelic to divine natures fundamentally misunderstands, for Augustine, the relationship between creator and creation.

Porphyry recommends commerce with demons, or theurgy, in his writings.[9] The purpose of Porphyry's recommendation of theurgy, according to Augustine, is so that "by means of certain 'theurgic consecrations,' which are called *teletae*, this spiritual element of the soul is put into a proper condition, capable of welcoming spirits and angels, and of seeing the gods."[10] These practices will result in "some

---

8. *Ciu. Dei*, 10.3.

9. Dodaro gives a concise explanation of theurgy: "The practice refers to the performance of ritual acts: prayers, hymns, and incantations, accompanied by meditation, which were intended to put the soul into contact with spirits and deities so that it would achieve moral purification and peace in an experience of spiritual ecstasy." Robert Dodaro, OSA, "Theurgy," in *Augustine through the Ages*, ed. Allan D. Fitzgerald (Grand Rapids, MI: Eerdmans, 1999), 827–8 at 827.

10. *Ciu. Dei*, 10.9.

sort of purification of the soul [*quasi purgationem animae*]."[11] Augustine says *quasi purgationem* because the purgation offered by Porphyry would only be partial, limited to the lower soul. Augustine counters that,

> [Porphyry] admits at the same time that those "theurgic rites" do not effect any purification of the intellectual soul which would fit it to see its God and to apprehend the true realities. From this one can gather what kind of gods and what kind of vision he is talking about in those "theurgic consecrations"; it is not a vision of the true realities. In fact, he says that the rational soul (or, as he prefers, the "intellectual" soul) can escape into its own sphere, even without any purification of the spiritual element by means of the "theurgic art," and further, that the purification of the spiritual part by theurgy does not go so far as to assure its attainment of immortality and eternity.[12]

Augustine's critique here is amazingly dense and requires a lot of unpacking. The full critique is present in only a few lines. First, Porphyry's theurgy offers only a partial purification of the spiritual or lower soul. The rational soul, on the other hand, is capable of the contemplation of intelligible reality without any purification of the spiritual soul. The lower soul seems to be the sensitive soul, the seat of the senses, the imagination, the passions, and the emotions. The higher soul is the seat of the intellectual or rational power, by which the mind can understand the truth. The division Augustine and Porphyry are talking about is the classic division Plato expressed in the image of the divided line[13] and the allegory of the cave.[14] The operations of the lower soul take place below the divided line and the operations of the intellectual soul take place above the divided line.

To see what Augustine is talking about in his own idiom, it may be helpful to think back to Augustine's *Confessions*. The most significant event in young Augustine's time in Africa is his introduction to the pursuit of wisdom through Cicero's *Hortensius*.[15] The *Hortensius*, Augustine remarks using striking language,

---

11. Ibid.
12. Ibid.
13. Plato, *Republic*, 509d–511e.
14. Ibid. 514a–517a.
15. Fortin comments on the influence of the *Hortensius* on the young Augustine:

> [*Hortensius*] held up the theoretical life as the highest human possibility and the philosopher as the highest human type. It thereby made a young and avid Augustine, who had more than his share of riot and high summer in the blood and for whom the familiar *cursus honorum* was the mandatory road to success, aware of the fact that one's whole life could be actuated, not by the love of pleasure, honor, or any of the other worldly goods to which the vast majority of human beings are drawn, but by that most unusual of all passions—a passion so rare that few people recognize it when they come face to face with it—the passion for the truth. (Fortin, *Birth of Philosophic Christianity*, 4)

"changed my affections. It turned my prayers to you, Lord, and caused me to have different purposes and desires. All my vain hopes forthwith became worthless to me. And with incredible ardor of heart I desired undying wisdom."[16] Augustine's change of affections, however, did not issue directly into a life lived in philosophy. His affections may have been turned toward wisdom, but his mind was crude. Because of his intellectual crudity, he fell in with the Manicheans, a sect that posited a good and an evil principle at war in the world. The Manicheans provided Augustine with seeming wisdom in the form of a superficially satisfying answer to the problem of evil and a way to exonerate God from responsibility for evil in the world: there is a good god and an evil god. Good is the responsibility of the good god, and evil the responsibility of the evil god. Augustine relates,

> I did not know that other being, that which truly is (*nesciebam enim aliud, uere quod est*), and I was as it were subtly moved to agree with those dull deceivers (*deceptoribus*) when they put their questions to me: "Whence is evil?" "Is God confined within a corporeal form?" "Does he have hair and nails?" "Are those to be judged just men who had many wives, killed other men, and offered sacrifices of animals?" Ignorant (*ignarus*) in such matters, I was disturbed by these questions, and while actually receding from the truth, I thought I was moving towards it. The reason was that I did not know that evil is only the privation of a good, even to the point of complete nonentity. How could I do this, when with eyes I could see only bodies, and with my soul only phantasms?[17]

It was in working through his dissatisfaction with Manicheanism that Augustine was able, eventually, to determine the source of his intellectual problems. He laments, "By what steps was I led down into the depths of hell, struggling and burning for want of the truth! For then I sought for you, not according to intellectual understanding [the understanding of the mind] (*intellectum mentis*), by which you willed to raise me above brute beasts, but according to carnal sense (*sensum carnis*)."[18] There is no indication that Augustine undertook, himself, the Chaldean-inspired theurgical rites that Porphyry recommends, but the Manichean rites he participated in and his crude, sub-philosophic investigations as a young man seem to be similar to the theurgy Porphyry recommends: the search for God or gods to purify the lower soul to the neglect of the higher soul. Augustine's criticism of Porphyry is therefore grounded not only on philosophical and theological arguments, but has an urgency and familiarity for Augustine based on his own personal experience.

---

16. "Mutavit affectum meum, et ad te ipsum, domine, mutavit preces meas, et vota ac desideria mea fecit alia. Veluit mihi repente omnis vana spes, et immortalitatem sapientiae concupiscebam aestu cordis incredibili." *Conf.*, 3.4.7.

17. *Conf.*, 3.7.12.

18. Ibid., 3.6.11. Intellectual understanding is better translated "understanding of the mind."

Augustine not only had experience seeking purifications for his lower soul. By working through his intellectual problems, Augustine is eventually led to the point of intellectual conversion. His intellectual problem as he narrates it in the *Confessions* is his inability to conceive of spiritual substance: that is, the very thing that allows one to operate above the divided line by the powers of the intellectual soul. It is no accident that he does so, as he tells us himself, under the tutelage of the "books of the Platonists."[19] It is a vexed question among scholars of Augustine about which books and authors Augustine means. Van Fleteren sums up the *status quaestionis* by saying, "Not either Plotinus or Porphyry, but both Plotinus and Porphyry."[20] On the basis of Augustine's own writing in the *City of God*, it may be possible to tip the scales a little to the side of Porphyry. When trying to decide which philosophers with whom to engage on the highest matters, the matters of "natural theology,"[21] he looks for the philosophers whose conception of God is closest to that of Christian faith. These are the "Platonists, Who are thus called on account of their teacher Plato."[22] Augustine later calls the Platonists *nobilissimos*, most noble.[23] He also calls Porphyry *philosophos nobilis*, a noble philosopher,[24] and *doctissimus philosophorum*, most learned of philosophers.[25] Augustine himself regards Porphyry as preeminent among philosophers. It is reasonable to assume, without in any way arguing that Plotinus was absent from Augustine's studies in the events narrated in Book 7 of the *Confessions*, that Porphyry's books were preeminent among those books of the Platonists under the tutelage of which Augustine had his intellectual conversion. In other words, it seems likely that Augustine had personal experience with both of the ways of salvation that Porphyry holds out.

From the standpoint of the Platonic philosopher and Augustine, the drawbacks to theurgy and related pursuits are obvious: they do not accomplish what they promise. What is sought is the liberation of the soul; what is delivered is nothing of the kind. Until Augustine has his intellectual conversion, the various measures he takes in order to attain wisdom do not accomplish the task: he does not attain to God in truth, he only attains to a phantasm (*phantasma*) instead of God.[26] But phantasms have no power to save in truth, although those who cannot distinguish between a phantasm and the true God—such as Augustine before his intellectual conversion—might be deceived into thinking that they either are saved or are on

---

19. Ibid., 7.9.13.
20. Frederick Van Fleteren, "Porphyry," in *Augustine through the Ages: An Encyclopedia*, ed. Allan D. Fitzgerald, OSA (Grand Rapids, MI: Eerdmans, 1999), 663.
21. As distinguished from the mythic and civil theology he discusses in early parts of the *City of God*.
22. "Platonicos appellatos a Platone doctore." *Ciu. Dei,* 8.1. My translation.
23. Ibid., 10.1.
24. Ibid., 7.25.
25. Ibid., 19.22.
26. *Conf.*, 7.17.23.

the way to being saved. In fact, falsity or deception is one of the main concerns of Augustine in Book 10: both the falsity of the philosopher who recommends theurgy and the falsity of the demons with whom the theurgist communicates.[27] Augustine's concern with the deception of the multitude by statesmen and philosophers in matters of religion is an ongoing concern throughout the *City of God*. It is on this basis that he criticizes the civil theology of Rome earlier. He says that the civil theology, which finds its home in the rites of the temples, hides the truth that the natural theology of the philosophers uncovers, thereby preventing its adherents from knowing the truth in religion and, therefore, barring access to any true deliverance or salvation. He says,

> But what are the elements which are harmful, if divulged to the general public? "The assertion," says Scaevola, "that Hercules, Aesculapius, Castor, and Pollux are not gods. The learned inform us that they were men, and that they died, in accordance with the human condition." And further, "The allegation that communities do not have true images (*vera simulacra*) of those who really are gods, because the true God (*verus Deus*) has neither sex nor age, nor has he a defined bodily form." The pontiff did not wish the people to be aware of this; he did not think the statements were untrue (*falsa*). Thus he held that it was expedient for communities to be deceived in matters of religion (*falli in religione*), and Varro himself has no hesitation in saying as much, even in his books on "Divine Affairs." What a splendid religion for the weak (*inifirmus*) to flee to for liberation (*liberandus*)! He asks for the truth (*ueritatem*) which will set him free; and it is believed that it is expedient for him to be deceived (*fallitur*)![28]

These strategies are not new. In the *Phaedo*, which takes place dramatically in the shadow of Socrates' impending execution, Socrates' friends worry about what they will do in the absence of their wise friend. The dramatic movement of the dialogue makes it clear that Socrates' presence and teaching moderates their fear of death and hatred of argument, or *misologia*. Socrates' ministrations are described as incantations, which hold the fear of death and the hatred of arguments at bay. Only Socrates the philosopher, the dialogue implies, is able to face up to the radical uncertainty of the individual's personal destiny beyond death. The many nonphilosophers must be soothed by myths. Joseph Cropsey explains, "Philosophy, the musical art, speaking with the voice of the poet Socrates singing his swan song, thus relieves the pains of profoundest ignorance and of the fear of death."[29] Through his incantations, Socrates seeks to impart some of his own

---

27. Some version of *fallo* occurs twenty-nine times and some version of *decipio* occurs six times throughout Book 10.

28. *Ciu. Dei,* 4.27.

29. Joseph Cropsey, *Plato's World* (Chicago: University of Chicago Press, 1997), 192. For Socrates' reference to his "swan song," see Plato, *Phaedo,* 84e–85b. Dodaro astutely observes that theurgy serves as "therapy for fear of death." Dodaro, *Christ and the Just Society*, 64.

serenity in the face of death to his friends. But it is by no means clear that Socrates actually believes the content of the swan song. Cropsey, for instance, interprets two of Plato's signature teachings, the immortality of the soul and the intelligible forms, as poetic therapy for the many given by Socrates who, after all, claims in the *Apology of Socrates* that he is the city's greatest benefactor.

In Porphyry's hands, theurgy is the Socratic swan song in a Neo-platonic key. The philosopher Socrates can lend his nonphilosophic friends some of the serenity that he himself has in the face of death on the basis of his poetic-philosophic incantation. Porphyry can likewise lend his nonphilosophic associates some of his own philosophic serenity by soothing their fears through the therapeutic ministrations of theurgy. Just like Socrates, Porphyry also seems to hold out hope that, through theurgy, the theurgist will have some kind of life after death. Augustine says, "[Porphyry] recommends us to cultivate the friendship of some demon, by whose assistance a man may be raised just a little above the earth after death."[30] But the strange way Augustine says Porphyry speaks of this existence after death ought to make us wonder about what he is saying. Later on, Augustine argues, "It is enough for our purpose that you admit that theurgic purification cannot purify the 'intellectual' soul—that is, our mind; and that while you assert that it can purify the 'spiritual' soul—that is, the part of the soul inferior to the reason—you confess that theurgic art cannot make it immortal [*immortalem*] and eternal [*aeternam*]."[31] In any case, needless to say, being raised a little above the earth after death falls far short of the philosophic achievement Porphyry says Plotinus achieved four times during his life and he himself once: merging with the One. Porphyry says,

> There was shown to Plotinus the Term ever near: for the Term, the one end, of his life was to become Uniate, to approach to the God over all: and four times, during the period I passed with him, he achieved this Term, by no mere latent fitness but by the ineffable Act. To this God, I also declare, I Porphyry, that in my sixty-eighth year I too was once admitted and entered into Union.[32]

There seems little doubt that Porphyry regards the true salvation of the soul to be in reach of the philosopher alone; the salvation of the soul able to be accomplished by theurgy is false. That is why Augustine says that the demons with whom the theurgists are encouraged to cultivate friendship are "either identical with that being who is called Deceiver, or else they are nothing but a figment of the human imagination."[33] Either the foolish theurgist is deceived by a demon or is saved only

---

30. "Admoneat utendum alicuius daemonis amicitia, quo subuectante uel paululum a terra possit eleuari quisque post mortem." *Ciu. Dei*, 10.9.

31. Ibid., 10.27.

32. Porphyry, "On the Life of Plotinus and the Arrangement of His Work," 17.

33. *Ciu. Dei*, 10.11. Augustine wonders later in the *City of God* whether Porphyry "falsely invented" the oracles he writes down in his book *Philosophy from Oracles. Ciu. Dei*, 19.23.

in his own imagination; in either case, he is not truly saved. His fear of death may be soothed, but not on the basis of truth. Augustine addresses Porphyry directly, saying, "You inveigle [*seducis*] those who are incapable of becoming philosophers to indulge in practices which, on your own showing, are of no use to you, because you are capable of higher things. Thus all those who cannot approach to philosophic virtue (a lofty ideal to which only a few attain) have your authority to seek out theurgists."[34]

But Augustine's criticism does not end at expressing concern for the deception of the multitude. In *Confessions*, he narrates that he himself was able to approach philosophic virtue, that "lofty ideal to which only a few attain," under the tutelage of the books of the Platonists. Here is how he describes that ascent:

> Thus I gradually passed from bodies to the soul, which perceives by means of the body, and thence to its interior power, to which the bodily senses present exterior things—beasts too are capable of doing this much—and thence to its interior power, to which what is apprehended by the bodily senses is referred for judgment. When this power found itself to be in me a variable thing, it raised itself up to its own understanding. It removed its thought from the tyranny of habit, and withdrew itself from the throngs of contradictory phantasms. In this way it might find that light by which it was sprinkled, when it cried out, that beyond all doubt the immutable must be preferred to the mutable. Hence it might come to know this immutable being, for unless it could know it in some way, it could in no wise have set it with certainty above the mutable. Thus in a flash of its trembling sight it came to that which is.[35]

This is the achievement at which Augustine has been aiming ever since his affections were turned toward wisdom by Cicero's *Hortensius*. It is a great achievement, and Augustine presents it as such. Even so, Augustine does not find the kind of satisfaction in it that he desired. He was incapable of sustaining the sight of *id, quod est*. His philosophic achievement turns out to be an anticlimax. Augustine explains himself, saying,

---

34. Ibid., 10.27.
35.

> Ita gradatim a corporibus ad sentientem per corpus animam atque inde ad eius interiorem uim, cui sensus corporis exteriora nuntiaret, et quousque possunt bestiae, atque inde rursus ad ratiocinantem potentiam, ad quam refertur iudicandum, quod sumitur a sensibus corporis; quae se quoque in me comperiens mutabilem erexit se ad intellegentiam suam et abduxit cogitationem a consuetudine, subtrahens se contradicentibus turbis phantasmatum, ut inueniret quo lumine aspergeretur, cum sine ulla dubitatione clamaret incommutabile praeferendum esse mutabili, unde nosset ipsum incommutabile—quod nisi aliquo modo nosset, nullo modo illud mutabili certa praeponeret—et peruenit ad id, quod est in ictu trepidantis aspectus. (*Conf.*, 7.17.23)

I was not steadfast (*non stabam*) in enjoyment of my God: I was borne up to you by your beauty. But soon I was borne down from you by my own weight, and with groaning, I plunged into the midst of those lower things. This weight was carnal custom (*consuetudo carnalis*). Still there remained within me remembrance of you: I did not doubt in any way that there was one to cleave to, nor did I doubt that I was not yet one who would cleave to him. "For the corruptible body is a load upon the soul, and the earthly habitation presses down upon the mind that muses upon many things."[36]

Augustine has not found at all that his "rational soul (or, as [Porphyry] prefers, the 'intellectual' soul) can escape into its own sphere, even without any purification of the spiritual element."[37] The problem is that he cannot separate his mind from the rest of himself and that the rest of himself is no less truly himself than his highest part.

Salvation of the intellectual part that does not provide salvation to the whole man is doomed to be as unstable as his own abortive contemplation of *id, quod est* under the tutelage of the books of the Platonists. That is why after Augustine's religious conversion, he and his mother, Monica, together ascend again "to touch eternal Wisdom which abides over all,"[38] but the experience is quite different from his abortive, Neo-Platonic ascent in Book 7. Here is how he describes his ascent with Monica:

And our conversation had brought us to this point, that any pleasure whatsoever of the bodily senses, in any brightness whatsoever of corporeal light, seemed to us not worthy of comparison with the pleasure of that eternal Light, not worthy even of mention. Rising as our love flamed upward towards that Selfsame, we passed in review the various levels of bodily things, up to the heavens themselves, whence sun and moon and stars shine upon this earth. And higher still we soared, thinking in our minds and speaking and marveling at your works: and so we came to our own souls, and went beyond them to come at last to that region of richness unending, where you feed Israel forever with the food of truth: and there life is that Wisdom by which all things are made, both the things that have been and the things that are yet to be. But this Wisdom itself is not made: it is as it has ever been, and so it shall be forever: indeed "has ever been" and "shall be forever" have no place in it, but it simply is, for it is eternal: whereas "to have been" and "to be going to be" are not eternal. And while we were thus talking of His Wisdom and panting for it, with all the effort of our heart we did for one instant attain to touch it; then sighing, and leaving the first fruits of our spirit bound to it, we returned to the sound of our own tongue, in which a word has both beginning and ending.[39]

36. *Conf.*, 7.17.23.
37. *Ciu. Dei*, 10.9.
38. *Conf.*, 9.10.25.
39. Ibid., 9.10.24.

The first difference between the two accounts is that the first ascent in Book 7 is undertaken by Augustine alone; the second in Book 9 is undertaken with another, namely, his mother Monica. Monica's inclusion is significant for two reasons: both because the second ascent is done in conversation with another and because of the specific character of the other: Monica is unlettered—she has definitely not read the books of the Platonists. The first, abortive ascent is like Porphyry's second way of salvation, concerning the intellectual soul alone. The second ascent is accomplished in common between Monica and Augustine, who are the two types of person that Porphyry thought needed two different ways of salvation. The second ascent in the *Confessions* therefore exemplifies the universal way of salvation Augustine holds forth as possible on the basis of Christ's mediation. The most significant difference between the two ascents is the goal. In both cases, God is the goal. But in the first ascent, God is described as *id, quod est*, a true but entirely impersonal description, suitable for the object of an ascent made purely on an intellectual plane. In the second ascent, God is addressed directly, as "You." God is therefore drawn into Augustine and Monica's conversation; or rather, Augustine and Monica's conversation is founded on a God who can be addressed as a person. Third, in the first ascent, Augustine's senses are relevant only as a beginning: he ascends beyond them to a flash of mental sight. But in the second ascent, Augustine and Monica also attain to God, but the flash of the mind allows them not just to see but to "touch" eternal wisdom.[40] Sensory descriptions abound as the final goal of their ascent is a region "where You feed Israel forever with the food of truth,"[41] a reference to the sacrament of the Eucharist. Indeed, Augustine makes sure to mention that all five senses are involved in the attainment of the goal of ascent, a reference to the humility of the Word of God[42] who condescends to subject himself to human senses in the Incarnation.[43]

At this point, it is possible to go back to Augustine's argument in *City of God* Book 10. Augustine does not simply argue against the philosophers' exclusion of the multitude from genuine salvation; he argues that the philosopher cannot achieve the salvation of the soul even through the operation of his intellect. Augustine begins Chapter 32 of Book 10 by saying, "This is the religion which contains the universal way for the liberation of the soul, since no soul can be freed by any other way."[44] Augustine's clear implication is that, while unbelieving philosophers may think that they are freed through philosophy, they are themselves deceived, since

---

40. Augustine repeats this twice: in attaining to God, Augustine and Monica "touch" eternal wisdom. He says this in *conf.*, 9.10.24 and 9.10.25.

41. Ibid., 9.10.24.

42. "The very possibility of this ascent rests with the conversion of the whole man effected by Christ as mediator on the cross." Thomas P. Harmon, "Reconsidering Charles Taylor's Augustine," *Pro Ecclesia* vol. 20, no. 2 (2011), 185–209 at 199–200.

43. On the role of the senses and the body in the Christian ascent to God, see also, inter alia, Augustine, *Jo. ev. tr.*, 2.16.

44. *Ciu. Dei*, 10.32.

no soul is freed except by Christ. The key to Augustine's argument is the universality of the way of salvation in Christianity. The two ways that Porphyry mentions are based on a division of men into two classes: those who are capable of philosophy, who are few; and those who are not capable of philosophy, who are many. The philosopher is capable of living his life according to his higher soul, the intellectual soul; while the nonphilosopher lives his life according to the lower, or spiritual, soul. The philosopher is capable of conceiving immaterial substance and therefore transcending the world of sense impressions and phantasms; the nonphilosopher is not. The fact of the matter is, however, that even though the nonphilosopher lives according to his lower soul, that does not mean that he has no intellect, only that he does not use it rightly. The fact that the philosopher is capable of using his intellect well and rightly regards it to be what is highest in him does not mean that his lower soul—or indeed even his body—is any less essentially constitutive of him as a human person. Augustine presses his case, saying, "For what is a universal way for the liberation of the soul, if it is not a way by which all souls are liberated, and therefore the only way for any soul?"[45] Christianity provides for the liberation of all souls, and is the only way of liberation for any soul, because it "purifies the *whole* man (*totum hominem*) and prepares his mortal being for immortality, in all the elements which constitute a man."[46] Theurgy claims to purify only part of a man, the spiritual soul, and therefore cannot claim really to liberate him in truth; Porphyry's philosophy claims to liberate the intellectual soul, which is also only part of a man, and therefore cannot claim to liberate him as a man in truth. The human person as human person involves body, lower soul, and higher soul. To neglect or excise one element is to be left with something that is not a man, not a human person.

Augustine's—and Christianity's—emphasis on the resurrection of the body is therefore a strong affirmation of the personal significance of each man as a man, as a person. The fear of death is so strong among men because they are right to fear it: it involves the sundering of the man's constitutive elements, which is a great evil. The incantations of the philosophic swan song, either in its Socratic or in its Porphyrean, theurgic manifestations, are essentially deceptive. Death, as Augustine knows St. Paul says, is the wages of sin.[47] To die without the forgiveness of sin would be not only to die the death of separation of soul and body, but to die what Augustine calls the second death, the eternal separation of the soul from God.[48] But St. Paul also says that "the free gift of God is eternal life in Christ Jesus our Lord."[49] Augustine therefore focuses on the gift of eternal life in Christ Jesus. He says,

---

45. Ibid.
46. Ibid. My emphasis.
47. Rom. 6:23.
48. See, inter alia, *ciu. Dei*, 10.6.
49. Rom. 6:23.

The grace of God could not be commended in a way more likely to evoke a grateful response, than the way by which the only Son of God, while remaining unchangeably in his own proper being, clothed himself in humanity and gave to men the spirit of his love by the mediation of a man, so that by this love men might come to him who formerly was so far away from them, far from mortals in his immortality, from the changeable in his changelessness, from the wicked in his righteousness, from the wretched in his blessedness. And because he has implanted in our nature the desire for blessedness and immortality he has now taken on himself mortality, while continuing in his blessedness, so that he might confer on us what our hearts desire; and by his sufferings he has taught us to make light of what we dread.[50]

To see how it is that there can be a universal way of salvation that offers eternal life, it is necessary to examine the mediation of Christ more closely.

There are three aspects of Christ's mediation that Augustine focuses on as the grounding of the universal way of salvation: first, who and what Christ is, namely the Incarnate Word who is true man and true God; second, what he does, namely, assumes a whole human nature without abandoning his divinity and offers a fitting sacrifice to the Father that reconciles man to God; third, the manner in which he does these things, namely, in humility. The three are, of course, inseparable. Augustine insists that there is one, universal way of salvation for all men. He says, "We have not to seek one purification for that element which Porphyry calls the 'intellectual' soul, another for the 'spiritual,' and yet another for the body itself. It was to avoid such quests that our Purifier and Savior (*mundator atque saluator*), the true Purifier and the all-powerful Saviour, took upon himself the man in his entirety (*totum suscepit*)."[51] True purification and, therefore, true salvation is by the Incarnate Word. The principle of purification is the Word, not the flesh; but it was necessary for the Word to take on the entirety of the human nature, including the flesh, so as to offer up the atoning sacrifice: the entirety of himself, including his flesh.[52] All of these things are possible because of Christ's humility.

The universal way of salvation first depends on the Incarnation, which involves the Word's assumption of the whole of human nature. Augustine's argument for the universal way of the salvation of the soul therefore depends on Trinitarian and Christological orthodoxy. In chapter 24 of Book 10, the chapter Augustine dedicates to his presentation of Christ as the true principle of purification,

---

50. *Ciu. Dei*, 10.29. Manent comments, "The point of Christianity is not to propose a God pure of all human contamination—Greek philosophy had already done that—but to announce that this God is the friend of humans to the point of assuming their condition." Manent, *Metamorphoses*, 316.

51. *Ciu. Dei*, 10.32.

52. Augustine is here faithful to the patristic soteriological principle that what is not assumed by Christ is not redeemed. If any part of a man is not assumed by Christ, then the whole man cannot be said to be redeemed. See, for example, Gregory Nazianzen, *Letter 101*.

he begins by emphasizing that, unlike Porphyry's talk of "principles" that are separate, Christians speak only of one principle, that is, the Holy Trinity who is three Persons in one God.[53] Augustine's criticism of Porphyry is that Porphyry emphasizes the plurality of the "principles" such that they cannot be spoken of as being one principle in the final account. To provide a clarification of his own position by contrast, he also brings up and criticizes Sabellianism, which makes the opposite error. The Sabellians, Augustine says, "identify the Father with the Son, and the Holy Spirit with both Father and Son."[54] In contrast, Augustine holds to the orthodox doctrine of the Trinity, which preserves the distinction of persons of the Father, Son, and Holy Spirit, but does not divide the divine substance. He also preserves the orthodox teaching on Christology, which requires the union of divine and human in Christ to be in the Person of the Word.

The hypostatic union is vital to the understanding of the universal way of salvation because it allows God to assume a human nature whole and entire and yet not diminish or corrupt his divinity. It was because the Word had taken a whole and entire human nature that he was able to be, in Augustine's words, "both the priest, himself making the oblation, and the oblation."[55] Christ himself offers the sacrifice that is himself to the Father. As Augustine says in the *De Libero arbitrio*, what the will lost through misuse, it cannot replace through its own efforts.[56] Only God who created man can restore what he lost through sin. But what God requires of man is himself. So it must be God who restores, and man who offers himself. Only the Incarnate Word, who is God, who can restore and man who can offer, is capable of doing so.

Nevertheless, it is not the flesh of Christ that is the principle of purification, Augustine is at pains to emphasize, nor the human soul of Christ, but the Word of God. Augustine says, therefore, "the flesh does not purify by itself, but through the Word by which it was assumed."[57] But the fact that the flesh, indeed the whole of human nature and every concrete man, which is purified is purified through the Word is the reason that Augustine can say that the Church, as the Body of Christ, is purified Eucharistically through the Word: "This is the reality, and he intended the daily sacrifice of the Church to be the sacramental symbol for this; for the Church, being the body of which he is the head, learns to offer itself through him. This is the true sacrifice."[58] It immediately follows from the wholeness and entirety of the human nature as perfected in Christ that Christ can assemble a whole and

---

53. Augustine does not seem entirely clear on the teaching of Porphyry or Plotinus on these principles, or at least his presentation of their positive teaching is not very clear. The sole point he wishes to make is that in some way or another, Porphyry's principles are plural, while the principle of purification for Christians is singular. See *ciu. Dei*, 10.23.
54. Ibid., 10.24.
55. Ibid., 10.20.
56. See *lib. arb.*, 3.18.177–9.
57. *Ciu. Dei*, 10.24.
58. Ibid., 10.20.

entire people composed of all manner of human beings, from the ranks of the wise or ignorant as the Neo-Platonists judge and from every nation and people. Augustine says, "What in fact is this universal way, unless it is one which is not the exclusive property of a particular nation but has been divinely imparted to be the common property of all nations?"[59] The universality Christ has in himself issues in the universality of the Church, which makes possible a sacrifice that offers universal salvation:

> The whole redeemed community, that is to say, the congregation and fellowship of the saints, is offered to God as a universal sacrifice, through the great Priest who offered himself in his suffering for us—so that we might be the body of so great a head—under "the form of a servant." For it was in this form he offered, and in this form he was offered, because it is under this form that he is the Mediator, in this form he is the Priest, in this form he is the Sacrifice … . This is the sacrifice of Christians, who are "many, making up one body in Christ."[60]

The phrase "form of a servant," from St. Paul,[61] brings up the final aspect of Christ's mediation that Augustine regards as indispensable: his humility.

Although it has been a matter of speculation among Christian theologians for centuries about whether God would have become man if man had not sinned, the New Testament confines itself to saying that the reason for the Incarnation was so that men might be saved from sin. As David Vincent Meconi puts it, commenting on the role the Incarnation plays in Augustine's conversion in the *Confessions*, "The Divine, born of a woman, participates in our nature so that we might more fully participate in Him as brothers and sisters. Christ came to partake of our fallen humanity not out of His greatness but on account of our wretchedness."[62] This teaching brings to light the reason why it might be said that the Platonists are simultaneously the closest to and the furthest away from Christianity of all men. One condition, the metaphysical condition, of the Incarnation is the absolute transcendence of God over the Creation. That is why, in *City of God* 8.4, Augustine chooses to have his discussion about natural theology with the Platonists as his philosophic interlocutors because they do not regard the human soul as divine. The other condition, not shared with his Platonic interlocutors, is the divine condescension to save human beings from sin. But the recognition of human sinfulness requires the recognition that our current condition is miserable. Augustine therefore observes that the Incarnation "is rejected, as folly and weakness, by those who think themselves wise and strong by their own virtue. But this in fact is grace, which heals the weakness of those who do not proudly boast

---

59. Ibid., 10.32.
60. Ibid., 10.6.
61. Phil. 2:7.
62. David Vincent Meconi, "The Incarnation and Participation in St. Augustine's *Confessions*," *Augustinian Studies*, vol. 29, no. 2 (1998), 61–75 at 71.

of their delusive happiness, but instead make a humble admission of their genuine misery."[63] Admission of *genuine* misery would include the truthful admission of fault for sin. But Augustine argues that Porphyry regards our condition to be evil because of the body, not because of sin, and so would despise Christ, who took on a body in part to show that "it is sin which is evil, not the substance or nature of flesh."[64] The humility of God in assuming human nature then ought to elicit the humility of man in confessing his responsibility for his own misery.

Instead, Augustine argues, Porphyry's pride makes him incapable of recognizing the principle of purification in Christ because of Christ's humility. Augustine says,

> The fact is that he despised [*contempsit*] Christ as he appeared in flesh, in that very flesh which he assumed in order to effect the sacrifice of our purification. It was of course his pride which blinded [*non intellegens*] Porphyry to this great mystery [*sacramentum*], that pride which our true and gracious Mediator has overthrown by his humility, in showing himself to mortals in the condition of mortality.[65]

Pride blinds Porphyry and presumably all philosophers who reject Christ. Augustine's general criticism of the pride of these philosophers is that "all these philosophers have wished, with amazing folly, to be happy here on earth and to achieve bliss by their own efforts."[66] The first part of Book 19 of the *City of God* is dedicated to the argument that it is impossible to be happy in this life due to the vicissitudes of chance. The only happiness that is available in this life is a happiness in hope—that is, a happiness that depends on confidence in Christ's mediation of eternal life to his followers. In contrast, Augustine says, "These philosophers refuse to believe in this blessedness because they do not see it; and so they attempt to fabricate for themselves an utterly delusive happiness by means of a virtue whose falsity is in proportion to its arrogance."[67] Even setting aside Augustine's very strong polemics, there is a deeply serious point he is making: ultimately, human happiness must be received from God and depends on divine agency rather than human agency. Pride is the refusal to receive happiness from God and the concomitant insistence that, whatever happiness one might attain to, one must attain to it based on one's own resources and those resources alone.[68] It is also the

---

63. *Ciu. Dei*, 10.28. Roberts Ogle eloquently explains, "To live in illusion cannot yield happiness in reality. Any time a creature seeks independence from God in order to claim happiness for itself, it severs itself from the source of happiness." Roberts Ogle, *Earthly City*, 31.
64. *Ciu. Dei*, 10.24.
65. Ibid.
66. Ibid., 19.4.
67. Ibid.
68. Fortin observes, "Aside from the fact that philosophers sometimes err in their teachings concerning God, however, there is still one crucial element which separates them from Christianity, and that is their refusal to accept Christ as mediator and redeemer. As a

refusal to countenance the thought that the root problem for all human beings—whether philosopher or nonphilosopher—is a common one, namely sin.[69]

Even if all of Augustine's arguments about the availability of a universal way of salvation based on the mediation of Christ are persuasive, there is still a question. What difference does it make? Classically, the division between the philosophers and the nonphilosophers appears in political philosophy when it is admitted that the wise—or the comparatively wise—are the ones who ought to rule.[70] The classical problem of the rule of the wise is based on the fact that there are few who are philosophers, it is difficult for the nonphilosophers to identify them, and it is an open question as to what would motivate the wise to want to rule, since that would presumably involve them in pursuits other than the pursuit of wisdom. But Augustine's argument about the universal way of salvation necessarily involves a different judgment about the availability of wisdom to the nonphilosopher. The reason why, classically, there are few true philosophers is that the kind of rational independence required to live the philosophic life requires massive intellectual effort combined with rare natural intelligence along with a desire to know the truth above everything else. Wisdom is a very high goal and reaching up to it requires much of anyone who tries. The number of potential philosophers is therefore already small; the number of actual philosophers would be vanishingly small. The problem is that nature distributes the natural qualities requisite to live the philosophic life only to a few, for which the Christian solution to the problem is the Incarnation. Instead of man needing to reach up to wisdom, eternal Wisdom

---

seeker after independent knowledge, the philosopher is basically proud and refuses to owe his salvation to anyone but himself. His whole endeavor is motivated in the final accounting by self-praise and self-admiration." Fortin, *Classical Christianity*, 18.

69. See Augustine's discussion of Victorinus in *conf.*, 8.2.

70. Leo Strauss puts it succinctly:

When attempting to guide the city, [the philosopher] knows then in advance that, in order to be useful or good for the city, the requirements of wisdom must be qualified or diluted. If these requirements are identical with natural right or with natural law, natural right or natural law must be diluted in order to become compatible with the requirements of the city. The city requires that wisdom be reconciled with consent. But to admit the necessity of consent, i.e., of the consent of the unwise, amounts to admitting a right of unwisdom, i.e., an irrational, if inevitable, right. Civil life requires a fundamental compromise between wisdom and folly, and this means a compromise between the natural right that is determined by reason or understanding and the right that is based on opinion alone. Civil life required the dilution of natural right by merely conventional right. Natural right would act as dynamite for civil society. In other words, the simply good, which is what is good by nature and which is radically distinct from the ancestral, must be transformed into the politically good, which is, as it were, the quotient of the simply good and the ancestral: the politically good is what "removes a vast mass of evil without shocking a vast mass of prejudice." (Strauss, *Natural Right and History*, 152–3)

reaches down by taking flesh. In principle, the Incarnation allows any human being to pursue wisdom even in the absence of the extraordinary personal resources required to live the philosophic life.

At least on the surface, that might lead us to believe that Augustine would regard the Christian, as a man who is apprenticed to Wisdom Incarnate, to be the natural ruler. If this were the case, it would be natural to find a sustained treatment of the two most outstanding Christian emperors up to that point, Constantine and Theodosius, in the *City of God*. But that is far from what Augustine presents. As Ernest L. Fortin points out, "It is significant that the *City of God* devotes barely more than two short chapters to Constantine and Theodosius, the most renowned of the Christian emperors, and that, in reviewing their reigns, Augustine stresses their private virtues to the virtual exclusion of their political virtues."[71] The reason Augustine gives such little attention to the most renowned Christian statesmen is because the wisdom that Christianity affords and the goal that the Christian seeks through the mediation of Christ is transpolitical.[72] Fortin says elsewhere, "This does not mean that the city of God has done away with the need for civil society. Its purpose is not to replace civil society but to supplement it by providing, over and above the benefits conferred by it, the means of achieving a goal that is higher than any to which civil society can lead."[73] The goal of the Christian is not a this-worldly goal[74] and so the wisdom of Christianity does not have direct and immediately applicable relevance for political life.

That Christianity is transpolitical does not mean that it has no relevance for political life. In light of transpolitical Christian faith, politics is able to appear in a different light: that is, in light of Christian faith, the limits of politics come into sight. The situation is similar to what happens in light of classical political philosophy, which also reveals the limits of politics. As Leo Strauss points out, the political philosopher "is ultimately compelled to transcend not merely the dimension of common opinion, of political opinion, but the dimension of political life as such; for he is led to realize that the ultimate aim of political life cannot be reached by political life, but only by a life devoted to contemplation, to philosophy."[75] Although the goal of the transcendence of the classical political philosopher and the Christian, respectively, is different, what their respective transcendence

---

71. Fortin, *Classical Christianity*, 128.

72. Roberts Ogle notices, "Augustine is not willing to speak of a Christian Empire or of the conversion of political rule (*regna*) to Christianity. Indeed ... all that he seems to advocate in *City of God* is a proper ordering of loves, encouraging Christian emperors to love God more than status and to use their position as a means of service, interpreting the responsibilities with which they are charged in light of the true good." Roberts Ogle, *Earthly City*, 157.

73. Ibid., 20.

74. "My kingship is not of this world," Jesus says in Jn 18:36.

75. Leo Strauss, *An Introduction to Political Philosophy: Ten Essays by Leo Strauss*, ed. Hilail Gildin (Detroit: Wayne State University Press, 1989), 74.

of political life does to their apprehension of the limits of political life is similar, especially from the standpoint of politics. Regardless of the presentation of Christ and Socrates that their kingship or contemplative life were not of this world, both were executed by the political authorities at least in part because of the limits they reveal about political life.

For Augustine, one of the clearest limitations of political life is that political life does not provide a final home—and not just for the philosopher, but for any human person. That judgment is what is behind his refusal to allow the earthly city to dictate to the city of God on matters of religion, especially about the worship of God,[76] and why he considered the witness of the martyrs against impiety to be so important.[77] That also provides a reason why he focuses on the private rather than political virtues of Theodosius and Constantine. Robert Dodaro points out, "Central to Augustine's conception of true piety as practiced by statesmen is their public acknowledgement of the limits of their virtue through prayer to God for forgiveness of their sins."[78] The public exercise of the private act of repentance of the emperor Theodosius reveals the limitations not only of his own virtue, but of political life itself through a clear acknowledgment of a standard that transcends the standards of ethics and politics that even an emperor must not only abide by, but from whom even the emperor must seek forgiveness if he sins, even in the exercise of his political power.

Through its rejection of the worship of false gods, Christianity has the effect of secularizing political authority. But that raises another problem. The authority of the laws of the city was classically understood to flow from some divine source. As Strauss puts it in his formulation of what he calls the theologico-political problem,

> Prephilosophic life is characterized by the primeval identification of the good with the ancestral … . One cannot reasonably identify the good with the ancestral if one does not assume that the ancestors were absolutely superior to "us," and this means that they were superior to all ordinary mortals; one is driven to believe that the ancestors, or those who established the ancestral way, were gods or sons of gods or at least "dwelling near the gods." The identification of the good with the ancestral leads to the view that the right way was established by gods or sons of gods or pupils of gods: the right way must be divine law.[79]

Along similar lines, Plato's *Laws* begins with the Athenian Stranger asking both of his interlocutors, "Is it a god or some human being, strangers, who is given the credit for laying down your laws?"[80] Both respond without hesitating that it is a

---

76. See *ciu. Dei*, 19.17.
77. See, inter alia, *ciu. Dei*, 10.23.
78. Dodaro, *Christ and the Just Society*, 57. See also ibid., 192–3.
79. Strauss, *Natural Right and History*, 83–4.
80. Plato, *Laws*, trans. Thomas L. Pangle (Chicago: University of Chicago Press, Chicago: 1988), 624a.

god. It is far easier for a citizen to devote himself wholeheartedly to the good of a community whose source is divine than to one that is merely human.

There is a risk here when Christians make up a significant enough proportion of the populace that Christianity will detach the Christian from his city in the name of a transpolitical good such that the city will be unable to flourish.[81] That judgment or intuition is what initially provokes Augustine to write the *City of God*. As Fortin observes, Augustine's response to the political critics of Christianity is that "Christianity does not destroy patriotism but reinforces it by making of it a religious duty,"[82] a religious duty grounded in Christ's commandment of love of neighbor. And while it is certainly true that Christianity reveals a transpolitical goal in principle accessible by all through grace, it is not true that Christianity necessarily detaches the members of the city of God from their duties in the earthly city. As Augustine points out, the New Testament in fact contains multiple exhortations to do one's civic duty.[83] But beyond that, even while claiming that the earthly city aims at an earthly peace based on what is merely a "Compromise between human wills about the things relevant to mortal life," which is contrasted to the city of God's eternal goal, he still affirms that the city of God

> Must needs make use of this peace also, until this mortal state, for which this kind of peace is essential, passes away. And therefore it leads what we may call a life of captivity in this earthly city as in a foreign land, although it has already received the promise of redemption, and the gift of the Spirit as a kind of pledge

---

81. Fortin points out that one of the main purposes for Augustine in writing the *City of God* was to show how a universal way of salvation could be shown not to dissolve the particularities of political life. Christianity, Fortin says, "engendered a tendency to regard the natural differences and traditional boundaries that set men off as separate groups leading separate lives as politically irrelevant, and thus stripped the city of its status as an exclusive community, as the all-embracing whole and unique expression of that common life which stands above its individual members and binds them together as fellow citizens." Fortin, *Classical Christianity*, 39.

82. Ibid., 24. Fortin says elsewhere, "Furthermore, any depreciation of the fatherland, if one can really speak of a depreciation, is amply compensated for by the fact that Christianity demands and very often obtains from its followers a higher degree of morality and virtue. It thus helps to counteract vice and corruption, which are the true causes of the weakness and decline of cities and nations." Fortin, "St. Augustine," 201.

83. To mention just a few: Christ's command to "Render to the things that are Caesar's, and to God the things that are God's" in Mk 12:17, echoed in Mt. 22:21 admits that there are things that the members of the city of God owe to Caesar, namely, in this instance, at least the paying of taxes; Jesus tells Pilate, "You would have no power over me unless it had been given you from above," in Jn 19:11, recognizing that Pilate's authority comes from God, even if he misuses it; and Paul's statements in Rom. 13:1-7 that Christians are to obey earthly authority, not just for expediency, but because political authority is "instituted by God." Rom. 13:1.

of it; and yet it does not hesitate to obey the laws of the earthly city by which those things which are designed for the support of this mortal life are regulated.[84]

But the city of God does not engage in these actions half-heartedly. Because the city of God also depends on the earthly peace of the earthly city, the city of God positively "makes use of the earthly peace and defends and seeks the compromise between human wills in respect of provisions relevant to the mortal nature of man, so far as may be permitted without detriment to true religion and piety."[85] The risk is adequately compensated for by the commandment of love and the transforming power of grace available, if not guaranteed, within the city of God. Augustine could therefore say in one of his letters,

> Therefore, let those who say that the teaching of Christ is opposed to the welfare of the state produce such provincial administrators, such husbands, such wives, such parents, such sons, such masters, such slaves, such kings, such judges, and finally such tax-payers and collectors of public revenue as Christian teaching requires them to be, and then let them dare to say that this teaching is opposed to the welfare of the state, or, rather, let them even hesitate to admit that it is the greatest safety of the state, if it is observed.[86]

Obviously, the last phrase is key: *if* it is observed. There is no guarantee that members of the city of God live up to their membership. But it is a much likelier starting point for virtue than the Roman temple.

The similarity between Augustine and Porphyry regarding their attitude toward the city is best examined by reference to the transpolitical good that each characteristically pursues. But there is a difference between their attitudes, too, grounded in the distinctive objects they pursue: union with the One and loving knowledge of the Triune God, respectively. The latter proceeds from and issues in a loving relationship with God and neighbor; the former requires divestment by degrees of personal attachments to particular beings. The Porphyrian attitude toward the city must finally be one of indifference. The Augustinian attitude toward the city cannot be indifferent, because of those who live in it: human beings who are actual or potential members of the city of God, whose image in them elicits the Christian's love. *City of God* 19.19 is the justly famous chapter where Augustine unveils this difference to its fullest degree.

City of God 19.19 is about the universality of the city of God. Augustine begins by highlighting the universality of the city of God with a statement by Augustine that the city of God does not require or exclude any particular habit or custom

---

84. *Ciu. Dei*, 19.17.
85. Ibid.
86. Augustine, *ep.* 138.

of living [*habitu vel more uiuendi*].[87] In particular, he says that a Christian may be a faithful Christian in the living of any of the three classical candidates for the best way of life: the life of leisure, the life of action, and the life that combines leisure and action. There is, of course, no reason to believe that Augustine does not have an opinion about how to rank those candidates on a scale of human nobility. In fact, right after his conversion, Augustine indicates his own preference by retiring into a leisured retreat at Cassiciacum once he is freed of the duties of his chair in rhetoric at Milan.[88] But in living any of these three ways of life, even—or especially—the life of leisure, Augustine makes clear that the Christian faith imposes two obligations on the Christian: that he love the truth and perform the duties of charity.[89] Augustine explains:

> For no one ought to live a life of leisure in such a way that he takes no thought in that leisure for the welfare of his neighbor; nor ought he to be so active as to feel no need for the contemplation of God. The delight offered by a life of leisure ought to consist not in idle inactivity, but in the opportunity to seek and find the truth, so that everyone may make progress in this regard, and not jealously withhold his discoveries from others.[90]

Augustine is articulating a theoretical point that is well illustrated in his own life. As a lover of the truth, Augustine is drawn to the life of contemplation. But precisely because of his learning, he is called into an active life as a priest and then a bishop, which office he was exercising at the time of the writing of the *City of God*. As he puts it, "It is on account of the life of truth that one seeks a holy leisure [*otium sanctum*]; it is on account of the necessity of charity that one takes up righteous work [*iustum negotium*]."[91] The bishop must both teach and rule. Unlike with the Platonic or Porphyrian philosopher, there is no open question as to what might make the Christian wise man want to rule.

Augustine and other Christian contemplatives are moved not by coercion or threats to take up these duties, but by love, grounded in their imitation of Christ the Word made flesh and by graced insertion into the loving relations of the Trinitarian persons. Unlike the non-Christian multitude, the nonphilosophic Christian seeks union with the same God by means of the same faith and the same sacraments as the Christian wise man.

---

87. *Ciu. Dei*, 19.19.
88. See Peter Brown, *Augustine of Hippo* (Berkeley: University of California Press, 1975), 101–27. Augustine says in *ciu. Dei* 19.19, "If this latter burden [of righteous work] is not imposed on us, we should devote our freedom to the search for and contemplation of truth."
89. *Ciu. Dei,* 19.19.
90. Ibid.
91. Ibid. My translation.

Chapter 8

CHRIST THE MEDIATOR OF THE UNIVERSAL WAY OF SALVATION

The Platonic philosophers Augustine engages are united in their opinion that the obstacles to human flourishing, which Augustine calls ignorance and difficulty, are the result of the limitations of nature: nature bestows her blessings variously and somewhat stingily, since very few, if any, are capable of becoming truly happy. But Augustine believes through faith that ignorance and difficulty are the result of history,[1] not nature: the obstacles to human flourishing are the punishments of original sin.[2] The clefts between body and soul and between the wise and the foolish are therefore the result of sin and not of nature. There might, therefore, be hope that the creator of human nature might mercifully heal human nature, once again making possible human flourishing not only for the few able to undergo philosophy's rigors but also for the whole mass of men.

Pierre Manent rightly observes that, for Augustine, human nature is social, whereas it is only human sin that tends toward disunity and discord.[3] But Manent also emphasizes the way in which some kinds of disunity were good and even necessary to prepare the ground for the universal way of salvation that Christ inaugurates. Manent is worth quoting in full:

> One could say that Jewish election and Greek philosophy break the course of humanity to raise its level. Neither the progress nor the rupture should be

---

1. Rist notes that "Unaided reason cannot give us a historical knowledge but only belief; indeed it is especially ineffectual … in generating knowledge about acts of God only revealed in Scripture and the traditions of the Church." Rist, "Christian Philosophy," 209.

2. Fortin highlights the dispute about origins as the crux of the disagreement between Augustine and his philosophic interlocutors on ignorance and difficulty. Fortin points to "the question of the perfect beginning, which forms an integral part of Augustine's anthropology and which is again diametrically opposed to the philosophic view according to which the origins of human history, assuming that one can even speak of them, are essentially barbaric, inasmuch as they are marked by the absence of philosophy, on which the attainment of human perfection was regarded as intrinsically dependent." Fortin, *Birth of Philosophic Christianity*, 103–4. See also Dodaro, *Christ and the Just Society*, 67.

3. See Manent, *Metamorphoses*, 279.

underestimated. In the perspective drawn by Augustine, one can say that Christianity preserves or confirms the advances achieved by these two ruptures while it overcomes them by restoring human unity on a higher plane through the mediation of the God-man. Augustine's presentation makes Christianity appear as the resolution of the most profound and fruitful fractures of human unity, the Jewish and the Greek.[4]

The way in which Christianity conjugates the soul and the body is directly related to the way in which it heals the rupture between the few and the many.[5] Only when the whole man is healed will man be happy. For this to happen, man must live in a right order with his fellow men. In order to live in right order with his fellow men, he must be rightly ordered in himself. To be rightly ordered in himself, his reason must rule his subrational soul, and his soul must rule his body. For his reason to rule his subrational soul and his soul to rule his body, his reason must be subject to God. In this way, every part of man and the whole society of men will be rightly ordered to God, which will result in perfect peace and happiness. True happiness and peace, and therefore true virtue and wisdom, involves the right order of the whole, which means the right order of every part of the whole and the order of the whole to God. Augustine can therefore say that "True virtues (*uerae uirtutes*), however, can only exist in those in whom there is true piety (*uera pietas*)."[6] Sin, Augustine says, disrupts that order and therefore sin must be healed. This is why

---

4. Ibid., 294. He says right beforehand, "The formation of the Jewish people, like the elaboration of philosophy, both mark a decisive qualitative progress of the 'self-awareness' of humanity. This progress in both cases comes at the price of a separation or rupture within humanity: the separation or rupture between the people of God and the 'nations' and the separation or rupture between the philosopher or wise man and the 'vulgar,' the latter deriving from the separation and even the rupture between the soul and the body that is the condition and achievement of philosophy." Ibid., 293–4.

5. This seems to be why Cavadini says that Augustine argues, "Porphyry and the other Platonists refuse to accept the Incarnation because they are proud. In order to accept the Incarnation and to submit to its purifying power in the Church, they would first have to admit that the link between body and soul, is something wondrous, marvelous, and humbling, rather than finally something to be left behind." Cavadini, "Ideology and Solidarity," 106.

6. *Ciu. Dei*, 19.4. My translation. See also *ciu. Dei*, 5.19. Ernest L. Fortin notes, "Just as for Plato the only virtue is philosophic virtue, so for Augustine the only virtue is Christian virtue." Fortin, *Birth of Philosophic Christianity*, 28. Dodaro fleshes out Augustine's meaning: "Central to Augustine's conception of true piety as practiced by statesmen is their public acknowledgement of the limits of their virtue through prayer to God for forgiveness of their sins." Dodaro, *Christ and the Just Society*, 57. This provides the reason for Augustine's noteworthy praise of the Christian emperor Theodosius in *ciu. Dei*, 5.26. See also Dodaro, *Christ and the Just Society*, 192–3.

man needs the grace of Christ, who is the *magister interior*,[7] and whose grace provides for human wholeness by healing man from within.

Augustine's engagement with Platonic political philosophy is based on his argument that Jesus Christ is the universally efficacious mediator of the universal way of salvation. Faith in Christ unites the simple and advanced believer, and Christ's charity unites all the members of the city of God, men and angels,[8] in love for the transcendent Triune God. The city of God is truly transpolitical, meaning that it does not destroy the way of life of the earthly city, but rather shares the goal of earthly peace and the harmony of men's wills, and therefore does not attempt to abolish the earthly political order or render irrelevant the various particularities of individuals and peoples that are important to political life.[9] Nevertheless, Augustine finds that the earthly city's total claims on its citizens must be resisted as idolatrous and impious. There is therefore no true justice to be found in the earthly city, and therefore no true peace, because of its love for temporal things to the exclusion of love of God.[10] The city of God, on the other hand, is able to provide true justice and true happiness as a foretaste in this earthly life.

Christ and the Church are central to Augustine's response to Porphyry. Christ, Augustine says, is the true mediator of the universal way of salvation, and the Church is the extension of Christ's mediation through history. The central act of mediation through time is the Church's celebration of the Eucharistic sacrifice, which depends on and makes present Christ's sacrifice on the Cross. Through participating in Christ's sacrifice in the Eucharist in the Church, and the Baptism that precedes and points to it, men are made part of Christ's mystical body and Christ's forgiveness, healing, and virtues are transmitted to the believer. Once again, Augustine articulates the goal of Christ's saving action: "To see him as he can be seen and to cleave to him, we purify ourselves from every stain of sin and evil desire and we consecrate ourselves in his name."[11] To see God and to cling to him are, Augustine has already said, the common aspiration of the Christian

---

7. *Ep. Jo.*, 3.13.2.

8. If angels, who are pure intellects, associate with men as fellow citizens in the city of God, then philosophers like Victorinus have no excuse not to.

9. And that were so important to Augustine's Roman interlocutors, such as Nectarius, Marcellinus, and Volusianus. See *epp.* 90, 103, 104, 132, 135, 136, 137, 138. On Christianity itself as transpolitical, see Fortin, *Birth of Philosophic Christianity*, 4. Or as Roberts Ogle puts it, "Just as Christ's coming did not nullify the diversity of languages, it seems that the coming of the Church does not nullify political communities." Roberts Ogle, *Earthly City*, 158.

10. Fortin notes that Augustine's thought on the city of God "is a rejection of the classical notion of the city or its equivalent as self-sufficient totalities capable of fulfilling all of one's basic needs and aspirations." Ernest L. Fortin, *Collected Essays*, vol. 4, *Ever Ancient, Ever New: Ruminations on the City, the Soul, and the Church*, ed. Michael P. Foley (Lanham, MD: Rowman and Littlefield, 2007), 71.

11. *Ciu. Dei*, 10.3.

and the Platonic philosopher. They are also frustrated by ignorance and difficulty. Ignorance frustrates knowledge of God and difficulty prevents clinging to him in love. Christ's sacrifice and mediation of the universal way of salvation therefore must overcome man's ignorance and difficulty in order to offer salvation to all men. Because man's body and soul, intellect and will are part of one whole, the salvation Christ offers must be accomplished in one act, in which ignorance and difficulty are overcome simultaneously.[12] The identity of Christ and the nature of the Church, for Augustine, are the keys to understanding how. As Robert Dodaro argues,

> Purification of the soul is not a gift that God bestows upon man "downward" through a hierarchy of intermediary, spiritual beings, as theurgists assume. Instead, by becoming man in Christ, God allows all human beings who are reborn in Christ to participate directly in his own divine nature, thus liberating them from mortality and misery by uniting them, not with angelic beings, but with himself.[13]

Christ's mediation, in other words, does not rely on any intermediaries. Divine and human are hypostatically united in Christ and all men are, in principle, able to participate in Christ's humanity through sacramental participation in the Church.[14] Christ therefore both shows the way to happiness and gives the strength necessary to travel the way. Members of the Church can therefore share in Christ's perfect sacrifice on the Cross, which decisively effects a reordering of man toward God.

Sacrifice establishes a hierarchical ordering by subordinating some goods to others. Pagan sacrifice does this incorrectly by leaving out the true creator of the world and giving the honors which only God the creator deserves to his creatures, at best, and to the works of man's imagination, at worst. The entire person is involved in sacrifice, and so sacrifices ought only to be made to a good to which the entire person ought to be ordered. Instead of sacrificing to demons, Augustine presents the sacrifice of Christ and its re-presentation in the Eucharistic sacrifice in the Church as a sacrifice to the eternal, transcendent, Creator God of gods (*Deum deorum*),[15] to whom it is appropriate to sacrifice because this God lacks no good, nor requires his worshippers finally to pit various goods against each other.

The sacrifice which Augustine says merits for men that they see and cling to God is love of God and love of neighbor as self. To love God is to cling to God in order to see God. To love one's neighbor is to "do all that [one] can to bring [one's] neighbour to love God."[16] This is why the good angels do not desire men's

---

12. See Dodaro, *Christ and the Just Society*, 74–5.

13. Dodaro, *Christ and the Just Society*, 96. Dodaro notes that, in relying on no intermediaries, Christianity avoids the inevitable spiritual rivalries that would arise through reliance on finite beings as intermediaries. Ibid., 102.

14. See *ciu. Dei*, 17.18.

15. Ibid., 10.3.

16. Ibid., 10.3.

worship: by truly loving men, the good angels will encourage men to worship God alone, just as they do. An angel who desires men's worship is immediately found to love neither God nor men. In encouraging nonphilosophers to worship beings other than God, the philosophers show that they do not love their neighbors as themselves, because they reserve natural theology to themselves.[17] Augustine calls the philosophers' dissimulation a vice [*vitium*] that he hopes to see healed, and which, being healed, "no one should deny that that would be an achievement worthy of all possible praise."[18] Therefore, they also do not truly love God, who desires men to love all those whom he loves. Pride is what prevents them from availing themselves of the grace of Christ, as manifested for example in Victorinus' erstwhile unwillingness to be counted among the multitude for the sake of his salvation. They must admit, as Victorinus and, eventually, Augustine did, that the obstacles to their happiness are deeper than the natural division between the wise and the foolish.

The sacrifice involved in love of God and love of neighbor unites all classes of men in the pursuit of the eternal God.[19] The question is, how does the mediation

---

17. Again, one senses that Augustine has in mind mostly the philosophers who wrote after Christ. He says of the pre-Christian followers of Plato, "So if these men could live their lives again today, they would see by whose authority measures are best taken for man's salvation, and, with the change of a few words and sentiments, they would become Christians, as many Platonists of recent times have done." *Uera rel.*, 4.7. He continues later, "However philosophers may boast, anyone can understand that religion is not to be sought from them. For they take part in the religious rites of their fellow-citizens, but in their schools teach divergent and contrary opinions about the nature of their gods and of the chief good, as the multitude can testify." Ibid., 5.8. This is Augustine's greatest criticism of the Platonists, whom he otherwise chooses as his preferred philosophic interlocutors. As John C. Cavadini observes about the Platonists' apparent recognition of the true God and concomitant refusal to worship Him alone, "It is this fundamental inconsistency, consistent only in its universality among Platonist philosophers, that is Augustine's primary criticism of them. It is a special unseemliness to have recognized and known the true God and yet to countenance worship of other gods, and it is the sort of inconsistency that prompts Augustine to search for the vested interest it reflects." John C. Cavadini, "Ideology and Solidarity," 101. No doubt there were vested interests; but the inconsistency is understandable if one recognizes the reserve of the Platonists regarding the nonexistence of the pagan gods to be a political action made necessary by the very division between the few and the many that Christ's mediation overcomes. After all, what good would public demythologization accomplish? Either the attachment of the people to their gods would have served to put philosophy into even lower repute, or the proclamation of the philosophers would have served to detach the people from the main source of the people's attachment to morality and civic harmony in favor of a philosophic ideal which they could not understand.

18. *Uera rel.*, 5.8.

19. See *ep.* 140.62.

of Christ allow even the man who is incapable of philosophy to live according to eternal wisdom? The beginning of an answer is given when Augustine says,

> A man consecrated in the name of God, and vowed to God, is in himself a sacrifice inasmuch as he "dies to the world" so that he may "live for God." For this also is related to compassion, the compassion a man shows towards himself. Hence the text, "have compassion on your own soul by making yourself acceptable to God." Our body also is a sacrifice when we discipline it by temperance, provided that we do this as we ought for the sake of God, so that we may not offer our bodily powers to the service of sin as the instruments of iniquity, but to the service of God as the instruments of righteousness. The Apostle exhorts us to this, when he says, "I entreat you, brothers, by the compassion of God, to offer your bodies as a living sacrifice, holy and acceptable to God, as the reasonable homage (*rationabile obsequium*) you owe him."[20]

The sacrifice of love of God and love of neighbor is therefore death to the world so that a man may live a life ordered to God. This is nothing other than the overcoming of the *consuetudo carnalis*, the disordered desire for temporal things, in order to love eternal things. As Augustine says elsewhere of the man who has died to the world and now lives oriented to God, "He does not obey the urge of sin, even though lusts still trouble him and seek his consent until the body is raised and death is swallowed up in victory. Thus because we do not consent to depraved longings, we are under grace, and sin does not reign in our mortal bodies."[21] Augustine, following Christ's example and St. Paul's exhortations, therefore affirms that the body itself can be a pleasing sacrifice to the eternal, incorporeal God. The body, and not just the mind, is fit for "reasonable service" to God, in the words of Rom. 6:16.

The patient endurance of suffering in resisting the temptation to sin is what converts the body into a suitable sacrifice or reasonable service, which is the lesson of the Incarnation:

> The good and true Mediator showed that it is sin which is evil, and not the substance or nature of the flesh, which could be assumed and held without sin together with a human soul, laid aside in death, and also changed for the better in the Resurrection; He showed that a body of flesh and a human soul could be assumed and held without sin, and laid aside at death, and changed into something better by resurrection; nor is death, although it be a punishment for sin—which nevertheless he paid off for us without sin—something to be avoided

---

20. *Ciu. Dei*, 10.6.
21. Augustine, *Propositions from the Epistle to the Romans*, trans. Paula Frederiksen Landes (Chico: Scholars Press, 1982), 35.1–2.

through sinning, but rather, if given the opportunity, it ought to be preferred for the sake of righteousness.[22]

Sin, which is a matter of the historical free choice of the will and not a result of man's composite nature or of the nature of the flesh, is what makes the body oppress the soul. Purification involves humble endurance of the consequences of sin by the believer's participation in grace. Further, the resurrection of the body is crowning affirmation of the body's place in the whole man's ascent to God.

The Incarnation, according to Augustine, accomplishes the cleansing of the flesh and the reordering of the body.[23] The way in which the cleansing of the flesh and reordering of the body is accomplished through the Incarnation is by the "sacrament of the altar,"[24] that is, the Eucharistic sacrifice.[25] Through participation in the Eucharist, which itself is intimately connected with the sacrament of Baptism, believers are more deeply incorporated into Christ's mystical body, so that Augustine can say, "The whole redeemed City (*redempta ciuitas*)—that is, the congregation and society of the saints—is offered to God as a universal sacrifice (*uniuersale sacrificium*) through the great priest who, in his Passion, offered his very self for us, so that we might be the body of so great a Head, according to the form of a servant."[26] When Christ assumed flesh, he assumed flesh that was "just and without sin [*iusta non paccatrix*],"[27] thereby showing that the flesh is not naturally opposed to the spirit. Even so, Augustine says, it was not the flesh which was the cause of the liberation of the whole man from sin and its consequences, but the Word of God, to whom Christ's human nature was hypostatically united.

---

22. "Bonus itaque uerusque Mediator ostendit peccatum esse malum, non carnis substantiam uel naturam, quae cum anima hominis et suscipi sine peccato potuit et haberi, et morte deponi et in melius resurrectione mutari; nec ipsam mortem, quamuis esset poena peccati, quam tamen pro nobis sine peccato ipse persoluit, peccando esse uitandam, sed potius, si facultas datur, pro iustitia perferendam." *Ciu. Dei*, 10.24. My translation.

23. "The 'Principle,' then, having assumed a soul and flesh, purifies the soul and the flesh of believers." Ibid., 10.24. Dodaro notes, "For Augustine, discourse about justice cannot sustain a just society unless the statesman who offers it is also capable of purifying his listeners' souls." Dodaro, *Christ and the Just Society*, 75. This is why Augustine criticizes pagan philosophers not for failing to show what happiness is, but for failing to provide a way of attaining and clinging to it.

24. *Ciu. Dei*, 10.6.

25. Cavadini explains, "The perfect worship of God is the Eucharistic life, the continual offering of Christ to us and for us, the continual formation of a *societas* whose loves and works are being transformed in Christ's compassion and configured to it." Cavadini, "Ideology and Solidarity," 104.

26. *Ciu. Dei*, 10.6. My translation. He continues, "This is the sacrifice of the Christians: 'The many are one body in Christ.'" "Hoc est sacrificium Christianorum: multi unum corpus in Christo." Ibid., 10.6. My translation.

27. Ibid., 10.24. My translation.

Christ's mediation therefore depends both on his true humanity and his true divinity, and man's salvation depends on right belief about Christ and his saving action so that he will be led to participate in the same sacrifice at the altar that Christ offered for the salvation of all men.

It is important to note that while Christ mediates universal salvation for all men, he does not abrogate the distinctions among men due to nature. Christ does not make all men capable of philosophy understood as the rigorous pursuit of wisdom through perfected reason. He does, however, mercifully present himself, the eternal wisdom, in the flesh, so that those who are incapable of the intellectual demands of the theoretical way of life can also, in following Christ humbly, live according to wisdom by attending to the words and deeds of Christ. Augustine observes, "By this grace of God, the evidence of his great mercy, we are guided in this life by faith, and after this life are brought to complete fulfilment by the vision of the unchanging truth (*speciem incommutabilis ueritatis*)."[28] The same Incarnation that makes wisdom available to the nonphilosopher also provides an antidote to the philosophic pride that puffs up, in the words of St. Paul, in the flesh of Christ. Faith in Christ therefore unites all classes of men, not in making all classes of men capable of contemplating highest wisdom in this life, but in presenting certain doctrines about God that exceed human reason and providing assistance to guard against error about the highest things so that man might live according to wisdom through discipleship in Christ. All classes of men are united in faith in the same God, which faith will give way to vision in the next life.

Ignorance and difficulty are the result of the disordered choice of the original sin. In choosing not to obey God, man's superior, man had, according to Augustine, justly lost the obedience of his own inferior parts to his superior part.[29] He says, "The soul, in fact, rejoiced in its own freedom to act perversely and disdained to be God's servant; and so it was deprived of the obedient service which its body had at first rendered. At its own pleasure the soul deserted its superior and master; and so it no longer retained its inferior and servant obedient to its will."[30] After original sin, man is buffeted by painful lusts. The death of the body becomes the just punishment for sin, which must be endured by those who wish to live well.[31]

---

28. Ibid., 10.22.

29. "In what is the punishment of that sin of disobedience unless it is disobedience itself as a consequence? For, of what is the misery of man unless it is his same disobedience as opposing himself, so that, because he did not will when he could, he now wills what he cannot?" "In illius peccati poena quid inoboedientiae nisi inoboedientia retributa est? Nam quae hominis est alia miseria nisi aduersus eum ipsum inoboedientia eius ipsius, ut, quoniam noluit quod potuit, quod non potest uelit?" Ibid., 14.15. My translation.

30. "Iam quippe anima libertate in peruersum propria delectata et Deo dedignata seruire pristino corporis seruitio destituebatur, et quia superiorem dominum suo arbitrio deseruerat, inferiorem famulum ad suum arbitrium non tenebat." Ibid., 13.13.

31. "For the corruption of the body, which weighs down the soul, is not the cause of the first sin but is its penalty; neither does the corruptible flesh make the soul to be sinful, but rather the sinful soul makes the flesh to be corruptible." "Nam corruptio corporis,

The Christian lives according to wisdom by undergoing bodily death in imitation of Christ's own sacrificial death on the Cross.[32] The original sin consisted in the preference of the temporal in favor of the eternal, the flesh over the spirit, and the self over God. The knowledge of mortality in the sinful man produces an inordinate attachment to his bodily life. He therefore ends up sacrificing higher things for lower things when he prefers those things that help him to secure his bodily life in safety and, as a matter of course, luxurious pleasure over justice and wisdom.

Christ's sacrificial death on the Cross and the sacrificial death of the members of his mystical body in communion with Christ manifest the preference for God's judgment over one's own judgment, eternal life over temporal life, and the spirit over the flesh. In addition to the preference of the eternal over the temporal, Christ's death as well as the death of Christian martyrs are public, for the many, and devoid of the dissimulation for which Augustine criticizes Varro, Seneca, and Porphyry. These deaths therefore combine love of God and love of neighbor. The death that the Christian undergoes out of just punishment and in reparation for sin is necessary, Augustine points out, to avoid what he calls the "second death,"

---

quae adgrauat animam, non peccati primi est causa, sed poena; nec caro corruptibilis animam peccatricem, sed anima peccatrix fecit esse corruptibilem carnem." Ibid., 14.3. My translation.

32.

It was then said to man, "You will die if you sin." Now it is said to the martyr, "Die, rather than sin." It was then said, "If you break the commandment you will certainly die." Now it is said, "If you shrink from death, you will break the commandment." What was then an object of fear, to prevent man from sinning, is now something to be chosen, to avoid sinning. So by the ineffable mercy of God even the penalty of man's offense is turned into an instrument of virtue, and the punishment of the sinner becomes the merit of the righteous. (Ibid., 13.4)

He says later on,

But whatever it is which in dying men takes away sensation with such a distressing sensation, it increases the merit of patience if it is endured with devout faith, though it does not cancel the term 'punishment.' And so, although death is perpetuated by propagation from the first man, and is without doubt the penalty of all who are born yet it becomes the glory of those who are reborn, if it is the price paid for piety and righteousness; and death, the recompense of sin, sometimes ensures that there is no sin to be recompensed.

"Quidquid tamen illud est in morientibus, quod cum graui sensu adimit sensum, pie fideliterque tolerando auget meritum patientiae, non aufert uocabulum poenae. Ita cum ex hominis primi perpetuata propagine procul dubio sit mors poena nascentis, tamen si pro pietate iustitiaque pendatur, fit gloria renascentis; et cum sit mors peccati retributio, aliquando inpetrat, ut nihil retribuatur peccato." Ibid., 13.6.

the death of the soul, in which the soul is separated from God forever, and which therefore includes the interminable, painful conflict among the parts of his own being. Man willingly undergoes the death of the body to avoid the death of the soul; he chooses eternal life over temporal life. Martyrdom, which is the form of every truly Christian death, is the preference of what is most universal and common, God and God's wise eternal law, over what is most his own, his bodily life. But since the Christian God is a "God of gods,"[33] the choice to undergo the just punishment of death does not require the hatred of the body, for the body will be returned to rightly ordered unity with the soul in the Resurrection. Indeed, it is precisely the death of the body for the sake of higher things that puts the body back into right order and shows its true worth. Worship of God therefore requires no dehumanizing mutilation or amputation of a part of human nature. The death of the body is the way of justification and healing for the sinner, after which he receives a glorified body.[34] The tension between body and soul will be overcome by means of complete harmony in the resurrection of the body.

The philosopher's judgment is that a life lived according to reason alone in pursuit of wisdom is the highest way of life. It is highest because it is most perfective of the highest part of man. Since human nature is limited and not divine, there is no possibility of choosing to perfect each part of man, so one must choose what is the best part. Even so, there is a kind of melancholy attached to the philosophic life among the pagan philosophers. James V. Schall remarks,

> The philosophic life is the quest for the truth, for the whole, for the explanation of what is. "The unexamined life is not worth living," Socrates told us in *The Apology*. But the examined life, the philosophic life, yields its own perplexities. It

---

33. Ibid., 10.3.
34. Augustine says,

> Just as the spirit is quite appropriately called carnal when it is the servant of the flesh, the flesh will with equal propriety be called spiritual, when it serves the spirit. This is not because the flesh will be converted into spirit (a notion which some people derive from the scriptural text: 'It is sown as an animal body: it will arise as a spiritual body') but because it will submit to the spirit with a ready obedience, an obedience so wonderfully complete that the body will fulfil the will of the spirit in such a way as to bring perfect assurance of indissoluble immortality, free from any feeling of distress, and relieved of any possibility of corruption, any trace of reluctance.

"Sicut enim spiritus carni seruiens non incongrue carnalis, ita caro spiritui seruiens recte appellabitur spiritalis, non quia in spiritum conuertetur, sicut nonnulli putant ex eo quod scriptum est: Seminatur corpus animale, surget corpus spiritale, sed quia spiritui summa et mirabili obtemperandi facilitate subdetur usque ad implendam inmortalitatis indissolubilis securissimam uoluntatem, omni molestiae sensu, omni corruptibilitate et tarditate detracta." Ibid., 13.20.

knows that it does not know. But knowing this, it still wants to know the highest things. What has the philosopher found when he has found all that he can find by his own methods? Can he call it happiness? Dare he call it happiness?[35]

As Augustine might ask, Given human limitations, could the philosophic life ever be completed satisfactorily? Schall continues later in the same essay, "What philosophers find maddening about Augustine finally is the fact that he questions their virtue on their own grounds. The virtues of the philosophers are in fact proud vices when they stand by themselves."[36] Augustine's critique is therefore an internal critique of classical philosophy and politics. He points out their limitations, of which their brightest practitioners would already have been aware even though they themselves are not able to provide a way to transcend those limitations.

Augustine even goes so far as to accuse at least some of his philosophic interlocutors of living according to the flesh.[37] He ascribes to "the Platonists" the view that "they hold that souls are so influenced by 'earthly limbs and dying members' that they derive from them their morbid desires and fears, joys and sadness."[38] Living according to the flesh is living according to man's own standards, or standards man has discovered or invented on his own rather than standards revealed to him by his creator.[39] The desire to perfect the best part of man—the soul—is praiseworthy, but not if those activities require the neglect of the whole man. Augustine insists that Christianity, when it is lived out faithfully, leads to the perfection of the whole of man through the perfection of each part in its proper ordering to the whole, which itself is under God.[40] Since the Christian God is

---

35. Schall, *Reason, Revelation, and Human Affairs*, 95.

36. Ibid., 111. Fortin similarly argues that "Augustine's critique … is based on his opponents' own principles." Fortin, *Birth of Philosophic Christianity*, 5.

37. He says, "Anyone who exalts the soul as the Supreme Good, and censures the nature of flesh as something evil, is in fact carnal alike in his cult of the soul and in his revulsion from the flesh, since this attitude is prompted by human folly, not by divine truth." "Nam qui uelut summum bonum laudat animae naturam et tamquam malum naturam carnis accusat, profecto et animam carnaliter adpetit et carnem camaliter fugit, quoniam id uanitate sentit humana, non ueritate diuina." *Ciu. Dei*, 14.5.

38. Ibid.

39.

It is in fact not by the possession of flesh, which the Devil does not possess, that man has become like the Devil: it is by living by the rule of self (*vivendo secundum se ipsum*), that is by the rule of man (*secundum hominem*). For the devil chose to live by the rule of self when he did not stand fast in the truth, so that the lie that he told was his own lie, not God's. The Devil is not only a liar; he is 'the father of lies.' He was, as we know, the first to lie, and falsehood, like sin, had its start from him. (Ibid., 14.3)

40. As a result, Augustine can take the side of the city of Athens in its accusation against Socrates in this limited sense: the body and man's moral life are integral to human

triune, the best way of life, the most divine way of life, is a life lived in charity in a communion of persons.

The distinction between those who live according to their own standards versus those who live according to God demarcates the two cities from each other, the earthly city and the City of God.[41] Classical political philosophy had traditionally undertaken to examine as its highest task what the best or wisest and most just regime is by determining who among the various parts of the city ought to rule in the city. Augustine relativizes this discussion by shifting attention to whether the city is ruled by God or by men.[42] If God does not rule in the city, then it cannot be just and it cannot live according to wisdom. He says,

> Although here are many great peoples throughout the world, living under different customs in religion and morality (*diuersis ritibus moribusque*), and

---

happiness. Despite the political way of life's limitations and the perils to which it is subject, there is an element of truth to its claims. Schall points out about moral or political virtue, "While Augustine is aware of the insufficiency of virtue, he does not denigrate virtue, even when he emphasizes the consequences of the Fall." Schall, *Reason, Revelation, and Human Affairs*, 110. As Fortin writes, Augustine's practice of considering things in light of their highest metaphysical principles is responsible for much of his extreme-sounding criticism of Roman virtue. See Fortin, *Birth of Philosophic Christianity*, 27–9. On this score, see also von Heyking, *Augustine and Politics as Longing in the World*, 18–19. Oliver O'Donovan also remarks, "What Augustine's reader carries away with him in the end is not a denigration of the role of virtue in politics (though there is a fair amount of deflation of pretension) but an ability to discern shadows cast by virtue in surprising places." O'Donovan, "Augustine's *City of God* XIX," 103. See also Manent's insightful observations about Augustine's treatment of Marcus Regulus as the high point of Roman virtue in *ciu. Dei* in *Metamorphoses*, 248–9.

41. See Markus' discussion of this distinction in Markus, *Saeculum*, 67–9. A discussion of Markus' central thesis, that there exists a neutral *saeculum* in Augustine's thought which is the arena in which the city of God and the city of man live their lives on earth, is outside the scope of our argument. He is surely right, however, that "Augustine's treatment of the sphere in which the state's function lies has the effect of endowing the realm of politics with a considerable degree of autonomy," if he avoids an absolute sense of "autonomy." Augustine would have found incoherent any notion of a sphere of human affairs that is undetermined either toward the end of eternal life with God or the second death in which the soul is irrevocably separated from God. An undetermined sphere of human affairs could only become a seemingly live option after the early modern rejection of teleology in nature and politics. In this regard, see O'Donovan, "Augustine's *City of God* XIX," 98–9.

42. Kevin Hughes notices, "It is not all that clear that 'political theory' as it is usually construed had any appeal or meaning to Augustine—forms of government, for example, do not seem to occupy him all that much." Kevin L. Hughes, "Local Politics: The Political Place of the Household in Augustine's *City of God*," in *Augustine and Politics*, ed. John Doody, Kevin L. Hughes, and Kim Paffenroth (Lanham, MD: Lexington Books, 2005), 145–64 at 145.

distinguished by a complex variety of languages, arms, and dress, it is still true that there have come into being only two main divisions (*genera*), as we may call them, in human society; and we are justified in following our Scriptures and calling them two cities (*civitates duas*). There is, in fact, one city of men who choose to live by the standard of the flesh (*secundum carnem*), another of those who choose to live by the standard of the spirit (*secundum spiritum*). The citizens of each of these desire their own kind (*generis*) of peace, and, when they achieve their aim, that is the kind of peace in which they live.[43]

The peace that each city seeks is different, both in terms of its content and for what the peace is used. The peace the earthly city seeks is a peace primarily about cessation of bodily violence, and, more subtly, the peace of subjection to the will of the ruler.[44] On the other hand, the peace the city of God seeks is the peace it has in eternal life in communion with God. The subjection to God's will as ruler in the city of God is also the subjection to wisdom since God's will is identical with wisdom. Life lived according to wisdom and life lived according to law are therefore one in the city of God as they never can be in the city of man or in any actual regime.

---

43. *Ciu. Dei*, 14.1. In perhaps the most extreme formulation of this principle about the transpolitical city of God, Augustine says, "As for this mortal life, which ends after a few days' course, what does it matter under whose rule [*imperio*] a man lives, being so soon to die, provided that the rulers do not force him to impious and wicked [*impia et iniqua*] acts?" Ibid., 5.17.

44. "We see, then, that all men desire to be at peace with their own people, while wishing to impose their will upon those people's lives. For even when they wage war on others, their wish is to make those opponents their own people, if they can—to subject them, and to impose on them their own conditions of peace." Ibid., 19.12.

Chapter 9

CHARITY, JUSTICE, AND RECONCILIATION IN THE TRANSPOLITICAL CITY OF GOD

Let us now consider the specific character of the way of life lived by the city of God in its pilgrimage on earth. For Augustine, the end of the whole man, body and soul, is transpolitical, in contrast to the Platonic philosopher for whom only the end of the soul is transpolitical, and the intellectual soul at that. The entirely transpolitical end of the city of God allows it to accept into itself all manner of men with all different customs and capacities. The earthly city is founded on disorder: dramatically, by the fratricide of Cain, and, at bottom, by the choice of self over God in the original sin. The disorder of the earthly city's founding influences its action and organization throughout history in the habitual preference of the lower over the higher, the temporal over the eternal, and vice over virtue. The earthly city prefers earthly peace to heavenly peace because it cares for temporal things inordinately. Its laws concern the dispensations of temporal things, which its citizens love inordinately. The men who rule the earthly city and the gods the earthly city worships flatter the earthly city's fundamental disorder. In its ignorant evaluation of goods and its incontinent or even vicious attachment to lower things over higher things, worse men are preferred to better in the allocation of offices and awards, and the city's will is preferred to God's will. The earthly city is therefore characterized by disorder through and through. The multitude of gods in the earthly city is a reflection of the multitude of desires and ways of life lived in that city, which, like their gods, are always warring.

In *City of God* 19.5–9, Augustine illustrates the deep disorders of the earthly city, its lack of the possession of true virtue and its insecure possession of any temporal blessing it might have for the moment by examining in successive chapters, starting with chapter 5, the family, the city, and the community of nations.[1] In Chapter 5, he shows the upheavals to which families are subjected, arising from "secret treachery" even among those who are tied together by the closest earthly

---

1. In these chapters, as well as in Book 19 as a whole, the problem of ignorance comes to the forefront and, while present as it must be, difficulty takes back stage, which reflects Augustine's more direct engagement with philosophers about the duty of the wise with respect to the rest of the city as indicated by his argument in the opening chapters of *ciu. Dei* about the divisiveness of philosophic knowledge.

bonds in the same household.² Augustine points out a twofold problem in the household arising from ignorance, which is in principle applicable to any temporal order: strife arises even between men whose love is "honourable,"³ and peace itself is insecure among men since "we do not know the hearts of those with whom we wish to maintain peace."⁴ And even if men's intentions were knowable today, none could know anything of what they will be tomorrow.

In Chapter 6, Augustine shows the disorders in the city, focusing on the maladies arising from ignorance in the matter of judgment of civil cases. He tells of the wise judge who, because of the deficiency of his wisdom, is incapable of seeing into the hearts of the men who come before him and who, because of his ignorance, is forced to condemn to death an innocent man. Sometimes the exigencies of a case may even require the judge to torture an innocent witness in order to determine the truth of his testimony. Torture of witnesses and the occasional condemnation of innocent men to death are unavoidable because of the ignorance of even a wise and just judge, and because of the prevalence of lies in the city that makes normal testimony habitually unreliable. Augustine therefore asks, "In view of this darkness (*tenebris*) that attends the life of human society, will our wise man (*sapiens*) take his seat on the judge's bench, or will he not have the heart to do so?"⁵ The question at stake is, do the manifold disorders of the earthly city not necessarily repel the wise man? Knowing, as he does, that political life is beset with such massive imperfection, will the wise man not withdraw from political life? Augustine says no: "Plainly, he will sit. For human society both constrains him and draws him to this duty, which he considers wicked to abandon."⁶ It is

---

2. *Ciu. Dei*, 19.5.
3. Ibid., 19.5.
4. Ibid., 19.5. Oliver O'Donovan argues,

> No one, perhaps, until Kierkegaard was so vexed at the difficulties we have in displaying to others our hearts, and of knowing what lies in theirs. It is this—not the pride of original sin, not the dazzle of glory or the iron rod of power, not the lure of sense, and most certainly not the temptations of sex—that cast a shadow over all social relations: we can be deceived in one another. (O'Donovan, "Augustine's *City of God* XIX," 109)

O'Donovan identifies ignorance, not difficulty or weakness, as the primary scourge of social life. The degree to which the scourges of ignorance and difficulty are interrelated may be lost in O'Donovan's generalization however.

5. *Ciu. Dei*, 19.6.
6. "Sedebit plane. Constringit enim eum et ad hoc officium pertrahit humana societas, quam deserere nefas ducit." Ibid., 19.6. My translation. The example is oddly shorn of particularities. We know nothing of the wise man in question. Is it, for example, the duty of the wise man to seek judicial office? Or is he merely constrained to accept such an office if forced upon him? Or does the very darkness Augustine describes, which infects social life, compel the city's best men to take up the office of judge as the men best able to do the job, albeit imperfectly, even in their case?

the wise man's duty to judge in hard cases, passing judgments that are necessarily imperfect, a fact that cannot fail to offend him both morally and intellectually. The duty of the wise judge is therefore a miserable one.[7] Augustine declares the necessary and, in popular opinion, noble office of judging civil cases to be, on the one hand, indispensable for earthly peace and, on the other hand, miserable for the judge. For the truly wise man will understand the deficiencies of his own knowledge and the possibility that he will end up rendering judgments that are objectively unjust. The duty of judging is necessary: the nature of human society after the Fall compels it. But the judge ought to pray to be freed from it.

In Chapter 7, Augustine shows the disorders to which the community of nations are subject. First, Augustine mentions the diversity of languages, which make human discussion among people who do not share the same tongue impossible. Even dumb animals have an easier time associating together, Augustine says, than human beings who do not speak the same language. Diversity of language results from the diversity of thoughts. The lack of union in language is a result of a lack of union in thought. True peace and justice among men is prevented when thoughts are not united, and thoughts cannot be united unless those thoughts are directed toward God the Creator rather than toward temporal goods like glory. The reader is supposed to think of the story of the Tower of Babel in Genesis at this juncture, but Pentecost, in which the Holy Spirit enables the Church to speak universally to all men by conversing with them in their own language, should also be in the back of the reader's mind for the sake of contrast. The imposition of common languages has only become possible through the wars necessary to establish empire. Those wars, says Augustine, even if they are just wars, are miserable necessities rather than glorious undertakings. He says,

> But the wise man, they say, will wage just wars. Surely, if he remembers that he is a human being, he will rather lament the fact that he is faced with the necessity of waging just wars; for if they were not just, he would not have to engage in them, and consequently there would be no wars for a wise man. For it is the injustice of the opposing side that lays on the wise man the duty of waging wars.[8]

7. Augustine comments,

> If it is through unavoidable ignorance (*necessitate nesciendi*) and the unavoidable duty of judging (*iudicandi*) that he tortures the innocent, are we to be told that it is not enough to acquit him? Must we grant him happiness as a bonus? How much more mature reflection (*consideratius*) it shows, how much more worthy of a human being it is when a man acknowledges this necessity as a mark of human wretchedness, when he hates that necessity in his own actions and when, if he has the wisdom of devotion, he cries out to God, "Deliver me from my necessities." (Ibid., 19.6)

8. Ibid., 19.7. See also ibid., 4.15 and 5.12. Dodaro remarks,

> When Augustine insists that the scriptural passages concerning just and unjust responses to violence are not intended to provide moral guidance for external acts but to train the heart, he refers, in effect, to this intellectual process of reconciling

Once again, sin and its consequence, the injustice of the opposing side, impose on the wise man the necessity of undertaking actions which would not be necessary before the Fall. The wise man does not shrink from his duty in waging just wars, but he views it as a miserable necessity. Just like the wise judge of the preceding chapter, presumably, he ought to pray to God to be delivered from his miserable necessity and not take pride in the empire he has formed as a response to evils he ought to wish never existed in the first place.

In Chapters 8 and 9, Augustine shows the disorders plaguing friendship both with human friends and with angels. Human friends can be imperiled or can turn against their friends. Sometimes, bad angels disguise themselves as good angels and, on their own, men are powerless to tell the difference without superior wisdom.[9] The effect of these five chapters is to show that no level of human society is free from disorder due to the fundamental disorder of original sin. Further, the stubborn disorders in the world due to sin compel even the man who is wise and just to undertake actions that make him miserable. The members of the earthly city regard waging war and judging in civil cases as great things and give honors and glory to those who undertake those offices, but the man who takes pleasure in them becomes depraved and forgets what it is to be a human being.[10] Augustine's discussion in Chapters 6–9 shows that any kind of earthly rule is, in Jean Bethke Elshtain's words, "always a tragic rule—necessarily so—involving the disciplining of sin."[11] These tragic duties are not the duties one would wish for; neither would one wish for a situation marked by original sin. But anyone who desires to do good must grapple with precisely these tragic necessities. Nevertheless, the observation of Augustine's mournfulness in light of the tragic necessities of earthly rulership

---

multiple interpretations of scriptural passages in order to produce a synthesis. Yet, even this intellectual effort does not guarantee that the resulting moral decision meets the divine standard of justice. Dodaro, *Christ and the Just Society*, 139

Ignorance and difficulty resist the human desire for moral perfection in this life. As Ernest L. Fortin perceptively remarks, Augustine's contribution to reflection on war is not so much the principle that "wars can ever be completely just, but that under more or less favorable circumstances they might become a trifle less unjust." Fortin, *Birth of Philosophic Christianity*, 31. Needless to say, that trifling improvement may appear trifling when evaluating a war's justice, but not at all trifling to concrete persons affected by any given war. In these cases, even "trifling" improvements can be quite significant to those whose lives are affected by war.

9. Which, as Augustine points out in *c. acad.*, 3.5.11–12, would have to be a divine wisdom.

10. Dodaro explains, "Augustine begins by asserting that by comparing their virtues with God's supreme mercy, blessedness, and justice, earthly judges can see that they are not sinless, despite the praise lavished upon them." Dodaro, *Christ and the Just Society*, 206.

11. Jean Bethke Elshtain, *Augustine and the Limits of Politics* (Notre Dame, IN: University of Notre Dame Press, 1995), 100.

should also be moderated by von Heyking's cautions about Augustine's political rhetoric, which aimed to "tame inordinate political passions and ambitions."[12] Augustine would have judged that most people would have erred in the direction of the zealous and unscrupulous exercise of power; his attempt to bridle the ambitions of the warlike and the judge who is intoxicated by his own office is an attempt to work against the tendencies of most people. That Augustine judged that most people's tendencies lie in this particular direction opens a way for Augustine's response to the disorder of the earthly city, which is predicated on the operation of charity in the city of God.

The breach between man and God caused by man's original sin causes man's lower nature to rebel against his mind and, in disordering the man himself, makes proper order among men impossible.[13] The proper order of man could not be regained by man's own efforts but must be restored to him by his creator. The grace of Christ is needed in order to heal the original breach between God and man, reestablishing man's proper order to God in charity. Charity, Augustine says, consists in love of God and neighbor. What this involves, he says, is that "In [these precepts], man finds three objects for his love: God, himself, and his neighbour; and a man who loves God is not wrong in loving himself."[14] When man loves these three things rightly, the original order lost when man sinned is regained: man in himself is rightly ordered because he is rightly ordered to God; man is rightly ordered to his neighbor because he is rightly ordered to God in himself. None of these three things can be loved in the absence of both of the other two. Disorder toward one necessarily implies a disorder with regard to the other two. Augustine draws the implication:

> It follows, therefore, that he should take care that his neighbor should love God, whom he is commanded to love as himself thus, to his wife, to his children, to his domestic servants, and for other men, so far as is possible. And, for the same

---

12. Von Heyking, *Augustine and Politics*, 20.
13. Augustine writes,

> The mind however rightly commands the body when it serves God, and in the mind itself the reason rightly rules the libido and other vices when it is subject to the Lord God. For that reason, when man does not serve God, what are we to think may be righteous in him? When indeed the mind is not serving God, in no way can the mind justly command the body or the human reason command the vices.
>
> Seruiens autem Deo animus recte imperat corpori, inque ipso animo ratio Deo Domino subdita recte imperat libidini uitiisque ceteris. Quapropter ubi homo Deo non seruit, quid in eo putandum est esse iustitiae? quando quidem Deo non seruiens nullo modo potest iuste animus corpori aut humana ratio uitiis imperare. Et si in homine tali non est ulla iustitia, procul dubio nec in hominum coetu, qui ex hominibus talibus constat. (*Ciu. Dei*, 19.21. My translation)

14. Ibid., 19.14.

end, he will wish his neighbor to care for him, if he happens to need that care. For this reason he will be at peace with all men, as much as lies within him, in that peace among men, that is, that ordered harmony.[15]

There are therefore two requirements for a universal way of salvation among men: a genuinely transcendent good and a good toward which all men can look. Philosophy provides the former but not the latter because of the exaltedness of the good it pursues, while the pagan city provides the latter but not the former because of the comparatively low good it habitually pursues. Only Christian faith, Augustine argues, provides for both conditions: a genuinely transcendent good accessible to all men through the mediation of the Incarnate Word. Charity, which is the gift of grace, reestablishes right order by directing man's love once again to the eternal God, whom man had despised in original sin.[16]

Yet the city of God does not do away with the natural particularities the earthly city finds significant in its own life; nor does it immediately heal the vices and folly that account for the "darkness"[17] of human social life Augustine observed earlier. Immediately following his account of love of God and neighbor, Augustine affirms that "to begin with, therefore, a man has responsibility (*cura*) for his own household—obviously, both in the order of nature and in the framework of human society (*uel naturae ordine uel ipsius societatis humanae*), he has easier and more immediate contact with them; he can exercise his concern (*consulendi*) for them."[18] Charity knows no bounds of particularity, and is therefore a duty bound on man toward all men; but the charity that moves the city of God itself moves through an order suited to man's station as both finite and still struggling with sin. Man's primary duty is still to those to whom he is closest by virtue of the most basic bodily ties: his family and household. The movement of charity therefore begins with those who are closest; the universality of charity is found in principle in

---

15. "Consequens est, ut etiam proximo ad diligendum Deum consulat, quem iubetur sicut se ipsum diligere (sic uxori, sic filiis, sic domesticis, sic ceteris quibus potuerit hominibus), et ad hoc sibi a proximo, si forte indiget, consuli uelit; ac per hoc erit pacatus, quantum in ipso est, omni homini pace hominum, id est ordinata concordia." Ibid., 19.14. My translation.

16. Fortin argues,

> The pagan philosophers correctly identify happiness in terms of virtue or excellence, that is to say, in terms of the highest goals to which human beings aspire, but they are unable to show the way to those goals. People are happy when they are at one with themselves and with one another, and they achieve this harmony when justice prevails both within and among them. Yet experience demonstrates that few of them ever manage to live perfectly just lives. (Fortin, *Birth of Philosophic Christianity*, 5)

17. *Ciu. Dei*, 19.6.
18. Ibid., 19.14.

each man through the presence of the Holy Spirit and in act in the whole Church universal.

Likewise, in the immediately following chapter, Augustine shows how the Christian balances membership in the city of God with a pilgrim existence in the earthly city by showing how the love of God and neighbor nevertheless does not negate the importance of family relationships. Households are composed of the father, the mother, the children, and the servants or slaves. The most basic distinction in the household, therefore, is between the family and the servants or between the free and the slaves. But all members of the household are human beings who may hope for happiness in eternal life with God. At first glance, therefore, Christianity might seem to destroy the foundation for the father's different treatment of son and slave. After all, as Augustine points out, slavery has its origin in warfare, which is a consequence of original sin, not nature; it is only natural by fallen nature.[19] Slavery is a punishment for sin.[20] Augustine's theological understanding of slavery certainly weakens the theoretical foundations of the institution. But it must be said that, considered in light of fallen nature, Augustine seems to understand slavery as a necessity of a similar kind to that which compels the just man to wage war.[21] There are some, Augustine might say, who must be ruled by a master. This necessity is a miserable one for both slave and master but both must endure it as a punishment and therefore as a path of purification, with the master's duty to rule the slave greater even than the slave's duty to obey the master. It is only in the next life that the miserable necessity of slavery will be overcome.[22] In this life, the consequences of sin may be moderated with the help

---

19. "However, no man by nature, in which God first established men, is a slave either to a man or to sin. Indeed, penal servitude is ordered by that law which commands the preservation of the natural order and forbids its disruption." "Nullus autem natura, in qua prius Deus hominem condidit, seruus est hominis aut peccati. Verum et poenalis seruitus ea lege ordinatur, quae naturalem ordinem conseruari iubet, perturbari uetat." Ibid., 19.15. My translation.

20. See ibid., 19.16.

21. In identifying slavery's origin with war, Augustine links their status. This also seems to indicate that Augustine's judgment is based on much more than prejudicial deference to his own society's conventions, as Wetzel asserts. See James Wetzel, *Augustine and the Limits of Virtue* (Cambridge, UK: Cambridge University Press, 1992), 65, and ibid., n. 36.

22.

> On the other hand, those who are genuine "fathers of their household" are concerned for the welfare of all in their households in respect of the worship and service of God, as if they were all their children, longing and praying that they may come to the heavenly home, where it will not be a necessary duty to give orders to men, because it will no longer be a necessary duty to be concerned for the welfare of those who are already in the felicity of that immortal state. But until that home is reached, the fathers have an obligation to exercise the authority of masters greater than the duty of slaves to put up with their condition as servants. (*Ciu. Dei*, 19.16)

of grace, but they will not finally be overcome until the Resurrection. As a result, the foundation of the different treatment of the son and the slave by the father is left intact by Christianity, although both master and slave long together for the Resurrection in which slavery is no longer necessary.

The Christian head of a household, Augustine says, should make decisions for his household that are informed by charity and directed to eternal goods. In this respect, the distinction between son and slave is preserved. On the other hand, the Christian head of the household has not just the temporal good of the members of his household under his care, but also their eternal good. Love of God and neighbor requires that he ought to desire that all members of his household love God rightly. The religious headship of the household therefore suffers no distinctions between son and slave; the Christian head ought to have equal concern for their immortal souls. Augustine therefore affirms the continuing relevance of the particularities of human life that are relevant in the household and in the city, which is why diversity of mode of dress and manner of life makes no difference in the city of God so far as the individuals share the same faith.[23] Just as the city of God does not do away with the relevant distinctions in the temporal governance of the household, so it does not do away with politically relevant distinctions in the governance of the city. In his specific role as theologian and bishop, therefore, Augustine has nothing to add to the discussion in classical political thought about who should rule the earthly city. The city of God, Augustine says, can have no doubts about the things revealed in the Scriptures for the sake of man's salvation, but man is not saved by the regime and its laws.[24] Salvation of the human being is possible under any number of different regimes. This explains Augustine's seeming indifference to the

---

23. Ibid., 19.19. Rowan Williams remarks, "Christians are to be indifferent to the *mores* of the nations among whom they live—and the word is wide enough to include many of the institutions of public or civil life." Rowan Williams, "Politics and the Soul: A Reading of the *City of God*," *Milltown Studies*, vols. 19/20 (1987), 55–72 at 67. Williams is right insofar as it is true that the universality of Christianity allows the Christian to live a faithfully Christian life under the exigencies of all manner of different *mores*. But the universality Augustine describes in the *City of God* does not encourage indifference to the particulars of earthly life. Rather, Christianity is a universal way in the sense that it is in principle open to all manner of *mores*; not that Christians are incapable of making distinctions or even making judgments of better and worse among them.

24.

> It believes also in the holy scriptures, the old and the new, which we call canonical, whence is derived the faith which is the basis of the just man's life, the faith by which we walk on our way without doubting, in the time of our pilgrimage, in exile from the Lord. So long as this faith is sound and certain we cannot justly be reproached if we have doubts about some matters where neither sense nor reason give clear perception, where we have received no illumination from the canonical Scriptures and where we have not been given information by witnesses whom it would be irrational to distrust. (*Ciu. Dei*, 19.18)

question of who ought to rule in the city when he says, "As for this mortal life, which ends after a few days' course, what does it matter under whose rule a man lives, being so soon to die, provided that the rulers do not force him to impious and wicked acts?"[25] On the other hand, James V. Schall argues,

> Augustine does not deny that some forms of rule are better than others. Rome was better than Carthage, not to mention better than the invading barbarians, even though those barbarians eventually became Christians and good Romans. Augustine's advice for those human beings caught in bad regimes is that the highest things are still possible for them, but only in *The City of God*.[26]

Earthly cities will never embody true justice, but they may in greater or lesser degrees reflect it and, even more probably, may in greater or lesser degrees allow individuals and households who are truly pursuing justice in piety to flourish within them.

Augustine concedes the earthly city's authority in temporal matters, but flatly denies that it has any authority to command actions for the sake of eternal ends contrary to those of the city of God. Christianity, Augustine says, removes from the city its decisive authority to shape men's souls altogether. Each individual man's destiny transcends the city because each man is directed toward communion with the Triune God. Both the earthly city and the city of God desire earthly peace, although for different ends. In the meantime, the city of God commands its members to do the things that conduce to earthly peace, especially obeying the earthly city's laws except for those contrary to the religious laws of the city of God. Civic obligations are therefore raised to the level of religious obligation by Christian teaching, without confusing the different orders of duties to city and duties to God. Augustine comments,

> Therefore, the heavenly city also makes use of earthly peace in this pilgrimage of its own and, within the limits of piety and religion, safeguards and desires the arrangement of human wills in matters pertaining to mortal human nature. It

---

Augustine mentions the origin of the soul among those things about which it is legitimate to have doubts, since any number of opinions might be compatible with Christian teaching. For a full discussion of this topic, see *lib. arb.*, 3.21–2. Knowledge of politics would then fall into this category of things about which it is legitimate for Christians to have doubts.

25. *Ciu. Dei*, 5.17. See also ibid., 5.10–15.

26. James V. Schall, *Reason, Revelation, and Human Affairs*, 102. Fortin concurs, writing that, "For Augustine, the choice was between civilization and barbarism, and it was in light of that choice that the decision to support one side or the other had to be made. No one had fewer illusions than Augustine about the justice of the Roman Empire. If his heart was still with it, it is because he thought that the prospects for justice, slim as they always are, were greater within it than outside of it." Fortin, *Birth of Philosophic Christianity*, 31.

relates this earthly peace to heavenly peace, which is truly such that it should be considered and spoken of as the only peace for rational creatures.[27]

The city of God desires the cooperation of men's wills with respect to the worship of God and the ordination of its members and their actions to God, which has true, eternal peace as its end and it also desires the cooperation of men's wills with respect to earthly peace.[28] The eternal end and the way to get there have been divinely revealed to the city of God, and it believes in what is revealed to it with the certainty of supernatural faith. On the other hand, Christianity is transpolitical and therefore has no crudely political teaching. James V. Schall explains, "In Augustine's terms, no existing civil society is *The City of God*. On the other hand, all members of any existing civil society have to choose the ultimate city to which they belong."[29] To a great degree, the Christian faith allows the earthly city to shape its own particular way of life, provided that its customs and laws do not directly interfere with the transcendent end of the city of God.

Paradoxically, Augustine implies that those whose souls are ultimately formed by Christian teaching rather than by the city have the chance to be better members of their earthly cities, since they will have a better sense for the true place of the city in God's providential ordering of the whole. The charity informing Christians' actions is—potentially, at least, since there is no necessity in matters of human choice—the best available chance for securing justice and peace. Augustine can therefore say in one of his letters,

> Let those who say that the teaching of Christ is opposed to the welfare of the state produce such provincial administrators, such husbands, such wives, such parents, such sons, such masters, such slaves, such kings, such judges, and finally such tax-payers and collectors of public revenue as Christian teaching requires them to be, and then let them dare to say that this teaching is opposed to the welfare of the state, or, rather, let them even hesitate to admit that it is the greatest safety of the state, if it is observed.[30]

The discussion of *City of God* 19.19 centers on three ways of life—"the life of leisure, the life of action, and the combination of both (*otioso, actuoso et ex utroque*

---

27. "Utitur ergo etiam caelestis ciuitas in hac sua peregrinatione pace terrena et de rebus ad mortalem hominum naturam pertinentibus humanarum uoluntatum compositionem, quantum salua pietate ac religione conceditur, tuetur atque appetit eamque terrenam pacem refert ad caelestem pacem, quae uere ita pax est, ut rationalis dumtaxat creaturae sola pax habenda atque dicenda sit." *Ciu. Dei*, 19.17. My translation.

28. See also *ep*. 138 where Augustine says in very strong language that the Christian counsel to turn the other cheek generates repentance and agreement, "than which nothing is more useful to the state (*qua nihil est utilius civitate*)." *Ep*. 138.2.11.

29. James V. Schall, *Reason, Revelation, and Human Affairs*, 97.

30. *Ep*. 138.2.15.

composito)"[31]—and their compatibility with the way of life lived by the city of God. The three ways of life are the three main contenders for the best way of life in classical thought: philosophy, politics, and the mixed life that engages in both. The way of life lived by the city of God is founded on charity. So far as the Christian does not neglect charity, he may pursue any of these three ways of life. Further, charity provides correctives to each of the ways of life and their characteristic excesses or deficiencies. Augustine emphasizes, "For no one ought to live a life of leisure in such a way that he takes no thought in that leisure for the welfare of his neighbour; nor ought he to be so active as to feel no need for the contemplation of God. The delight offered by a life of leisure ought to consist not in idle inactivity, but in the opportunity to seek and find the truth, so that everyone may progress in this regard, and not jealously withhold his discoveries from others."[32] Charity compels the man who lives the theoretical life to benefit his neighbor whenever he sees that he can be of help. He ought to share the fruits of his pursuit of wisdom, insofar as is prudent and possible, with those who are unable to undertake the search. In other words, the man who learns has a corresponding duty to teach, although he is never compelled to teach imprudently.[33] On the other hand, men who hold political office ought to view their office as a service to those subject to them. Augustine remarks, "In the active life, on the other hand, we are not to love the honour or power which this kind of life affords, since 'all things under the sun are vanity.' Rather, as we have explained above, we should seek to use that same honour or power righteously and beneficially, for the wellbeing of those under us, according to the will of God."[34] Charity works to counteract the pride of the philosopher and the lust for glory of the political man by ordering their characteristic ways of life under the love of God and of neighbor.

In speaking of the active way of life, Augustine mentions the bishop, who he says ought to take delight in doing good rather than in ruling itself. Augustine does not specifically mention any particular officeholder in the city. The bishop's

---

31. *Ciu. Dei*, 19.19.

32. "Nec sic esse quisque debet otiosus, ut in eodem otio utilitatem non cogitet proximi, nec sic actuosus, ut contemplationem non requirat Dei. In otio non iners uacatio delectare debet, sed aut inquisitio aut inuentio ueritatis, ut in ea quisque proficiat et quod inuenerit ne alteri inuideat." *Ciu. Dei*, 19.19.

33. See, for example, ibid., 1.9:

> If anyone refrains from rebuking and correcting evildoers because he is waiting for a more propitious time, or for fear of making matters worse for doing so, or because he fears that, if he does so, others who are weak may be discouraged from living a good and godly life and driven and turned away from the faith: this restraint is clearly occasioned not by greed, but by the counsel of love.

> On the other hand, one may not hold back to correct an evildoer for fear of the loss of temporal goods, which is the lesson of the martyrs.

34. Ibid., 19.19.

task is immediately transpolitical, concerning as it does directly the worship of God and the teaching of the faith. A Christian holding political office himself has transpolitical ends as an individual man and as a member of the city of God and he would be responsible for ordering the earthly peace he is duty bound to pursue to eternal peace; but this further ordering is just that: a *further* ordering. Augustine's task is similar to that of Socrates in Plato's *Republic*: to explain why a man who has begun to understand himself in terms of a good that transcends the city might willingly return to the city in order to serve its citizens. Augustine argues that Christianity requires its adherents to regard their political obligations as a religious duty.[35] Marc D. Guerra explains,

> Christianity's injunction to love one's neighbor as himself—the exact opposite of the antisocial and antipolitical stance that the ancient city claimed the classical philosophers struck—did not mean that Christians should slight their responsibilities within civil society. Instead, the theological virtue of charity demanded that Christians were obliged to devote themselves to the good of their fellow citizens with an intensity that was unknown and unimaginable in the Greek polis.[36]

The philosopher in Plato's *Republic* must be forced to leave behind his contemplations in order to rule; the Christian, Augustine argues, does so willingly out of love for his neighbor. In this respect, Augustine's own call to the priesthood and episcopacy and away from his life in leisure exemplifies the charitable service of neighbor Christianity solicits even from those who are able to live the philosophic way of life. Augustine's position rests on what the new context brings: eternal life and the resurrection of the body due to the mediation of Christ, which allows Augustine to choose a mixed life of contemplation and action grounded on faith, hope, and charity.

As Augustine's use of the words necessity and compulsion throughout Book 19 testify,[37] there are tensions between the earthly city and the city of God due to sin that are irresolvable. The city of God desires to convert not the earthly city as such, but rather the members of the earthly city by drawing them into its own distinctive, graced way of life. Membership in the city of God offers to the Christian the wisdom to understand that the imperfections of the earthly city are precisely that: imperfections. The Christian knows that his end lies in eternal life with God, and so the imperfections of the earthly city are punishments for sin that are to be endured for the sake of purification and sanctification so that the believer may merit that eternal life which is his true end. The nature of social life after the

---

35. See *ex. Prop. Rm.*, 74.

36. Marc D. Guerra, *Christians as Political Animals* (Wilmington, DE: ISI Books, 2010), 116.

37. Versions of *necessaria* are used thirty-three times throughout Book 19, while versions of *cogere* are used ten times.

Fall compels the good man to resist evil, which the Christian does out of love for the men his actions can help in imitation of Christ. The good man's resistance causes him to take an active part in the disorders of the fallen world, in which perfect wisdom and justice are not available. Nevertheless, he does his best to love God and his neighbor. He is happy in hope, however, for he aims at true peace and true happiness in eternal life, which Christ promises to his followers.[38] When the city of God finally rests, it will rest in true wisdom and justice. The knowledge that transpolitical wisdom and justice, available now in foretaste by faith and through hope, will be possessed in eternal life guards the Christian against the twin temptations of fanaticism and cynicism that threaten man through the temptation of despair. Just as Christ descended to take part in the imperfections of human history through the Incarnation, the Christian has confidence that his participation in human social and political life can be done well if it is viewed as the path of charity that purifies and sanctifies the believer, accompanied by the prayer, "From my necessities deliver Thou me."[39] Vices will be vanquished utterly only after the Resurrection, in which the destruction of the *consuetudo carnalis* is accomplished completely. Having endured bodily death humbly as the ultimate punishment of sin, the resurrected man receives back his body as a spiritual body.[40] Ignorance will give way to wisdom as the mind beholds God face to face

---

38.

> Nonetheless, if any man uses this life in such a way that he directs it towards that end which he so ardently loves and for which he so faithfully hopes, he may without absurdity be called happy even now, though rather by future hope than in present reality. Present reality without that hope, however, is a false happiness and a great misery, since, in that case, the true goods of the soul are not enjoyed. For no wisdom is true wisdom if it does not direct all its prudence, fortitude, temperance, and justice towards that final state where God shall be all in all in an assured eternity and perfect peace.
>
> Quam tamen quicumque sic habet, ut eius usum referat ad illius finem, quam diligit ardentissime ac fidelissime sperat, non absurde dici etiam nunc beatus potest, spe illa potius quam re ista. Res ista uero sine spe illa beatitudo falsa et magna miseria est; non enim ueris animi bonis utitur, quoniam non est uera sapientia, quae intentionem suam in his quae prudenter discernit, gerit fortiter, cohibet temperanter iusteque distribuit, non ad illum dirigit finem, ubi erit Deus omnia in omnibus, aeternitate certa et pace perfecta. (*Ciu. Dei*, 19.20)

39. Ibid., 19.6. See also ibid., 19.27: "For such a prayer is needed by righteous men because the reason, though subjected to God, does not have complete command over the vices in this mortal state and in the 'corruptible body which weighs down the soul.' In fact, even though command be exercised over the vices it is assuredly not by any means without a conflict [*sine conflictu*]."

40. Augustine continues,

> But in that final peace, to which this justice must be referred and for the sake of which it must be possessed, since nature will be healed by immortality and incorruption

and difficulty will give way to peace in the completion of the conquest of the vices, which are extirpated. Human wholeness is accomplished in the resulting harmony of a way of salvation open to all.

In providing a universal way of salvation for all men, Christianity overcomes the division between the philosophic few and the nonphilosophic many. Through the incarnation, passion, death, and resurrection of Christ, the simple are granted a way to love wisdom that does not exceed their natural capacities and the wise are freed from their pride and from the necessity of lying to the multitude and submitting to humiliating rites honoring deities they know to be false. The advanced believer does not need to fear harming the many in speaking the truth of the Gospel or to fear for his safety, both because the simple believers will have some reliable assurance that the advanced believer shares the same faith with them and because the advanced believer knows that death in the service of the truth is a noble act of sanctity that will purify him further and make him prepared to enter communion with God in eternal life.

and will have no vices, and nothing at all, in ourselves or in any other will be in conflict with any one of us, there will be no need for reason to rule vices that will not exist. Instead, God will rule man, the soul will rule the body and the sweetness and ease of obedience will be as great as our felicity in living and reigning.

In illa uero pace finali, quo referenda et cuius adipiscendae causa habenda est ista iustitia, quoniam sanata inmortalitate atque incorruptione natura uitia non habebit nec unicuique nostrum uel ab alio uel a se ipso quippiam repugnabit, non opus erit ut ratio uitiis, quae nulla erunt, imperet; sed imperabit Deus homini, animus corpori, tantaque ibi erit oboediendi suauitas et facilitas, quanta uiuendi regnandique felicitas. (Ibid., 19.27. My translation)

Part III

THE UNIVERSAL WAY OF SALVATION AND
AUGUSTINE HIMSELF

Chapter 10

HUMAN WHOLENESS IN THE *CONFESSIONS*

The universal way of salvation unites every human type, in principle, through the mediation of the Incarnate Word. In previous chapters, the ways in which the way of salvation offered in Christ operates to bring together the few and the many has been explored. In addition to operating among human beings, Christ's universal way of salvation also operates in and through human beings. The internal integration of this particular human being and the integration of this particular human being into the body of Christ are linked intimately. Both integrations happen as part of the same movement of grace. Whereas, for instance, the soteriological paradigm of Porphyry only sought to cleanse a human being's constituent parts piecemeal, "Augustine argues," Simmons observes, "that Christ alone cleanses each of a human being's constituent parts, body, soul, and spirit, at the same time, and not by separate means as Porphyry taught."[1] In the following chapters, therefore, attention will turn from an exploration of the ways in which the universal way of salvation operates among men primarily through a reading of select parts of the *City of God*, to the ways in which Christ's universal way of salvation operates within a man—namely, within the man Augustine of Hippo—through a reading of select parts of the *Confessions*. Ignorance and difficulty in the *Confessions* will be examined in four sections. The first will provide a brief overview of the effects of ignorance and difficulty in Augustine's early life and Manichean stage as Augustine tells it in Books 1–4 of the *Confessions*. The second examines Augustine's intellectual conversion, in which, through reading the "books of the Platonists,"[2] Augustine is able to conceive of a spiritual substance, thereby freeing him from the crude dualism of Manicheanism and the unreasonable skepticism of the Academics. The third will explicate the ways in which philosophy helps Augustine to overcome the effects of ignorance and difficulty, and the ways in which Augustine is still left bound by ignorance and difficulty. The fourth will examine Augustine's religious conversion, in which Augustine humbly acknowledges his sins, asks for the Savior's help, and is given the strength to overcome his ignorance and difficulty insofar as it is possible in this life.

1. Simmons, *Universal Salvation*, 107.
2. Platonicorum libros. *Conf.*, 7.9.13.

From the time Augustine reads Cicero's *Hortensius* in his nineteenth year, he says that his affection was changed from bodily pleasure and vain honors to wisdom.[3] Yet for all his learning, Augustine finds that philosophy is not able to grant him what he most desires: complete freedom to pursue wisdom and the sustained contemplation of God. He finds that carnal custom (*consuetudo carnalis*),[4] his share in the inheritance of original sin, weighs him down and prevents him from living a life seeking wisdom. Carnal custom accounts for the other "law in my members"[5] St. Paul talks about. His will is divided between love for eternal and temporal goods, preventing him from making the full act of will that is necessary to abandon the worldly way of life that he finds so unsatisfying and that makes him frustrated and miserable. In the *Confessions*, therefore, the *consuetudo carnalis* sums up ignorance and difficulty under one heading.

As a result of the punishment of ignorance, Augustine is unable to distinguish what is false from what is true. He is unable to conceive of an incorporeal substance and is therefore unable to distinguish corporeal from incorporeal. Augustine explains that his inability to conceive of an incorporeal substance is due to the distraction among lower things imposed on him by the *consuetudo carnalis*, which causes him to mistake his mind for another material thing and to imagine God as limited by extension and duration. Augustine's ignorance and difficulty make it impossible for him to pursue wisdom in a stable way and to free himself from the miserable, disordered love of temporal things. In order to pursue knowledge of God and the soul, Augustine must be able to clearly distinguish God and the soul from lower things and to distinguish the soul as the highest temporal thing from the eternal things of God. Augustine has to learn that his soul is different from and higher than his body, and that God in his eternity is different from and infinitely higher than temporal things, his soul included. If he does not, he would be condemned to repeat the same theoretical errors and remain enslaved by his worldly ways and the custom of the flesh, prevented from pursuing wisdom as he

---

3. Ibid., 3.4.8.
4. Ibid., 7.17.23. Carl G. Vaught observes,

In anticipation of his later reflections about the distortion of the will, Augustine identifies the weight to which he refers with "carnal habit." This is important; for if we assume that Augustine is simply a Neoplatonist, we might be tempted to identify the weight to which he calls our attention with the body and with the evil that derives from the fact that the soul falls into it. However, in referring to habit as the source of evil, the author of the *Confessions* points once more to a volitional analysis of the problem of evil, which is more obviously compatible with Christianity than with the Neoplatonic strand in his thinking that so many commentators have chosen to emphasize.

Carl G. Vaught, *Encounters with God in Augustine's* Confessions: *Books VII–IX* (Albany: State University of New York Press, 2004), 49.

5. Rom. 7:23.

desires. But he also needs to overcome his pride and submit to the ministrations of the humble savior, Jesus Christ, who condescends to appear in the flesh, in the midst of human affairs.

In the *Confessions*, Augustine tells how his slavery to the *consuetudo carnalis*, while inherited, is also freely chosen. The content of the *consuetudo carnalis* is Augustine's habitual preference of temporal goods over eternal goods,[6] which violates the eternal law according to which "it is just that everything be ordered in the highest degree."[7] He is able to distinguish between temporal and eternal goods only after his intellectual conversion under the tutelage of Platonist philosophers when he is finally able to conceive of an incorporeal substance. This watershed moment in Augustine's life shows him what has been the goal for all his striving: God, now understood as incorporeal substance and Creator. Augustine's conversion to the understanding of incorporeal substance also provides the decisive difference between his and Evodius' intellectual lives.[8] Before his intellectual conversion, Augustine is condemned to seeking wisdom among the Manichees, whom Augustine the author characterizes as a sect of proud men who believe in false fables. Philosophy helps him to distinguish the Manichean fables from the truth about the world and the soul by helping him to conceive of an incorporeal substance.[9] Augustine's philosophic conversion does not,

---

6. Kathleen Roberts Skerrett, apparently following Chadwick, misleadingly translates *consuetudo carnalis* as "sexual habit," and thereby misses the broader implications of the term. See Kathleen Roberts Skerrett, "*Consuetudo Carnalis* in Augustine's *Confessions*," *Journal of Religious Ethics*, vol. 3, no. 37 (2009), 495–512 at 497 and Augustine, *Confessions*, trans. Henry Chadwick (Oxford: Oxford University Press, 1992), 7.17.23. Wetzel notes that the *consuetudo carnalis*, at base, describes a situation in which there is a shift in "attention away from what is and toward what is not." James Wetzel, "The Question of *consuetudo carnalis* in Confessions 7.17.23," *Augustinian Studies* vol. 3, no. 2 (2000), 165–71 at 166. Wetzel's observation is much more adequate.

7. *Lib. arb.*, 1.6. See also *c. Faust.*, 22.27.

8. See Book 2 of *lib. arb.* and *quant.*

9. Fortin explains why a knowledge of the soul is so critical for Augustine, saying,

> The reason is simple. Anyone who would seek the truth must know something about the instrument with which he seeks. The goal of philosophy is self-knowledge, which the divine oracle enjoins upon us and without which the philosopher cannot give an adequate account of his own doings. Unlike Theodorus, the mathematician in Plato's *Theaetetus* whose science is unaccompanied by any awareness of his needs as a human being, the philosopher cannot remain blind to the reasons that motivate his quest for knowledge. He owes it to himself to gain an insight into the nature of the soul and therewith an understanding of its place within the whole, its relationship to the other beings in the universe, both above and below it, and the many factors which, unless one is aware of them, are liable to interfere with its operations, such as inveterate habits, unexamined opinions, and the promptings of a disordered appetite. (Fortin, *Birth of Philosophic Christianity*, 43)

however, heal his pride or overcome the *consuetudo carnalis*. Philosophy partially overcomes Augustine's ignorance but is not able to overcome his difficulty. His pride, which philosophy exacerbates by separating him from human affairs and abstracting him from temporal concerns, along with his divided will make it impossible for Augustine to pursue wisdom in a stable or habitual way. It is only when Augustine humbly accepts the grace of Christ and begins to desire baptism that he is able to overcome carnal habit and to be liberated from the punishments of ignorance and difficulty. The manner of liberation would be surprising to the pre-conversion Augustine. The gift of grace will soothe the pain of Augustine's alienation from the vision of God not by allowing him, in the midst of his earthly pilgrimage, to see God face to face in intellectual vision, but to be united to him in ways more appropriate to his earthly station: in faith and through bonds of love in the Church. The virtue of hope moderates Augustine's strivings by allowing him to recognize simultaneously that he is bound to God through faith and sacrament, but also that the full consummation of his desire for wisdom will be found in eternal life.

Subjection to the *consuetudo carnalis*, or carnal custom, inclines Augustine to various created goods over and against eternal goods. This divides his will and makes it "half-maimed (*semisauciam*)."[10] He is also not free to pursue what is good for him even if he is not ignorant as to what that is. Ignorance is overcome in vain if difficulty is not also overcome, for one who knows the good but cannot act for the good is still unable to attain the good. If affliction with ignorance and difficulty is the inescapable condition of all men by nature, strictly understood,[11] then overcoming them would be the same as overcoming nature, a humanly impossible task. If ignorance and difficulty have been earned as punishments, then there is some hope that the one who set the punishment may be able to help, which is precisely Augustine's claim.[12] Until sin is acknowledged and confessed, it is impossible for man to receive salvation from God. As Augustine says in the *De libero arbitrio*, what the will lost through misuse, it cannot replace through its own efforts.[13] Only God who created man can restore what he lost through sin. Once Augustine is humbled enough to accuse himself of his own sins, he can confess

---

10. *Conf.*, 8.8.19. This translation is from the more dramatic rendition offered by John K. Ryan. See: Augustine, *Confessions*, trans. John K. Ryan (New York: Image, 1960).

11. Rather than "*quodam modo naturaliter*," as Augustine puts it in *lib. arb.*, 3.18.177.

12. Rist argues, "Not that Augustine considers our 'penal' weakness itself to be sinful; rather it is a fault in human nature as we now experience it. Viciousness and sin arise when we assent to the temptations which this weakness presents and to the sweetness of the pleasures, and hence their 'weight,' to which we are all exposed." Rist, *Augustine*, 176. This is true enough in one sense, but Rist does not discuss the extended sense of sin which arises directly from the *consuetudo carnalis*, by which Augustine can accuse even his infant self of being a sinner. See *conf.*, 1.7.11.

13. See *lib. arb.*, 3.18.177–9.

his sins, pray for God's help, put on the whole Christ, and accept Christ's grace through baptism into the Church.[14]

Plato's *Phaedo* is at least partially an attempt to address what Augustine calls the problems of ignorance and difficulty. Comparing Plato's approach in the *Phaedo* to Augustine's approach brings out more clearly the difference Augustine thinks the Incarnation makes. In the *Phaedo*, which takes place dramatically in the shadow of Socrates' impending execution, Socrates' friends worry about what they will do in his absence. The dramatic movement of the dialogue makes it clear that Socrates' presence and teaching moderates their fear of death and hatred of argument, or *misologia*. Socrates' ministrations are described as incantations, which hold the fear of death and the hatred of arguments at bay. Only Socrates the philosopher, the dialogue implies, is able to face up to radical uncertainty regarding the individual's personal destiny beyond death. The nonphilosopher must be soothed by myths. Joseph Cropsey explains, "Philosophy, the musical art, speaking with the voice of the poet Socrates singing his swan song, thus relieves the pains of profoundest ignorance and of the fear of death, at the price of belief in the immortality of the soul and of the existence of the intelligible things in themselves."[15] Cropsey interprets two of Plato's signature teachings, the immortality of the soul and the intelligible forms, as poetic therapy for the many given by Socrates who, after all, claims in the *Apology of Socrates* that he is the city's greatest benefactor.[16] Cropsey notes one effect of the soothing song of the philosopher: "We sense that the solidity of Socrates' conclusions is affected by the weight of the questions that are left unaddressed by the philosopher chanting his song."[17] In the process of spinning out his therapeutic (but uncertain) incantations, Socrates is at pains to reorient his friends' piety away from the false beliefs in the gods as presented by the unphilosophic poets to the Good as presented by the poetic philosopher. Cropsey says that Socrates presents the notion that

> The coming into being of each thing is consummated in the participation of that thing in the cause of its being, that is, in the transcendent entity in which it participates in order to be the precise thing that it is (101C). Put otherwise, the *becoming* of each thing is governed by the *being* of the unchanging transempirical essence in which the thing "participates" at last, toward which it is so to speak drawn in the course of the process that we call becoming. The transempirical which resembles a final cause is what Socrates calls the cause of the thing whose becoming has been perfected. Everything that is, is and is what it is by reason of

---

14. Peter Brown observes that the capacity to ascend to God in Christianity, as opposed to Platonist ascent, "has been made available to the mass of men by an act of *popularis clementia*—that is, by the Incarnation of Christ and by the preservation of divine scriptures in a universal church." Brown, *Augustine of Hippo*, 106.
15. Cropsey, *Plato's World*, 192.
16. Socrates' incantations are analogous to Porphyry's recommendation of theurgy.
17. Cropsey, *Plato's World*, 195.

its cause, which is its end. It comes into being and becomes what it becomes in order to be what it comes to be. Its end is at its beginning and its beginning is of its end, alpha and omega, world without god ... On such terms, "good" bears a definition that perfectly reconciles the "goodness" of the whole with the god's abandonment of the whole to its natural disposition. We might see this as the replacement of theodicy by physiodicy. If cause defines good rather than good governing cause, we can do no better than to be resigned to what is as "good." Such a physiodicy or optimism offers the bittersweet consolation of seeing "the good" in the infinite chain of causes that brings bloodshed, wickedness, and calamity as well as genius, serenity, charity, and sacrifice. With little effort, the moral neutrality of nature can be converted into a benediction, perhaps as an invisible hand, a principle of population, a process of evolution, or an object of contemplation.[18]

Through his incantations, Socrates seeks to impart some of his own serenity in the face of death to his friends. The *Phaedo*'s teaching about resignation to evil, reflected in Plotinus' *Enneads* and Cicero's *Dream of Scipio* from *De Republica*, is precisely what Augustine seeks to overcome. The fear of death, Augustine argues, and the common but usually untutored outrage at evil are important signals that nature has been marred; death, after all, is the wage of sin.[19] What is needed is not resignation to evils, but confession of sins and the charitable will to oppose evil. For Augustine, the *Phaedo*'s physiodicy would be despair.

Augustine famously says at the beginning of his *Confessions*, "Thou hast made us for Thyself and our hearts are restless until they rest in Thee."[20] Man's restless heart is the result of his evil will, which separates him from God. Man is separated from God because he does not love God. As Augustine says a little later, "What rather am I to thee, that Thou shouldst demand my love and if I do not love Thee be angry and threaten such great woes? Surely not to love Thee is already a great woe."[21] Failure to love God is a great punishment because that failure shackles Augustine to the love of lower, temporal things, which cannot satisfy him and can only make him more and more miserable. The first three books of the *Confessions* cover Augustine's infancy, childhood, and youth. In each stage, he seeks happiness. But his search is tainted in each case by ignorance and difficulty. The source of Augustine's ignorance and difficulty is his prideful preference for lower things over higher things, and his sinful attachment to what is his own.[22] The choice to pursue

---

18. Ibid., 210.
19. Rom. 6:23. See also Manent, *Metamorphoses*, 289.
20. "Fecisti nos ad te et inquietum est cor nostrum, donec requiescat in te." *Conf.*, 1.1.1.
21. Ibid., 1.5.5.
22. N. Joseph Torchia notes,

The proud soul turns to a good proper to itself alone (*ad proprium*), desiring self-mastery and self-determination. But *superbia* introduces an additional difficulty: the proud soul directs itself to inferior levels of reality, choosing lesser goods as objects of

lower instead of higher things is proud because it is a preference for one's own will[23] over the wise order set up by God in which the higher ought to be preferred over the lower. To prefer the higher over the lower is therefore an act of humility, because it is a recognition of an order that is already given by God and is by no means a result of one's own actions or desires. The proud man, however, is not satisfied to conform himself to God's wisely given order, but rather seeks his own will. As Augustine remarks in *De libero artbitrio*, "Those who are happy, who also ought to be good, are not happy because they desire to live happily, which even evil men desire, but rather because they will to live rightly—which evil men do not."[24] To will to live rightly is to will to conform oneself to God's wisely given order. Augustine desires happiness, but he does not know the happy life; nor would he be able to choose it if he did know it. As he chooses in accord with his disordered inclinations, he adds voluntary consent to what he inherits without choice, the state of original sin all men receive from their first parents. As his evil choices build up vicious habits, his freedom contracts until his habits become a kind of necessity from which he can no longer deviate, let alone liberate himself. Fallen nature therefore brings with it fallen natural necessity. That being said, the restless heart, which man has because he fails to love God, is also the spur by which he can begin to seek God instead of the lower things he otherwise attempts to put into God's place. This is the character of punishment for wayfarers in Augustine's writings. Those punishments are certainly evil, but not unqualifiedly so: they hold out the possibility of openness to God's grace, repentance, and conversion.

The most significant event in young Augustine's time in Africa is his introduction to the pursuit of wisdom through Cicero's *Hortensius*.[25] The *Hortensius*, Augustine

> desire, devotion, and love. It exalts those things which it should rightfully govern and use as a means of attaining spiritual perfection and lasting happiness ... By shifting the soul's focus from God to oneself, *superbia* opens the individual to the pull of curiosity (the lust for experiential knowledge through the mediation of the bodily senses) and to the influence of carnal concupiscence (the lust for the gratification of the flesh). If the soul had not succumbed to *superbia*, it might never experience the lust of the eyes (*concupiscentia oculorum*) and the lust of the flesh (*concupiscentia carnis*).

N. Joseph Torchia, "St. Augustine's Treatment of *superbia* and Its Plotinian Affinities," *Augustinian Studies*, vol. 18 (1987), 66–80 at 66-7. Torchia might also have mentioned that pride, as disordered self-regard, opens the soul to the temptation of the pride of life, or *ambitio saeculi*, the disordered desire for temporal glory and honors. These three disordered desires are found in 1 Jn 2:16 and are also manifested narratively in the wilderness temptation of Christ in Mt. 4:1-11. For a succinct explanation of Augustine's utilization of these concepts in the *Confessions*, see Foley, "Glossary," 332–3.

23. Rist remarks, "Pride rejoices in private goods, and it is perverse self-love to identify what is common and for all with the private and therefore divisive." Rist, *Augustine*, 155.

24. *Lib. arb.*, 1.14.100–1.

25. Fortin comments on the influence of the Hortensius on the young Augustine:

remarks using striking language, "changed my affection, changed my prayers to You, O Lord, and gave me a new undertaking and desire. Suddenly I repented of the vanity I had hoped in, and with an incredible agitation of heart I longed after the immortality of wisdom."[26] Before Augustine's encounter with Cicero's *Hortensius*, his desire had been for goods lower than wisdom, for "earthly things (*terrenis*)."[27] Afterwards, he desires "the immortality of wisdom (*immortalitatem sapientiae*)."[28] His immediate falling in with the Manichees indicates otherwise. His affection may have been changed, but he was too ignorant and incontinent to pursue philosophy steadfastly *as a way of life*. Nor was his will healed. As Augustine says in *De libero arbitrio*,[29] one must not merely seek happiness, but also seek it rightly, which distinguishes the good man from the bad. Likewise, one must not merely seek wisdom, but seek it rightly, which distinguishes the philosopher from the believer of fables. In order to pursue philosophy, one must have both a changed affection and the steadfast will to pursue the object of that changed affection.[30] Augustine sought wisdom, but did not have enough of a grasp of wisdom to know how to seek it rightly.

> [*Hortensius*] held up the theoretical life as the highest human possibility and the philosopher as the highest human type. It thereby made a young and avid Augustine, who had more than his share of riot and high summer in the blood and for whom the familiar *cursus honorum* was the mandatory road to success, aware of the fact that one's whole life could be actuated, not by the love of pleasure, honor, or any of the other worldly goods to which the vast majority of human beings are drawn, but by that most unusual of all passions—a passion so rare that few people recognize it when they come face to face with it—the passion for the truth. (Fortin, *Birth of Philosophic Christianity*, 4)

26. "Mutavit affectum meum, et ad te ipsum, domine, mutavit preces meas, et vota ac desideria mea fecit alia. Veluit mihi repente omnis vana spes, et immortalitatem sapientiae concupiscebam aestu cordis incredibili." *Conf.*, 3.4.7. My translation.

27. Ibid., 3.4.8. My translation.

28. Ibid., 3.4.7. Yet it is too much to say, as Todd Breyfogle does, that Augustine's "soul was ripe for philosophy." Todd Breyfogle, "No Changing Nor Shadow," in *A Reader's Companion to Augustine's Confessions*, ed. Kim Paffenroth and Robert P. Kennedy (Louisville, KY: Westminster John Knox, 2003), 33–52 at 42. Vaught describes the situation astutely, noticing "the initial indeterminacy of wisdom" as it appears to the young Augustine. Carl G. Vaught, *The Journey Toward God in Augustine's* Confessions: *Books I–VI* (Albany: State University of New York Press, 2003), 76.

29. *Lib. arb.*, 1.14.100–1.

30. Breyfogle goes on to say, "His love had been dislodged—temporarily, yet decisively—from temporal to eternal things." Breyfogle, "'No Changing Nor Shadow,'" 42. But to call it decisive is to misunderstand Augustine's subsequent conversions in Books 5, 7, and 8, and to underestimate the disappointment with which Augustine looks back on this event years hence when he realizes that he has not been able steadfastly to live a life of philosophy. See, for example, *conf.*, 8.7.17.

Augustine lays out three choices for how he could proceed after his introduction to Cicero's *Hortensius*: First, to enter into a study of the Scriptures; second, to enter into a study of philosophy as presented in the *Hortensius*; third, to become a superstitious Manichean. The direction of his mind was turned toward wisdom, but he did not at that point know how to seek wisdom; all he knew, or suspected, was that "with [God] there is wisdom."[31] The contest among the three groups and the reasons for which the Manicheans initially won Augustine's loyalty reveal Augustine's character at the time. The three groups are divided in two ways as Augustine presents them: pride versus humility and falsehood versus truth. The Bible is humble in its presentation, while the Manicheans and the philosophers are proud. The Manicheans speak falsehoods not only of God but also of God's creation, while the philosophers and the Bible speak the truth. Manicheans are both false and proud, neither knowing the good nor inclining their devotees to do the good. They promised Augustine wisdom about God and, because of his ignorance about the nature of God, he was unable to answer their criticisms of Catholicism or to formulate answers to their perplexing questions. As Augustine relates,

> I did not know that other reality which truly is (*nesciebam enim aliud, uere quod est*), and through my own sharpness I let myself be taken in by fools, who deceived (*deceptoribus*) me with such questions as: "Whence comes evil?" "Is God bounded by a bodily shape and has he hair and nails?" And are those [patriarchs] to be esteemed righteous who had many wives at the same time and slew men and offered sacrifices of living animals? By all this my ignorance (*ignarus*) was much troubled, and it seemed to me that I was coming to the truth when I was in fact going away from it. I did not know that evil has no being of its own but is only an absence of good, so that it simply is not. How indeed should I see this, when the sight of my own eyes saw no deeper than bodies and the sight of my soul no deeper than images [*phantasma*] of bodies?[32]

As a result of his ignorance, he laments, "Alas, by what stages was I brought down to the deepest depths of the pit, giving myself needless labour and turmoil of spirit for want of the truth: in that I sought You ... not according to the understanding of the mind (*intellectum mentis*), by which you have set us above the beasts, but according to the sense of the flesh (*sensum carnis*)."[33] Augustine's inability to conceive of spiritual substance left him only carnal sense by which to judge.

---

31. Ibid., 3.4.8.
32. Ibid., 3.7.12.
33. Ibid., 3.6.11. Breyfogle astutely notices that Augustine's inability to conceive of spiritual substance is partially responsible for his repulsion by the Scriptures: "Having learned the lesson that eloquent words conveying substance are to be preferred to empty eloquence, Augustine has not yet learned to prefer spiritual substance, however inelegantly expressed." Breyfogle, "'No Changing Nor Shadow,'" 232, n. 37.

Augustine does not say explicitly in Book 3 why he chooses the Manicheans over philosophy, but the above passages give the answer: in order to say true things about God and creation, one has to be able to judge according to the *intellectum mentis*, which distinguishes between incorporeal and corporeal. Being unable to conceive of a spiritual substance at this point in his life, he is more readily inclined toward Manicheanism, by which he is "taken in,"[34] because it presents answers to his questions that flatter his pride but are not too difficult for his brilliant but untrained mind. Perhaps because of his upbringing, Augustine also tells the reader that he was somewhat suspicious of the *Hortensius* and the way of life it praises because of the absence of the name of Christ, an absence he did not find in the religion of the Manicheans.[35]

As for why Augustine does not choose to study the Bible and become a Christian, he says that he was too proud:

> So I resolved to make some study of the Sacred Scriptures and find what kind of books they were. But what I came upon was something not grasped by the proud, not revealed either to children, something utterly humble in the hearing but sublime in the doing, and shrouded deep in mystery. And I was not of the nature to enter into it or bend my neck to follow it. When I first read those Scriptures, I did not feel in the least what I have just said; they seemed to me unworthy to be compared with the majesty of Cicero. My conceit was repelled by their simplicity, and I had not the mind [*acies*] to penetrate into their depths. They were indeed of a nature to grow in your little ones. But I could not bear to be a little one; I was only swollen with pride, but to myself I seemed a very big man [*grandis*].[36]

---

34. *Conf.*, 3.7.12.
35. Ibid., 3.4.8.
36. Ibid., 3.5.9. O'Donnell remarks, "Augustine, falling in with that crowd [of Manicheans] in Carthage, had the feeling of being just a little ahead of his time and among the true elites of the world." James J. O'Donnell, *Augustine: A New Biography* (New York: Harper, 2005), 48. Michael C. McCarthy observes,

> The scriptural "books" circulating in fourth- and fifth-century North Africa constitute what we now call the "Old Latin" (*Vetus* Latina) version of the Bible, an exceedingly awkward and literal translation of the Septuagint from the late-second century. To someone of Augustine's rhetorical background, the "voice" of such books must have sounded very peculiar. The vulgar soul of the Latin marked a serious fall from the *Latinitas* cultivated by *rhetores* and *grammatici*, and we must not underestimate the effect of this distinctive speech either in the social identity of a unique religious community or in the psychic formation of a member of that community.

Michael C. McCarthy, "Augustine's Mixed Feelings: Vergil's *Aeneid* and the Psalms of David in the *Confessions*," *Harvard Theological Review*, vol. 102, no. 4 (October 2009), 453–79 at 468.

It is entirely possible that a humble Augustine who took up the Scriptures directly after reading *Hortensius* may have been able to find what he sought. As matters stood, the Augustine who thought of himself as a great fellow desired to read books that flattered his pretensions. Cicero's book attracted the proud Augustine to a noble way of life by appealing to his desire for wisdom—which at that point was intermingled with his pride—but did not transform him into the kind of man who could live well. The Bible attracts the humble and discloses its meaning only to the humble, winnowing the proud by demanding humility. The false but easier fables of the Manicheans were able to appear plausible to Augustine, since the crudity of the Manichean fables matched the crudity of his own mind at that point.

The Manicheans therefore won young Augustine's loyalty as he started out on his search for wisdom.[37] He chose neither philosophy nor Christianity because they demanded an intellectual excellence Augustine lacked and a humility he disdained. It was, therefore, a result of Augustine's own faults that he chose the Manicheans, whose superstitions were to make him ever more miserable. Augustine burns to find wisdom; instead, he receives "splendid phantasms (*phantasmata splendida*)."[38] Augustine's desire for wisdom, awakened by reading *Hortensius*, is cruelly frustrated as a punishment for his sins, as Augustine tells it. He says, "You punish the sins men commit against themselves, because though their sin is against You, they are wronging their own souls and their iniquity gives itself the lie."[39] The sufferings Augustine endured in his state of frustration as a Manichean spurred him on to look beyond the Manicheans and their carnal doctrines to find the truth. Augustine's restlessness eventually led him to take up

---

37. Fortin calls Augustine's "nine-year flirtation" with Manicheanism "implausible," "explained only by the fact that it promised a rational solution to his nagging intellectual perplexities." Fortin, *Birth of Philosophic Christianity*, 4. Fortin's interpretation stands in stark contrast to O'Donnell's, who even goes so far as to say that Augustine's flirtation with the Manichees was a "great love affair." O'Donnell, *Augustine: A New Biography*, 47. O'Donnell seems sympathetic to the view that, in light of his enthusiasm for Manicheanism early in life, it is rather his conversion to Christianity which may seem implausible. The disagreement between Fortin and O'Donnell can be settled on the basis of the importance Augustine assigns to the theoretical life.

38. *Conf.*, 3.6.10. My translation. A little later on at the end of Book 4, Augustine tells of his attempt to understand God by recourse to Aristotle's *Categories*. Augustine uses this as an occasion to illuminate his crudity of mind and to highlight his fundamental mistake: he cannot understand the difference between creator and creature. For an excellent discussion of this part of Augustine's intellectual problem, see Michael P. Foley, "Augustine, Aristotle, and the *Confessions*," *The Thomist*, vol. 67 (2003), 607–22.

39. "Hoc uindicas, quod in se homines perpetrant, quia etiam cum in te peccant, impie faciunt in animas suas." *Conf.*, 3.8.16.

the books of the philosophers. He is at least partially aware of his own intellectual failings and inability to judge according to the *intellectum mentis*, and thereby to live a life in philosophy. He therefore needs an intellectual conversion whereby he might be enabled to live according to wisdom—to become one of the few capable of treading Porphyry's most rarefied soteriological way.

Chapter 11

AUGUSTINE'S PHILOSOPHIC ASCENT

As mentioned in previous chapters, Simmons outlines three ways to salvation in the writing of Porphyry of Tyre: the way of the multitude through theurgy; the way of the neophyte philosopher through continence and the practice of moral virtue; and the way of the mature philosopher through rigorous, ascetical contemplation of the highest things. Each way corresponds to the part of the soul that dominates in the person in question: appetites, spiritedness, and reason. Augustine speaks in *City of God* primarily about the first and third ways. There are phases of his own life, as he narrates it in the *Confessions*, that correspond to those ways. His Manichean phase, which Augustine characterizes as a chasing after fables, corresponds to Porphyry's first way. The philosophic ascent accomplished under the tutelage of the *libri Platonicorum* in *conf.* 7 corresponds to the way of the mature philosopher.[1] In this chapter, Augustine's intellectual ascent, which can be considered a genuine conversion from phantasms (*phantasma*)[2] to reality (*id, quod est*),[3] will be explored.

The story of Augustine's intellectual conversion moves through several stages. First, he must be detached from Manicheanism and its superstitions. The agent of his detachment from Manicheanism is his study of natural philosophy, which gives Augustine the standards by which to discern knowledge from myth. Next, Augustine meets Ambrose, whose teaching on the spiritual sense of the Scriptures enables Augustine to judge that the tales contained in the Bible are able to be understood as true rather than as false fables. Finally, Augustine must directly confront the problem of evil. The solution to the problem of evil requires the distinction between being and nonbeing, the knowledge of nature and its

---

1. Interestingly enough, if Augustine can be said to have trodden something similar to the second way of Porphyry, the way of the Neophyte philosopher involving the practice of continence, it must be located in *conf.* 8, in which Augustine cannot make progress toward continence until he has been transformed by the grace of Christ through his reading of Paul's Letter to the Romans in the Milanese Garden and set on the path toward Baptism. The order Augustine presents himself as treading the Porphyrian ways is not the order in which Porphyry would have presented them.
2. *Conf.*, 7.17.23.
3. Ibid.

defects, and an understanding that the immaterial is not the material. Augustine's intellectual conversion consists in his genuinely metaphysical breakthrough to an understanding of intelligible substance. Augustine's intellectual conversion, his turning toward the light in terms of Plato's allegory of the cave, is a genuine and impressive accomplishment. But he does not find that it allows him finally to live happily, as had been his expectation since his reading of Cicero's *Hortensius* as a younger man because it both fails to address his divided will and also makes his pride worse. His intellectual conversion at least partially overcomes his ignorance but it does nothing to heal his difficulty. But without healing his difficulty, Augustine's intellectual conversion is unstable at best and at worst actually exacerbates his problems by bringing him so close to his goal but leaving him puffed up with pride and frustratingly without the strength to attain it consistently and reliably.[4]

Despite his pride and his errors, Augustine continued to have a real, if flawed, love for wisdom. When Augustine began to study natural philosophy, he started to compare their books to the books of the Manicheans. The divergence he noticed accomplished a final separation from the Manicheans. He says,

> Now I had read many works of the philosophers and retained a great deal in my memory, and I compared certain of these with the long-winded fables of the Manichees. What the philosophers taught seemed to me the more probable, though their power was limited to making judgment of this world and they could not pierce through to its Lord. For the Lord is high and looks on the low: and the proud he knows afar off.[5]

Augustine takes Mani, the founder of Manicheanism, to task for presumption. Mani, it seems, wrote widely on matters also considered by natural philosophy, especially on the heavens, but his writings on these matters were often incorrect and Augustine even mentions some evidence that Mani falsified astrological data.[6] Augustine observes, "Thus [Mani] had gone astray and spoken much of these things: to the sole end that he might be convicted of ignorance by those who had learned them aright, and so his incompetence upon other more abstruse matters could be readily judged."[7] Because Mani claimed divine authority,[8] if he were to be

---

4. Wetzel observes that, for Augustine, "We can be wretched in one of two ways. We can either lack what we want or we can have what we ought not to have wanted." Wetzel, *Augustine and the Limits of Virtue*, 45. Augustine's pain as he narrates it in Book 7 results from his new realization of what he ought to want and does not have.

5. *Conf.*, 5.3.3. See also Ps. 137:6.

6. See Brown, *Augustine of Hippo*, 56–7.

7. *Conf.*, 5.5.8.

8. Mani claimed that the Holy Spirit "was resident in him personally, with plenary authority." *Conf.*, 5.5.8. "*Auctoritate plenaria personaliter in se*."

shown to have taught falsely on one matter, his authority would be undermined on any matter on which he propounded a teaching.

Yet Augustine is also quick to censure the natural philosophers he favorably compares to the Manicheans. He notes, "Much that they say of the created universe is true, but they do not religiously seek the Truth, the architect of the created universe; so that they either do not find him, or if they find Him and know Him to be God, they do not honor Him as God or give Him thanks."[9] The Manicheans are worse than the natural philosophers because they do not even say true things about God's creation. There is even a hint in Augustine's censure that, like the Manicheans, the natural philosophers, or at least some of the natural philosophers, do not acknowledge a difference between their own substance and God. Augustine is at pains to say that knowledge of God in the absence of praise of God and thanksgiving offered to him is not pleasing to God. One who offers praise and thanksgiving to the true God but lacks erudition is happier than the learned but impious.[10] The distinction is important: one offers praise and thanksgiving only to persons. Augustine's criticism here is that these philosophers are not treating God as a person.

Augustine can find no one nearby to answer his questions adequately about the Manichean teachings he has begun to doubt. All of his Manichean friends assure him that Faustus, a Manichean bishop and sage, will be able to help him. But when Faustus himself comes, he is a massive disappointment. Augustine praises his eloquence but finds him unlearned. Unable to find anyone among the Manicheans to answer his questions, even the famous Faustus, he begins to abandon the sect and its teachings, although he did not separate "myself from them entirely; but simply, not finding anything better than the course upon which I had somehow or other stumbled, I decided to look no further for the time unless something more desirable should chance to appear."[11] Even though he is now liberated by the study of natural philosophy from the Manicheans' fables, Augustine is not freed from the main theoretical errors that had made the Manicheans attractive in the first place. First, he still thinks of God as a body.[12] Second, he is still unwilling to accuse

---

9. "Multa uera de creatura dicunt et ueritatem, creaturae artificem, non pie quaerunt et ideo non inueniunt, aut si inueniunt, cognoscentes deum non sicut deum honorant aut gratias agunt." Augustine, *Conf.*, 5.3.5.

10. Augustine's censure of the natural philosopher foreshadows the appearance of St. Anthony of the Desert and his monks in Book 8, who lack the knowledge of created things that the natural philosopher possesses, but live according to wisdom in a higher way through Christian discipleship.

11. *Conf.*, 5.7.13.

12. He laments,

It seemed to me degrading to believe that You had the shape of our human flesh and were circumscribed within the bodily outlines of our limbs. When I desired to think of my God, I could not think of Him save as a bodily magnitude, for it seemed

himself of wrongdoing, preferring instead to blame some erring part of his own nature lying out of his control and, therefore, responsibility.[13]

Having been liberated from the Manichean fables, Augustine is still proud and has not acquired much in the way of real wisdom. Now he turns to the skeptics: "The notion began to grow in me that the philosophers whom they call Academics were wiser than the rest, because they held that everything should be treated as matter of doubt and affirmed that no truth can be understood by men."[14] Augustine first fell victim to the Manicheans and their false tales, in which he gave assent to opinions too hastily, committing an intellectual vice of excess. Now, under the influence of the Academic skeptics, he commits the intellectual vice of defect by refusing to give his assent when it is reasonable, demanding of all opinions that they demonstrate the same degree of certainty as that present in mathematics. He remarks, "I held back my heart from accepting anything, fearing that I might fall once more, whereas in fact the hanging in suspense was more deadly."[15] Augustine has partially succumbed to what Plato calls *misologia* in the *Phaedo*.[16] According to Plato's Socrates, the danger is "when somebody trusts some argument to be true without the art of arguments, and then a little later the argument seems to him to be false, as it sometimes is and sometimes isn't, and this happens again and again with one argument after another. And, as you know, those who've spent their days in debate-arguments end up thinking they've become the wisest of men

> to me that what was not such was nothing at all: this indeed was the principal and practically sole cause of my inevitable error. (*Conf.*, 5.10.19)

"Multumque mihi turpe videbatur credere figuram te habere humanae carnis et membrorum nostrorum liniamentis corporalibus terminari. Et quoniam cum de deo meo cogitare uellem, cogitare nisi moles corporum non noueram—neque enim uidebatur mihi esse quidquam, quod tale non esset—ea maxima et prope sola causa erat ineuitabilis erroris mei."

13. "I still held the view that that it was not we that sinned, but some other nature sinning in us; and it pleased my pride to be beyond fault, and when I did any evil not to confess that I had done it, that You might heal my soul because I had sinned against You." *Conf.*, 5.10.18. "Adhuc enim mihi uidebatur non esse nos, qui peccamus, sed nescio quam aliam in nobis peccare naturam et delectabat superbiam meam extra culpam esse et, cum aliquid mali fecissem, non confiteri me fecisse, ut sanares animam meam, quoniam peccabat tibi." Wetzel describes the Manichean doctrine of the two souls as offering "a seductive avoidance of the need for theodicy." Wetzel, *Augustine and the Limits of Virtue*, 89.

14. *Conf.*, 5.10.19.

15. Ibid., 6.4.6. James J. O'Donnell comments, "Serious people now and then would argue that the suspension of imprudent belief represents an ascent rather than a descent." O'Donnell, *Augustine: A New Biography*, 43. No doubt this is true. What Augustine objects to retrospectively is the suspension of *prudent* belief.

16. Plato, *Phaedo*, 89d. Augustine's *Contra Academicos* is an extended argument against the skepticism he himself employed during this time, and a warning about the dangers of misology.

and that they alone have detected that there's nothing sound or stable—not in the realm of either practical matters *or* arguments—but all the things that *are* simply toss to and fro."[17] Augustine's experience with the Manicheans, in which he too quickly gave his assent to their false tales, made him suspicious not only of false tales, but of any opinion whatsoever, insofar as it is able to offer less certainty than mathematics. One who has succumbed to *misologia*, the *Phaedo* says, is in danger of blaming *logoi* rather than "his own artlessness" and, in his distress, is "only too pleased to push the blame off himself and onto the arguments, and from that moment on should finish out the rest of his life hating and reviling arguments and should be robbed of the truth and knowledge of the things that are."[18] While not yet in these dire straits, Augustine would be in danger of reaching them if he were to persist in his demand that the standard for all kinds of judgment be identical to the standards demanded in mathematics. Even though his study of natural philosophy has helped to liberate him from the false tales of the Manicheans, he has not moved closer to understanding his mind or God. The Manicheans had promised certainty about matters of religion and ridiculed Christians for relying on belief.[19] Augustine abandons Manicheanism as soon as he determines that the Manichean promise of certainty is foolish, although he retains his contempt for belief and desire for strict certainty. He explains, "By believing I might have been cured; for then the eye of my mind would have been clearer and so might in some way have been directed towards Your truth which abides for ever and knows no defect. But as usually happens, the man who has tried a bad doctor is afraid to trust even a good one; so it was with the health of my soul."[20] The poor physician of Manichean fables had disappointed him and so he distrusts the good physician, Christ, who demands faith. Augustine's ignorance leads him credulously to accept false Manichean tales as true; when he discovers their falsity, he abandons them. He had discovered one tale to be false, but not yet whether any opinions about God and the soul might be true. His pride, which had not at all been ameliorated by natural philosophy, still makes it difficult for him to bend his neck to belief.

At about the same time that Augustine starts to prefer the Academic skeptics, he also begins to listen to Ambrose of Milan expound the Scriptures. As a result of Ambrose's preaching, especially his use of the spiritual sense in interpreting the Old Testament,[21] Augustine becomes convinced that Manichean arguments against the Catholic faith based on accusations against the Old Testament do not compel. He

---

17. Plato, *Phaedo*, 90b–c. Cropsey remarks, "Misology is the hostility to reason harbored by those who incompetently accept and then renounce arguments with equal incontinence until they end vaunting as their wisdom that all is flux in reason and throughout all things." Cropsey, *Plato's World*, 200.

18. Plato, *Phaedo*, 90d.

19. See *util. cred.* 1.2 and *b. vita* 1.4. See also Rist, "Christian Philosophy," 206–7.

20. *Conf.*, 6.4.6.

21. For a helpful study of the influence of Ambrose on Augustine's ability to read the Old Testament fruitfully, see Cameron, *Christ Meets Me Everywhere*, 23–42.

says, "I began to see that the Catholic faith, for which I thought nothing could be said in the face of the Manichean objections, could be maintained on reasonable grounds: this especially after I had heard explained figuratively several passages of the Old Testament which had been a cause of death for me when taken literally."[22] Ambrose's preaching did not present Augustine with the certain evidence he was seeking, so he did not assent to the faith of the Church, but an obstacle was removed: one line of Manichean attack against the Catholic faith had been cut off.[23] Augustine had to learn from Ambrose to apply the rhetorical technique of accommodation of speech, a technique whereby a rhetor adapts his words for the capacity of a given audience, when interpreting the difficult passages of the Old Testament. God, too, acts as something of a rhetor in fashioning speech suitable to an audience (the ancient Israelites) who are quite different from Augustine's contemporary Romans. This shows Augustine that he had not been reading the Old Testament even with the degree of rigor that his own rhetorical training demands. Michael Cameron also rightly points out that Augustine's newfound ability to read the Bible spiritually preceded and prepared the way for his ability to conceive of spiritual substance.[24]

Gradually, belief began to seem more acceptable and necessary to Augustine. Augustine observes,

---

22. *Conf.*, 5.14.24. Peter Brown remarks about what attracted Augustine to the Manicheans:

> This "new" Christianity had sloughed off the Old Testament as unspiritual and disgusting. In such a Christianity, Christ did not need the witness of the Hebrew prophets: He spoke for Himself, directly to the soul, by His elevated message, by His Wisdom and His miracles. God needed no other altar than the mind, particularly a mind such as the young Augustine's: "A mind imbued with good arts and education." (Brown, *Augustine of Hippo*, 43)

As a result, Augustine's encounter with Ambrose ought not to be underestimated. Ambrose taught Augustine how to read the Old Testament spiritually and showed Augustine that he needed to be taught through the preaching of a holy bishop rather than relying on his own judgment. Augustine's own judgment had been insufficient to avoid gross errors about how to read the Scriptures despite Augustine's excellent education. An example of underestimating Ambrose's influence and the importance it played in Augustine's intellectual conversion is O'Donnell, who thinks it more likely Augustine was impressed with Ambrose's cultural sophistication and the aristocratic circles in which he moved rather than the excellence of his thought. See O'Donnell, *Augustine: A New Biography*, 54–5.

23. See *conf.* 5.14.25: "But because these philosophers were without the saving name of Christ, I refused utterly to commit the cure of my soul's sickness to them. Therefore, I determined to continue as a catechumen in the Catholic Church, commended to me by my parents, until something certain would enlighten me, by which I might direct my course."

24. See Cameron, *Christ Meets Me Everywhere*, 25–30.

I considered the countless things that I believed, although I had not seen them nor was I present when they took place, just as there were so many events in the history of peoples, so many things about places and cities that I had not seen, so many things about my friends, so many things with respect to physicians, so many things about countless other men, which, unless we were to believe, we would be able to do nothing at all in this life.[25]

Things to be done fall within the purview of morals. Faith, or belief, Augustine points out, is necessary for the moral and political life.[26] Augustine has come to judge the Catholic faith to be more modest (*modestius*) and honest "in requiring things to be believed which could not be proved—whether they were in themselves provable though not by this or that person, or were not provable at all," rather than the Manicheans, who "derided credulity and made impossible promises of certain knowledge, and then called upon men to believe so many utterly fabulous and absurd things because they could not be demonstrated."[27] Acknowledging the modesty of the Catholic faith is in no way the same as assenting to its truth. Nevertheless, Augustine's approval of the faith on moral matters allows him to consider Catholicism in a new light. The Catholic faith does command belief in necessary things that are not demonstrable, either to some or to all, but Catholicism does not command demonstrably false or absurd beliefs, as the Manicheans do. Ambrose's teaching on the spiritual interpretation of Scripture was the key to Augustine's distinction between the Catholic faith and Manichean credulity. Catholicism is therefore capable, in Augustine's judgment, of upholding both justice and truth. It upholds justice by moderately commanding belief in things that are necessary for the living of a human life and it upholds truth by commanding only those things that do not offend reason by their demonstrable falsity.

In addition to his newfound approval of the Scriptures' moderation, Augustine also approves of the Scriptures' justice. He says,

> Indeed the authority of Scripture seemed to be more to be revered and more worthy of devoted faith in that it was at once a book that all could read and read easily, and yet preserved the majesty of its mystery in the deepest part

---

25. My translation. *Conf.*, 6.5.7.

26. "Ah, what great men are the Academic philosophers! Nothing certain can be discovered for the conduct of life! But no, we must search more diligently; we must not fall into despair." *Conf.* 6.11.18. Augustine also says elsewhere, "Many examples can be cited which show that absolutely nothing would remain intact in human society if we should determine to believe only what we can grasp by perception." Augustine, *The Advantage of Believing*, trans. Luanne Meagher, OSB, in *Writings of Augustine*, vol. 2, ed. Ludwig Schopp (New York: CIMA Publishing, 1947), 12.26. All translations from *util. cred.* are from Meagher.

27. *Conf.*, 6.5.7.

of its meaning: for it offers itself to all in the plainest words and the simplest expressions, yet demands the closest attention of the most serious minds. Thus it receives all within its welcoming arms, and at the same time brings a few direct to you by narrow ways: yet these few would be fewer still but for this twofold quality by which it stands so lofty in authority yet draws the multitude to its bosom by its holy lowliness.[28]

The many can safely read the Scriptures, but they also contain deeper secrets to which the many simple believers cannot gain access, yet which do not contradict what the simple can know. The Scriptures themselves, like Christ and his body the Church, constitute a kind of universal way.

Augustine had begun work as a teacher of rhetoric after he finished his schooling in Africa. Grouping his profession as teacher of rhetoric with his Manicheanism, Augustine tells what he and his associates pursued:

> I was astray myself and led others astray, was deceived and deceived others in various forms of self-assertion, publicly by the teaching of what are called the liberal arts, privately under the false name of religion; in the one proud, in the other superstitious, in both vain. On the one side of my life I pursued the emptiness of popular glory and the applause of spectators ... , on the other side I was striving to be made clean of all this same filth.[29]

Augustine's pride and superstition feed each other. At this point, Augustine says that what he most desires are wealth and marriage. He says, "Among those desires I suffered most bitter difficulties [*difficultates*], but your favor was so much the greater forasmuch as you permitted nothing to become sweet to me which was not you."[30] The pain and misery, the punishment of the *difficultates* resulting from his sinful pride manifested now in his pursuit of temporal goods apart from God, show that his liberation from false tales has not freed him from ignorance and

---

28.

Mihi illa uenerabilior et sacrosancta fide dignior apparebat auctoritas, quo et omnibus ad legendum esset in promptu et secreti sui dignitatem in intellectu profundiore seruaret, uerbis apertissimis et humillimo genere loquendi se cunctis praebens et exercens intentionem eorum, qui non sunt leues corde, ut exciperet omnes populari sinu et per angusta foramina paucos ad te traiceret, multo tamen plures, quam si nec tanto apice auctoritatis emineret nec turbas gremio sanctae humilitatis hauriret. (*Conf.*, 6.5.8)

29. "Seducebamur et seducebamus, falsi atque fallentes in uariis cupiditatibus et palam per doctrinas, quas liberales uocant, occulte autem falso nomine religionis, hic superbi, ibi superstitiosi, ubique uani, hac popularis gloriae sectantes inanitatem ... illac autem purgari nos ab istis sordibus expetentes." Ibid., 4.1.1.

30. Ibid., 6.6.9. My translation.

difficulty even on the eve of what should have been the highlight of his rhetorical career: an oration to the imperial court in Milan in praise of the emperor.

His speech in praise of the emperor would be filled with lies, which his audience would know were lies. The honor he would receive would be founded on lies, which makes him miserable. He even compares himself unfavorably with a drunk beggar, who has none of the honors, wealth, or marriage prospects Augustine has. He refuses to count his erudition in his favor, since "I got no joy from my learning, but sought only to please men by it ... For my glory was no truer than his joy, and it turned my head even more. That very night he would sleep off his drunkenness: but how often and often I had gone to bed and woken up with it, and would in the future go to bed with it and wake up with it."[31] The consequences of the drunk's base pursuit of drunkenness would vanish overnight: he would get sober again. The consequences of Augustine's supposedly noble pursuit of empty, temporal glory, on the other hand, results in a long-lasting corruption of his mind.

Augustine's horrifying realization that he is in a more miserable position than the drunken beggar is a key moment in his coming to self-knowledge. Recall, Augustine tells his friend Romanianus[32] that it is a worse punishment to endure ignorance and difficulty but not understand that ignorance and difficulty is unnatural. The scene with the drunken beggar shows Augustine coming to grips with the fact that the situation he finds himself in is an affliction that he deserves for his own bad choices. He describes God as acting "to bring home to me the realization of my misery," by presenting to him the contrast between the "pleasure of a temporary happiness" enjoyed by the beggar and the "utter misery" of Augustine who was about to give "an oration in praise of the Emperor in which I was to utter any number of lies to win the applause of people who knew they were lies."[33] He is starting to admit that he is responsible for his *difficultates*. He asks plaintively, "'How long shall these things be?' This question was ever on our lips, but for all that we did not give up our worldly ways, because we still saw no certitude which it was worth changing our way of life to grasp."[34] Augustine's observation shows the mutual reinforcement of ignorance and difficulty. In order for Augustine to embark on the pursuit of wisdom, he must relinquish worldly ways; but in order to relinquish worldly ways, he waits for something certain to appear. The increasing recognition of his afflictions narrated in Book 6 allows Augustine to reflect more honestly about his way of life and to take stock of himself. Remembering back to his introduction to philosophy by Cicero's *Hortensius*, Augustine is distressed, lamenting,

---

31. Ibid., 6.6.9–10. Augustine now desires *true* glory, a reversal of his Book 2 desire to receive glory from his vicious associates. See ibid., 2.3.5–8.

32. See *c. acad.*, 1.2.2.

33. *Conf.*, 6.6.9.

34. "'Quam diu haec?' Et hoc crebro dicebamus, et dicentes non relinquebamus ea, quia non elucebat certum aliquid, quod illis relictis apprehenderemus." My translation. Ibid., 6.10.17.

I was much exercised in mind as I remembered how long it was since that nineteenth year of my age in which I first felt the passion or true knowledge and resolved that when I found it I would give up all the empty hopes and lying follies of vain desires. And here I was going on for thirty, still sticking in the same mire, greedy for the enjoyment of things present though they ever eluded me and wasted my soul.[35]

The mere change in the direction of his mind has proven to be insufficient to acquire the wisdom he desires so that he can relinquish his worldly ways. He still loves temporal things and hesitates to pursue eternal things. His love for eternal things is not strong enough to withdraw him from his disordered love for temporal things, and his pride still prevents him from seeking the remedy in the Church.

Vacillating, Augustine even finds himself on the brink of agreeing with Epicurus about the nature of virtue. He says he "did not realize that it belonged to the very heart of my wretchedness to be so drowned and blinded (*demersus et caecus*) in it that I could not conceive that light of honor, and of beauty loved for its own sake, which the eye of the flesh (*oculus carnis*) does not see but only the innermost soul."[36] The standard of moral judgment, what Augustine calls the "lights of virtue" in *De libero arbitrio*, is precisely what Augustine does not know and is prevented from knowing by his ignorance of incorporeal substance. The eye of flesh cannot see the lights of virtue. Only the intellect can see them, but Augustine thus far is not able properly to distinguish between the body's sight and the mind's sight. His note on his sorry intellectual state provides the transition between Books 6 and 7. Book 6 treats of Augustine's liberation from Manicheanism by natural philosophy, subsequent descent into misology and his falling under the sway of Academic skepticism, and details his building frustration with his inability to forsake his worldly ways due to his inordinate love of temporal things and his weak love for eternal things or, in other words, his slavery to the *consuetudo carnalis*. Augustine has painted himself into a corner by eschewing faith while excessively raising the standards of assent and, self-servingly, making his abandonment of his worldly ways dependent on finding a wisdom capable of guiding his life that will pass his new, skeptic-influenced test of certainty. Book 7 starts with a rearticulation of the problem with which he ends Book 6, indicating that the quest to conceive an incorporeal substance will be the topic of Book 7. In Book 7, Augustine takes direct aim at his ignorance. With Augustine's introduction to the books of the Platonists, he finally finds a way to conceive an incorporeal substance, which allows him to contemplate the nature of his mind and to discover the incorporeal

---

35. "Ego maxime mirabar satagens et recolens, quam longum tempus esset ab undeuicensimo anno aetatis meae, quo feruere coeperam studio sapientiae, disponens ea inuenta relinquere omnes uanarum cupiditatum spes inanes et insanias mendaces. Et ecce iam tricenariam aetatem gerebam in eodem luto haesitans auiditate fruendi praesentibus fugientibus et dissipantibus me." Ibid., 6.11.18.

36. Ibid., 6.16.26. See also *lib. arb.*, 2.10.

truth above his mind by which his mind judges,[37] without making errors founded on an untutored materialism.

Book 7 narrates the breakthrough that allowed Augustine to achieve this lofty accomplishment. The ability to conceive of an incorporeal substance allows Augustine to distinguish the soul from lower, material things. Based on his ability to distinguish the soul from lower material things, what Augustine calls in *De libero arbitrio* middle and lower goods, respectively, Augustine is then able to distinguish the soul from God. The ability to make this latter distinction is the reason Augustine places the Platonists above all other philosophic sects in the *De ciuitate Dei* 8.1.[38] The distinction of lower corporeal things from the soul, and then the soul from God, is the foundation of the ability to distinguish temporal from eternal goods. The mind is able to base moral decisions on a solid ground only when temporal and eternal goods are known unconfusedly for what they are. Decisions about what is to be done must rest on knowledge of the Good, and knowledge of the Good must be specified by a ranking of the various, particular goods, and various particular goods must be understood in their relation to God, the universal Good and the source of all good things.[39] Decisions about which goods to pursue in preference over which other goods constitute the rational side of morality. Augustine's intellectual breakthrough in Book 7 allows Augustine to begin to rank goods well in accordance with wisdom about the whole.

Book 7 is divided into three parts. The first part details the effects of Augustine's ignorance about incorporeal substance, frustrating both his intellectual and moral life. The second part of Book 7 narrates Augustine's introduction to the books of the Platonists, which help Augustine finally to conceive an incorporeal substance. His intellectual breakthrough, in which he is finally able to discern a difference between eternal and temporal things, allows him to grasp the order of the whole creation and his own place in it;[40] it also provides a neat parallel to his introduction to Cicero's *Hortensius* back in Book 3. As Stephany puts it, "In Book 3, Augustine's reading of Cicero leads him to dedicate himself to the love of wisdom, and in

---

37. See *Conf.*, 7.17.23.

38. See also, inter alia, *doctr. chr.*, 2.40.60 for Augustine's preference of the Platonists.

39. Jesus Christ, as the eternal wisdom who enters time, brings together universal and particular in his person. But Augustine has not, as of Book 7, assented to the Catholic faith in Christ. The distinctions made by Catholic Christology rest on the kind of intellectual breakthrough that Augustine narrates in Book 7. See Thomas Williams's essay, "Augustine vs Plotinus: The Uniqueness of the Vision at Ostia," for an insightful argument about the necessity of Christ as mediator for Augustine's full conversion. See Thomas Williams, "Augustine vs Plotinus: The Uniqueness of the Vision at Ostia," in *Medieval Philosophy and the Classical Tradition: In Islam, Judaism and Christianity*, ed. John Inglis (London: Routledge, 2013), 169–81.

40. "For Augustine the world is an intelligible whole, not in its own being, to be sure, but in the divine intellect, and that it is rightly construed only when seen as a 'universe,' organized by a single unifying principle." Fortin, *Birth of Philosophic Christianity*, 104.

Book 7, his reading of the Platonists leads him to seek that wisdom within himself, to reject the Manichees and so to clear away all intellectual obstacles to his final conversion to Christianity."[41] This discovery helps him to come to an adequate grasp of evil as a privation and a realization that he suffers the evils of ignorance and difficulty as a punishment for the acts of his own will. The third part of Book 7 tells about the immediate effects of Augustine's intellectual discoveries, which, instead of allowing him to become more morally virtuous, end up further corrupting his moral life by exacerbating his pride. Book 7 ends with Augustine's miserable realization that his newfound knowledge has not made him fit to seek wisdom in a stable way and has not given him the moral strength to abandon his worldly ways.[42] He is still bound by the *consuetudo carnalis*, which he identifies as the "other law" "in my members" of which St. Paul speaks.[43] He now suffers more acutely because of the tantalizing glimpses of eternal things he is able to gain, which exacerbate his frustration because he cannot in his current state pursue those eternal things continently. The temporal things he continues to love inordinately become even harsher scourges; his lessened but persistent ignorance still binds him to temporal things and underscores the depth of his difficulty, manifesting his persistent slavery to lower things despite his newfound superior knowledge. At the end of Book 7, Augustine is finally ready to hear the words of St. Paul, "For though a man be delighted with the law of God according to the inward man, what shall he do about that other law in his members, fighting against the law of his mind and captivating him in the law of sin that is in his members?"[44] The liberation in mind he receives by virtue of the tutelage of the Platonists is an extraordinary accomplishment, but it is not enough to overcome this other law St. Paul and Augustine find in their members, the *consuetudo carnalis* or inheritance of original sin, and the accompanying twin punishments of ignorance and difficulty.

Augustine explores the link between his inability to conceive an incorporeal substance and his enslavement to the *consuetudo carnalis* or disordered love of temporal things in Book 7. Book 7 therefore provides the clearest indication of the link between ignorance and difficulty as they effect Augustine's soul, or between

---

41. William A. Stephany, "Thematic Structure in Augustine's *Confessions*," *Augustinian Studies*, vol. 20 (1989), 129–14 at 135. Stephany astutely calls Augustine's encounters with Cicero and the books of the Platonists the two "intermediate plateaus in his spiritual ascent." Ibid.

42. Matthew L. Lamb puts it concisely, saying that Augustine "might know the good but still could not live it." Lamb, "Wisdom Eschatology in Augustine and Aquinas," in *Aquinas the Augustinian*, ed. Michael Dauphinais, Barry David, and Matthew Levering (Washington, DC: Catholic University of America Press, 2007), 258–76 at 259.

43. Rom. 7:23.

44. "Etsi condelectetur homo legi dei secundum interiorem hominem, quid faciet de alia lege in membris suis repugnante legi mentis suae et se captiuum ducente in lege peccati, quae est in membris eius?" *Conf.*, 7.21.27.

Augustine's moral and theoretical problems. He says at the beginning of Book 7, "Thus I was so gross of mind[45]—not seeing even myself clearly—that whatever was not extended in space, either diffused or massed together or swollen out or having some such qualities or at least capable of having them, I thought must be nothing whatsoever."[46] To the pre-Platonic Augustine, the world is composed of a differentiated corporeal mass. There is no metaphysical distinction between corporeal and incorporeal things; there is no substantial distinction between God and creatures, at least that he can account for theoretically. There is no theoretically accountable distinction between time and eternity. There is, therefore, no theoretically sustainable distinction between body and soul, or man's soul and divine substance, and no way to rank eternal goods over temporal or creator over creature in any intelligible way. Augustine's piety militates against his theoretical errors: he thinks it unfitting to identify his own substance with God's substance, and he desires to distinguish between what is mutable and what is immutable. Without a genuinely metaphysical grasp of the different orders in creation, and the order of creator and creature or eternity and time, his piety and his understanding remain at loggerheads.

Augustine is perplexed by evil and its cause, but knows that he must avoid believing that God is mutable. He says, "I did not see, clear and unraveled, what was the cause of evil. Whatever that cause might be, I saw that no explanation would do which would force me to believe the immutable God mutable; for if I did that I should have been the very thing I was trying to find,"[47] that is, lest Augustine himself become evil through his false belief. He accuses the Manicheans of having undertaken the search for the cause of evil maliciously,[48] since they preferred to think of God's substance as being mutable—rather than that they themselves were responsible for their own evil desires and deeds. Out of a desire to understand God in the noblest way possible, Augustine attempts to understand how it could be that men are responsible for their own evil desires and deeds, this time in investigating an opinion he had heard about: that the free human will is the source of evil.[49] In order to understand how it is that man's free will is responsible for his evil deeds, Augustine needs an understanding of man's will as one of the goods he

---

45. As Foley points out, this is rendered literally, "fattened in heart," *incrassatus corde*. That rendering makes clear Augustine's biblical references, especially to Isa. 6:10, Mt. 13:15, and Acts 28:27. See Foley's note in Augustine, *Confessions*, trans. F. J. Sheed (Indianapolis, IN: Hackett, 2006), 117, n. 6.

46. "Ego itaque incrassatus corde nec mihimet ipsi uel ipse conspicuus, quidquid non per aliquanta spatia tenderetur uel diffunderetur uel conglobaretur uel tumeret uel tale aliquid caperet aut capere posset, nihil prorsus esse arbitrabar." *Conf.*, 7.1.2. Just as Augustine's confusion centers around what kind of greatness is indicated by "magnum," so Augustine plays with the ambiguity of what quantity might mean in the *De animae quantitate*.

47. Ibid., 7.3.4.

48. Ibid.

49. Ibid., 7.3.5. What Augustine says here is similar to what he says in the opening conversation of *lib. arb.*:

classes as "intermediate goods (*media bona*)" in the *lib. arb.*[50] What Augustine needs is knowledge of the nature of the human soul as a principle of moral agency. Knowledge of the soul's nature is what Augustine is trying to prod Evodius into acquiring in *De libero arbitrio* 3.1 when Augustine draws attention to the difference between the movement of a stone and the movement of the soul.[51] Augustine is incapable of seeing how man could be responsible for his evil desires and deeds and therefore he is incapable of seeing how man's creator is innocent of what the evil man does because he is ignorant of the incorporeal nature of the soul and, therefore, ignorant of the will as a principle of moral agency.

Augustine is left for the meantime in the position of holding that man is responsible for his own evil desires and deeds and simultaneously holding that God is innocent of man's evil desires and deeds but being unable to provide a theoretical account for his positions. All of the theoretical options he has explored have proven to be inadequate, and the theoretical option left on the table, that God the creator is responsible for man's evil desires and deeds, is impious. Perplexed, Augustine says, "By such thoughts I was cast down again and almost stifled; yet I was not brought down so far as the hell of that error, where no man confesses unto You, the error which holds rather than You suffer evil than that man does it."[52] Augustine is left tormented by the tension he feels between piety toward God and his theoretical ignorance, which did not allow him to affirm what he desired to believe about God. Augustine therefore tries to find the cause of evil. In searching, Augustine relates,

> I sought for the origin of evil, but I sought in an evil manner, and failed to see the evil that there was in my manner of enquiry. I ranged before the eyes of my mind the whole creation, both what we are able to see—earth and sea and air and stars and trees and mortal creatures; and what we cannot see—like the firmament of the heaven above, and all its angels and spiritual powers: though even these I imagined as if they were bodies disposed each in its own place. And I made one great mass of God's creation, distinguished according to the

---

> But if you know or believe that God is good (and it is not right to believe otherwise), God does not do evil. Also, if we admit that God is just (and it is sacrilege to deny this), He assigns rewards to the righteous and punishments to the wicked—punishments that are indeed evil for those who suffer them. Therefore, if no one suffers punishment unjustly (this too we must believe, since we believe that the universe is governed by divine Providence), God is the cause of the second kind of evil, but not of the first. (*Lib. arb.*, 1.1.1)

50. Ibid., 2.19.191.
51. Ibid., 3.1.6–13.
52. *Conf.*, 7.3.5. It is likely that Augustine's choice to speak of a hell of error where no one makes confession to God is meant to unite both the Manicheans and the philosophers, and among the philosophers, both the natural philosophers, the skeptics, and even the Platonists, none of whom makes "confession to" God.

kinds of bodies in it, whether they really were bodies, or only such bodies as I imagined spirits to be. I made it huge, not as huge as it is, which I had no means of knowing, but as huge as might be necessary, though in every direction finite. And I saw You, Lord, in every part containing and penetrating it, Yourself altogether infinite.[53]

Since Augustine's mind's eye is distracted among corporeal things, he is incapable of conceiving the infinite except as an infinity of duration or extent. He conjures an imaginary infinity of all created things, which God encompasses and soaks up like a great sponge. The remainder of Section 7.5 attests that Augustine's crude cosmology raised many more questions than it answered, and led to the ridiculous absurdity that a larger body would contain more of the divine substance than a smaller body.

Lacking answers to his pressing questions, Augustine describes himself as a man in torment. He says, "Such thoughts I revolved in my unhappy heart, which was further burdened and gnawed at by the fear that I should die without having found the truth."[54] In his perplexity and painful subjection to his disordered love of temporal things, Augustine feels his unhappiness keenly. He is subjected to "torments (*tormenta*)," "griefs (*contritiones*)," and "groaning (*gemitus*)" and is never able to find "relief (*laxamentum*)," a victim as he is of his "wound (*uulnere*)."[55] Augustine is left thoroughly miserable because he seeks rest among temporal things, which cannot grant rest to his restless heart. Yet if Augustine is correct that the bitterness of ignorance and difficulty "followed from your mercy,"[56] then Augustine's increasing awareness of his own misery is a hopeful sign. He is increasingly aware that his ignorance and difficulty are not, strictly speaking, natural and that his pain is an indication that his way of life is the cause of his unhappiness. God's mercy bestows the punishments of ignorance and difficulty, which are experienced as suffering in the transgressor of the eternal law. Augustine's increasing self-knowledge is a fruit of God's punishments. If ignorance and difficulty were natural, they would not be experienced as suffering by the sufferer. A realization of the penal condition under which he is subjected to ignorance and difficulty is the merciful assistance the transgressor needs in order to recognize his sufferings as penalties and his sins as sins, rather than an indication of the imperfection of nature or the incoherence of the order of the

---

53. Ibid., 7.5.7.

54. "Talia uoluebam pectore misero, ingrauidato curis mordacissimis de timore mortis et non inuenta ueritate." Ibid., 7.5.7. Rist notes that the "fear of death," according to Augustine, is a natural fear "in accordance with our second nature" which "is the fruit of our habits." Rist, *Augustine: Ancient Thought Baptized*, 138. In other words, fear of death is attendant upon our fallen nature. The fear of death is itself the strongest indication that human beings are inordinately attached to temporal things and prefer them over eternal things.

55. *Conf.*, 7.7.11. My translations.

56. "De misericordia tua sequebatur." My translation. Ibid., 6.10.17.

world. In other words, "You kept stirring me with your secret goad so that I should remain unquiet until You should become clear to the gaze of my soul."[57] Augustine refers to these *stimuli internis* as *proficiendi admonitio* and *perfectionis exordium*, an admonition to make progress and a beginning of perfection, in the De libero arbitrio.[58] These penalties are "for the sake of expiating the misery of the soul; but in [the descendants of Adam] however they are also the key to the ministry for the recovery of the body's incorruption."[59] The penal misery of Augustine's ignorance and difficulty spurs him on in his search for wisdom and continence.[60]

Augustine is now aware of his own misery, and is also convinced that the answers he seeks are to be found in faith in Christ.[61] Yet he is still proud. Therefore, Augustine says, "You brought in my way by means of a certain man—an incredibly conceited man—some books of the Platonists translated from Greek into Latin."[62] The books of the Platonists help Augustine at least partially to overcome his ignorance by helping him learn to conceive an incorporeal substance. Yet Augustine's introduction to the books of the Platonists, he says, was brought about by God because, "you willed to show me how You resist the proud and give grace to the humble, and with how great mercy You have shown men the way of humility in that the Word was made flesh and dwelt among men."[63] Even after learning how to conceive an incorporeal substance, Augustine is still not able to gain what he desires. He is not able to consummate the desire that was awakened in his soul when he read Cicero's *Hortensius* for the first time in his nineteenth year. What follows is Augustine's narration of his intellectual progress under the tutelage of those Neoplatonic books together with his increasing pride. His intellectual ascent turns his gaze toward the transcendence truth of metaphysics, which is genuinely

---

57. "Stimulis internis agitabas me ut impatiens essem donec mihi per interiorem aspectum certus esses." Ibid., 7.8.12. My translation. The "*interiorem aspectum*" is contrasted with the imagination, which arises from exterior things and external stimuli. The *interior aspectus* is the mind's sight, or intelligence.

58. *Lib. arb*., 3.20.191.

59. "Ad animi expendendam miseriam, in istis autem ianua ministerii ad reparandam corporis incorruptionem." My translation. Ibid., 3.20.194.

60. As Augustine says in the *lib. arb.*, "God gave to the soul the power of good works for duties that are toilsome; He gave it the way to faith for the blindness caused by forgetfulness. He also gave to every soul the power of judgment, by which it affirms that it must seek what, to its disadvantage, it does not know; that it must struggle patiently amidst toilsome duties, to overcome the difficulty of right action; and that it must beg the Creator for help in its endeavor." Ibid., 3.20.195–6.

61. "Yet the faith of your Christ, our Lord and Savior, the faith that is in the Catholic Church was firmly fixed within my heart." "Stabiliter tamen haerebat in corde meo in catholica ecclesia fides Christi tui, domini et saluatoris nostri." *Conf*., 7.5.7.

62. "Procurasti mihi per quendam hominem immanissimo typho turgidum quosdam Platonicorum libros ex graeca lingua in latinam uersos." *Conf*., 7.9.13.

63. Ibid.

where he needs to seek in order to find an answer to his theoretical questions about evil and the substance of God. But he also finds his pride exacerbated, which has the effect of taking him further from God even while he comes to know certain things about God—namely his relation to evil and his spiritual substance—better.

In the books of the Platonists, Augustine narrates, he finds all manner of true things about the nature of God and the soul. Augustine uses the language of the prologue to John's Gospel to compare and contrast the teaching of the Platonists to that of the Christian faith.[64] He seems to be using a deliberate rhetorical strategy to downplay the differences between Christianity and Neoplatonism about God himself, especially the Trinity, by choosing to focus on the difference between Neoplatonism and Christianity regarding the Incarnation.[65] Augustine finds that

---

64. Lamb remarks, "Augustine makes clear how his intellectual conversion moves far beyond what any of the Platonists could sustain. For when he narrates in Book VII of his *Confessions* what he has learned from the Platonists, he never quotes them but only Scripture." Matthew L. Lamb, *Eternity, Time, and the Life of Wisdom* (Naples, FL: Sapientia, 2007), 8. Augustine's approach underscores his claim that, whatever of use he found in the Neoplatonic books, he found—or could have found—in the Scriptures.

65. Augustine especially seems to mute his difference with the Neoplatonists on the topic of creation *ex nihilo*. As Vaught observes, "Neoplatonists and Christians agree that God makes the world in a suitably broad sense of the term, but this scarcely entitles us to assume that Augustine believes that the way this occurs is identical in the two cases." Vaught, *Encounters with God in Augustine's* Confessions: *Books VII–IX*, 39. Vaught later describes Augustine's commitment to creation *ex nihilo* as "unequivocal," in a way that is quite distinct from the Neoplatonic category of emanation. Ibid., 41. Vaught argues, "Augustine departs from Neoplatonism in the realization that both creation *ex nihilo* and the redemptive work of Christ are expressions of the grace of God without which the metaphysical chasm between God and the world could neither be generated nor mediated." Ibid. Then what is Augustine's purpose in muting this particular disagreement? What Augustine wants to do is to highlight the humility of God and his intimacy with his creation. Now, these things are part and parcel with the Christian doctrine of creation *ex nihilo*, but to understand how or why that is requires great deal of philosophical acumen, which might not be expected of the reasonably broad audience for whom Augustine is writing his *Confessions*. For an outstanding presentation of the metaphysics involved in this issue, see Robert Sokolowski's chapter, "The Incarnation and the Christian Distinction" in his *The God of Faith and Reason* (Washington, DC: Catholic University of America Press, 1995), 31–40. Sokolowski's chapter also gives a sense for how difficult these matters are. In the absence of something like Sokolowski's relatively difficult argument, the Christian doctrine of creation *ex nihilo* has the risk of making God seem even more distant from the world than the Neoplatonist doctrine of emanation. For this kind of effect, see Frank J. Sheed's attempt to explain creation from nothing in a more popular account, where he says, "The first effect of realizing that one is made of nothing is a kind of panic-stricken insecurity." Frank J. Sheed, *Theology and Sanity* (San Francisco: Ignatius Press, 1978), 23. In this context, since a focus on the Incarnation can do all the work necessary, Augustine wisely deems it acceptable to mute disagreements with the Neoplatonists about creation.

God is *verbum*, and that God the Word made all things; he finds that man's soul is not the light, that is, is not the standard of judgments of truth, but rather gives testimony to the light that is above it and made it; he reads that the Word of God is born of God and therefore coequal with God by nature; that wisdom remains with God and that men's souls are enlightened by participating in the wisdom that dwells with God. On the other hand, Augustine does not read anything about the humble condescension of God in mercifully accomplishing man's salvation: he finds no reference to the Incarnation, God's special condescension to a particular people in Israel, Christ's humble obedience unto the sacrificial death on the Cross, or that he died for the ungodly, or hid these things from the wise while revealing them to little ones. He finds no reference to God's meekness and humility, his forgiveness of sins, and his special care for men who are meek. In other words, as Augustine quotes Rom. 1:21-22, "And if they know God, they have not glorified him as God or given thanks: but became vain in their thoughts; and their foolish heart is darkened. Professing themselves to be wise they became fools."[66] Augustine's progress under the tutelage of the Platonic books is testament to the divine truth contained therein; the instability of his accomplishment is due to the fact that those books lack Christ's humanity and humility.[67] Only when Augustine's flesh is healed by the flesh of the Incarnate God will he be able to live according to the highest wisdom in a stable way.

While Augustine's genuine accomplishment is not sufficient to liberate him to pursue eternal things, his later religious conversion depends on his prior intellectual conversion.[68] The books of the Platonists allow Augustine to think of the soul without mistakenly importing corporeality into his contemplation of the nature of the soul. His understanding of the incorporeality of the soul allows him to understand that truth itself is incorporeal and stands above the mind, as the creator stands to the creature. Augustine says,

> Being admonished by all this to return to myself, I entered into my own depths, with You as my guide; and I was able to do it because You were my helper. I entered, and with the eye of my soul, such as it was, I saw Your unchangeable Light shining over that same eye of my soul, over my mind … . Nor was it above my mind as oil above the water it floats on, nor as the sky is above the earth; it

---

66. *Conf.*, 7.9.14.

67. They also lack a fulsome doctrine of creation. Frederick Crosson argues, "Contrary to the only way in which Cicero could conceive of it, the epiphany of the divine is not just an event within the whole, it is the whole itself as epiphany. The vehicle of God's presence *is* the created world, the world experienced as telling of God." Crosson, "Structure and Meaning in St. Augustine's *Confessions*," 92–3.

68. Lamb observes, "Only when his intellectual conversion was taken up into the grace of his conversion to Christ Jesus did the infinite spiritual reality of the Word Incarnate enable him to overcome the disordered desires that darkened and distracted his mind." Lamb, "Wisdom Eschatology," 260.

was above because it made me, and I was below because made by it. He who knows the truth knows that Light, and he that knows the Light knows eternity.[69]

His ability to conceive an incorporeal substance allows him to distinguish the incorporeal soul from corporeal things and to be able to understand the distinction between creator and creature; the ability to understand the distinction between creator and creature allows him to understand the difference between time and eternity. He no longer thinks of eternity as endless duration or infinity as endless extent. Augustine is now capable of approaching an understanding of the whole world as composed of various orders of goods and having been made by God.

In light of his newfound knowledge of the whole, Augustine is able to see that each thing in its order is good: higher things are better than lower things and the whole taken together as a whole is better even than the higher things taken by themselves. The nature of evil begins to become clear. Augustine realizes that, although certain things in creation do not agree with others, but taken in the context of the whole of reality, there is a higher-order wisdom in which all things find their proper place.[70] Since all things that exist, insofar as they exist, are good in their own order, evil cannot be a substance. Augustine consequently affirms, "When I now asked, What is iniquity, I realized that it was not a substance but a swerving of the will which is turned towards lower things and away from You, O God, who are the supreme substance: so that it casts away what is most inward to it and swells greedily for outward things."[71] Evil only comes about through a disruption of order, a disordered abuse of things in themselves good by the will of free creatures.

69.

Inde admonitus redire ad memet ipsum intraui in intima mea duce te et potui, quoniam factus es adiutor meus. Intraui et uidi qualicumque oculo animae meae supra eundem oculum animae meae, supra mentem meam lucem incommutabilem, non hanc uulgarem et conspicuam omni carni nec quasi ex eodem genere grandior erat, tamquam si ista multo multoque clarius clarescerbrt totumque occuparet magnitudine. Non hoc illa erat, sed aliud, aliud ualde ab istis omnibus. Nec ita erat supra mentem meam, sicut oleum super aquam nec sicut caelum super terram, sed superior, quia ipsa fecit me, et ego inferior, quia factus ab ea. Qui nouit ueritatem, nouit eam, et qui nouit eam, nouit aeternitatem. (*Conf.* 7.10.16)

Lamb admonishes, "Note the crucial discovery of Augustine that while his mind generated endless images, it was not itself an image but a spiritual presence or light." Matthew L. Lamb, *Eternity, Time, and the Life of Wisdom*, 35, n. 16.

70. *Conf.*, 7.13.19. See also *lib. arb.*, 2.19.191–2.

71. "Quaesiui, quid esset iniquitas, et non inueni substantiam, sed a summa substantia, te deo, detortae in infima uoluntatis peruersitatem proicientis intima sua et tumescentis foras." *Conf.*, 7.16.22.

Augustine has finally attained some part of what he desired when Cicero's *Hortensius* set him ablaze with love of wisdom. Delighted, Augustine observes, "I marveled that now I loved you, not a phantasm instead of you."[72] Augustine is able to attempt to cling to God, where before all he could do was to try to embrace a phantasm constructed by his own imaginations and carnal understanding. Augustine narrates his philosophic ascent:

> Thus by stages I passed from bodies to the soul which uses the body for its perceiving, and from this to the soul's inner power, to which the body's senses present external things, as indeed the beasts are able; and from there I passed on to the reasoning power, to which is referred for judgment what is received from the body's senses. This too realized that it was mutable in me, and rose to its own understanding. It withdrew my thought from its habitual way. Abstracting from the confused crowds of phantasms that it might find what light suffused it, when with utter certainty it cried aloud that the immutable was to be preferred to the mutable, and how it had come to know the immutable itself: for if it had not come to some knowledge of the immutable, it could not have known it as certainly preferable to the mutable. Thus in the thrust of a trembling glance my mind arrived at That Which Is.[73]

This is the moment Augustine has been striving for. He took a long, circuitous journey through Manichaeism because he was incapable of judging according to *intellectum mentis* in his nineteenth year after reading Cicero's *Hortensius*. His

---

72. "Mirabar, quod iam te amabam, non pro te phantasma." My translation. *Conf.*, 7.17.23.

73.

Ita gradatim a corporibus ad sentientem per corpus animam atque inde ad eius interiorem uim, cui sensus corporis exteriora nuntiaret, et quousque possunt bestiae, atque inde rursus ad ratiocinantem potentiam, ad quam refertur iudicandum, quod sumitur a sensibus corporis; quae se quoque in me comperiens mutabilem erexit se ad intellegentiam suam et abduxit cogitationem a consuetudine, subtrahens se contradicentibus turbis phantasmatum, ut inueniret quo lumine aspergeretur, cum sine ulla dubitatione clamaret incommutabile praeferendum esse mutabili, unde nosset ipsum incommutabile—quod nisi aliquo modo nosset, nullo modo illud mutabili certa praeponeret—et peruenit ad id, quod est in ictu trepidantis aspectus. (*Conf.*, 7.17.23)

Lamb maintains that the grasp of *id, quod est* indicates Augustine's emphasis of the importance of judgment as second act of the mind for the life in philosophy. The ability to grasp being, which is the object of the science of metaphysics, is what sets wisdom apart from fable. Not merely understanding, but judgment that the understanding is true, is key to seeing Augustine's breakthrough for what it is. Lamb, *Eternity, Time, and the Life of Wisdom*, 31–2.

arrival at "that which is" signals that he has overcome that intellectual problem. The moment of triumph, however, reverses quickly as Augustine finds,

> Yet I did not stably (*non stabam*) enjoy my God, but was ravished to You by Your beauty, yet soon was torn away from You again by my own weight, and fell again with torment to lower things. Carnal habit (*consuetudo carnalis*) was that weight. Yet the memory of You remained with me and I knew without doubt that it was You to whom I should cleave, though I was not yet such as could cleave to You.[74]

What should have been the climax turns into an anticlimax. The *consuetudo carnalis* defeats Augustine. Once again, he is punished with ignorance and difficulty for his disordered love of temporal things. Now his defeat is even more bitter, since he has been able at least to glimpse that which he desires. Now he experiences the misery of knowing what he wants, but also knowing that he is not in any condition to attain it. Augustine's intellectual conversion, accomplished with the help of the Platonic books, has accomplished a partial liberation in him insofar as he has been liberated from a corporeal understanding of incorporeal things. Augustine as a whole man, however, body and soul, passions and mind, has not been set free from carnal custom.

Augustine emphasizes the frustration of his situation, saying, "But I lacked the strength to hold my gaze fixed, and my weakness was beaten back again so that I returned to my old habits, bearing nothing with me but a memory of delight and a desire as for something of which I had caught the fragrance but which I had not yet the strength to eat."[75] Augustine needs to imitate the humility of Christ. But he has yet to acknowledge Jesus as the Incarnate Word: "I was not yet lowly enough to hold the lowly Jesus as my God, nor did I know what lesson His embracing of our weakness was to teach."[76] As yet, he still only acknowledges the divinity of the

---

74. *Conf.*, 7.17.23. Lamb remarks, "He immediately adds that this discovery was not yet habitual. For he could not live the theoretic or contemplative life demanded by the discovery until Christ gave him the strength to do so." Lamb, *Eternity, Time, and the Life of Wisdom*, 32.

75. *Conf.*, 7.17.23. Vaught mentions that Augustine's failure suggests "that he must undergo a further stage of development that transcends intellectual apprehension." Vaught, *Encounters with God in Augustine's Confessions: Books VII–IX*, 52.

76. *Conf.*, 7.18.24. Meconi explains,

> The Divine, born of a woman, participates in our nature so that we might more fully participate in Him as brothers and sisters. Christ came to partake of our fallen humanity not out of His greatness but on account of our wretchedness. This self-abasement of the divine is something Augustine's Neoplatonism could never have articulated on its own. No Platonist could ever hold that the Forms actually condescend to participate in this world of mutable particulars, an insight which

Word and not his humble humanity. He begins to grow proud as he progresses in knowledge of the higher things. He says,

> I was at a standstill, yet I felt what through the darkness of my mind I was not able actually to see; I was certain that You are and that You are infinite, but not as being diffused through space whether finite or infinite: that You truly are and are ever the same, not in any part or by any motion different or otherwise; and I knew that all other things are from You from the simple fact that they are at all. Of these things I was utterly certain, yet I had not the strength to enjoy You. I talked away as if I knew a great deal; but if I had not sought the way to You in Christ our Savior, I would have come not to instruction but to destruction. For I had begun to wish to appear wise, and this indeed was the fullness of my punishment; and I did not weep for my state, but was badly puffed up with my knowledge.[77]

The fullness of his punishment comes with being puffed up with knowledge. This is a fitting punishment because it flows out of what he has wanted so much: wisdom. It is a punishment because it almost perfectly closes him off from the humility he really needs in order to be saved. It appears to him that his quest is at an end: he has been able to grasp That Which Is. But he is not able to enjoy his contemplations! His disordered love for lower things weighs him down, and his contemplations cannot heal him. What he needs is a wholistic integration of his loves and himself. But the ascent to That Which Is he makes under the tutelage of the *libri platonicorum* does not suffice. Augustine still loves God, the supreme substance, in a way that competes with his love of lower things. The ascent he has tried to undertake, it can be presumed, grasps God *only* as supreme and therefore above, transcendent, having no way to understand God's presence in creation, including in the lower things. That is why Augustine's emphasis on the Incarnation and the humility of the Word in becoming incarnate being missing from the *libri platonicorum* is so crucial. And that is what Augustine will address next.

It may help to pause here for a moment to dig more deeply into what Augustine has described in his philosophic ascent. It seems to me that what Augustine illustrates in these chapters gets to the heart of the philosophic way of life and accords well with what Manent calls "the portrait of the superhuman philosopher."[78] This portrait shows us, according to Manent, a philosopher who "turns away from human things."[79] Manent explains this figure of the philosopher further, saying, "Man, or at least a certain type of man, is capable of distancing

---

prepares the way for Augustine's full acceptance of Christ's dual nature. (Meconi, "Incarnation and Participation in St. Augustine's *Confessions*," 61–75 at 71)

77. *Conf.*, 7.20.26.

78. Pierre Manent, *Seeing Things Politically*, trans. Ralph C. Hancock (South Bend, IN: St. Augustine's Press, 2015), 59.

79. Ibid., 56.

himself from the urgent interests of human life, of suspending these interests in order to raise questions to which he will not find certain answers, and ultimately of suspending and, as it were, dismissing the fear of death in order to reflect on the articulations of being."[80] This is why the context of Augustine's ascent is important. His ascent is by abstraction, by removing himself from the necessities and interests of human life. His ascent is accomplished alone and with no references to his body. When he is finished with his ascent, that is also why he characterizes the aftermath as a turning away and a going back. This also explains why his ascent, abortive as it was, has the effects on him that it does: namely, why his ascent increases his pride, or "puffs him up," in Pauline language.[81] Pride, or *superbia*, is essentially a holding of oneself over and against. That stance requires a certain vertical distance, which Augustine now has in spades through his philosophic ascent. His philosophic activity distances himself from the urgent interests of human life, including those with whom he shares human life.[82] The very life in philosophy provides the

---

80. Ibid., 57. Fortin comments,

[The philosophers'] model is Socrates, whose aloofness from the affairs of the city is a better index of his fundamental disposition than his public declarations of piety or his professed concern for the welfare of Athens. If Socrates can boast of his ignorance, it is not because he is humble but because he has learned what true knowledge is and can distinguish it from its opposite ... Philosophers follow their personal bent, associating with their own kind and mingling with others only as necessity dictates. A gulf separates their arrogance (*praesumptio*) from the humble "confession" of the believer. (Fortin, *Birth of Philosophic Christianity*, 8)

81. For Brian Harding, "In Augustine's eyes, the philosophical project is largely a pursuit of glory; even when the philosopher makes a show of disdaining glory (we may think of Diogenes the Cynic) that is a backhanded way of striving after it." Brian Harding, *Augustine and Roman Virtue* (London: Continuum, 2008), 106. Augustine nowhere provides a clearer picture of what he takes the philosophic project to be than in the philosophic ascent of Book 7. But glory does not enter into the picture until afterwards. Augustine's objective, and we may say the objective of the "philosophic project," is knowledge, especially of the highest things. That is not to say that there is no link between philosophy and glory. John von Heyking puts things more carefully, saying, "Philosophers glory in wisdom." Von Heyking, *Augustine and Politics*, 29. But even here, it would be better to say that blameworthy glory-seeking among philosophers happens when philosophers glory in *their own* wisdom, as something they themselves possess. Glorying in highest wisdom is not something Augustine would have blamed. As von Heyking himself points out, Augustine says that "among the disciples of Socrates, and not however without merit, who shone with a most outstanding glory [*Gloria claruit*] so that he overshadowed all the others, was Plato." *Ciu. Dei*, 8.4. My translation. In other words, "Plato's glory was just." Von Heyking, *Augustine and Politics*, 30.

82. "Augustine reads the tendency to scapegoat the body," Roberts Ogle argues, "as an attempt to shift the blame to something other, something with which philosophers do not identify." Roberts Ogle, *Earthly City*, 93. See also *ciu. Dei,* 14.5.

opportunity for his pride to increase.[83] That also means, of course, that his act of distancing functions to remove himself from the parts of himself that are more taken up with the urgent affairs of human life: namely, his body and the lower powers of his soul;[84] but it will be the vices associated with those lower parts of him that will remain the most tenacious.

What Augustine the author has been telling us he has been seeking since the beginning of the *Confessions* is a way to collect himself back from being scattered among the many, a reintegration. But now, in turning away from the many and toward the One under the tutelage of the *libri Platonicorum*, he has not accomplished anything of the sort. In fact, what he has accomplished is an even more severe disintegration both in himself and with his fellow human beings through his pride. In short, he ascends (pride) first when he needs first to descend (humility). He can only ascend to God after he has first become humble. God himself models the correct order of descent followed by ascent in the Incarnation. The philosophic way of ascent to contemplate the highest things has turned out not to be salvific after all. What Augustine needs in order to be whole is a way of approaching the One that does not distance him from the human, a way of communion with God that also incorporates his neighbor. The abortive philosophic ascent of Book 7 foreshadows another ascent that Augustine narrates in Book 9 after his conversion, to which attention will turn a little later. Book 8 narrates Augustine's moral training in humility and continence. What Augustine finds he needs is a way of salvation that incorporates the whole of his being; only this type of way of salvation can also and simultaneously incorporate him into a universal way with other men—including other types of men than himself.

---

83. J. Patout Burns lists hatred of the body created by God and demonic glorying "in the complacency of their minds" as ways in which philosophic pride subverts philosophic accomplishment. See Burns, "Augustine on the Origin and Progress of Evil," *The Journal of Religious Ethics*, vol. 16, no. 1 (Spring 1988), 9–27 at 23–4.

84. Cavadini argues, "Platonism nurtures pride by imagining salvation as fleeing from the body, that is, as something I, not being in any essential way linked to the body, can do on my own." Cavadini, "Ideology and Solidarity," 106.

Chapter 12

SALVATION FOR THE PHILOSOPHER AND THE NONPHILOSOPHER: THE CASES OF VICTORINUS AND ANTHONY

Augustine's intellectual conversion, abortive and frustratingly anticlimactic as it turned out to be for him, was a necessary preparation for his religious conversion. His ignorance and difficulty are rooted in the same underlying problem: sin. Trying to solve his problems piecemeal without addressing sin cannot but fail. He cannot live a happy life by hyperfocusing on his mind, even if the mind is the highest part of him. He cannot live a happy life if he attempts to study God as an object rather than to love him as a person. For these reasons, Augustine finds Porphyry's way of salvation for the mature philosopher wanting. Augustine needs to have his divided will, by which he loves temporal things and eternal things incontinently and in conflict with each other, healed. His loves need to be brought together into one, full act that can encompass all of the good things to which he is drawn. He needs a way to harmonize his body and soul, to heal his broken relationships, and to establish communion with God. For that, he will need the grace of Christ and a humility that beats back his alienating pride. For that, he needs a genuinely universal way of salvation.

Only now, Augustine emphasizes, is he prepared to read St. Paul. As a younger man, before his intellectual conversion, he misunderstood what the Catholic faith holds about God and the soul. After his intellectual conversion, when he begins to be able to distinguish between material and incorporeal things, created and uncreated things, time and eternity, he is able to understand the exaltedness of the Scriptures' teaching. He now finds in the Scriptures pure and noble teachings about God and the soul in accord with reason. Augustine has now had the experience of overcoming his own ignorance to a degree, but he is still prevented from attaining what he desires, that is, liberation from disordered love of temporal things and freedom to seek wisdom in a stable, habitual way. He knows that he is too weak to seek wisdom and the knowledge of God by himself, and he acknowledges that

> I set about finding a way to gain the strength that was necessary for enjoying You. And I could not find it until I embraced the Mediator between God and man, the man Christ Jesus, who is over all things, God blessed forever, who was calling unto me and saying, I am the Way, the Truth, and the Life; and who

brought into union with our nature that Food which I lacked the strength to take: for the Word was made flesh that Your Wisdom, by which You created all things, might give suck to our souls' infancy.[1]

Augustine merges language relating to each of the three ways of salvation: he utilizes the concern for the body and the senses present in the first way for the multitude; he utilizes the language of strength that characterizes the second way of the neophyte philosopher; and he speaks of the truth, the Word, and Wisdom, which characterize the third way of the mature philosopher. He finds in Christ and his Church one way that incorporates the substance and concerns of each of the separate ways of salvation Porphyry speaks of.

Even though he is delighted with God and God's law in his understanding, he is still enslaved to base desires and prevented from seeking out Christ the mediator by pride, which rejects the necessity of mediation, and he is too weak in such a condition to abandon the carnal custom and worldly ways that he perversely finds so sweet.[2] He observes, "For though a man may be delighted with the law of God according to the inward man, what shall he do about that other law in his members, fighting against the law of his mind and captivating him in the law of sin that is in his members?"[3] He finds no answer to this question in the books of the Platonists.[4] Specifically, they do not speak of Christ the mediator or about confession, Christ's sacrifice, contrition, humility, and the economy of salvation revealed in the Bible, and so on. Those books speak of God and the soul, but not of "the body of this death."[5] Augustine seeks the knowledge of God and the soul, just

---

1. *Conf.*, 7.18.24.

2. Rist notes, "Augustine only describes one conversion in the *Confessions*: to Christianity. The Platonic books could only give him a notional assent, an assent to propositions, not a real commitment to a way of life." John M. Rist, *Augustine: Ancient Thought Baptized*, 152, n. 3. It depends on what Rist means by conversion. It is certainly true that Augustine's life changed to some degree when he read the Platonic books. If Rist simply means that there is only one fully effective conversion in the *Confessions*, that is certainly true. But Augustine's conversion to philosophy, begun when he read the *Hortensius* and brought to its highest point in his conception of incorporeal substance in Book 7, involved the change of affections, the (at least partial) change of his mode of life, the withdrawal from belief in fables and superstitious religion, and real intellectual accomplishment. Presumably Rist is reacting, quite rightly, to the claims of other twentieth-century scholars to the effect that Augustine's real conversion in the *Confessions* is to Platonism and not to Christianity. For example, James J. O'Donnell claims, "Manicheism was with him early and late, and was the one truly impassioned religious experience of his life." O'Donnell, *Augustine: A New Biography*, 47.

3. "Etsi condelectetur homo legi dei secundum interiorem hominem, quid faciet de alia lege in membris suis repugnante legi mentis suae et se captiuum ducente in lege peccati, quae est in membris eius?" *Conf.*, 7.21.27.

4. Ibid.

5. Ibid. See also Rom. 7:24.

as his Platonic books do. They cannot fully account for the difficulty in reaching that goal because they cannot account for the obstacles to human happiness due to sin, which affect philosophers and nonphilosophers alike.

The Platonists find the body and its loves distracting, just as Augustine does, but Augustine begins to discern a difference at the end of Book 7: for the Platonists, the life of the mind is what is important, and the body contributes little to the philosophic life that is positive. In the *Phaedo*, as Joseph Cropsey explains,

> We—[Socrates] means our soul—think better when our soul is less impeded by the burden of the body, which we may take to mean when we are undistracted by itchings and uproar. Thus we may understand the yearnings of the philosopher, i.e., of his soul, for his singular solitude, which is the abstraction of his soul from all consciousness that arises in the body. The purest concentration of the mind is the nearest approximation to death that we can enjoy on earth. His soul having simulated flight, the philosopher is dead to the world. His figurative death is the condition for his approach, which is to say his soul's approach, to the truths. The incorporeal truth admits the approach only of the incorporeal soul.[6]

Pierre Manent points out, "The hero of philosophy, the new Achilles, is only a soul that is indifferent to his mortal body, a soul that does not cease to reason and to speak until the moment of death."[7] For the Socrates presented by Plato in the *Phaedo*, philosophy involves the separation of word and flesh so that word remains and flesh dissolves. For Christianity, the Word becomes flesh so that the flesh becomes, as it were, logified. When Christ is preparing for his death, he makes sure with the institution of the Eucharist and the foundation of the Church, the mystical body of Christ, to leave behind a way for his own logified flesh to live on in history.

What is needed, Augustine starts to see, is a wholly new kind of way of life that satisfies the mind, but does not dismiss the body and its desires.[8] John Rist remarks,

> But the Platonists, and Plotinus in particular, taught that the soul returns to God as "the alone to the Alone" (*Enneads* 6.9.11.50), and it is widely recognized

---

6. Cropsey, *Plato's World*, 184. One must always be on the lookout for Plato's poetic exaggeration. Nevertheless, there is nothing in the *Phaedo* or in Cropsey's account of the *Phaedo* to lead us to believe that, while the *Phaedo*'s teaching on the relation between soul and body is an exaggeration, that the exaggeration is not rooted in a fundamentally instrumental view of the relation between soul and body.

7. Manent, *Metamorphoses*, 46–7.

8. Roberts Ogle, following Cavadini, argues that, "It was, after all, the rational soul with which the philosophers truly identified themselves. For the Platonists in particular, the body was a mere prison, while the soul was the true locus of personhood." Roberts Ogle, *Earthly City*, 93, n. 37.

that, despite the often exemplary kindness of Neoplatonic philosophers towards their fellow-men, such behaviour does not fit entirely consistently into their ethical system as a whole. At best it will appear as part of the necessary, but only preliminary, purification of the soul, a setting of the stage for one's own elevation. The problem is to see how ordinary moral action (whether or not motivated by love, or kindness, or obligation, or duties), could itself be constitutive of, rather than merely necessary for, the "religious" life summed up as a return to God.[9]

The problem is how to reconcile love of God and love of neighbor without making love of neighbor a mere condition for or preliminary step to the love of God, which might eventually be dispensed with. Augustine finds in St. Paul knowledge of God, the glorification of and thanksgiving to him, and the truths about God and the soul spoken with humility and not pride; he also finds that it is Christ who frees us from this body of death and who transforms the body into a spiritual body through the Resurrection. An anticipation of that freedom and transformation is available in the Church to his disciples even in their earthly lives. Christ, who is both God and neighbor, Augustine begins to see, is able to heal both his intellectual pride and his concupiscence.

At the beginning of Book 8, Augustine's doubts concerning incorruptible substance have been defeated. He says, "My desire was not to be more sure [*certior*] of You but more steadfast (*stabilior*) in You. But in my temporal life all was uncertain; my heart had to be purged of the old leaven. The way, our Savior himself, delighted me; but I still shrank from actually walking a way so strait."[10] Augustine had learned to conceive an incorporeal substance and from this breakthrough he was able to grasp the hierarchy of creation, including the place of the human will, and that evil is a privation rather than a substance. A better understanding of God, the will, and evil, however, did not automatically usher Augustine into a virtuous or holy life. His contemplations were unstable and he continued to love temporal things over eternal things, even though his main intellectual problem had been dealt with. After he escaped the foolish fables of the Manicheans and found wanting the perilous—because only partial—intellectual liberation he achieved under the tutelage of the Platonists, Augustine still hesitates to enter the Church. His Platonist ascent was insufficient to free him from his disordered love of temporal things and was ultimately more frustrating than satisfying because of his inability to persevere. In the context of answering the provocative question, "Where exactly was Platonist philosophy at fault?," Ernest L. Fortin comments,

> By reason of their bodily nature, human beings are necessarily attached to what belongs to them as individuals and, when conflicts of interest arise, almost always prefer themselves to others. The love of their own cannot be eradicated from their souls and in virtually all cases proves stronger than their love of the true or

---

9. Rist, *Augustine: Ancient Thought Baptized*, 149.
10. *Conf.*, 8.1.1.

the beautiful. To make matters worse, less than perfect laws combine with bad inclination and tyrannical habit to prevent them from becoming true lovers of justice. To this problem the pagan philosophers have no solution to offer. They are right in stressing the need for virtue but cannot secure its performance. They themselves are the first to admit that their model of the most desirable society cannot be translated into action. It exists in speech or "private discussion" only ... . As [Augustine] saw it, pagan philosophy was bound to fail, not because it made unreasonable demands on human nature, but because its proponents did not know or were unwilling to apply the proper remedy to its congenital weakness. That remedy consists in following Christ, apart from whom one can do nothing (cf. John 15.5), for he alone both reveals the true goal of human existence and furnishes the means whereby it may be attained.[11]

The pagan philosophers are well aware of ignorance and difficulty, but are incapable of overcoming them. The best they can do is to sing incantations to purge the fear of death,[12] or to tell the noble lie[13] in attempting to ally wisdom, justice, the gods, and the city's laws. Joseph Cropsey remarks,

Perhaps philosophy and poetry in union can draw the sting of death by giving it bright and promising features. If this could be made part of a teaching that the cosmos is a single realm of justice and clarity, a great boon would be offered to humanity, who need only reject the easily disparaged testimony of the senses in order to accept it. All good things will devolve from the immortality of the soul.[14]

At the end of the *Phaedo*, Socrates "will construct an immense geological myth that illustrates the caring deed of the man who knows what he and his fellow human beings cannot know at the same time that he knows what they need and yearn to know and what they incline, perhaps one should say incline naturally, to believe that they know."[15] Socrates' superiority consists in his knowledge that he cannot know what he and his fellow men yearn most to know: whether they will persist as persons beyond death; his goodness consists in the fact that he cares enough for his fellow men to incant away their fears with a salutary but false myth. Cropsey's "perhaps naturally" can underscore the two senses in which Augustine uses nature: before or after the Fall. Is the inclination to know what happens after death natural or not? Is death natural or not? In what sense? These are the nagging questions to which Plato's Socrates gives voice and which take on new importance for Augustine.

11. Fortin, *Birth of Philosophic Christianity*, 5.
12. Plato, *Phaedo*, 77e.
13. Plato, *Republic*, 414b–c.
14. Cropsey, *Plato's World*, 182.
15. Ibid., 218.

Just as Cicero's *Hortensius* had changed Augustine's affections toward the love of wisdom, so reading St. Paul's epistles had changed Augustine's affections toward the way of the Savior. But just as his newly changed affections were not sufficient to transform him wholly into a true lover of wisdom after reading the *Hortensius*, so his reading of the Epistle to the Romans was not sufficient to move him from being merely pleased by Christ to being a follower of Christ or, in other words, to move him from his catechumenate to baptism. To take this next step, Augustine needs to be converted and, to be converted, he needs to learn something new: humility. Only with humility can Augustine confess his sins and beseech God's help for himself.

Book 8 tells the story of Augustine's education in humility after he has become displeased with his way of life and his enslavement to disordered temporal loves, his worldly ways and the custom of the flesh, and after he has been moved to approve of the way of Christ. Book 8 has three main episodes: the story of the conversion of Victorinus, the story of St. Anthony of the Desert, and Augustine's travails in the garden, in which he is finally moved by grace to decide to accept baptism. The first story about Victorinus tells about a famous philosopher who learns humility and enters the Church; the second story about Anthony tells about an unknown (to Augustine), unlettered, humble monk who managed to achieve what Augustine could not in spite of all his learning: liberation from disordered love of temporal things and a chaste love of eternal things in accord with highest wisdom. Both stories together combine to provoke a crisis in Augustine's soul serious enough finally to break down his pride and allow him to accept the grace of Christ. The two stories are complementary. Victorinus' conversion appeals to Augustine's desire to live the theoretical life well, but it takes the story of St. Anthony to lead Augustine to understand that the way of life he is called to live as a Christian regards the flourishing of the body, not just the soul, to be crucial. The flourishing of both the body and soul in their right order is required for full, human happiness.

The structure of the *Confessions* leaves little doubt that Augustine's philosophic studies had to come before his religious conversion in Book 8. He had to learn in a vivid way that God resists the proud before he could embrace humility.[16] He says,

---

16. A passage from *De Trinitate* perfectly captures Augustine's plight: "There are certain ones, however, who think themselves capable by their own strength of being purified, so as to see God and to inhere in God, whose very pride defiles them above all others. For there is no vice which the divine law resists more, and over which that most proud spirit, the mediator to things below and the obstacle to things above, receives a greater power of domination ... For they promise a purification of themselves by their own power, because some of them have been able to penetrate with their mind's eye beyond all created things and to touch, though it be ever so small a part, the light of unchangeable truth, while many Christians, as they mockingly assert, who live in the meantime by faith alone, have not yet been able to do so." *Trin.*, 4.15.20. After he conceives of an incorporeal substance, Augustine is simultaneously at his closest point to Christianity and furthest away; he is closest by virtue of his understanding of God, and furthest away by virtue of the pride he takes in his

12. The Cases of Victorinus and Anthony 191

> Yet I think it was Your will that I should come upon these books before I had made study of the Scriptures, that it might be impressed on my memory how they had affected me; so that, when later I should have become responsive to You through Your books with my wounds healed by the care of your fingers, I might be able to discern the difference that there is between presumption (*praesumptionem*) and confession (*confessionem*), between those who see what the goal is but do not see the way, and [those who see] the Way which leads to that country of blessedness, which we are meant not only to know but to dwell in.[17] If I had been first formed by Your Holy Scriptures so that You had grown sweet to me through their familiar use, and had later come upon these books of the Platonists, they might have swept me away from the solid ground of piety.[18]

It is precisely the gulf between *praesumptio* and *confessio* that Simplicianus wanted both Victorinus and Augustine to cross. Without experiencing the effects of *praesumptio* in himself, the prideful swelling and the frustrating, unstable contemplation of wisdom, he would not have been able to recognize the necessity and usefulness of *confessio*. Augustine's constant refrain that the punishments

---

understanding. See again St. Paul's statement that "Knowledge puffs up, but love builds up" in 1 Cor. 8:1, which is a constant undertone throughout *conf*. 7.

17. "Those who see where they must travel, but do not see the way" are the Platonists, whom Augustine praises in *ciu. Dei*, 8.1 for their knowledge of God, but also criticizes them because they despise Christ, the universal way to salvation. "Those who see the way that leads not only to beholding our blessed fatherland but also to dwelling therein" are men like himself at the time and Victorinus before his public profession of faith. In Book 8, Augustine narrates his movement from being one who knows where he must travel and the way to get there, to one who actually travels the way.

18.

> In quos me propterea, priusquam scripturas tuas considerarem, credo uoluisti incurrere, ut imprimeretur memoriae meae, quomodo ex eis affectus essem et, cum postea in libris tuis mansuefactus essem et curantibus digitis tuis contrectarentur uulnera mea, discernerem atque distinguerem, quid interesset inter praesumptionem et confessionem, inter uidentes, quo eundum sit, nec uidentes, qua, et uiam ducentem ad beatificam patriam non tantum cernendam sed et habitandam. Nam si primo sanctis tuis litteris informatus essem et in earum familiaritate obdulcuisses mihi et post in illa uolumina incidissem, fortasse aut abripuissent me a solidamento pietatis. (*Conf.*, 7.20.26)

Augustine's narration of the necessity of his coming to know the consequences of his sinful presumption is strongly redolent of his discussion of the knowledge of good and evil gained by Adam after committing the original sin. Adam's newfound knowledge, Augustine says, is an experiential knowledge of the difference between evil, which he now experiences in the punishments for sin, and good, which he knows by comparing his present punishments with the happiness he has lost. See *Gn. Adu. Man*, 2.9.12 and *Gn. Litt*, 8.6.12.

of ignorance and difficulty that he experienced were a sign of God's mercy are reminiscent of Heb. 12:4-12, in which the author of Hebrews exhorts his readers to regard discipline for sins as signs that God has adopted them as sons. The severity of his punishments, which Augustine leads the reader to believe are very great, works to Augustine's benefit. One could conceive of a different result if, for example, Augustine had been the beneficiary of a better disposition from the beginning, or had received a better education as a small child. If the young Augustine had been more serene and less troubled by ignorance and difficulty, he may never have experienced the difference between *praesumptio* and *confessio* because he never would have recognized the necessity of *confessio*. For instance, unlike Augustine, Plato never tells us of any struggles with the flesh Socrates had to endure, although Porphyry does say that Plotinus "seemed ashamed of being in the body."[19]

The stories of Victorinus and Anthony combine to open Augustine to a religious conversion and are parallel to Augustine's earlier reading of the books of the natural philosophers in Book 6 and the Platonists in Book 7, which provided decisive assistance in Augustine's intellectual conversion. Like the books of the philosophers, these tales were true; like the stories of the Manicheans, they were tales. Augustine's acquisition of the knowledge of astronomy and metaphysics was done with the help of books, but ultimately was a private task accomplished through the exercise of Augustine's own mind. The knowledge he gained through his philosophic studies was speculative: the knowledge itself was the point. On the other hand, the stories about Victorinus and St. Anthony were stories he had to be told by another and could not have learned through private study. Indeed, Augustine is told these stories by his friends, emphasizing further the ways in which human social life is used by Providence to prepare Augustine for conversion.[20] For these stories to be beneficial, he had to abandon his insistence on essentially private certainty founded on his own private judgments in favor of the reasonable reliance on the judgment and testimony of another. The knowledge he gained about the deeds of Victorinus and Anthony was practical knowledge, useful for moving him to deeds, accusing himself of sin, and confessing his sins to God. Yet that practical knowledge was the condition for Augustine's progress in the theoretical life, since he could not heal his divided will without confession to God and the reception of grace. In order for those stories to move him, he needed to believe they were true on the testimony of another. The speculative knowledge he gained in his philosophic studies paved the way for his religious conversion, but was not sufficient in order to provoke him to act, to overcome the carnal custom and worldly ways that were making him miserable. The true tales of Victorinus and Anthony brought together intellectual and moral excellence and displayed both in

---

19. Porphyry, "Life of Plotinus," #1.

20. Stephany has astutely noted the connection between the theft of the pears done partly to impress his companions in Book 2 and the "friendship that leads to salvation and liberation" in Book 8. See Stephany, "Thematic Structure in Augustine's *Confessions*," 135.

the lives of historical men and show that the characteristic struggles of both the few and the many were present in Augustine and both demanded address.

These stories attacked Augustine's attachment to carnal custom and his subjection to ignorance and difficulty from different directions. Augustine's pride made him hesitate on the threshold of the Church. He relates that his friend and mentor, Simplicianus, told him the story of Victorinus because he had diagnosed Augustine's problem as a lack of humility.[21] By relaying Simplicianus' narration of the story of Victorinus, Augustine seems clearly to be adopting Simplicianus' judgment that Augustine's and Victorinus' cases were similar as far as each man's motivations for remaining outside the Church. Augustine describes his appraisal of the Church: "For I saw the whole Church, and one man went this way, while another went that way."[22] The Church was full of men who lived different ways of life: both the wise, like Ambrose, and the simple, like his mother Monica.[23] Yet he hesitated, like Victorinus, because he disapproved of the multitude, the mixed mass of believers who worshipped God together in the Church. His disapproval was at bottom a failure of charity. He was repulsed by the mixture of the few and the many, inflated by his pride. To enter the Church would be to admit that his problems were, at root, the same problems of the many, who lacked Augustine's intelligence and learning. Simplicianus related Victorinus' thinking, saying, "[Victorinus] said not publicly but to Simplicianus privately and as one friend to another: 'I would have you know that I am now a Christian.' Simplicianus answered: 'I shall not believe it nor count you among Christians unless I see you in the Church of Christ.' Victorinus asked with some faint mockery; 'Then

---

21. *Conf.*, 8.2.3.

22. "Videbam enim plenam ecclesiam, et alius sic ibat, alius autem sic." Ibid., 8.1.2. My translation.

23. Fortin remarks, "Monica and Augustine share the same faith but not in the same way." Fortin, *Birth of Philosophic Christianity*, 100. Fortin continues: "If philosophy is a preparation for death, a *melete thanatou* in the Platonic sense, then Monica, who can face death courageously, is indeed a true philosopher; but her strength obviously comes from a source other than the disinterested contemplation of the eternal order of the universe." Monica's strength comes from her Christian discipleship. The way of life she lives as a Christian, following after the eternal wisdom becomes flesh in Christ, has allowed Monica to overcome her inordinate attachment to her own indicated by her prior preoccupation with the place of her grave. Monica tells her sons near the time of her death, "Lay this body wherever it may be. Let no care of it disturb you. This only I ask of you: that you should remember me at the altar of the Lord wherever you may be." Ibid. See also *conf.*, 9.11.27. Monica's faith in the Resurrection has allowed her to stop worrying about the resting place of her bodily remains, but it is not because she thinks that the body is somehow an unimportant part of who she is; on the contrary, she says a little later, "Nothing is far from God and I have no fear that He will not know at the end of the world from what place He is to raise me up." *Conf.*, 9.11.28. Monica's faith in the resurrection of the body gives her hope that God will provide her with wholeness of body and soul in the Resurrection.

is it walls that make Christians?'"[24] Victorinus desired the acknowledgement of Simplicianus, his intellectual peer, but was troubled by the necessity of confessing himself to be a sinner in front of those who were decidedly his inferior in learning.[25] His assumption is that becoming a Christian is primarily a matter of the mind's assent to a set of doctrines or, in other words, that Christianity is like a philosophic sect. Christianity, however, is not just a matter for the mind, but concerns the body as well. In a decisive sense, walls do make a Christian. As Frederick Crosson argues, "For Augustine ... first, the encounter with the God of Jesus occurs in the world, not within the soul, and second, coming to Him is entering a community sharing in His life."[26] In the absence of the willingness to be present bodily in the Church, to receive the bodily sacraments, and to confess the same faith in the same, universal savior with other Christians, one is not a Christian.

Man's corporate nature and the inherited character of original sin mean that sinfulness is a condition to which all men are subject. The effects of sin manifest differently in different men, but the root of all men's sinfulness is the same.[27] The theoretical man and the man who is not theoretically inclined are both sinful. Augustine's ability to undertake philosophic investigations, to free himself from the errors of Manichean fables, to conceive on his own power an incorporeal substance, simply means that he is affected by sin differently from the nontheoretical man, who is not able to undertake philosophic investigations or conceive an incorporeal substance. But without the grace of Christ in the Church, neither man is able to be free of a disordered love of temporal things and for a rightly ordered love of eternal things. The nontheoretical man would not be able even to make the attempt to be steadfast in love of eternal things, while Augustine's attempts are doomed to failure by the weight of carnal custom, the other law in his members that St. Paul discusses; his superior powers of mind are still too weak to overcome that other law. His pride in despising the humble savior Jesus Christ prevents his liberation through the ministrations of Christ. But on an even deeper level, his pride prevents him from even looking for God in the right place: in the Church, the body of Christ.

---

24. Ibid., 8.2.4. Given Simplicianus' choice of stories to tell Augustine and that Augustine relays them early in Book 8, it is safe to say that Augustine recognized his own fears in the hesitations of Victorinus.

25. Fortin says, "One cannot love God without loving those whom God loves, and God loves all his creatures. This is what Augustine did not find in the books of the Platonists, however much he may have felt indebted to them for other reasons." Fortin, *Birth of Philosophic Christianity*, 8.

26. Crosson, "Structure and Meaning in St. Augustine's *Confessions*," 92.

27. Rist observes in this idea Augustine's "'Christian egalitarianism': a recognition of the equal plight of mankind, but in a very non-classical sense." Rist, *Augustine: Ancient Thought Baptized*, 139. One might also add that Augustine's egalitarianism is quite non-modern, as well, and is perhaps even less modern than it is classical in the sense Rist means.

After much hesitation, Simplicianus tells Augustine, Victorinus did eventually enter the Church. Augustine relates,

> He preferred to make his profession of his salvation in the sight of that holy multitude [*sanctae multitudinis*]. For it was not salvation which he was teaching in rhetoric, and yet he professed it publicly. How much less, therefore, should he fear your gentle flock when pronouncing your Word, which he never feared to pronounce in his own words before crowds of the mad [*turbas insanorum*]?[28]

The holy multitude within the Church is contrasted with the mad crowd outside the Church. The fundamental division among men, Augustine reveals in this passage, is not between the wise and the foolish or the few and the many, but between the holy multitude and the mad crowd or the city of God and the earthly city. The teaching of the Scriptures and the Church about God, which is both humble and true, is able to keep believers from making harmful errors, while the grace of Christ received in the sacraments of the Church is able to heal the will and empower even the many to be morally good, at least insofar as is possible in earthly life. Augustine then says that the story had the effect to set him on fire ("*exarsi*") with the desire to imitate Victorinus.[29] Augustine burned previously to pursue wisdom; now he burns to confess like Victorinus. The latter burning specifies the former burning rather than replaces it; he recognizes that a confession like that of Victorinus is the necessary road for the pursuit of wisdom.

Despite his burning desire to imitate Victorinus, Augustine still finds himself enslaved. He says, "The enemy held my will; and of it he made a chain and bound me. Because my will was perverse it changed to lust [*libido*], and lust yielded to become habit, and habit not resisted became necessity."[30] The lust Augustine speaks of stands in for all disordered desire.[31] The sins Augustine originally committed in ignorance as an infant and a child when he was not in command of his own reason, he later did as a believer of false Manichean tales, then did afterwards as a skeptic, and then as a proud, puffed up student of Platonist philosophy. His bad deeds built up the carnal custom that, over time, became necessity for him even when he understood that the way of life he was living was evil. Carnal habit or custom imposed itself on Augustine's will as a necessity even when he no longer wished to live by it. Nevertheless, Augustine confesses, "My hostile habit was made more

---

28. "Illum autem maluisse salutem suam in conspectu sanctae multitudinis profiteri. Non enim erat salus, quam docebat, in rhetorica, et tamen eam publice professus erat. Quanto minus ergo uereri debuit mansuetum gregem tuum pronuntians uerbum tuum, qui non uerebatur in uerbis suis turbas insanorum?" *Conf.*, 8.2.5. My translation.

29. Ibid., 8.5.10.

30. "Velle meum tenebat inimicus et inde mihi catenam fecerat et constrinxerat me. Quippe ex uoluntate peruersa facta est libido, et dum seruitur libidini, facta est consuetudo, et dum consuetudini non resistitur, facta est necessitas." Ibid., 8.5.10.

31. See *lib. arb.*, 1.3.

obstinate by me, since I had come willingly to this point where I now did not will. And who can with right speak against it, when a just punishment follows upon sinning?"[32] As Augustine says in the *De libero arbitrio*,

> It is not to be wondered at either that by ignorance man might not have free choice of the will for choosing rightly what he ought to do: or by a resisting carnal habit, which has grown in a certain way naturally by the violence of mortal succession, he may see what he rightly ought to do, and will, but not be able to fulfill [his willing]. For that is the most just penalty for sin, that he lose everything which he does not will to use well, when he is able without any difficulty, if he were to will it. That is, he who, knowing, does not do rightly, he loses to know what is right: and he who does not will to do rightly when he is able, he loses to be able when he wills.[33]

Augustine therefore affirms that the necessity of doing evil to which he was subject by the bonds of carnal custom was a just punishment due to him for his sins. He continues, saying, "For the law of sin is the fierce force of habit, by which the mind is drawn and held even against its will, and yet deservedly because it had fallen willfully into the habit."[34] The delight for God and the eternal law Augustine had in his understanding was insufficient to overcome the law in his members without the grace of Christ.

The story of Victorinus is about a lettered man who bowed his neck in humility and received healing from Christ in the Church for his sins. The story of St. Anthony of the Desert, on the other hand, shows Augustine an unlettered man whose humility allows him to live his life according to the highest wisdom. Augustine learns of Anthony by hearing of Anthony's story as told in a particular book, St. Athanasius' *Life of Anthony*. The major problem in Plato's political philosophy

---

32. "Sed tamen consuetudo aduersus me pugnacior ex me facta erat, quoniam uolens quo nollem perueneram. Et quis iure contradiceret, cum peccantem iusta poena sequeretur?" *Conf.*, 8.5.11. My translation.

33.

> Nec mirandum est quod vel ignorando non habet arbitrium liberum uoluntatis ad eligendum quod recte faciat: uel resistente carnali consuetudine, quae uiolentia mortalis successionis quodam modo naturaliter inoleuit, uideat quid recte faciendum sit et uelit nec possit implere. Illa est enim peccati poena iustissima, ut amittat quisque quod bene uti noluit cum sine ulla posset difficultate si uellet; id est autem ut qui sciens recte non facit amittat scire quid rectum sit, et qui recte facere cum posset noluit amittat posse cum uelit. (*Lib. arb.*, 3.18.177–8. My translation)

34. "Frustra condelectabar legi tuae secundum interiorem hominem, cum alia lex in membris meis repugnaret legi mentis meae et captiuum me duceret in lege peccati, quae in membris meis erat. Lex enim peccati est uiolentia consuetudinis, qua trahitur et tenetur etiam inuitus animus eo merito, quo in eam uolens inlabitur." *Conf.*, 8.5.12.

is the degree to which wisdom can rule the city, a problem that is analogous to the problem of reason's rulership of the passions and the body.[35] Plato and other thinkers who are broadly part of the Platonic tradition in political philosophy were never particularly optimistic on either score. Unlike Plato's *Republic*, in which the best regime is said to be founded only in speech or private discussion, Athanasius stresses that the events and deeds he records in the *Life of Anthony* really happened. Anthony's way of life, unlike Plato's *Republic*, existed in deed, not just in speech. The distinguishing mark of Anthony's way of life is that he lived a life according to the highest wisdom by following Christ. Anthony's life was not merely a life dedicated to the satisfaction of his intellectual longings, although Athanasius is at pains to show that Anthony is a wise man;[36] his life demonstrates that a life lived in Christ is capable of producing men, individually and living in community, in whom and over whom wisdom rules. Athanasius lists both Anthony's virtues and his temptations toward vice, writing that the devil attacked Anthony through his flesh. It was Christ, the God who took on flesh, who defeated the devil by making the flesh godly. Christ defeated Anthony's *difficultas* by making it susceptible to highest wisdom in faith as taught through the Scriptures and the Church. Athanasius characterizes Anthony as "a man guided by reason and stable in his character,"[37] which is precisely what Augustine is striving to be. Anthony's faith in the work of Christ on the Cross, which brings eternal life through the resurrection of the whole man, frees him from the fear of death by freeing him from disordered love of temporal things. As a result, Anthony derides the philosophers he meets, who are constrained by fear of persecution into acknowledging idols as gods, for their dismissal of the Cross, which frees from death and the fear of death.[38] Christ's Cross is neither a Socratic incantation nor an exhortation to philosophic resignation in the face of evil. For Athanasius, the crucifixion is a historical event that heals human nature from its wounds due to sin and in which men can share through the extension of Christ's humanity in the Church. Anthony's peace with his own flesh is illustrated dramatically by Athanasius, who tells that even the wild beasts, animals who do not possess reason and who have not been tamed by men, do not bother Anthony.[39]

The two stories are juxtaposed: one tells of a wise man who accepts humility and the other tells of a humble man who lives according to wisdom, providing historical evidence that a philosopher's pride can yield to Christ's humility and a Christian monk's humility can attain to a life of wisdom in Christ. Ponticianus tells Augustine about Anthony, and also tells him about how hearing the story of

---

35. See, for example, Plato, *Republic*, 434d–435b.
36. See Athanasius, *The Life of Saint Anthony*, trans. Robert T. Meyer, Newman (New York: 1950), 72–80. All quotations from the *Life of Saint Anthony* will be from the Meyer translation.
37. Ibid., 14.
38. See ibid., 75.
39. Ibid., 15.

Anthony had affected Ponticianus and his three companions. After hearing about Anthony, they turned aside from the *cursus honorum* to the pursuit of holiness, two of them taking up the monastic life. One of Ponticianus' companions, he relates, pointedly asks the question,

> Tell me, please, what is the goal of our ambition in all these labours of ours? What are we aiming at? What is our motive in being in the public service? Have we any higher hope at court than to be friends of the Emperor? And at that level, is not everything uncertain and full of perils? And how many perils must we meet on the way to this greater peril? And how long before we are there? But if I should choose to be a friend of God, I can become one now.[40]

The positions at the emperor's court that the friends had coveted, which would be the highest achievement of their pursuit of honors, are insecure because they are subject to the mutable will of a sinful man, namely the emperor. Becoming God's friend, on the other hand, can be accomplished in an instant through a good will and can never be taken away against the will.[41]

---

40. *Conf.*, 8.6.15.
41. See *lib. arb.*, 1.15.112.

Chapter 13

AUGUSTINE'S MORAL AND RELIGIOUS CONVERSION: SOUL AND BODY, FEW AND MANY

Augustine's unstable intellectual ascent in Book 7 convinced him that he was not such a man as could steadfastly contemplate eternal things and live according to them. The story of Victorinus had set Augustine ablaze to imitate Victorinus' entry into the Church. Now the story of St. Anthony, together with hearing about how St. Anthony's example had affected other men who, like him, were leading a life devoted to honors, combine to confront Augustine with his own difficulty in overcoming the law in his members. Anthony and his monks live lives dedicated to wisdom through faith, hope, and charity. Christ has conquered the devil in their flesh and has overthrown their ignorance and difficulty so that they can live guided by wisdom. The Christian asceticism of Anthony, Athanasius emphasizes, was a boon for his body, helping to moderate the desires of his body, bringing them under the direction of reason, and therefore allowing them to satisfy those newly reasonable desires.[1] Christ's conquest of the devil in their flesh allows them to satisfy the desires of their flesh in a well-ordered, reasonable way, in accord with wisdom. The way of life in Christ lived by Anthony allows Anthony to be satisfied in body and soul, morally and intellectually, without having to choose one over

---

1. After twenty years of solitary asceticism, Anthony's followers are astonished when they see him "to see that his body had kept its former appearance, that it was neither obese from want of exercise, nor emaciated from his fastings and struggles with demons: he was the same man they had known before his retirement." Athanasius, *The Life of Saint Anthony*, 14. At the end of his life, Athanasius describes Anthony's remarkable wholeness in body that resulted from its harmony with Anthony's soul:

> He never made old age the excuse for yielding to the desire for lavish foods, nor did he change his form of clothing because of his body's infirmity, nor did he as much as wash his feet with water. And yet his health remained entirely unimpaired. For instance, even his eyes were perfectly normal so that his sight was excellent; and he had not lost a single tooth, only they had worn down near the gums through the old man's great age. He also kept healthy hands and feet, and on the whole he appeared brighter and more active than did all those who use a diversified diet and baths and a variety of clothing. (Ibid., 93)

and against the other. The unlettered Anthony's way of life can even be said to include Victorinus' way of life because he follows Christ, who is wisdom incarnate.

Directly after Augustine listens to Ponticianus relate the story of St. Anthony, for a third and final time he recalls his experience reading *Hortensius*. But he still finds that he delays.[2] He had convinced himself that he should continue in his worldly ways until something certain would appear, but now he finds that he hesitates to abandon his worldly ways even after his doubts have been removed. He becomes aware of a great fear within himself, followed by great shame. He says, "All [my soul's] arguments had already been used and refuted. There remained only trembling silence; for it feared as very death the cessation of that habit of which in truth it was dying."[3] The eloquent rhetor has run out of arguments and been rendered speechless. Augustine's perverse passions are revealed as he finds that he fears what could lead him to life as if it were death because it would keep him from the worldly ways that he now knows are leading him toward death.[4] He knows that the *consuetudo carnalis* leads to death, but still loves all the bad habits that constitute it and cannot yet bear to part from them. Augustine's reflection on his theft of the pear in *conf.* 2.4 illuminates his condition: "Let that heart now tell You what it sought when I was thus evil for no object, having no cause for wrongdoing save my wrongness. The malice of the act was base and I loved it—not the thing for which I did the evil, simply the evil."[5] The preference for the temporal over the eternal is implicitly a preference of death over life, for temporal things pass away while eternal things remain, which shows the irrationality of evil. Augustine fears death but loves the worldly ways that lead him to death, while his mind loves and approves the eternal law that leads to eternal life but he fears the way that leads there.

On top of his fear, he is shamed by the example of the unlettered men who, he has now heard, are living according to wisdom while he himself is unwilling to do so. He exclaims, "The unlearned arise and take heaven by force, and here are we with all our learning, stuck fast in flesh and blood!"[6] Salvation, Augustine now admits, begins with the humble acknowledgment and confession of sin and the acknowledgment that one needs to receive healing from Christ through the Church. Simplicianus refused to count Victorinus as a Christian because walls

---

2. *Conf.*, 8.7.17.

3. Ibid., 8.7.18. The death Augustine is primarily concerned about is the death of the soul, what he elsewhere calls the "second death." *Ciu. Dei*, 14.1.

4. Augustine's state of speechless dread in the face of death is similar to the state of the group of men conversing with Socrates in the middle of the *Phaedo* (88c–91c) when the fear of death threatens to overwhelm the conversation. Socrates tells his friends that what they need is someone to incant away the fear of death, which Socrates himself begins to do in the rest of the dialogue.

5. *Conf.*, 2.4.9.

6. "Surgunt indocti et caelum rapiunt, et nos cum doctrinis nostris sine corde ecce ubi uolutamur in carne et sanguine!" *Conf.*, 8.8.19. My translation.

do make Christians in a decisive sense: everyone within the walls acknowledges that he is a sinner in need of the grace of Christ. Victorinus and Augustine do not constitute a special case because of their learning.[7] Augustine's learning, after all, does not free him from the weight of the *consuetudo carnalis* that makes him miserable, from his disordered love of temporal things.

The problems of the few and the many are both rooted in ignorance and difficulty, but ignorance and difficulty have different effects on different kinds of souls. The fundamental problem that Augustine has to overcome before he is finally able to accept the assistance of Christ is in recognizing that his problems have the same root as those of the multitude and, therefore, the same remedy. Augustine's pride will therefore have to be overcome in order to accept the ministrations of Christ through the Church, the home of the "holy multitude."[8] Both Augustine and his nonphilosophic interlocutor in the *De libero arbitrio*, Evodius, are afflicted with difficulty that springs from pride, and both men's pride consists in disordered attachment to their own. Evodius' pride consists in his attachment to the opinions with which he grew up under the education of Rome and its laws and therefore to the judgments of his countrymen. Augustine's pride consists in a disordered attachment to his own judgment, which makes him disdain faith, which itself rests on the judgments of another. Augustine is in a genuinely better situation with respect to knowledge of the truth than his nonphilosopher friend, for philosophy has allowed him to chip away at his ignorance, and the laws of Rome no longer constitute the complete horizon for his judgments about justice. As a result, Augustine is able to transcend the city and her laws in thought in a way that his nonphilosopher fellow citizens are not. But, as his misery about the lies he has to tell in the praise of the emperor show, the transcendence of the city he has attained in mind through philosophy still leaves him bound by the city in body. If he were to tell the truth about the emperor in his laudatory speech, he would be subject to dire temporal penalties. As the story of Victorinus shows, it is only the reception into the Church that frees the whole man, so that after his public profession of faith and baptism, Victorinus is liberated in order to address the many and to tell the truth about man's salvation. It is only the man who loves temporal things inordinately whom the temporal law can punish efficaciously.

Joining the Church indicates Victorinus' final liberation from love of temporal things, because it indicates that he does not fear temporal reprisals. His own life, which is a temporal good, is subject to the police power of the city. A fully converted Christian, however, who is not afraid of martyrdom is free from the penalties of the city, in the sense that they have lost their coercive force over him. Athanasius narrates that St. Anthony said to the Greek philosophers, "And

---

7. Fortin argues, "He may know vastly more than his less learned listeners and is thus often compelled to adapt himself to their limited intellectual capacities, but what he knows is not something other than what every Christian knows or should know." Fortin, *The Birth of Philosophic Christianity*, 7.

8. *Conf.*, 8.2.5.

regarding the Cross, which would you say is better: when treachery is resorted to by wicked men, to endure the Cross and not to flinch from death in any manner or form, or to fabricate fables about the wanderings of Osiris and Isis, the plots of Typhon, the banishment of Cronus, the swallowing of children, and the slaying of fathers? Yes, here we have your wisdom!"[9] Augustine must learn the lesson that Anthony learned, that Christ's death on the Cross puts "the body of this death"[10] to death in giving eternal life.

Following the stories of Victorinus and St. Anthony, Augustine presents an examination of the state of his will, on which he lays the blame for his continuing hesitations. He is seeking a change in his whole way of life and he says that that change is something "which I could have done as soon as I willed to, given that willing means willing wholly."[11] But he does not will wholly; Augustine's will is divided against itself, and so when he wills to live according to the highest wisdom, he does not will completely. He is still encumbered by disordered love for temporal things. The body is not at fault, for Augustine has no trouble commanding the body to do whatever he wishes. Instead there are, as it were, two wills, neither of them whole.[12] The evil will is "weighed down by custom (*consuetudine praegrauatus*)."[13] Nor is the conflict within Augustine's soul a result of two conflicting natures. Augustine ascribes this error to the Manichean confusion of the human soul with the divine substance.[14] Man has no evil element in his constitution; rather, human evil is due to a privation for which he is himself responsible. Augustine cannot attain what he wills because his will is incomplete; his will is incomplete because of his own disordered love for temporal things.[15] Nor are Augustine's two wills evidence of "another mind (*mentis alienae*),"[16] by which Augustine indicates

---

9. Athanasius, *The Life of Saint Anthony*, 75.
10. *Conf.*, 7.21.27. See also Rom. 7:24.
11. *Conf.*, 8.8.20.
12. "Una earum tota non est et hoc adest alteri, quod deest alteri." Ibid., 8.9.21.
13. Ibid., 8.9.21. My translation.
14. Ibid., 8.10.22.
15. Dodaro observes, "For Augustine, ignorance and weakness, like the intellect and will to which they correspond, ought not to be considered as separate spiritual disorders. Although he describes them both as defects (*uitia*) which restrict the scope of the will in the practice of justice, he understands the two conditions to interact with each other." Dodaro, *Christ and the Just Society*, 29. See also ibid., 73–4. A comparison of Christ's ministrations to Augustine in the *Confessions* and Socrates' ministrations to Alcibiades in the Platonic corpus demonstrates Augustine's contention that, what Platonic philosophy was missing was not so much a true apprehension of virtue so much as a way to hold fast to virtue.
16. *Conf.*, 8.10.22. My translation. Charles T. Matthewes comments, "The dissenting will is not an alien force, but as much part of the self as is the properly desiring will. It cannot be eliminated or evaded, but must be converted. You cannot fully identify with part of yourself against another part of yourself; you are helpless before the dis-integrity of your loves." Mathewes, "Augustinian Anthropology: Interior intimo meo," *The Journal of Religious Ethics*, vol. 27 (Summer 1999), 195–221 at 207.

that his failure to live well is not a problem arising out of his nature. The pain caused by Augustine's failure to live well is therefore "My punishment [*poenam meae*]."[17] Augustine's sin, not Augustine's nature, is the cause of his misery. He was prevented from living well since he still could not wholly forsake his disordered love of temporal things in order to pursue eternal things wholeheartedly. He could not fully live the life in philosophy presented in the *Hortensius* and then as exemplified in the lives of Christian wisdom of Victorinus and St. Anthony. Thanks to his tutelage at the hands of the Platonists, he has begun to glimpse what it means to live according to wisdom; but his philosophic training is not enough to free him from the habit of his worldly ways. What he needs is to be liberated from his carnal custom so that he can finally live according to the highest wisdom. Augustine's will is bad and he needs assistance in order to have a good will.[18] Until then, he will continue to be scourged by his ignorance and difficulty.

The stories of Victorinus and Anthony provoke a profound examination of conscience in Augustine, which leads to the famous scene in the garden in which, wracked by shame and fear, Augustine weeps over himself and tries to move himself to cast aside his carnal custom. He knows that he ought to, but cannot. There is still a niggling voice in his mind, the vocalization of his "old friends [*antiquae amicae*],"[19] the temporal pleasures he enjoys inordinately, which taunt him and remind him that he will no longer enjoy them once he decisively changes his way of life. In contrast, he also narrates that he had a vision of an apparition of the "chaste dignity of continence,"[20] the foe of his difficulty, who shows him "young men (*pueri*)" and "maidens (*puellae*)"[21] who have become continent where the mature and learned Augustine has failed. Then, withdrawing deeper within the garden away from his friend Alypius, Augustine casts himself down underneath a fig tree like Nathanael in John's Gospel.[22] Augustine comments in his *Tractates on John* that Nathanael's presence under the fig tree combined with his guileless character indicates that Nathanael is a man who acknowledges his sins and, therefore, his need for a savior.[23] Augustine therefore indicates that he has become like Nathanael, a man who acknowledges his sins, confesses them, and seeks salvation from God. Weeping, Augustine prays the words of the Psalms: "'And Thou, O Lord, how long? How long, O Lord; wilt Thou be angry forever? Remember not our former iniquities.' For I felt that I was still bound by them. And I continued my miserable complaining, 'How long, how long shall I go on saying tomorrow

---

17. *Conf.*, 8.10.22. My translation.

18. Recall that Augustine defines a good will in *lib. arb.* as "a will by which we seek to live rightly and honorably and to come to the highest wisdom." *Lib. arb.*, 1.12.

19. *Conf.*, 8.11.26. My translation.

20. "Casta dignitas continentiae." Ibid., 8.11.27. My translation.

21. Ibid., 8.12.27.

22. See Jn 1:48.

23. Jn 1:47. See *Jo. ev. tr.*, 7.15–22. Augustine remarks that Adam and Eve used the leaves of the fig tree to cover the evidence of their sins in the Garden of Eden.

and again tomorrow? Why not now, why not have an end to my uncleanness this very hour?'"[24] In the *De libero arbitrio*, Augustine makes it clear that ignorance and difficulty are punishments for sin, not sins themselves. One does not sin because of what one suffers, but because of what one does. He writes there, "You are not considered at fault if you, against your will, are ignorant; however, if you are ignorant because you fail to ask, you are at fault. You are not blamed because you do not bind up your wounded limbs. Your sin is that you despise Him who wishes to heal you."[25] Until the point that Augustine prays those words of the Psalms, he had been despising "Him who wishes to heal you," by hesitating to ask for his help and his healing. As soon as Augustine prays these words, he hears a voice as if of a child who says "Take and read (*tolle lege*)."[26] Taking the command as divine, Augustine picks up a copy of St. Paul's epistles, where he reads: "Not in rioting and drunkenness, not in chambering and impurities, not in contention and in envy, but put ye on the Lord Jesus Christ and make not provision for the flesh in its concupiscences."[27] The passage addresses the impurities of Augustine's sexual lust and the envy and strife of his lust after honors. It says that the remedy is Christian baptism and that baptism, or putting on the Lord Jesus Christ, is the way to make no provision for the flesh in its concupiscence or, in other words, to love eternal things and to turn away from the carnal habit of disordered love for temporal goods.

As Augustine says at the beginning of Book 8, "My desire now was not to be more sure of you but be more steadfast in you that I desired."[28] Khaled Anatolios argues that a key teaching of Athanasius on creation is that

> Perseverance, endurance, fixity are not *per se* creaturely qualities; indeed the Word protects creation from its inherent lack of fixity and makes it "firm" (*Bebaios*) by granting it a participation in His own power. This principle applies equally to the second level of grace whereby humanity is enjoined to "remain" in this grace. But, of course, as Athanasius tells it, the whole story of salvation history up to the coming of the Word-made-flesh is precisely the story of humanity's failure to remain in grace.[29]

Augustine's affinity with Athanasius' teaching is manifest in *conf.* 7.9.14, in which Augustine emphasizes the eternity of the second person of the Trinity, identical

---

24. *Conf.*, 8.11.28. See also Pss. 6:3 and 79:5-8.

25. "Non tibi deputatur ad culpam, quod inuitus ignoras, sed quod neglegis quaerere quod ignores, neque illud quod uulnerata membra non colligis, sed quod uolentem sanare contemnis, ista tua propria peccata sunt." *Lib. arb.*, 3.19.181.

26. *Conf.*, 8.12.29.

27. Ibid. See Rom. 13:13-14.

28. *Conf.*, 8.1.1.

29. Khaled Anatolios, "The Soteriological Significance of Christ's Humanity in St. Athanasius," *St Vladimir's Theological Quarterly*, vol. 40, no. 4 (1996), 265–86 at 273.

13. Augustine's Moral and Religious Conversion

with wisdom, and that wisdom is always "remaining in herself." Augustine has also demonstrated in his own actions his solidarity with the rest of sinful humanity in his inability to persevere in the right way of life; hence his search for steadfastness. Anatolios presents Athanasius' theology of the Incarnation as God providing a recourse for his creatures from their creaturely tendency toward nonbeing; but man refuses God's protection. Anatolios says, "It is the union of the Word with humanity, effected by the Word becoming flesh, that is presented as the decisive resolution between God's giving and securing of grace on the one side, and humanity's turning away from grace, on the other."[30] This same Christ, Anatolios says further, "continues to work, to enliven, to exercise providence and manifest his power, to be revealed as God by his works."[31] Christ, Anatolios continues to say, receives the Holy Spirit on our behalf, and "it is precisely in the Incarnation, through Christ's human receptivity on our behalf, that our reception of the grace of the Spirit finally becomes securely united with our flesh."[32] The stability of our reception in grace is secured by Christ's humanity and grounded in his divinity. Men become sharers in Christ's virtuous stability through communion with Christ's body in the Church. Augustine's search for steadfastness therefore ends in his conversion to Christ and is accomplished through his baptism, which is his entrance into the body of Christ, the Church. Further, the lines before and after this quotation from Romans refer to an entire way of life lived by the grace of Christ, in which love of God and love of neighbor are combined so that the Christian lives on earth as a servant to his fellow members of the earthly city, and as a pilgrim journeying toward heaven where his true citizenship lies. This man described by St. Paul obeys the laws of the earthly city, but also fulfills God's law, by obeying the commandments and loving his neighbor.[33] The strength to carry out this new kind of way of life is given to the man who puts on the Lord Jesus Christ.

Christology underlies Augustine's conversion. Christ and the Catholic faith in Christ's hypostatic union, and the corresponding sacramental theology and ecclesiology, provide the difference between the way of life of the philosopher and the Manichean and the way of life of the Christian. Augustine's prayer here at this point marks the first time in the *Confessions* that the character of Augustine invokes the power of Christ through prayer to make him whole. Augustine narrates his reaction: "I had no wish to read further, and no need. For in that instant, with the very ending of the sentence, it was as though a light of utter confidence shone in all my heart, and all the darkness of uncertainty vanished away."[34] It is no accident

---

30. Ibid., 278.
31. Ibid., 279.
32. Ibid., 284.
33. Rom. 13:1-7.
34. *Conf.*, 8.12.29. Wetzel expresses disappointment. Augustine, he says, has set up the reader to expect a moment of choice as constituting his conversion:

> If free choice of his calling were the hinge on which his conversion turned, we might have expected Augustine to dramatize the moment of choice. But as the "tolle,

that he has just read the story of St. Anthony, who himself performs a similar act.[35] Anatolios emphasizes that, for Athanasius,

> The proper human activity of Antony is prayer—in the large sense of the term, which includes all of Antony's ascetical "discipline," insofar as it is understood to derive from his invocation of divine assistance. Prayer, understood as the invocation of divine presence and assistance, is the human counterpart to the divine power which is operative in Antony's life of holiness ... Antony wants therefore to reinforce the point that, as a mere man, the only thing he can do is invoke the power of Christ through prayer.[36]

Augustine receives peace for his erstwhile restless heart and banishes even the shadows of doubt. As for the troubling vestiges of the *consuetudo carnalis*, he has finally become continent. With Augustine's resolve to put on Christ, he announces that the promise of the voice he heard on high after his unstable philosophic ascent in 7.10.16 is being accomplished in him: "I am the food of grown men: grow, and you shall eat Me. And you shall not change Me into yourself as bodily food, but

> lege" episode stands, can we even tell when the moment occurs? It is hard enough deciding at what point an offer of the spirit has been tendered to Augustine. He seems to identify the voice as God's point of entry into the scene, but it is in reading the verse from Paul that his torment ends. He gives no indication, however, that he chose with deliberation to respond to either. His obedience to the command to take up and read follows as a matter of course from his interpretation of the voice as a personal address. It does not emerge as a discrete moment of decision. When he encounters the book of the apostle, he is all receptivity. He does not have to consent to the spirit's presence, because after he has read the verse, no shadow of hesitation or irresolution remains over his will. This moment of inner clarity and conversion is memorable precisely because it is the moment when Augustine no longer needs to choose. (Wetzel, *Augustine and the Limits of Virtue*, 153–4)

But Wetzel seems to be expecting God's offer to come to Augustine the same way any other offer might: an external agent proposes, Augustine deliberates among options, and then chooses. But that would make God and the grace of God an agent like any other agent, and the choice Augustine makes a choice among competing goods roughly on the same plane. But the banishing of hesitation and irresolution is the precise response to the erstwhile half-maimed character of his will. The fact that his will was half-maimed meant that he was not capable of putting his whole energy into a choice. The banishing of hesitation and irresolution is precisely the moment of choosing. It is a choosing done in total cooperation with the grace of God, requested by Augustine in prayer and received through the healing of his half-maimed will.

    35. See Athanasius, *The Life of Saint Anthony*, 2.
    36. Khaled Anatolios, *Athanasius: The Coherence of His Thought* (London: Routledge, 1998), 186.

into Me you shall be changed."[37] To be changed into God is to put on Christ, and the Eucharistic imagery indicates the ecclesial context of Augustine's conversion.[38] With one prayer and the resolution to receive baptism, Christ's grace heals Augustine's ignorance and difficulty, making him peaceful and banishing his hesitation. The healing that grace accomplishes within Augustine begins to make him whole via Christ's universal way of salvation.

Sin distracts man among the lower things, the many created things. At the beginning of *conf.* 2, Augustine says that God is the "Loveliness that does not deceive, Loveliness happy and abiding: and I collect myself out of that broken state in which my very being was torn asunder because I was turned away from Thee, the One, and wasted myself upon the many."[39] Augustine dissipates himself among the many created things that are beautiful, becoming blind because of his distraction among them. In this state, he cannot affirm what he hints at in *Confessions* 1.2–3, that God is present to his entire creation, while not being contained in any sense by creation. Among the created things, no one good compels man's love; there are higher and lower created goods, but only by gradation. Bodies and the pleasures of the body are good, although not as good as the glory given to great souls; glory is good and indicates the goodness of the soul worthy of honor, but is not as good as wisdom and the soul that pursues it. Yet a way of life seeking any of these goods necessarily closes off avenues to the attainment of the other goods. Augustine cannot love all the goods he finds within his field of view in one act; a piecemeal approach just leads to a fractured way of life. He cannot live a way of life aimed at the good of his whole self without an object of love that itself can harmonize all of those good things into a wise order. Any effective way of salvation cannot divide these goods up, as do the ways recommended by Porphyry.

Christ, who is true God and true man, unifies Creator and creature and appears among temporal things so that he is a proper object of knowledge and love for

---

37. *Conf.*, 7.10.16.

38. Wetzel comments on this passage, "The words speak to gestation, not digestion." James Wetzel, "Life in Unlikeness: The Materiality of Augustine's Conversion," *The Journal of Religion*, vol. 19, no. 1 (January 2011), 43–63 at 62. Wetzel is surely right about gestation, but perhaps hasty in dismissing digestion. Augustine clearly draws parallels between the philosophic ascent under the tutelage of the books of the Platonists in Book 7 and the ascent at Ostia that Augustine undertakes with his mother in Book 9. Boersma says that the Ostia ascent has "unmistakable eucharistic overtones." Boersma, "Monica as Mystagogue: Time and Eternity at Ostia," in *Wisdom and the Renewal of Catholic Theology: Essays in Honor of Matthew L. Lamb*, ed. Thomas P. Harmon and Roger W. Nutt (Eugene: Pickwick Publications, 2016), 104–24 at 120, n. 69. John C. Cavadini calls the second ascent, "Eucharistic remembering." See Cavadini, "Eucharistic Exegesis in Augustine's *Confessions*," *Augustinian Studies*, vol. 41, no. 1 (2010), 87–108 at 89. See also Michael P. Foley, "The Sacramental Topography of the *Confessions*," *Antiphon*, vol. 9, no. 1 (2005), 31–64 at 42–3.

39. *Conf.*, 2.1.1. "Dulcedo non fallax, dulcedo felix et secura, et conligens me a dispersione, in qua frustatim discissus sum, dum ab uno te auersus in multa euanui."

sinful men who are distracted and dissipated among temporal things, thereby placing all goods in context within his universal way of salvation.[40] Christ's passion and death puts to death "this body of death."[41] Christ is a whole man, body and soul, and as a whole man he undergoes passion, death, and resurrection. In the Resurrection, the whole man is raised to eternal life, body and soul. The sinful Augustine had been no longer able to love the incorporeal God because of the disorder of his mind distracted among temporal things. He is, however, able to love Christ who mercifully condescends to appear in the flesh among temporal things. Augustine is not able to love every created good worthy of human love in one act and as the object of a single, unified, universal way of life. He is, however, able in one act to love Christ who is divine wisdom united to a whole man. He begins to do so when he humbly asks for God's help under the fig tree. That humble prayer and God's response to it frees him from his enslavement to the *consuetudo carnalis* as expressed in his lowly and intractable bodily lusts. Christ sums up and contains in himself every created good, and unites created good to uncreated good by his hypostatic union. Loving Christ, which is accomplished in the Church, therefore constitutes a universal way of life in the one act of love for Christ that encompasses the love for all the goods human beings legitimately desire. Christ therefore unites the whole man by harmonizing and giving proper order to all of man's loves, especially the crucially important love of God and love of neighbor. There can be no divided will in loving Christ, because, in loving Christ, there is no genuine good that is not loved. This wholeness was what Augustine found was lacking in the books of the Platonists: the mediator that brings together Creator and creature, divinity and humanity, Word and flesh and can therefore alone offer a genuinely universal way of salvation.

The wholeness of right order that Christ accomplishes within Augustine is what Joseph Cropsey calls, "the rule of the better over the worse, of soul over body," and which "is ordained by nature itself."[42] The problem is,

---

40. As Augustine later affirms, "Now clearly a mediator between God and men should have something in common with God, something in common with men; if he were in both points like men, he would be too far from God; if he were in both points like God, he would be too far from men: and in neither event could be a mediator." "Mediator autem inter deum et homines oportebat ut haberet aliquid simile deo, aliquid simile hominibus, ne in utroque hominibus similis longe esset a deo, aut in utroque deo similis longe esset ab hominibus atque ita mediator non esset." *Conf.*, 10.42.67. Meconi argues that Augustine's recognition of the Word's divinity in 7.9.14, his recognition of a "downward participation" of the Word in 7.18.24, and his recognition of Jesus Christ's full humanity in 7.19.25 all contribute to the removal of objections to the Catholic faith. See Meconi, "The Incarnation and the Role of Participation in St. Augustine's *Confessions*," 61–75. The theological judgment, made in faith, that this man, Christ, is also the divine Word of God allows Augustine to cling to Christ steadfastly.

41. See *conf.*, 7.21.27; Rom. 7:24.

42. Cropsey, *Plato's World*, 196.

We observe that it is scarcely ever to be seen. Socrates is not pressed to explain the imperfection of the rule of the soul over the body among mankind ... The soul's rule over the body is brought to its peak as the soul simulates withdrawal from the body, much as the philosopher practices on the city by withdrawing from it as well and as far as he is able. The power of the higher varies inversely with its proximity to its object. By this light, the rule that is effectual manifestly must be that which is imposed by like upon like or equal upon equal, the palpable rule of the statesman.[43]

Needless to say, the principle Cropsey enunciates, while true in its own order, undergoes a remarkable transposition in Augustine's Christology, in which the absolutely higher takes on flesh to be like the lower, so that the higher will act on the lower both through its being higher and through equality. Augustine's conversion scene in the garden in *conf.* 8.12 is therefore entirely undergirded by Christology, in which the high and the low are hypostatically united in Jesus Christ who, through the divine mercy, effects a whole transformation of the believer through grace.

Having been healed, Augustine is able to tell his mother that he "no longer sought a wife nor any of this world's promises,"[44] indicating that he would put away his mistresses once and for all and abandon his chair of rhetoric, finally overcoming the two most visible manifestations of the weight of carnal custom in his life, and thereupon embarking on the pursuit of wisdom he had desired since reading the *Hortensius* but which he was only strong enough to do after receiving the grace of Christ and resolving to be baptized. Under the tutelage of the Platonists, Augustine achieves a liberation in mind when he is able to conceive an incorporeal substance, which indicates his ability to transcend the world of sense and opinion through dialectic and contemplation. But this liberation in mind does not fully liberate his mind, for he is still distracted by his disordered loves and, therefore, is scourged by ignorance and difficulty. He needs to ask for Christ's mercy in conquering the devil in his flesh like St. Anthony did. Augustine exults, "Now my mind was free from the cares that had gnawed it, from aspiring and getting and weltering in filth and rubbing the scabs of lust."[45] With his conversion and intention to receive baptism, he is finally liberated in his whole self, soul and body, mind and will, like Victorinus and Anthony before him. That liberation eluded him even in the midst of his philosophic ascent in *conf.* 7.

Augustine describes another ascent in Book 9, after his conversion. This ascent contrasts with his Neoplatonic ascent in Book 7 in several ways.[46] Importantly,

---

43. Ibid.

44. "Nec uxorem quaererem nec aliquam spem saeculi huius." *Conf.*, 8.12.30. My translation.

45. *Conf.*, 9.1.1.

46. Vaught makes an sharp comparison between Augustine and Plotinus. Vaught observes, "In disrupting the continuity of his narrative by discussing the death of his mother, Augustine is moving in a Christian rather than a Neoplatonic direction. Plotinus

it is done not privately, but with his mother, Monica, and in the context of their shared faith in Christ and their membership in his body.[47] Now Augustine's ascent is accomplished not only with another person, but with an unlettered person. They ascend by virtue of a conversation about "what the eternal life of the saints could be like."[48] Their ascent and their goal are both marked by fellowship with others. This is no "flight of the alone to the alone."[49] Just as in the Neoplatonic ascent, he attains to eternal wisdom through a "flash" of the mind.[50] But at Ostia, it is also marked by reference to the other senses: taste, touch, smell, hearing, and vision are all fully engaged throughout the entire ascent.[51] The Neoplatonic ascent leaves him beaten back and frustrated. The ascent at Ostia leaves him straining forward in hope.[52] The social context and the constant references to the bodily senses show that the Ostia ascent is not accomplished through distance from human affairs, but by way of an immersion in human affairs purified by humility and done in the context of the ecclesial body of Christ.[53]

---

never mentions his family or his earthly origins … . By contrast, after Augustine says that he must hasten, he pauses for six paragraphs to describe the death of his mother." Vaught, *Encounters with God in Augustine's* Confessions: *Books VII–IX*, 120.

47. Boersma argues that Monica herself functions as an "ecclesial symbol" both here and in the Cassiciacum dialogues. See Boersma, "Monica as Mystagogue," 116.

48. *Conf.*, 9.10.23.

49. Plotinus, *Enneads*, 6.9.11.

50. *Conf.*, 9.10.25.

51. Brian Stock observes, "In his earlier accounts of Plotinian ascent, Augustine stresses the manner in which a neoplatonic hierarchy of the senses proceeds from images of hearing toward those of outer and inner sight. At *Confessions* 9.10 the order is reversed. A visual framework—the sight of the garden outside the house—acts as a background for an ascent described largely in auditory terms." Brian Stock, *Augustine the Reader: Meditation, Self-Knowledge, and the Ethics of Interpretation* (Cambridge, MA: Belknap Press of Harvard University Press, 1998), 119.

52. Boersma describes Augustine and Monica's experience as "a hope-filled ascent to eternal wisdom." Boersma, "Monica as Mystagogue," 114. Boersma continues, "This hope … sets the Ostian narrative apart from that of Milan. While both ascents are fleeting experiences, that of Ostia is described as a foretaste of heaven, to which they remain bound (*religatas*) in hope even after the conclusion of the experience. In contrast, after the experience in Milan Augustine crashes back down, back into the *regio dissimilitudinis*; at Ostia Augustine and Monica experience the *region ubertatis indeficientis*: the 'region of inexhaustible abundance where you feed Israel eternally with truth for food.'" Ibid., 116.

53. Cavadini points out, "The Eucharist is the sacrifice of the Word made flesh, and those bound to the Eucharist by the bond of faith cannot be 'wrenched away' from the Father's protection." Cavadini, "Eucharistic Exegesis," 89. The prideful reliance on his own powers in Book 7 is replaced by what Cavadini calls "an eschatological sacrament that mediates an identity suffused with hope in God's economy of mercy instead of in one's own ability to create an identity out of whole cloth." Ibid. Cavadini insightfully links memory and hope

The Neoplatonic ascent operates under the assumption that God is the highest substance, perhaps the highest part of the whole. God is to be sought, therefore, at the highest reachable point. But what Augustine actually found was quite surprising. Crosson observes that Augustine "did not find anything in the Platonists about the appearance of that divine Word within the world. What he finds missing in the eternal, immutable, transcendent One of Plotinus is *not* ubiquity or omnipresence, for he had learned that spirit is not localized as matter is; rather, what is missing is that in the writings of the Platonists, 'no man hears [God] *calling* to us' (7.21.27). But Augustine's experience was that '[the *man* Christ Jesus] called to me, and said "I am the way of truth and the life."'"[54] The answer, as Crosson points out, is that God does not speak to man merely through some epiphany within the whole order of creation: he speaks to man through the whole order of creation, as a whole and as its creator: and not only through the whole as whole, but also in every part. As Crosson puts it, "The vehicle of God's presence *is* the created world, the world experienced as telling of God. The illumination of the moment of epiphany, occurring in a particular locus of space and time, radiates outward, suffusing and transmuting the meaning of the whole of finite beings."[55] It is this wholistic apprehension of the transcendence and immanence of God that Augustine finds through meditating on the Incarnation and the mediation of the Word made flesh.[56] This apprehension makes it possible for Augustine to ascend through the whole order of creation and never leave aside the contributions of the flesh or the conversation of his unlettered mother. He finds himself bound to God now through faith, hope, and love in such a way that he will not be beat back as he was in his abortive ascent in Book 7. Hope moderates Augustine's intellectual strivings, transfiguring his search for wisdom and putting it into a new and fruitful context. As Books 10–13 of the *Confessions* show, Augustine's conversion does not shut down his intellectual search for God.[57] Far from it, Augustine is free to pursue the highest and most intimate questions about the inner life of the Trinity after

in the Eucharist. The Eucharist is for the believer a cause of reintegration grounded in the worship of the Triune God.

54. Crosson, "Structure and Meaning," 91.

55. Ibid., 93.

56. What the reader may find through meditating on Augustine's two ascents and the place of humility and the Incarnation in the Ostia ascent strikes me as quite similar to Robert Sokolowski's articulation of the "Christian distinction" in his book, *The God of Faith and Reason*. Sokolowski says, for example, "The Christian distinction between God and the world, the denial that God in his divinity is a part of or dependent on the world, was brought forward with greater clarity through the discussion of the way the Word became flesh." Sokolowski, *The God of Faith and Reason*, 37.

57. Mathewes observes, "Augustine suggests that questioning, and 'seeking' more generally, is not simply a prolegomenon to faith or praise but, in fact, a vital expression of it." Charles T. Mathewes, "The Liberation of Questioning in Augustine's *Confessions*," *Journal of the American Academy of Religion*, vol. 70, no. 3 (September 2002), 539–60 at 542.

his conversion. The difference is that he now does so in the context or prayer and together with the praise of God. Indeed, he begins Book 10 with the prayer, "Let me know thee who knowest me, let me know thee even as I am known."[58]

Christ's ministrations succeeded where the books of the Platonists could not. Augustine's conversion is brought about through the mediation of the Word made flesh. James V. Schall argues, "Augustine realized that one also had to address the question of what should, or could, be changed first, the man or his state. Indeed, it might be argued that Augustine has elaborated for us the most radical political philosophy possible by the fact that he changed himself, as he states in the *Confessions*, by the grace of God."[59] The internal transformation worked by the grace of Christ allows Augustine to live according to wisdom in some measure of continent peace and overcomes the twin punishments of ignorance and difficulty as far as possible in this life. Augustine's transformation through grace is what reorders his disorder and makes possible right relationships with God, within himself among his various parts, and with his neighbor. The internal wholeness grace effects within Augustine is both required for and leads to the universal way of salvation in which all manner of human beings are united within the city of God.

---

58. *Conf.*, 10.1.1. Augustine cites 1 Cor. 13:12.
59. Schall, *Reason, Revelation, and Human Affairs*, 102.

CONCLUSION

For Augustine, Jesus Christ mediates the universal way of salvation through his incarnation, passion, death, and resurrection. Christ heals man internally by inserting him once again into the proper order, wherein he is subjected to God through right worship. Through the grace of Christ, the subjecting of the whole man to God makes it possible to heal the ignorance and difficulty that plague man's soul and, through setting the soul back into its correct order, also sets the soul and body back into correct order. Through the reconciliation of man's various parts, the individual is prepared to be reconciled in the Church with his fellow citizens of the city of God.

Christ's way of salvation is universal because it heals the whole man in one movement and is, therefore, in principle open to all human beings and all types of human being. Christ himself embodies and sums up the universal good: through the hypostatic union he is both creator and creature and provides satisfaction for the mind, will, and body. Through his own humility, he can heal the pride of those who prioritize the nobler good of wisdom; through his Incarnation he proves the goodness and indispensability of embodied, human life; through his condescension, he is able to allow even the vulgar to transcend the world of common opinion and live according to wisdom; through his grace, he is able to gather up the scattered will and strengthen it.

Nevertheless, the grace of Christ and the universal way of salvation based on it do not do away with the fallen, human condition altogether. The life lived by Christ's followers is still one of pilgrimage on the way to the heavenly homeland, and is therefore beset with both external and internal difficulties. The effects of sin have not vanished from the world. The situation noticed by the Platonic political philosophers in which wisdom is sparsely distributed among human beings still pertains; the investigations and even conclusions of classical political philosophy, therefore, remain largely intact, according to Augustine, even if Augustine marks out the limits of politics and political philosophy differently. While the city of God is still on the way, there is no rest from temptation, and therefore no final escape from the risk of sin and vice yet.

More particularly, in the preceding pages several things have been accomplished. First, the importance of the universal way of salvation as a theme in the thought of Augustine has been demonstrated. Its significance in the pagan-Christian debates before Augustine's time and in less developed forms in Augustine's own early thought, especially as he wrestled with the philosophic strategy of esotericism, has been seen. Esotericism, he thought, was important given the real division between philosophers and nonphilosophers; but the need for esotericism, if not some reserve and prudence in gauging one's audience, vanishes in light of the Incarnation, at least concerning religion and the highest things. Christ's mediation provides a way for the type of human being who is suited to philosophy and the type of human being who is not to come together in the pursuit of wisdom through discipleship in Christ in the Church. Viewing Augustine's argument with Porphyry about what it would mean for a way of salvation to be genuinely universal through the lens of the Platonic division between the few and the many illuminated the real stakes of the argument: whether it was nature or historical sin grounding human division and, correspondingly, whether there might be a remedy.

Second, it has been established that Augustine thinks the universal way of salvation is capable of healing the divisions between the few and the many in the transpolitical city of God by showing, in detail, how the pursuit of different human goods divides human beings and how ignorance and difficulty afflict different types of human beings differently. Christ's mediation, it has been seen, provides a way to address both types of human beings through one movement and to reconcile them through charity and Christ's example of humility.

Third, the way in which the universal way of salvation flows through an individual has been illustrated by focusing on Augustine's narration of his own life in the *Confessions*. The soul of Augustine, it has been seen, is itself dominated by each of the three main classes of goods and so, at different points, Augustine is himself dominated by his appetites, his willful spiritedness, and his intellectual quest to know wisdom. But in each case, Augustine is painfully afflicted by sin and its consequences and, until he is converted to Christ, cannot find a way to reconcile his disparate longings and the various objects of his half-maimed will. The internal reconciliation wrought by grace is the key to the reconciliation among men in the city of God, both of which are accomplished by the same movement of Christ's salvific work mediated through the Incarnation and the Church that provides an extension of Christ's Incarnation through time.

In the end, Augustine remains a critic of particular Platonic philosophers, especially the ones who lived and worked after the Gospel was widely available, for refusing to acknowledge the genuinely universal way of salvation Christ provides. These philosophers exaggerate and exacerbate human division unnecessarily now that there is a remedy. But first even the philosopher must bow his head and accept the necessity of grace, rooted in an acknowledgment that all human beings and all types of human beings suffer from what is at root the same, common problem: sin. Nevertheless, Augustine remains a friend of the wisdom-seeking activity that characterizes Platonic philosophy at its best, and a friend of the human excellences cultivated in the dedicated pursuit of wisdom, as long as that pursuit of wisdom does not lead to the inhuman vivisection of the human being, in which mind is pitted against body, or the lower parts of the man are seen as entirely instrumental and, therefore, as in principle dispensable with respect to human flourishing.

BIBLIOGRAPHY

Abbreviations

CCSG   Copus Christianorum, Series Graeca
CCSL   Corpus Christianorum, Series Latina
CSEL   Corpus Scriptorum Ecclesiasticorum Latinorum
SC   Sources Chrétiennes

Primary Texts

Aquinas, Thomas. *Summa Theologiae*, ed. John Mortensen and Enrique Alarcón. Lander, WY: The Aquinas Institute for the Study of Sacred Doctrine, 2012, volumes 13–20.
Aristotle. *Poetics. Aristotelis Opera*, vol. 5, ed. Immanuel Bekker. Berlin: Walter de Gruyter, 1960 [facsimile of the 1831 ed.].
Aristotle. *Politics. Aristotelis Opera*, vol. 5, ed. Immanuel Bekker. Berlin: Walter de Gruyter, 1960 [facsimile of the 1831 ed.].
Athanasius. *Vitae Antonii Versiones latinae. Two Versions of the Life of Anthony.* CCSL 170.
Augustine. *Confessiones (conf.). Confessions.* CCSL 27.
Augustine. *Confessions*, trans. Henry Chadwick. Oxford: Oxford University Press, 1992.
Augustine. *Contra Academicos (c. acad.). Against the Academics.* CCSL 29.
Augustine. *Contra Mendacium (c. mend.). Against Lying.* CSEL 41.
Augustine. *Contra Faustum Manicheum (c. Faust.). Against Faustus, a Manichee.* CSEL 25.2.
Augustine. *De animae quantitate (quant.). On the Greatness of the Soul.* CCEL 89.
Augustine. *De beata vita (b. vita). On the Happy Life.* CSEL 63.
Augustine. *De ciuitate Dei (ciu. Dei). City of God.* CCSL 47–8.
Augustine. *De Genesi ad litteram (Gn. Litt). On the Literal Interpretation of Genesis.* CCEL 28.
Augustine. *De Genesi aduersus Manicheos (Gn. Adu. Man.). On Genesis, against the Manichees.* CCEL 91.
Augustine. *De libero arbitrio (lib. arb.). On Free Choice of the Will.* CCSL 29.
Augustine. *De magistro (mag.). On the Teacher.* CCSL 29.
Augustine. *De ordine (ord.). On Order.* CCSL 29.
Augustine. *De sermone Domini in monte (s. Dom. Mon.). On the Lord's Sermon on the Mount.* CCSL 35.
Augustine. *De Trinitate (Trin.). On The Trinity.* CCSL 50/50A.
Augustine. *De utilitate credenda (util. cred.). On the Advantage of Believing.* CSEL 25.

Augustine. *De uera religione (uera rel.). On True Religion.* CCSL 32.
Augustine. *Enchiridion ad Laurentium de fide spe et caritate (ench.). A Handbook on Faith, Hope, and Love.*
CCSL 46. *Epistulae (ep./epp.). Letters.* CSEL 34, 44, 57, 58, 88.
CCSL 46. *Expositio Quarundam propositionum ex epistula Apostoli ad Romanos (ex. Prop. Rm.).*
CCSL 46. *Commentary on Statements in the Letter to the Romans.* CSEL 84.
CCSL 46. *In epistulam Joannis ad Parthos tractatus (ep. Jo.). Tractates on the First Letter of John.* SC 75.
CCSL 46. *In Johannis evangelium tractatus (Jo eu. tr.). Tractates on the Gospel of John.* CCSL 36.
CCSL 46. *Rectractationes (retr.). Retractations.* CCSL 57.
CCSL 46. *Soliloquia (sol.). Soliloquies.* CSEL 89.
Gregory Nazianzen. *Epistulae 102 et 101. Letters 102 and 101.* CCSG 99.
Lactantius. *De Mortibus Persecutorum*, ed. and trans. J. L. Creed. Oxford: Clarendon, 1984. CSEL 27.2.
Origen of Alexandria. *Traité Des Principes*, vol. 1, ed. Henri Crouzel and Manlio Simonetti. Paris: Les Éditiones du Cerf, 1978. SC, no. 252.
Origen of Alexandria. *Traité Des Principes*, vol. 3, ed. Henri Crouzel and Manlio Simonetti. Paris: Les Éditiones du Cerf, 1980. SC, no. 268.
Plato. *Apologia*, in *Platonis Opera Omnia*, vol. 1, ed. Godofredus Stallbaum. New York: Garland Publishing, Inc., 1980.
Plato. *Crito*, in *Platonis Opera Omnia*, vol. 1, ed. Godofredus Stallbaum. New York: Garland Publishing, Inc., 1980.
Plato. *Leges*, in *Platonis Opera Omnia*, vol. 10, ed. Godofredus Stallbaum. New York: Garland Publishing, Inc., 1980.
Plato. *Meno*, in *Platonis Opera Omnia*, vol. 6, ed. Godofredus Stallbaum. New York: Garland Publishing, Inc., 1980.
Plato. *Phaedo*, in *Platonis Opera Omnia*, vol. 1, ed. Godofredus Stallbaum. New York: Garland Publishing, 1980.
Plato. *Politia sive De Republica libri decem*, in *Platonis Opera Omnia*, vol. 3, ed. Godofredus Stallbaum. New York: Garland Publishing, Inc., 1980.
Plato. *Symposium*, in *Platonis Opera Omnia*, vol. 1, ed. Godofredus Stallbaum. New York: Garland Publishing, 1980.
Plotinus. *Enneads*, in *Plotini Opera*, 3 vols., ed. Paul Henry and Hans-Rudolf Schwyzer. Oxford: Oxford University Press, 1978.
Porphyry of Tyre. *Porphyrii Vita Plotini*, in *Plotini Opera*, vol. 1, ed. Paul Henry and Hans-Rudolf Schwyzer. Oxford: Oxford University Press, 1978.
Porphyry of Tyre. *Porphyry the Philosophy to Marcella*, text and trans. Kathleen O'Brien Wicker. Atlanta: Scholars Press, 1987.
Shakespeare, William. *Antony and Cleopatra*, in *The Complete Works of William Shakespeare*, ed. David Bevington, 1293–344. New York: Longman, 1997.
Shakespeare, William. *Coriolanus*, in *The Complete Works of William Shakespeare*, ed. David Bevington, 1345–95. New York: Longman, 1997.
Shakespeare, William. *Julius Caesar*, in *The Complete Works of William Shakespeare*, ed. David Bevington, 1021–59. New York: Longman, 1997.

Primary Texts in Translation

Aquinas, Thomas. *Summa Theologiae*, trans. Laurence Shapcote, OP, ed. John Mortensen and Enrique Alarcón. Lander, WY: The Aquinas Institute for the Study of Sacred Doctrine, 2012, vols. 13–20.
Aristotle. *Poetics*, trans. Seth Benardete and Michael Davis. South Bend: St. Augustine's Press, 2002.
Aristotle. *Politics*, trans. Carnes Lord. Chicago: University of Chicago Press, 1985.
Athanasius. *The Life of Saint Anthony*, trans. Robert T. Meyer. New York: Newman, 1950.
Augustine. *The Advantage of Believing*, trans. Luanne Meagher, OSB, in *Writings of St. Augustine*, vol. 2, ed. Ludwig Schopp. New York: CIMA Publishing, 1947.
Augustine. *Against the Academics*, trans. Michael P. Foley. New Haven, CT: Yale University Press, 2019.
Augustine. *City of God*, trans. Henry Bettenson. London: Penguin Books, 2003.
Augustine. *The City of God against the Pagans*, trans. R. W. Dyson. Cambridge: Cambridge University Press, 1998.
Augustine. *Confessions*, trans. John K. Ryan. New York: Image Books, 1960.
Augustine. *Confessions*, trans. F. J. Sheed. Indianapolis, IN: Hackett, 2006.
Augustine. *The Enchiridion*, trans. J. B. Shaw. Washington, DC: Gateway Editions, 1996.
Augustine. *On Free Choice of the Will*, trans. Anna S. Benjamin and L. H. Hackstaff. Upper Saddle River, NJ: The Library of Liberal Arts, 1964.
Augustine. *The Greatness of the Soul*, trans. Joseph M. Colleran, CSSR. Westminster, MD: The Newman Press, 1950.
Augustine. *Letters*, vol. 1, trans. Wilfrid Parsons, SND. New York: Fathers of the Church, 1951.
Augustine. *Letters*, vols. 2–3, trans. Wilfrid Parsons, SND. New York: Fathers of the Church, 1953.
Augustine. *Letters*, vol. 4, trans. Wilfrid Parsons, SND. New York: Fathers of the Church, 1955.
Augustine. *Letters*, vol. 5, trans. Wilfrid Parsons, SND. New York: Fathers of the Church, 1956.
Augustine. *The Lord's Sermon on the Mount*, trans. John J. Jepson, SS. Westminster, MD: The Newman Press, 1948.
Augustine. *On Order*, trans. Michael P. Foley. New Haven, CT: Yale University Press, 2020.
Augustine. *Soliloquies*, trans. Kim Paffenroth. New York: New City Press, 2000.
Augustine. *Soliloquies*, trans. Michael P. Foley. New Haven, CT: Yale University Press, 2020.
Augustine. *The Teacher*, trans. Peter King, in *Against the Academicians and the Teacher*, ed. Peter King. Indianapolis, IN: Hackett, 1995.
Augustine. *The Trinity*, trans. Stephen McKenna, CSSR. Washington, DC: Catholic University of America Press, 2002.
Augustine. *Of True Religion*, trans. J. H. S. Burleigh. Chicago: Henry Regnery Company, 1959.
Benedict XVI. *Deus Caritas Est*. Rome: Libreria Editrice Vaticana, 2006.
Cicero. *De Officiis*, trans. Walter Miller. Cambridge, MA: Loeb Classical Library, 1975.
Cicero. *On the Commonwealth*, trans. George Holland Sabine and Stanley Barney Smith. New York: Macmillan, 1976.
Cicero. *On Duties*, trans. Walter Miller. Cambridge, MA: Loeb Classical Library, 2005.

Cicero. *Tusculan Disputations*, trans. J. E. King. Cambridge, MA: Loeb Classical Library, 1966.
Constantine. *Oration to the Saints*, trans. Mark Edwards, in *Constantine and Christendom*, ed. Mark Edwards, 1–62. Liverpool: Liverpool University Press, 2003.
Origen of Alexandria. *On First Principles*, trans. G. W. Butterworth. Gloucester, MA: Peter Smith, 1973.
Plato. *Apology of Socrates*, in *Four Texts on Socrates*, trans. Thomas G. West and Grace Starry West, 63–98. Ithaca, NY: Cornell University Press, 1998.
Plato. *Crito*, in *The Trial and Death of Socrates*, trans. G. M. A. Grube, 43–54. Indianapolis, IN: Hackett, 2000.
Plato. *Laws*, trans. Thomas Pangle. Chicago: University of Chicago Press, 1988.
Plato. *Meno*, trans. George Anastaplo and Laurence Berns. Newberry, MA: Focus Philosophical Library, 2004.
Plato. *Phaedo*, trans. Eva Brann, Peter Kalkavage, and Eric Salem. Newberry, MA: Focus Philosophical Library, 1998.
Plato. *Republic*, trans. Allan Bloom. New York: Basic Books, 2016.
Plato. *Symposium*, trans. Seth Benardete. Chicago: University of Chicago Press, 2001.
Plotinus. *Enneads*, trans. Stephen MacKenna. London: Faber and Faber, 1930.
Porphyry of Tyre. *On Abstinence from Killing Animals*, trans. Gillian Clark. London: Bloomsbury, 2014.
Porphyry of Tyre. *Porphyry the Philosophy to Marcella*, ed. and trans. Kathleen O'Brien Wicker. Atlanta: Scholars Press, 1987.
Porphyry of Tyre. "On the Life of Plotinus and the Arrangement of His Work," in Plotinus, *Enneads*, trans. Stephen Mackenna, 1–20. London: Faber and Faber Limited, 1966.
Porphyry of Tyre. *Porphyry's Against the Christians: The Literary Remains*, ed. and trans. R. Joseph Hoffmann. Lanham, MD: Prometheus Books, 1994.
Virgil. *Aeneid*, trans. Robert Fitzgerald. New York: Alfred A. Knopf, 1992.

Secondary Texts

Alulis, Joseph. "'The Very Heart of Loss': Love and Politics in *Antony and Cleopatra*," in *Shakespeare and the Body Politic*, ed. Bernard J. Dobski and Dustin Gish, 31–48. Lanham, MD: Lexington Books, 2013.
Anastaplo, George. "Human Being and Citizen: A Beginning to the Study of Plato's *Apology of Socrates*," in *Ancients and Moderns: Essays on the Tradition of Political Philosophy in Honor of Leo Strauss*, ed. Joseph Cropsey, 16–49. New York: Basic Books, 1964.
Anatolios, Khaled. *Athanasius: The Coherence of His Thought*. London: Routledge, 1998.
Anatolios, Khaled. "The Soteriological Significance of Christ's Humanity in St. Athanasius," *St Vladimir's Theological Quarterly*, vol. 40, no. 4 (1996), 265–86.
Arquillière, Henri-Xavier. *L'Augustinisme Politique: Essai sur la Formation des Theories Politiques du Moyen Age*. Paris: Vrin, 1933.
Asiedu, F. B. A. "Following the Example of a Woman: Augustine's Conversion to Christianity in 386," *Vigiliae Christianae*, vol. 57, no. 3 (Aug. 2003), 276–306.
Ayres, Lewis. "Augustine on the Spirit as the Soul of the Body, or, Fragments of a Trinitarian Ecclesiology," *Augustinian Studies*, vol. 41 (2010), 165–82.

Ayres, Lewis. *Augustine and the Trinity*. Cambridge: Cambridge University Press, 2010.
Ayres, Lewis. "Into the Poem of the Universe: *Exempla*, Conversion, and Church in Augustine's *Confessions*," *Zeitschrift für Antikes Christentum* vol. 13, no. 2 (September 2009), 263–81.
Balot, Ryan. "Truth, Lies, Deception, Esotericism: The Case of St. Augustine," in *Augustine's Political Thought*, ed. Richard J. Dougherty, 173–99. Rochester, NY: University of Rochester Press, 2019.
Balthasar, Hans Urs von. *Dare We Hope "That All Men Be Saved?"* San Francisco: Ignatius Press, 2014.
Barnes, Peter. "Augustine's View of History in His *City of God*," *The Reformed Theological Review*, vol. 71, no. 2 (Aug. 2012), 90–108.
Barnes, T. D. *Athanasius and Constantius: Theology and Politics in the Constantinian Empire*. Cambridge, MA: Harvard University Press, 1993.
Barnes, T. D. *Constantine: Dynasty, Religion, and Power in the Later Roman Empire*. Oxford: Wiley-Blackwell, 2011.
Battenhouse, Roy. *Shakespeare's Christian Dimension: An Anthology of Commentary*, ed. Roy Battenhouse. Bloomington: Indiana University Press, 1994.
Battenhouse, Roy. "Shakespeare's Augustinian Artistry," in *Shakespeare's Christian Dimension: An Anthology of Commentary*, ed. Roy Battenhouse. Bloomington: Indiana University Press, 1994.
Beatrice, Pier Franco. "*Quosdam Platonicorum Libros*: The Platonic Readings of Augustine in Milan," *Vigiliae Christianae*, vol. 43 (1989), 248–81.
Benestad, J. Brian. *Church, State, and Society: An Introduction to Catholic Social Doctrine*. Washington, DC: Catholic University of America Press, 2011.
Blits, Jan A. *Spirit, Soul, and City: Shakespeare's Coriolanus*. Lanham, MD: Lexington Books, 2006.
Bloom, Allan. "The Morality of the Pagan Hero: *Julius Caesar*," in Allan Bloom with Harry V. Jaffa, *Shakespeare's Politics*. Chicago: University of Chicago Press, 1981.
Bloom, Allen, with Harry V. Jaffa. *Shakespeare's Politics*. Chicago: University of Chicago Press, 1981.
Boersma, Gerald. *Augustine's Early Theology of Image: A Study in the Development of Pro-Nicene Theology*. Oxford: Oxford University Press, 2016.
Boersma, Gerald. "Monica as Mystagogue: Time and Eternity at Ostia," in *Wisdom and the Renewal of Catholic Theology: Essays in Honor of Matthew L. Lamb*, ed. Thomas P. Harmon and Roger W. Nutt, 104–24. Eugene: Pickwick Publications, 2016.
Brachtendorf, Johannes. "Augustine on the Glory and the Limits of Philosophy," in *Augustine and Philosophy*, ed. Phillip Cary, John Doody, and Kim Paffenroth, 3–22. Lexington Books: Lanham, 2010.
Breyfogle, Todd. "No Changing Nor Shadow," *A Reader's Companion to Augustine's Confessions*, ed. Kim Paffenroth and Robert P. Kennedy, 33–52. Louisville, KY: Westminster John Knox Press, 2003.
Brown, Peter. *Augustine of Hippo*. Berkeley: University of California Press, 1975.
Brown, Peter. *Religion and Society in the Age of St. Augustine*. London: Faber and Faber, 1972.
Buchheit, Vinzenz. "Augustinus unter dem Feigenbaum," *Vigiliae Christianae*, vol. 22 (1968), 257–71.
Burger, Ronna. "Socratic Eironeia," *Interpretation: A Journal of Political Philosophy*, vol. 13, no. 2 (May 1985), 143–9.

Burnell, Peter. "The Status of Politics in St. Augustine's *City of God*," *History of Political Thought*, vol. 13, no. 1 (1992), 13–29.
Burns, Daniel E. "St. Augustine on the Nature and Limits of Human Law," PhD diss., Boston College, 2012.
Burns, Daniel E. "Augustine on the Moral Significance of the Human Law," *Revue d'études augustiniennes et patristiques*, vol. 61 (2015), 273–98.
Burns, J. Patout. "Augustine on the Origin and Progress of Evil," *The Journal of Religious Ethics*, vol. 16, no. 1 (Spring 1988), 9–27.
Burns, Timothy W. *Shakespeare's Political Wisdom*. New York: Palgrave Macmillan, 2013.
Burns, Timothy W. "Philosophy and Poetry: A New Look at an Old Quarrel," *American Political Science Review*, vol. 109, no. 2 (May 2015), 326–38.
Burrell, David. "Reading *The Confessions* of Augustine: An Exercise in Theological Understanding," *The Journal of Religion*, vol. 50, no. 4 (October 1970), 327–51.
Cameron, Averil. *Christianity and the Rhetoric of Empire: The Development of Christian Discourse*. Berkeley: University of California Press, 1991.
Cameron, Averil. *The Later Roman Empire*. Cambridge, MA: Harvard University Press, 1993.
Cameron, Michael. "Augustine and Scripture," in *A Companion to Augustine*, ed. Mark Vessey, 200–14. Malden, MA: Wiley-Blackwell, 2012.
Cameron, Michael. *Christ Meets Me Everywhere*. Oxford: Oxford University Press, 2012.
Cantor, Paul A. "Shakespeare and Politics: *Julius Caesar*," lecture 1 of 3. https://thegreatthinkers.org/shakespeare-and-politics/lecture-course/?video=4, accessed September 1, 2021.
Cantor, Paul A. *Shakespeare's Roman Trilogy: The Twilight of the Ancient World*. Chicago: University of Chicago Press, 2017.
Cantor, Paul A. *Shakespeare's Rome: Republic and Empire*. Chicago: University of Chicago Press, 2017.
Cary, Phillip, John Doody, and Kim Paffenroth. *Augustine and Philosophy*, ed. Phillip Cary, John Doody, and Kim Paffenroth. Lanham, MD: Lexington Books, 2010.
Cavadini, John. "The Darkest Enigma: Reconsidering the Self in Augustine's Thought," *Augustinian Studies*, vol. 38, no. 1 (2007), 119–32.
Cavadini, John. "Eucharistic Exegesis in Augustine's *Confessions*," *Augustinian Studies*, vol. 41, no. 1 (2010), 87–108.
Cavadini, John. "Ideology and Solidarity in Augustine's *City of God*," in *Augustine's City of God: A Critical Guide*, ed. James Wetzel, 93–110. Cambridge, UK: Cambridge University Press, 2014.
Cavanaugh, William T. "From One City to Two: Christian Reimagining of Political Space," *Political Theology*, vol. 7, no. 3 (2006), 299–321.
Chadwick, Henry. "Self-Justification in Augustine's *Confessions*," *The English Historical Review*, vol. 118, no. 479 (2003), 1161–75.
Chadwick, Henry. *The Sentences of Sextus*, ed. Henry Chadwick. Cambridge, UK: Cambridge University Press, 1959.
Clark, Gillian. "Augustine's Porphyry and the Universal Way of Salvation," in *Studies on Porphyry*, ed. George Karamanolis and Anne Sheppard, 127–40. London: Institute of Classical Studies, University of London, 2007.
Clemmons, Thomas. "Augustine and Porphyry," in *Augustine and Tradition: Influences, Contexts, Legacy: Essays in Honor of J. Patout Burns*, ed. David G. Hunter and Jonathan P. Yates, 153–79. Grand Rapids, MI: Eerdmans, 2021.

Cochrane, Charles. *Christianity and Classical Culture*. Indianapolis, IN: Liberty Fund, 2003.
Conybeare, Catherine. *The Irrational Augustine*. Oxford: Oxford University Press, 2006.
Corrigan, Kevin. "'Solitary' Mysticism in Plotinus, Proclus, Gregory of Nyssa, and Pseudo-Dionysius," *The Journal of Religion*, vol. 76, no. 1 (January 1996), 28–42.
Courcelle, Pierre. *Recherches sur les Confessions de Saint Augustin*. E. de Boccard: Paris, 1951.
Crawford, Dan D. "Intellect and Will in Augustine's *Confessions*," *Religious Studies*, vol. 24, no. 3 (1988), 291–302.
Cropsey, Joseph. *Ancients and Moderns: Essays on the Tradition of Political Philosophy in Honor of Leo Strauss*, ed. Joseph Cropsey. New York: Basic Books, 1964.
Cropsey, Joseph. *Plato's World*. Chicago: University of Chicago Press, 1997.
Crosson, Frederick. "Esoteric versus Latent Teaching," *The Review of Metaphysics*, vol. 59, no. 1 (September 2005), 73–93.
Crosson, Frederick. "Religion and Faith in Augustine's *Confessions*," in *Rationality and Religious Faith*, ed. C. F. Delaney, 152–68. Notre Dame, IN: University of Notre Dame Press, 1979.
Crosson, Frederick. "Structure and Meaning in St. Augustine's *Confessions*," *Proceedings from the American Catholic Philosophic Association*, vol. 63 (1989), 84–97.
Crouse, R. "*Paucis Mutatis Verbis*: St. Augustine's Platonism," in *Augustine and His Critics*, ed. R. Dodaro and G. Lawless, 37–50. London: Routledge, 2000.
Daley, Brian E., SJ. "A Humble Mediator: The Distinctive Elements of St. Augustine's Christology," *Word and Spirit*, vol. 9 (1987), 100–17.
Deane, Herbert. *The Political and Social Ideas of St. Augustine*. New York: Columbia UP, 1963.
Den Boer, Willem. "A Pagan Historian and His Enemies: Porphyry against the Christians," *Classical Philology*, vol. 69, no. 3 (1974), 198–208.
Digeser, Elizabeth DePalma. "Christian or Hellene? The Great Persecution and the Problem of Identity," in *Religious Liberty in Late Antiquity*, ed. Robert M. Frakes and Elizabeth DePalma Digeser, 36–57. Campbellville, ON: University of Toronto Press, 2006.
Digeser, Elizabeth DePalma. "Lactantius, Porphyry, and the Debate over Religious Toleration," *The Journal of Roman Studies*, vol. 88 (1998), 129–46.
Digeser, Elizabeth DePalma. *A Threat to Public Piety: Christians, Platonists, and the Great Persecution*. Ithaca, NY: Cornell University Press, 2012.
Dodaro, Robert. *Christ and the Just Society in the Thought of Augustine*. Cambridge, UK: Cambridge University Press, 2008.
Dodaro, Robert. "Theurgy," in *Augustine through the Ages*, ed. Allan D. Fitzgerald, 827–8. Grand Rapids, MI: Eerdmans, 1999.
Doody, John, Kevin L. Hughes, and Kim Paffenroth. *Augustine and Politics*, ed. John Doody, Kevin L. Hughes, and Kim Paffenroth. Lanham, MD: Lexington Books, 2005.
Dougherty, Richard. *Augustine's Political Thought*, ed. Richard J. Dougherty. Rochester, NY: University of Rochester Press, 2019.
Dougherty, Richard. "St. Augustine and the Problem of Political Ethics in *The City of God*," in *Augustine's Political Thought*, ed. Richard J. Dougherty, 13–35. Rochester, NY: University of Rochester Press, 2019.
Dupont, Anthony, and Mateusz Stróżyński. "Augustine's Ostia Revisited: A Plotinian or Christian Ascent in *Confessiones* 9?," *International Journal of Philosophy and Theology*, vol. 79, nos. 1–2 (2018), 80–104.

Edwards, Mark. "Porphyry and the Christians," in *Studies on Porphyry*, ed. Mark Edwards, 111–26. London: Institute of Classical Studies, School of Advanced Study, University of London, 2007.
Edwards, Mark. *Studies on Porphyry*, ed. Mark Edwards. London: Institute of Classical Studies, School of Advanced Study, University of London, 2007.
Elshtain, Jean Bethke. *Augustine and the Limits of Politics*. Notre Dame, IN: University of Notre Dame Press, 2005.
Evans, G. R. *Augustine on Evil*. Cambridge, UK: Cambridge University Press, 1993.
Ferrari, Leo Charles "The 'Food of Truth' in Augustine's Confessions," *Augustinian Studies*, vol. 9 (1978), 1–14.
Ferrari, Leo Charles. "The Gustatory Augustin," *Augustiniana*, vol. 29 (1979), 304–15.
Ferrari, Leo Charles. "Paul at the Conversion of Augustine," *Augustinian Studies*, vol. 11 (1980), 5–20.
Fichter, Andrew. "*Antony and Cleopatra* and Christian Quest," in Roy W. Battenhouse, *Shakespeare's Christian Dimension: An Anthology of Commentary*. Bloomington: Indiana University Press, 1994.
Foley, Michael P. "Augustine, Aristotle, and the *Confessions*," *The Thomist*, vol. 67 (2003), 607–22.
Foley, Michael P. "Cicero, Augustine, and the Philosophical Roots of the Cassiciacum Dialogues," *Revue d'études augustiniennes et patristiques*, vol. 45 (1999), 51–77.
Foley, Michael P. "Commentary," in Augustine, *Against the Academics*, trans. Michael P. Foley, 115–215. New Haven: Yale University Press, 2019.
Foley, Michael P. "The Fruit of Confessing Lips," *Augustinianum*, vol. 59, no. 2 (2019), 425–52.
Foley, Michael P. "Glossary of Select Terms," in Augustine, *Confessions*, trans. F. J. Sheed, 327–34. Indianapolis, IN: Hackett, 2006.
Foley, Michael P. "The Other Happy Life: The Political Dimensions to St. Augustine's Cassiciacum Dialogues," *Review of Politics*, vol. 65, no. 2 (Spring 2003), 165–83.
Foley, Michael P. "St. Augustine: *The Confessions*," in *Finding a Common Thread: Reading Great Texts from Homer to O'Connor*, ed. Robert C. Roberts, Scott H. Moore, and Donald D. Schmeltekopf, 81–97. South Bend, IN: St. Augustine's Press.
Foley, Michael P. "The Sacramental Topography of the *Confessions*," *Antiphon*, vol. 9, no. 1 (2005), 31–64.
Fortin, Ernest, AA. *Collected Essays*, vol. 1, *The Birth of Philosophic Christianity: Studies in Early Christian and Medieval Thought*, ed. J. Brian Benestad. Lanham, MD: Rowman and Littlefield, 1996.
Fortin, Ernest, AA. *Collected Essays*, vol. 2, *Classical Christianity and the Political Order*, ed. J. Brian Benestad. Lanham, MD: Rowman and Littlefield, 1996.
Fortin, Ernest, AA. *Collected Essays*, vol. 4, *Ever Ancient, Ever New: Ruminations on the City, the Soul, and the Church*, ed. Michael P. Foley. Lanham, MD: Rowman and Littlefield, 2007.
Fortin, Ernest, AA. "Justice as the Foundation of the Political Community: Augustine and His Pagan Models," in *Augustinus, De Civitate Dei*, ed. Christoph Horn, 41–62. Berlin: Akademie Verlag, 1997.
Fortin, Ernest, AA. "St. Augustine," in *History of Political Philosophy*, ed. Leo Strauss and Joseph Cropsey, 176–205. Chicago: University of Chicago Press, 1987.
Fuhrer, Therese. "Das Kriterium der Wahrheit in Augustins *Contra Academicos*," *Vigiliae Christianae*, vol. 46 (1992), 257–75.

Fustel de Coulanges, Numa Denis. *The Ancient City*. Baltimore, MD: The Johns Hopkins University Press, 1980.
Gerson, Lloyd. *Plotinus*. London: Routledge, 1994.
Gildin, Hilail. *An Introduction to Political Philosophy: Ten Essays by Leo Strauss*, ed. Hilail Gildin. Detroit: Wayne State University Press, 1989.
Gilson, Étienne. *The Christian Philosophy of St. Augustine*. New York: Random House, 1960.
Gilson, Étienne. *The Metamorphoses of the City of God*, trans. James C. Colbert. Washington, DC: Catholic University of America Press, 2020.
Gnilka, Christian. "Kritische Bemerkung zu Augustinus Conf. 7,5,7," *Hermes*, vol. 137 (2009), 386–8.
Gregory, Eric. "Politics and Beatitude," *Studies in Christian Ethics*, vol. 30, no. 2 (2017), 199–206.
Greenwood, David Neal. "Porphyry, Rome, and Support for Persecution," *Ancient Philosophy*, vol. 36 (2016), 197–207.
Guerra, Marc D. *Christians as Political Animals*. Wilmington, DE: ISI Books, 2010.
Guerra, Marc D. "The One, the Many, and the Mystical Body," *The Heythrop Journal*, vol. 53 (2012), 904–14.
Guerra, Marc D. *Reason, Revelation, and Human Affairs: Selected Writings of James V. Schall*, ed. Marc D. Guerra. Lanham, MD: Lexington Books, 2001.
Hagendahl, Harald. *Augustine and the Latin Classics*, 2 vols. Stockholm, Sweden: Gothenburg, 1967.
Hammer, Dean. *Roman Political Thought: From Cicero to Augustine*. Cambridge: Cambridge University Press, 2014.
Harding, Brian. *Augustine and Roman Virtue*. London: Continuum, 2008.
Harding, Brian. "Skepticism, Illumination and Christianity in Augustine's *Contra Academicos*," *Augustinian Studies*, vol. 34, no. 2 (2003), 197–212.
Harmon, Thomas P. "Augustine and the Ancient Quarrel between Poetry and Philosophy," *Antonianum*, vol. XC (2015), 249–74.
Harmon, Thomas P. "The Few, the Many, and the Universal Way of Salvation: Augustine's Point of Engagement with Platonic Political Thought," in *Augustine's Political Thought*, ed. Richard J. Dougherty, 129–51. Rochester, NY: University of Rochester Press, 2019.
Harmon, Thomas P. "Reconsidering Charles Taylor's Augustine," *Pro Ecclesia*, vol. 20, no. 2 (2011), 185–209.
Harmon, Thomas P., and Roger W. Nutt. *Wisdom and the Renewal of Catholic Theology: Essays in Honor of Matthew L. Lamb*. Eugene, OR: Pickwick Publications, 2016.
Harrison, Carol. *Christian Truth and Fractured Humanity*. Oxford: Oxford University Press, 2000.
Harrison, Carol. *Rethinking Augustine's Early Theology: An Argument for Continuity*. Oxford: Oxford University Press, 2006.
Harrison, Simon. *Augustine's Way into the Will: The Theological and Philosophical Significance of De Libero Arbitrio*. Oxford: Oxford University Press, 2006.
Hart, David Bentley. *That All Shall Be Saved*. New Haven, CT: Yale University Press, 2021.
Hathaway, R. F. "The Neoplatonist Interpretation of Plato: Remarks on Its Decisive Characteristics," *Journal of the History of Philosophy*, vol. 7, no. 1 (January 1969), 19–26.
Heil, John. "Augustine's Attack on Skepticism: The *Contra Academicos*," *Harvard Theological Review*, vol. 65 (1972), 99–116.

Hollingsworth, Miles. *The Pilgrim City: St. Augustine of Hippo and His Innovation in Political Thought*. London: T&T Clark International, 2010.
Hughes, Kevin L. "Local Politics: The Political Place of the Household in Augustine's *City of God*," in *Augustine and Politics*, ed. John Doody, Kevin L. Hughes, and Kim Paffenroth, 145–64. Lanham, MD: Lexington Books, 2005.
Hunt, Maurice. "A New Taxonomy of Shakespeare's Pagan Plays," *Religion and Literature* 43:1 (Spring 2011), 29–53.
Kaufman, Peter Iver. *Incorrectly Political*. Notre Dame, IN: University of Notre Dame Press, 2007.
Kaufman, Peter Iver. "The Lesson of Conversion: A Note on the Question of Continuity in Augustine's Understanding of Grace and Human Will," *Augustinian Studies*, vol. 11 (1980), 49–64.
Kennedy, George. *Classical Rhetoric and Its Christian and Secular Tradition from Ancient to Modern Times*. Chapel Hill, NC: University of North Carolina Press, 1999.
Kenney, John Peter. "'None Come Closer to Us Than These': Augustine and the Platonists," *Religions*, vol. 7, no. 9 (2016); https://doi.org/10.3390/rel7090114, accessed July 26, 2018.
Keys, Mary M. *Aquinas, Aristotle, and the Promise of the Common Good*. Cambridge: Cambridge University Press, 2007.
Keys, Mary M. "Books 6 & 7: Nature, Convention, Civil Religion, and Politics," in *The Cambridge Companion to Augustine's* City of God, ed. David Vincent Meconi, SJ, 102–21. Cambridge: Cambridge University Press, 2021.
Keys, Mary M. *Pride, Politics, and Humility in Augustine's City of God*. Cambridge: Cambridge University Press, 2022.
Kolbet, Paul R. *Augustine and the Cure of Souls*. Notre Dame, IN: University of Notre Dame Press, 2010.
Kojève, Alexandre. "The Emperor Julian and His Art of Writing," in *Ancients and Moderns: Essays on the Tradition of Political Philosophy in Honor of Leo Strauss*, ed. Joseph Cropsey, 95–113. New York: Basic Books, 1964.
Kries, Douglas. "On the Intention of Cicero's *De Officiis*," *The Review of Politics*, vol. 65, no. 4 (2003), 375–93.
Kries, Douglas. "Reason in Context: Augustine as Defender and Critic of Leo Strauss' Esotericism Thesis," *Proceedings of the American Catholic Philosophical Association*, vol. 83 (2009), 241–52.
Kries, Douglas. "Augustine's Response to the Political Critics of Christianity in the *ciu. Dei*," *American Catholic Philosophical Quarterly*, vol. 74, no. 1 (2000), 77–93.
Kries, Douglas. "Echoes and Adaptations in Augustine's *Confessions* of Plato's Teaching on Art and Politics in the *Republic*," in *Augustine's Political Thought*, ed. Richard J. Dougherty, 152–72. Rochester, NY: University of Rochester Press, 2019.
Lamb, Matthew L. *Eternity, Time, and the Light of Wisdom*. Naples, FL: Sapientia, 2007.
Lamb, Matthew L. "Lonergan's Transpositions of Augustine and Aquinas: Some Exploratory Suggestions," in *The Importance of Insight: Essays in Honor of Michael Vertin*, ed. John J. Liptay and David S. Liptay, 3–21. Toronto: University of Toronto Press, 2007.
Lamb, Matthew L. "Wisdom Eschatology in Augustine and Aquinas," in *Aquinas the Augustinian*, ed. Barry David, Michael Dauphinais, and Matthew Levering, 258–76. Washington, DC: Catholic University of America Press, 2007.
Lamb, Michael. "Between Presumption and Despair: Augustine's Hope for the Commonwealth," *American Political Science Review*, vol. 112, no. 4 (218), 1036–49.

Lamb, Michael. *A Commonwealth of Hope: Augustine's Political Thought*. Princeton, NJ: Princeton University Press, 2022.
Lawler, Peter Augustine. "Esotericism and Living in the Truth," *Perspectives on Political Science*, vol. 44, no. 3 (2015), 199–203.
Leake, James. "On the *Lesser Hippias*," in *The Roots of Political Philosophy*, ed. Thomas L. Pangle. Ithaca, NY: Cornell University Press, 1987, 300–6.
Lendon, J. E. *The Empire of Honor: The Art of Government in the Roman World*. Oxford: Oxford University Press, 2001.
Levering, Matthew. *The Theology of Augustine: An Introductory Guide to His Most Important Works*. Grand Rapids, MI: Baker Academic, 2013.
Liebert, Hugh. *Plutarch's Politics: Between City and Empire*. Cambridge: Cambridge University Press, 2016.
Liebeschuetz, J. H. W. G. *Continuity and Change in Roman Religion*. Oxford: Clarendon Press, 1979.
Lössl, Josef. "The One (*unum*)—A Guiding Concept in *De uera religione*: An Outline of the Text and the History of Its Interpretation," *Revue des Études Augustiniennes*, vol. 40 (1994), 79–103.
Louth, Andrew. *The Origins of the Christian Mystical Tradition from Plato to Denys*. Oxford: Clarendon, 1981.
Lowenthal, David. *Shakespeare's Thought: Unobserved Details and Unsuspected Depths in Thirteen Plays*, Lanham, MD: Lexington Books, 2017.
Manent, Pierre. "Birth of the Nation," *City Journal* (Winter 2013), https://www.city-journal.org/html/birth-nation-13529.html, accessed September 2, 2021.
Manent, Pierre. *Metamorphoses of the City: On the Western Dynamic*, trans. Marc LePain. Cambridge, MA: Harvard University Press, 2013.
Manent, Pierre. *Seeing Things Politically*, trans. Ralph C. Hancock. South Bend, IN: St. Augustine's Press, 2015.
Manent, Pierre. "The Tragedy of the Republic," *First Things* (May 2017), https://www.firstthings.com/article/2017/05/the-tragedy-of-the-republic, accessed December 29, 2021.
MacDonald, Scott. "The Paradox of Inquiry," *Metaphilosophy*, vol. 39, no. 1 (2008), 20–38.
Markus, R. A. *Christianity and the Secular*. Notre Dame, IN: University of Notre Dame Press, 2006.
Markus, R. A. *Saeculum: History and Society in the Thought of Augustine*. Cambridge, UK: Cambridge University Press, 1970.
Marrou, H. I. *Saint Augustin et la Fin de la Culture Antique*. Paris: E. De Boccard, 1938.
Mathewes, Charles T. "Augustinian Anthropology: Interior intimo meo," *The Journal of Religious Ethics*, vol. 27 (Summer 1999), 195–221.
Mathewes, Charles T. "The Liberation of Questioning in Augustine's *Confessions*," *Journal of the American Academy of Religion*, vol. 70, no. 3 (September 2002), 539–60.
McCarthy, Michael C. "Augustine's Mixed Feelings: Vergil's *Aeneid* and the Psalms of David in the *Confessions*," *Harvard Theological Review*, vol. 102, no. 4 (October 2009), 453–79.
McLynn, Neil. "Augustine's Roman Empire," *Augustinian Studies*, vol. 30, no. 2 (1999), 29–44.
McMahon, Robert. *Augustine's Prayerful Ascent*. Athens, GA: University of Georgia Press, 1989.
Meconi, David Vincent. *The Cambridge Companion to Augustine's City of God*, ed. David Vincent Meconi, SJ. Cambridge: Cambridge University Press, 2021.

Meconi, David Vincent. "The Incarnation and the Role of Participation in St. Augustine's *Confessions*," *Augustinian Studies*, vol. 29, no. 2 (1998), 61–75.

Meconi, David Vincent. *The One Christ*. Washington, DC: Catholic University of America Press, 2013.

Melzer, Arthur M. *Philosophy between the Lines: The Lost History of Esoteric Writing*. Chicago: University of Chicago Press, 2014.

Menchaca-Bagnulo, Ashleen. "Deeds and Words: *Latreia*, Justice, and Mercy in Augustine's Political Thought," in *Augustine's Political Thought*, ed. Richard J. Dougherty, 74–104. Rochester, NY: University of Rochester Press, 2019.

Menchaca-Bagnulo, Ashleen. "Tragic Glory? Human Excellence in Pierre Manent and St Augustine," *The European Legacy*, vol. 27, no. 1 (2022), 20–38.

Miles, Margaret. *Desire and Delight*. New York: Crossroads, 1992.

Mosher, David L. "The Argument of St. Augustine's *Contra Academicos*, *Augustinian Studies*, vol. 12 (1981), 89–113.

O'Connell, Robert J., SJ. "*De Libero Arbitrio* I: Stoicism Revisited," in *Augustinian Studies*, vol. 1 (1970), 49–60.

O'Connell, Robert J., SJ. *St. Augustine's Confessions: The Odyssey of Soul*. Cambridge, MA: The Belknap Press of Harvard University Press, 1969.

O'Daly, Gerard. *St. Augustine's City of God: A Reader's Guide*. Oxford: Clarendon Press, 1999.

O'Donnell, James J. *Augustine: A New Biography*. New York: Harper, 2005.

O'Donovan, Oliver. "Augustine's *City of God* XIX and Western Political Thought," *Dionysius*, vol. XI (1987), 89–110.

O'Grady, Desmond. *Beyond the Empire: Rome and the Church from Constantine to Charlemagne*. New York: Crossroad, 2001.

O'Meara, Dominic. *Platonopolis: Platonic Political Philosophy in Late Antiquity*. Oxford: Oxford University Press, 2003.

O'Meara, John J. *Porphyry's Philosophy from Oracles in Augustine*. Paris: Études Augustiniennes, 1959.

Ogle, Veronica Roberts. *Politics and the Earthly City in Augustine's* City of God. Cambridge, UK: Cambridge University Press, 2021.

Ogle, Veronica Roberts. "Therapeutic Deception: Cicero and Augustine on the Myth of Philosophic Happiness," *Augustinian Studies*, vol. 50, no. 1 (2019), 13–42.

Oort, Johannes van. *Jerusalem and Babylon: A Study into Augustine's City of God and the Sources of His Doctrine of the Two Cities*. Leiden, The Netherlands: Brill, 1991.

Pang-White, Ann A. "The Fall of Humanity: Weakness of the Will and Moral Responsibility in the Later Augustine," *Medieval Philosophy and Theology*, vol. 9 (2000), 51–67.

Paffenroth, Kim, and Robert P. Kennedy. *A Reader's Companion to Augustine's Confessions*, ed. Kim Paffenroth and Robert P. Kennedy. Louisville, KY: Westminster John Knox Press, 2003.

Parens, Joshua. *Leo Strauss and the Recovery of Medieval Political Philosophy*. Rochester, NY: University of Rochester Press, 2016.

Peterson, Erik. "Monotheism as a Political Problem: A Contribution to the History of Political Theology in the Roman Empire," trans. Michael J. Hollerich, in Peterson, *Theological Tractates*, ed. Michael J. Hollerich, 68–105. Palo Alto, CA: Stanford University Press, 2011.

Platt, Michael. *Rome and Romans according to Shakespeare*. Lanham, MD: University Press of America, 1983.

Pranger, Burcht. "Augustine and the Silence of the Sirens," *The Journal of Religion*, vol. 91, no. 1 (January 2011), 64–77.
Ratzinger, Joseph. *Introduction to Christianity*, trans. J. R. Foster. New York: Herder and Herder, 1969.
Ratzinger, Joseph. *Volk und Haus Gottes in Augustins Lehre von der Kirche*. St. Ottilien: EOS Verlag, 1992.
Rist, John M. *Augustine: Ancient Thought Baptized*. Cambridge: Cambridge University Press, 2000.
Rist, John M. *Augustine Deformed: Love, Sin, and Freedom in the Western Tradition*. Cambridge: Cambridge University Press, 2014.
Rist, John M. "On the Nature and Worth of Christian Philosophy: Evidence from the *City of God*," in *Augustine's City of God: A Critical Guide*, ed. James Wetzel, 205–24. Cambridge: Cambridge University Press, 2012.
Roberts, Veronica. "Augustine's Ciceronian Response to the Ciceronian Patriot," *Perspectives on Political Science*, vol. 52, no. 2 (2016), 113–24.
Roberts, Veronica. "Idolatry as the Source of Injustice in Augustine's *De Ciuitate Dei*," *Studia Patristica LXXXVIII*, vol. 14, no. 1 (2017), 69–78.
Schall, James V., SJ. *Political Philosophy and Revelation: A Catholic Reading*. Washington, DC: Catholic University of America Press, 2013.
Schall, James V., SJ. *Reason, Revelation, and Human Affairs: Selected Writings of James V. Schall*, ed. Marc D. Guerra. Lanham, MD: Lexington Books, 2001.
Schall, James V., SJ. "The 'Realism' of Augustine's 'Political Realism': Augustine and Machiavelli," *Perspectives on Political Science*, vol. 25, no. 3 (1996), 117–23.
Schall, James V., SJ. *Roman Catholic Political Philosophy*. Lanham, MD: Lexington Books, 2006.
Schott, Jeremy M. *Christianity, Empire, and the Making of Religion in Late Antiquity*. Philadelphia: University of Pennsylvania Press, 2008.
Sehorn, John "Monica as a Synecdoche for the Pilgrim Church in the *Confessiones*," *Augustinian Studies*, vol. 46, no. 2 (2015), 225–48.
Sheed, Frank J. *Theology and Sanity*. San Francisco: Ignatius Press, 1978.
Simmons, Michael Bland. *Universal Salvation in Late Antiquity*. Oxford: Oxford University Press, 2016.
Simmons, Michael Bland. "Graeco-Roman Philosophical Opposition," in *The Early Christian World*, vol. 2, ed. Philip Esler, 840–68. London: Routledge, 2000.
Simmons, Michael Bland. "Julian the Apostate," in *The Early Christian World*, vol. 2, ed. Philip Esler, 1251–72. London: Routledge, 2000.
Simmons, Michael Bland. "Porphyrian Universalism: A Tripartite Soteriology and Eusebius's Response," *The Harvard Theological Review*, vol. 102, no. 2 (April 2009), 169–92.
Skerrett, Kathleen Roberts. "*Consuetudo Carnalis* in Augustine's *Confessions*," *Journal of Religious Ethics*, no. 37, vol. 3 (2009), 495–512.
Sokolowski, Robert. *The God of Faith and Reason*. Washington, DC: Catholic University of America Press, 1995.
Squires, Stuart. "*Contra Academicos* as Autobiography: A Critique of the Historiography on Augustine's First Extant Dialogue," *Scottish Journal of Theology*, vol. 64, no. 3 (2011), 251–64.
Stephany, William A. "Thematic Structure in Augustine's *Confessions*," *Augustinian Studies*, vol. 20 (1989), 129–42.

Stock, Brian. *Augustine the Reader: Meditation, Self-Knowledge, and the Ethics of Interpretation*. Cambridge, MA: The Belknap Press of Harvard University Press, 1998.

Strand, Daniel. "Augustine's *City of God* and Roman Sacral Politics," in *Augustine's Political Thought*, ed. Richard J. Dougherty, 222–44. Rochester, NY: University of Rochester Press, 2019.

Strauss, Leo. *An Introduction to Political Philosophy: Ten Essays by Leo Strauss*, ed. Hilail Gildin. Detroit, MI: Wayne State University Press, 1989.

Strauss, Leo. *Natural Right and History*, Chicago: University of Chicago Press, 1965.

Strauss, Leo. *Persecution and the Art of Writing*. Chicago: University of Chicago Press, 1988.

Strauss, Leo. *The Rebirth of Classical Political Rationalism*, ed. Thomas L. Pangle. Chicago: University of Chicago Press, 1989.

Strauss, Leo. *Studies in Platonic Political Philosophy*. Chicago: University of Chicago Press, 1986.

Strauss, Leo. *What Is Political Philosophy?* Chicago: University of Chicago Press, 1988.

Tell, Dave. "Augustine and the 'Chair of Lies': Rhetoric in *The Confessions*," *Rhetorica: A Journal of the History of Rhetoric*, vol. 28, no. 4 (Autumn 2010), 384–407.

TeSelle, Eugene. "Porphyry and Augustine," *Augustinian Studies*, vol. 5 (1974), 113–47.

Theiler, Willy. *Porphyrios und Augustin*. Berlin: Halle, 1933.

Thomas, Adam. "The Investigation of Justice in Augustine's *Confessions*," in *Augustine's Political Thought*, ed. Richard J. Dougherty, 105–26. Rochester, NY: University of Rochester Press, 2019.

Topping, Ryan N. S. "Augustine on Liberal Education: Defender and Defensive," *The Heythrop Journal*, vol. 51 (2010), 377–87.

Topping, Ryan N. S. *Happiness and Wisdom: Augustine's Early Theology of Education*. Washington, DC: Catholic University of America Press, 2012.

Topping, Ryan N. S. "The Perils of Skepticism: The Moral and Educational Argument of *Contra Academicos*," *International Philosophical Quarterly* vol. 49, no. 3 (September 2009), 333–50.

Torchia, N. Joseph. "St. Augustine's Treatment of *Superbia* and Its Plotinian Affinities," *Augustinian Studies*, vol. 18 (1987), 66–80.

Trainor, Brian T. "Augustine's Glorious City of God as Principle of the Political," *The Heythrop Journal*, vol. 51 (2010), 543–53.

Troup, Calvin L. *Temporality, Eternity, and Wisdom: The Rhetoric of Augustine's Confessions*. Columbia, SC: University of South Carolina Press, 1999.

Van Fleteren, Frederick. "Augustine's Ascent of the Soul in Book VII of the Confessions: A Reconsideration," *Augustinian Studies*, vol. 5 (1974), 29–72.

Van Fleteren, Frederick. "Augustine's *De vera religione*: A New Approach," *Augustinianum*, vol. 16, no. 3 (1976), 476–97.

Van Fleteren, Frederick. "The Cassiciacum Dialogues and Augustine's Ascents at Milan," *Mediaevalia*, vol. 4 (1978), 59–82.

Van Fleteren, Frederick. "Plato, Platonism," in *Augustine through the Ages: An Encyclopedia*, ed. Allan D. Fitzgerald, OSA, 651–4. Grand Rapids, MI: Eerdmans, 1999.

Van Fleteren, Frederick. "Porphyry," in *Augustine through the Ages: An Encyclopedia*, ed. Allan D. Fitzgerald, OSA, 661–3. Grand Rapids, MI: Eerdmans, 1999.

Van Oort, Johannes. "The Young Augustine's Knowledge of Manichaeism: An Analysis of the 'Confessiones' and Some Other Relevant Texts," *Vigiliae Christianae*, vol. 62, no. 5 (2008), 441–66.

Vander Valk, Frank. "Friendship, Politics, and Augustine's Consolidation of the Self," *Religious Studies*, vol. 45, no. 2 (2009), 125–46.
Vaught, Carl G. *Encounters with God in Augustine's Confessions: Books VII–IX*. Albany, NY: State University of New York Press, 2004.
Vaught, Carl G. *The Journey toward God in Augustine's Confessions: Books I–VI*. Albany, NY: State University of New York Press, 2003.
Von Heyking, John. *Augustine and Politics as Longing in the World*. Columbia, MO: University of Missouri Press, 2001.
Wetzel, James. *Augustine and the Limits of Virtue*. Cambridge, UK: Cambridge University Press, 1992.
Wetzel, James. *Augustine's City of God: A Critical Guide*, ed. James Wetzel. Cambridge, UK: Cambridge University Press, 2012.
Wetzel, James. "Life in Unlikeness: The Materiality of Augustine's Conversion," *The Journal of Religion*, vol. 19, no. 1 (January 2011), 43–63.
Wetzel, James. "The Question of *consuetudo carnalis* in *Confessions* 7.17.23," *Augustinian Studies*, vol. 3, no. 2 (2000), 165–71.
Wilken, Robert L. *The Christians as the Romans Saw Them*. New Haven, CT: Yale University Press, 1984.
Williams, Rowan. "Augustine's Christology: Its Spirituality and Rhetoric," in *In the Shadow of the Incarnation: Essays on Jesus Christ in the Early Church in Honor of Brian E. Daley, S.J.*, ed. Peter Martens. Notre Dame, IN: University of Notre Dame Press, 2008, 176–89.
Williams, Rowan. "Politics and the Soul: A Reading of the *City of God*," *Milltown Studies*, vols. 19/20 (1987), 55–73.
Williams, Stephen. *Diocletian and the Roman Recovery*. New York: Routledge, 1997.
Williams, Thomas. "Augustine vs Plotinus: The Uniqueness of the Vision at Ostia," in *Medieval Philosophy and the Classical Tradition: In Islam, Judaism and Christianity*, ed. John Inglis. London: Routledge, 2013, 143–52.

INDEX OF NAMES

Achilles 187
Adam 5, 176, 191, 203
Aesculapius 86, 104
Alaric 48, 63
Alcibiades 78, 202
Alulis, Joseph 28
Ambrose of Milan 161, 165–7, 193
Ammonius Sacchus 40
Anastaplo, George 76, 78
Anatolios, Khaled 204–6
Anaxagoras 77
Anthony of the Desert 163, 190, 192, 196–203, 206, 209
Antonius, Marcus 20–1, 25–9
Anytus 77
Apuleius 8, 20, 73, 85, 92
Aquinas, Thomas 69
Arcesilaus 51
Aristophanes 76–8
Aristotle 21–2, 37, 94, 159
Arnobius 32, 39
Athanasius of Alexandria 196–206
Athenian Stranger 116
Augustine
    anthropology of 120
    arguments with Neoplatonists 59, 150, 177, 181–2
    attitude toward Scripture 158
    Baptism of 48, 152–3, 161, 190, 205, 20, 209
    as bishop 90, 119, 140, 144
    as catechumen 166
    Christology of 209
    confession of 203
    conversion to Christianity of 195, 199–212
    and the drunk beggar 169
    familiarity with Platonic texts 7–8, 85, 91, 103
    on households 134
    on lying 48, 82
    manner of writing 4, 47, 82
    philosophic ascent of 7, 188, 199, 209–10
    as priest 144
    as philosopher 149, 156
    as political thinker 131–2, 140
    as rhetorician 59, 71–2, 89, 137, 168–9, 209
    and the theft of the pears 200
Augustus Caesar 28, 43, 45
Aurelian, Lucius Domitius 16, 32
Ayres, Lewis 8

Balot, Ryan 48
von Balthasar, Hans Urs 11
Barnes, Timothy 39
Battenhouse, Roy W. 21, 28
Benedict XVI 69
Benestad, J. Brian 36, 77
Blits, Jan H. 22
Bloom, Allan 18, 23–4, 27, 82
Den Boer, Willem 42
Boersma, Gerald 8, 59–61, 63, 207, 210
Brachtendorf, Johannes 9
Breyfogle, Todd 156–7
Brown, Peter 119, 153, 162, 166
Brutus, Marcus Junius 18
Burger, Ronna 2
Burns, J. Patout 184
Burns, Timothy W. 18

Caesar, Julius 17–18, 20, 23–7
Cain 133
Cameron, Averil 32
Cameron, Michael 4, 165–6
Cantor, Paul A. 15–16, 22–7
Carneades the Cyrene 9, 50–1
Cary, Phillip 9
Cassius, Gaius 20, 24
Cavadini, John 91, 94–5, 121, 124, 126, 184, 187, 207, 210

Celsus 38
Chadwick, Henry 39, 151
Christ
  grace of 73–4, 85–6, 124
  humility of 208
  incarnation of 6, 10–12, 15, 49, 53, 60, 62, 67, 99, 110, 125, 176, 187, 205
  mercy of 209
  mediation of 3, 11–12, 15, 20, 31, 33, 42, 50, 53, 67, 70–1, 93, 99, 108, 112–13, 120–32, 171, 185–6, 211–14
  name of 158, 166
  passion of 3
  as physician 165
  priesthood of 112, 126
  redemptive action 6, 10, 12, 53–4, 70, 110, 113, 194
  as rhetorician 54, 56–7
  as savior 73, 85, 100, 109–10, 123, 200
  as teacher 122
  as wisdom 200, 204
  as without sin 126
Cicero 5–6, 8, 18–19, 50–1, 73, 80, 85, 92, 158, 171–2, 178
Clark, Gillian 35–6
Cleopatra 20, 25–9
Clement of Alexandria 48
Constantine the Great 16, 30, 32, 40–5, 115–16
Coriolanus, Caius Marcus 20, 22–5, 28
Corrigan, Kevin 59
Cropsey, Joseph 45, 47, 76, 104–5, 153, 165, 187, 189, 208–9
Crosson, Frederick 3–4, 178, 194, 211
Crouse, Robert D. 8

Damascene Studites 32
Digeser, Elizabeth DePalma 39–40
Diocletian 15, 38–9, 41, 50
Diotima 83
Dodaro, Robert 67–8, 70, 74, 87, 92, 96, 100, 104, 116, 120–1, 123, 126, 135–6, 202
Doody, John 9, 131
Dougherty, Richard J. 48, 83

Edwards, Mark 42
Elshtain, Jean Bethke 136
Epicurus 170
Eusebius of Caesarea 16, 39, 43–4

Evans, Gillian R. 48–9
Eve 5, 203
Evodius 86, 151, 174, 201

Faustus 163
Fichter, Andrew 21
Van Fleteren, Frederick 8, 48, 54, 58, 61, 85, 103
Foley, Michael P. 1, 9, 51–2, 60–2, 90, 122, 155, 159, 173, 207
Fortin, Ernest L. 9, 36–7, 4, 47–8, 70, 73–4, 77, 79, 81–5, 93, 101, 113–15, 117, 120–2, 130–1, 136, 138, 141, 151, 155–6, 159, 171, 183, 188–9, 193–4, 201
Fustel de Coulanges, Numa Denis 78

Galerius 41
Gallienus, Publius 39
Gibbon, Edward 16
God
  as creator 7, 69, 151, 171
  as eternal 58, 60, 63, 93, 107–8, 123–5, 138, 150, 171, 193, 204, 211
  Father 60, 62–3, 111
  Holy Spirit 6, 60–3, 87–8, 111
  as immaterial 163
  knowledge of 186
  as love 69
  mercy of 53, 62, 120, 210
  providence of 192, 205
  as rhetorician 166
  Son (or Word) 60–3, 110–11, 204–5, 208
  as Trinity 44–5, 59–62, 74, 76, 110–11, 118
  vision of 127
Gildin, Hilail 115
Greenwood, David Neal 38
Gregory Nazianzen 110
Guerra, Marc D. 74, 144

Harding, Brian 183
Harmon, Thomas P. 77, 108, 207
Hart, David Bentley 11
Hathaway, R. F. 36–7
Hera 76
Hercules 16, 27
Hermogenianus 49, 51
Herod 28
von Heyking, John 71, 87–8, 131, 137, 183

Hierocles, Sossianus 39
Hughes, Kevin L. 9, 131
Hunt, Maurice 28

Iamblichus 40
Isis 202

Julian the Apostate 45
Jupiter 16–17, 21, 92

Kennedy, Robert P. 156
Kenney, John Peter 8
Keys, Mary M. 38, 86
Kierkegaard, Søren 134
Kojève, Alexandre 45
Kries, Douglas 1, 4, 47, 73, 85, 90

Lactantius 39, 41, 58
Lamb, Matthew L. 172, 177–81
Leake, James 82–3
Levering, Matthew 172
Liebert, Hugh 23, 29
Liebeschuetz, John H. W. G. 16–17, 21, 32, 43
Lössl, Josef 48, 58–60
Louth, Andrew 59
Lowenthal, David 18
Lycon 77

MacDonald, Scott 69
Manent, Pierre 1, 5–10, 15–21, 28–9, 37–8, 68, 88–91, 98, 110, 120, 131, 154, 182, 187
Mani 162–3
Manlius Theodorus 49
Marcellinus 122
Markus, Robert A. 74, 131
Mary, mother of Jesus 62
Mathewes, Charles T. 202, 211
McCarthy, Michael C. 158
Meconi, David Vincent 38, 71, 112, 181–2, 208
Meletus 76–9
Menenius, Agrippa 24
Miles, Margaret 67
Milton, John 27
Monica 59, 86, 107, 108, 193, 207, 210
Montaigne, Michel de 21
Moses 3

Nathanael 203
Nectarius 122
Nietzsche, Friedrich 16
Nutt, Roger W. 207

O'Donnell, James J. 158–9, 164, 186
O'Donovan, Oliver 88, 131, 134
Octavia 26
Ogle, Veronica Roberts 3, 10, 71–2, 74, 86, 88–9, 113, 115, 122, 183, 187
Onatus 42
Origen of Alexandria 11, 48
Osiris 202

Paffenroth, Kim 9, 131, 156
Pangle, Thomas 1, 83, 116
Paul the Apostle 109, 112, 117, 124, 127, 150, 172, 185, 188, 194, 205–6
Pausanias 83
Parens, Joshua 7–8
Peterson, Erik 17, 42–5
Philostratus 42
Pilate 117
Platt, Michael 23–6, 28
Plato 1, 8, 20–1, 34, 36–8, 50–9, 72–85, 90–2, 96, 99–104, 116, 121, 124, 164–5, 183, 187, 189, 192, 197
Plotinus 8, 36, 39, 49–50, 52, 59–60, 103, 105, 111, 154, 187, 192, 209–11
Plutarch 15, 21, 23
Pompeius, Gnaeus 26
Ponticianus 197–8, 200
Porphyry of Tyre 2, 4, 8, 10–12, 15, 31–46, 49–50, 52, 57–8, 64, 70, 73, 85, 91–119, 121–2, 128, 149, 161, 186, 192, 207, 215
Proclus 8
Proteus 96

Ratzinger, Joseph 44–5
Regulus, Marcus 131
Rist, John M. 9, 85, 120, 152, 155, 165, 175, 186–8, 194
Rousseau, Jean-Jacques 21

Satan 95
Scaevola 86, 104
Schall, James V., SJ 9, 74, 80–1, 83, 129–31, 141–2, 212

Schott, Jeremy M. 39–41, 45
Saturn 86
Seneca 89–90, 128
Shakespeare, William 15–28
Sheed, Frank J. 4, 61, 173, 177
Simmons, Michael Bland 2, 15, 28, 31–5,
　39–42, 45, 50, 94, 97, 149, 161
Simplicianus 191, 193–5, 200
Skerret, Kathleen Roberts 151
Socrates 1, 4, 38, 52, 54, 71, 74–84, 90–1,
　99, 104–5, 116, 129–30, 144, 153,
　154, 164, 183, 187, 189, 192, 200,
　202, 209
Sokolowski, Robert 177, 211
Sol Invictus 16, 21, 32
Stephany, William A. 171–2, 192
Stock, Brian 210
Strauss, Leo 1, 8, 22–3, 37, 39, 45, 47,
　49–50, 72–3, 75, 78–9, 81–2, 114–16

Theiler, Willy 58
Theodorus 151
Theodosius 43, 115–16, 121

Thomas, Adam 83
Topping, Ryan N. S. 54
Torchia, N. Joseph 154–5
Typhon 202

Varro, Marcus 4, 8, 38, 40, 85–92, 104,
　128
Vaught, Carl G. 150, 156, 177, 181, 209–10
Victorinus, Caius Marius 57, 69, 114, 122,
　124, 190–6, 199–203, 209
Virgil 8, 43
Volusianus 122

Wetzel, James 9, 91, 139, 151, 162,
　164, 205–7
Wilken, Robert L. 32, 39
Williams, Rowan 140
Williams, Stephen 32, 38
Williams, Thomas 171

Zeno of Citium 51
Zenobius 49
Zeus 76

INDEX OF SUBJECTS

angels 93, 95, 100, 122–4, 136, 174
apologetics 2, 64
Apostle's Creed 60
appetite 10, 22, 26, 33–4, 151, 161, 214
Arianism 17, 44, 62–3
asceticism 56, 199, 206
atheism 76, 78
Athens 38, 75, 77–80, 130, 183

Babel, Tower of 135
baptism 60–1, 69, 122, 126, 153, 201, 204
belief 1, 9, 45, 54, 56, 58, 75–6, 83, 90, 113, 116, 120, 127, 151, 153, 163–7, 173–4, 186, 189, 192
blasphemy 95
books of the Platonists (*libri Platonicorum*) 51, 59, 103, 106–8, 149, 161, 170–2, 176–8, 181–2, 184, 186, 191, 194, 207–8, 212

Carthage 141, 158
Cassiciacum 119
Catholic Church 11
    as body of Christ (or *totus Christus*) 6, 62, 71, 76, 111–12, 122, 126, 187, 194, 197, 205, 209
    foundation by Christ 187
    as mediating institution 122, 214, 188, 194, 196, 201, 214
    as political form 29
    sacraments of 11, 61, 122, 195
    salvation through 123, 170, 190, 193, 195, 200–1
    as universal 29, 59, 63, 168, 186, 193, 195, 201, 208, 213
charity 69–70, 73–4, 87, 119, 122, 128, 131, 137–8, 140, 142–5, 152, 154, 193–4, 199, 205, 208, 214
    order of 138
citizenship 19, 117, 205
city of God 67–9, 71
    as an actual city 74
    end of 68–9, 132–3, 142, 145
    as pilgrim 74, 133, 138, 141–2, 213
    relationship to the earthly city 29–30, 68, 74, 87–9, 116–18, 122, 131–4, 136–42, 144, 195, 205
    as a sacrifice 126
    as transpolitical 30, 44–6, 69, 74, 88–9, 115–19, 122, 132–3, 138, 140–4, 214
    as universal 67, 118, 122, 212
concupiscence 188
    of the eyes 155
    of the flesh 155, 204
consuetudo carnalis 55, 70, 107, 125, 145, 150–2, 170, 172, 181, 186, 190, 192–6, 200–3, 206, 208–9
contemplation 1–2, 7, 34–5, 55, 81, 92, 101, 107, 115, 119, 143–4, 150, 154, 161, 178, 191, 193, 209
continence 34–5, 107, 161, 176, 184, 188, 203, 206, 212
creation, Christian doctrine of 92, 177–8, 211
Cronus 202
curiosity 58, 155
cursus honorum 101, 156, 198
custom 31, 38, 41–2, 58, 72, 75–8, 80, 82, 84, 86, 88, 90, 98, 118, 131, 133, 142
cycle of regimes 17

death
    of the body 84, 104, 127, 197
    Christian attitude toward 193
    fear of 154, 175, 189, 197, 200
    of the soul 128–9, 131, 20
demons 22, 35, 40, 48, 56, 58, 73, 92–4, 100, 104–5, 123, 199
    as liars 96, 104–5, 130
despair 49, 84, 145, 154, 167
despotism 1
discipline of the secret 60

divination 35
dream of Scipio 84, 154

Edict of Toleration 41
emotion 95–6, 101
episcopacy 143–4
eros 25–6, 28, 75
eschatology 34, 45, 210
esotericism 1–3, 47–54, 73, 90, 93–5, 214
eternity 42, 55–8, 63, 70, 72, 74, 93, 101, 145, 173, 179, 185
Eucharist 40, 60–1, 108, 111, 122–3, 126, 187, 207, 210–11
Europe 21
evil
   cause of 102, 150, 157, 173–4, 202–3
   as privation of good 52, 102, 113, 125, 157, 172, 177, 179, 188, 200, 202
   problem of 102, 150, 154, 161, 164, 172

faith 3–6, 9–10, 41, 44–5, 56, 67–8, 74, 95, 103, 115, 119–20, 122, 127–8, 138, 140, 142–6, 152, 165–7, 170–1, 176–7, 190, 193–4, 197, 199, 201, 205, 208, 210–11
Fall 5, 60, 67–8, 131, 135–6, 143, 145, 189
fraternal correction 143
friendship 105, 136, 192, 198

glory 1, 24, 70–2, 91, 134–6, 155, 168–9, 183, 207
gnosticism 32
grace 5, 33, 59–60, 62, 67–8, 70, 73–4, 86, 110, 112, 117–18, 122, 124–7, 137–40, 149, 152–3, 155, 161, 176–8, 186, 190–6, 201, 204–9, 212–14
Great Persecution 17, 38–9, 41, 50

homoousios 44
honor 17, 22–6, 79, 101, 156, 163, 169–70, 207
hope 11, 72, 94, 113, 139, 144–5, 152, 193, 199, 210–11
humility 7, 10, 53, 59–60, 68, 74, 92, 108, 110, 112–13, 126–7, 145, 149–52, 155, 157–9, 176–178, 181–6, 188, 190, 193–7, 200, 208, 210–11, 213–14
hypostatic union 15, 62, 111, 123, 126, 182, 205, 207–9, 213

idolatry 122, 197
ignorance and difficulty 5–7, 67–8, 70–5, 85–97, 120, 123, 127, 134, 136, 149–54, 169, 172, 175–6, 181, 185, 189, 192–3, 199, 201–4, 207, 209, 212–14
image of God 63
imagination 6, 23, 95, 101, 105–6, 123, 176
inequality 10, 18, 98
intellect 3, 10, 49, 58, 63, 95, 99, 108–9, 123, 170–1, 202
Israel 44, 107–8, 178, 210

joy 69–70
Judaism 6, 45, 76, 120–1
justice 49, 73–4, 79, 83, 88, 98, 122, 126, 128, 133–46, 167, 189, 201–2
justification 129

law
   divine 74, 116–17, 132, 186, 190, 205
   eternal 129, 151, 175, 196, 200
   natural 72–3, 114, 139
   regarding religion 88, 94, 141
   of sin 150, 172, 186, 194, 196, 199
   temporal (or civil) 43, 73, 75–6, 78–9, 82, 84, 90, 92, 114, 116–18, 140, 189, 201, 205
leisure 119, 142–4
liberal arts 168
libido dominandi 71, 93
liturgy 60
logos 35, 165
lying
   impossibility for the Christian 48, 82
   morality of 48, 73, 82
Lord's Prayer 60

Manicheanism 5, 102, 149, 151, 157–70, 173–4, 192–5, 202, 205
marriage 168
martyrdom 116, 128–9, 143, 201
materialism 51, 171
meekness 178
memory 210
metaphysics 33, 60, 92, 112, 131, 162, 173, 176–7, 180, 192
misologia 81, 104, 153, 164–5, 170
mystery religions 27, 31–2

myth (or fable) 5, 25, 38, 41–2, 45, 58, 70, 82–3, 86, 104, 151, 153, 156, 159, 161–5, 168, 180, 186, 188–9, 194, 202

natural right 72, 114
nature
  effects of sin on 4–5
  fallen 70, 73, 83, 139, 155, 175, 213
  as guide 86
  teleology of 131, 154
  weakness (or limits) of 84, 95, 120, 129, 214
Neoplatonism
  as apolitical 36–8
  description of 7–8, 36, 59
  ethics of 188
Nicomedia 39
noble lie 48, 56, 70, 73, 82–7, 99

The One 35, 59–62, 105, 118, 184
oracle of Apollo 78
Origenists 40
Ostia 69, 86, 171, 207, 210–11

passions 18, 20, 24, 35, 49, 63, 71, 92, 101, 137, 156, 181, 197, 200
patriotism 46, 117
peace
  eternal, 27–8, 121, 132–3, 135, 138, 142–6, 197
  temporal 27, 29, 69, 73–4, 88, 96–7, 117–18, 122, 132–5, 138, 141–5
phantasms 55, 102–3, 106, 109, 159, 161, 180
philosophers
  academic 49–53, 73, 164, 167
  indirect rule of 81–2, 85, 99
  as liars 47, 82–3, 86–7, 99, 104, 124, 146
  natural 174
  philosopher king 1, 84
  pre-Socratic 80, 90
  as proud 114, 127, 130, 143, 176–7, 183–4, 197
  sins of 73
  their duty to the city 133
philosophy
  as divisive 1, 91, 95, 133, 214
  and denigration of the body 187, 192, 209–10

limits of 81, 88–9, 126, 129–30, 188
natural 161–3, 170
Platonic 1, 90, 93
philosophic ascent 35–6, 49, 59, 69, 80, 105–6, 161–84
as setting the limit to political life 81, 115–16
as transpolitical 79–80
as a way of life 49, 79, 81, 114, 129, 144, 156, 180, 183–4
Photinianism 62–3
piety 40, 78, 116, 118, 121, 128, 141, 153, 163, 173–4, 183, 191
poetry
  ancient quarrel between philosophy and 77, 86, 91–2
  and religion 76
political theology 44–5
prayer 54, 116, 121, 145, 205–8, 212
pride 60–1, 68, 74, 91, 93, 95, 112–13, 124, 127, 134, 146, 151–2, 155–9, 162–72, 176–7, 183–90, 193–4, 201, 213
pride of life 91, 155
prophecy 45
prudence 40, 47, 52, 79, 82, 88, 143, 145, 214
Pythagoreanism 42

repentance 116, 142, 155
republicanism 18, 20, 23
resurrection of the body 94, 109, 125–6, 129, 140, 144–5, 188, 193, 197, 208, 213
revelation 5, 58, 81
Rome
  Augustine's evaluation of 141
  desire for conquest 25
  foundation of 25
  pax Romana 28–9, 43
  religion of 2, 15–16, 19–20, 23–6, 29–32, 38–45, 54, 56, 85–6, 88, 97
  sack of 48, 63
  transition from city to empire 2, 15–23, 25, 28–32, 43, 46

Sabellianism 111
sacraments 11, 60–2, 119, 123, 152, 194–5
sanctification 144
Scripture
  authority of 167, 177

mode of expression 167–8
New Testament 112, 117
Old Testament 45, 165–6
Porphyry's critiques of 40
spiritual senses 166–7
universality of 168
sin
  as choice 126, 151, 196
  confession of 113, 152–4, 190, 194, 200
  consequences of 5–6, 62, 67, 69, 73, 96, 127–8, 137, 139, 154, 185, 187, 191, 196
  forgiveness of 116, 121
  original 3, 5, 60, 67–8, 114, 128, 138, 194, 214
  social consequences of 144, 214
skepticism 51, 53, 149, 164–5, 170
slavery 139–40
Sophists 77
soul
  as divine 90
  immortality of 105
  incorporeality of 178–9
  knowledge of 151, 186
  nature of 151
  origin of 141
  proper order of 5, 67, 79, 121, 130, 137, 146, 197, 199, 213
  in relation to the body 145, 150, 187, 190, 197, 213
  tripartition of 67
spiritedness 10, 22, 25–6, 33, 161, 214
superstition 5, 94, 157, 159, 168

theologico-political problem 75, 88
theology
  civil 16–17, 39, 44–5, 54, 73, 85, 88–90, 103–4, 118, 124
  natural 86, 103–4, 112
  poetic (or theatrical) 89–90, 9, 103
theurgy 33–6, 40, 50, 57–8, 71, 73, 85, 92–5, 98–105, 109, 153, 161
time 28, 42, 58, 70, 122, 171, 173, 179, 185, 211, 214
transmigration of the soul 36

vices 22, 58, 87, 89, 117, 124, 130, 133, 137–8, 145–6, 164, 184, 190, 197, 203, 213
virtues
  civic 88
  cultivation of 40, 117–18, 128
  false 80, 83, 113
  intellectual 35, 84, 192
  knowledge of 79–80, 170
  limits of 22, 116, 121, 131, 136, 138
  moral 34, 49, 70, 78, 83, 115, 117, 131, 161, 192
  pagan 93, 112, 189
  philosophic 83, 106, 121, 130, 202
  political 36, 115–16, 131
  Roman 26, 41, 131
  theological 36, 87
  true 1, 56, 80, 83, 121, 133

war 24, 132, 135–6, 139
worship 35, 38, 41, 43, 54, 62–3, 73, 89–93, 96, 99–100, 116, 124, 126, 129, 139, 142, 144, 211, 213

www.ingramcontent.com/pod-product-compliance
Lightning Source LLC
Chambersburg PA
CBHW051520230426
43668CB00012B/1683